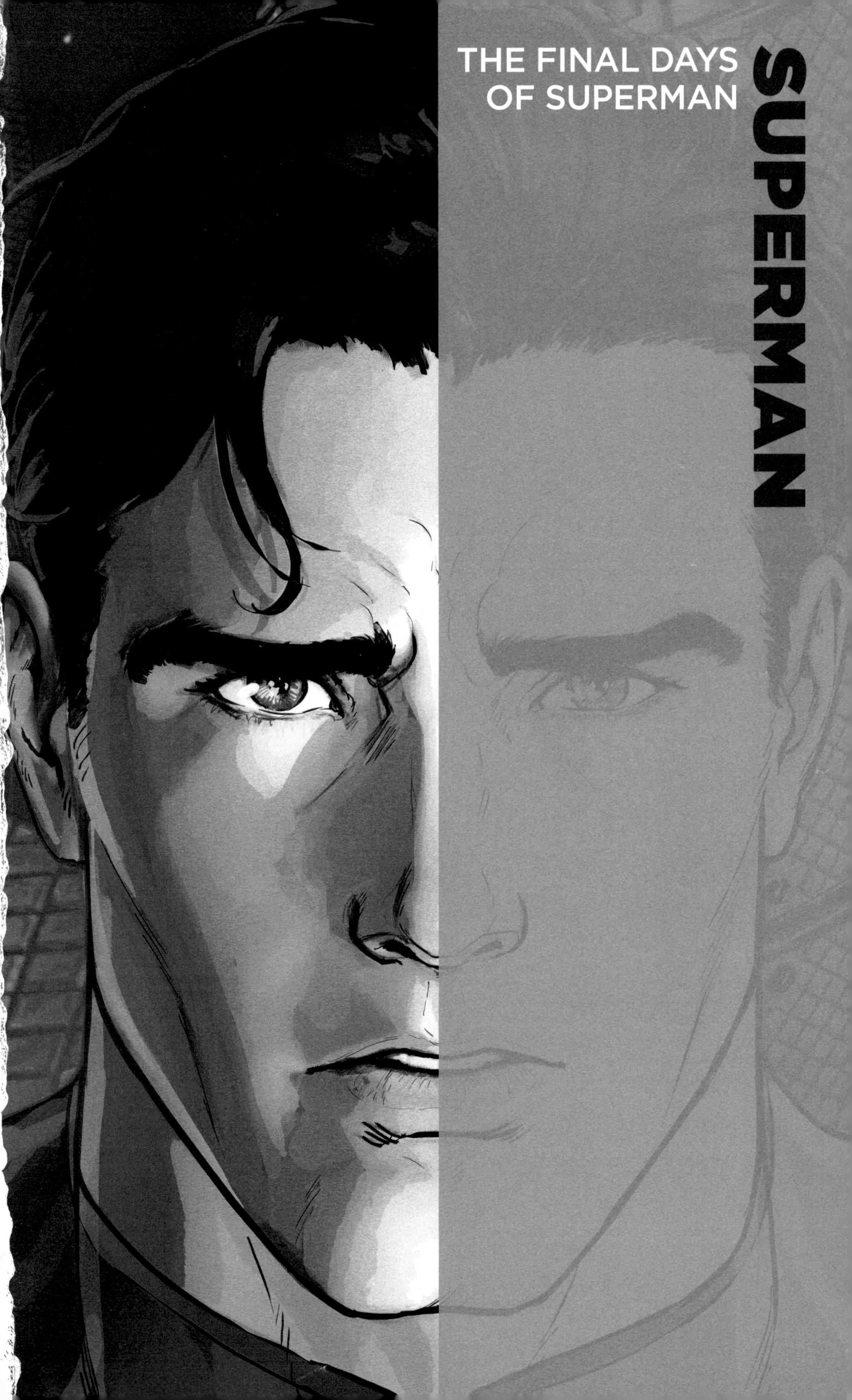
THE FINAL DAYS
OF SUPERMAN
SUPERMAN

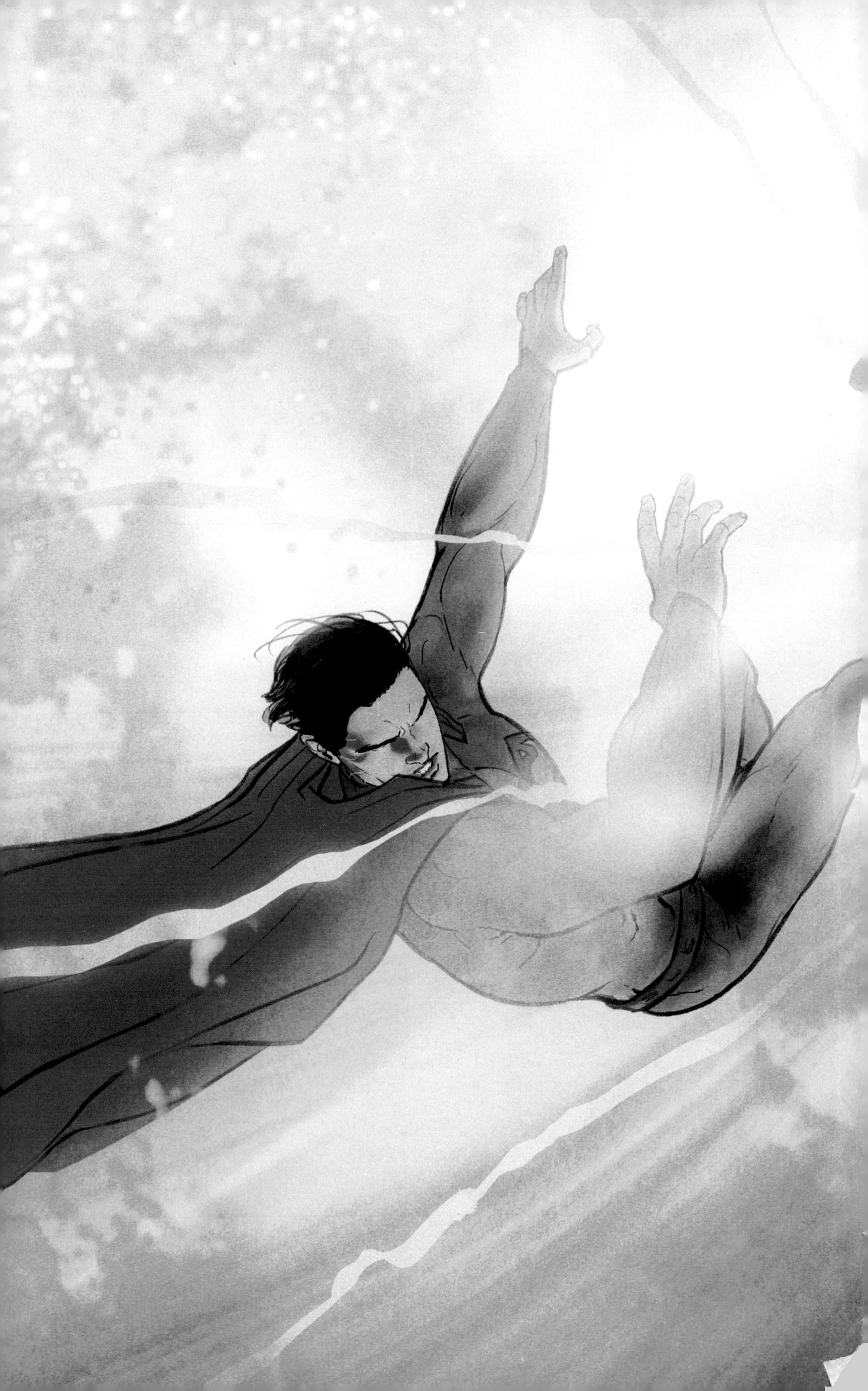

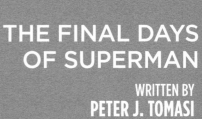

THE FINAL DAYS OF SUPERMAN

WRITTEN BY
PETER J. TOMASI

PENCILS BY
ED BENES
DALE EAGLESHAM
SCOT EATON
MIKEL JANÍN
JORGE JIMÉNEZ
DOUG MAHNKE
PAUL PELLETIER

COLOR BY
JEROMY COX
MIKEL JANÍN
TOMEU MOREY
WIL QUINTANA
ALEJANDRO SÁNCHEZ
ALEX SINCLAIR

INKS BY
CHRISTIAN ALAMY
SANDRA HOPE ARCHER
ED BENES
DALE EAGLESHAM
WAYNE FAUCHER
MIKEL JANÍN
JORGE JIMÉNEZ
JOHN LIVESAY
JAIME MENDOZA
TOM NGUYEN

LETTERS BY
ROB LEIGH

COLLECTION COVER ART BY
MIKEL JANÍN

SUPERMAN CREATED BY
JERRY SIEGEL & JOE SHUSTER
BY SPECIAL ARRANGEMENT
WITH THE JERRY SIEGEL FAMILY

WONDER WOMAN CREATED BY
WILLIAM MOULTON MARSTON

BATMAN CREATED BY
BOB KANE WITH **BILL FINGER**

ANDREW MARINO Assistant Editor – Original Series
EDDIE BERGANZA Group Editor – Original Series
JEB WOODARD Group Editor – Collected Editions
SUZANNAH ROWNTREE Editor – Collected Edition
STEVE COOK Design Director – Books
DAMIAN RYLAND Publication Design

BOB HARRAS Senior VP – Editor-in-Chief, DC Comics

DIANE NELSON President
DAN DIDIO and JIM LEE Co-Publishers
GEOFF JOHNS Chief Creative Officer
AMIT DESAI Senior VP – Marketing & Global Franchise Management
NAIRI GARDINER Senior VP – Finance
SAM ADES VP – Digital Marketing
BOBBIE CHASE VP – Talent Development
MARK CHIARELLO Senior VP – Art, Design & Collected Editions
JOHN CUNNINGHAM VP – Content Strategy
ANNE DEPIES VP – Strategy Planning & Reporting
DON FALLETTI VP – Manufacturing Operations
LAWRENCE GANEM VP – Editorial Administration & Talent Relations
ALISON GILL Senior VP – Manufacturing & Operations
HANK KANALZ Senior VP – Editorial Strategy & Administration
JAY KOGAN VP – Legal Affairs
DEREK MADDALENA Senior VP – Sales & Business Development
JACK MAHAN VP – Business Affairs
DAN MIRON VP – Sales Planning & Trade Development
NICK NAPOLITANO VP – Manufacturing Administration
CAROL ROEDER VP – Marketing
EDDIE SCANNELL VP – Mass Account & Digital Sales
COURTNEY SIMMONS Senior VP – Publicity & Communications
JIM (SKI) SOKOLOWSKI VP – Comic Book Specialty & Newsstand Sales
SANDY YI Senior VP – Global Franchise Management

SUPERMAN: THE FINAL DAYS OF SUPERMAN

DC Comics, 2900 West Alameda Ave., Burbank, CA 91505
Printed by RR Donnelley, Salem, VA, USA. 9/23/16. First Printing.
ISBN: 978-1-4012-6722-3

Library of Congress Cataloging-in-Publication Data is available.

PEFC Certified

Printed on paper from
sustainably managed
forests and controlled
sources

PEFC/29-31-75

www.pefc.org

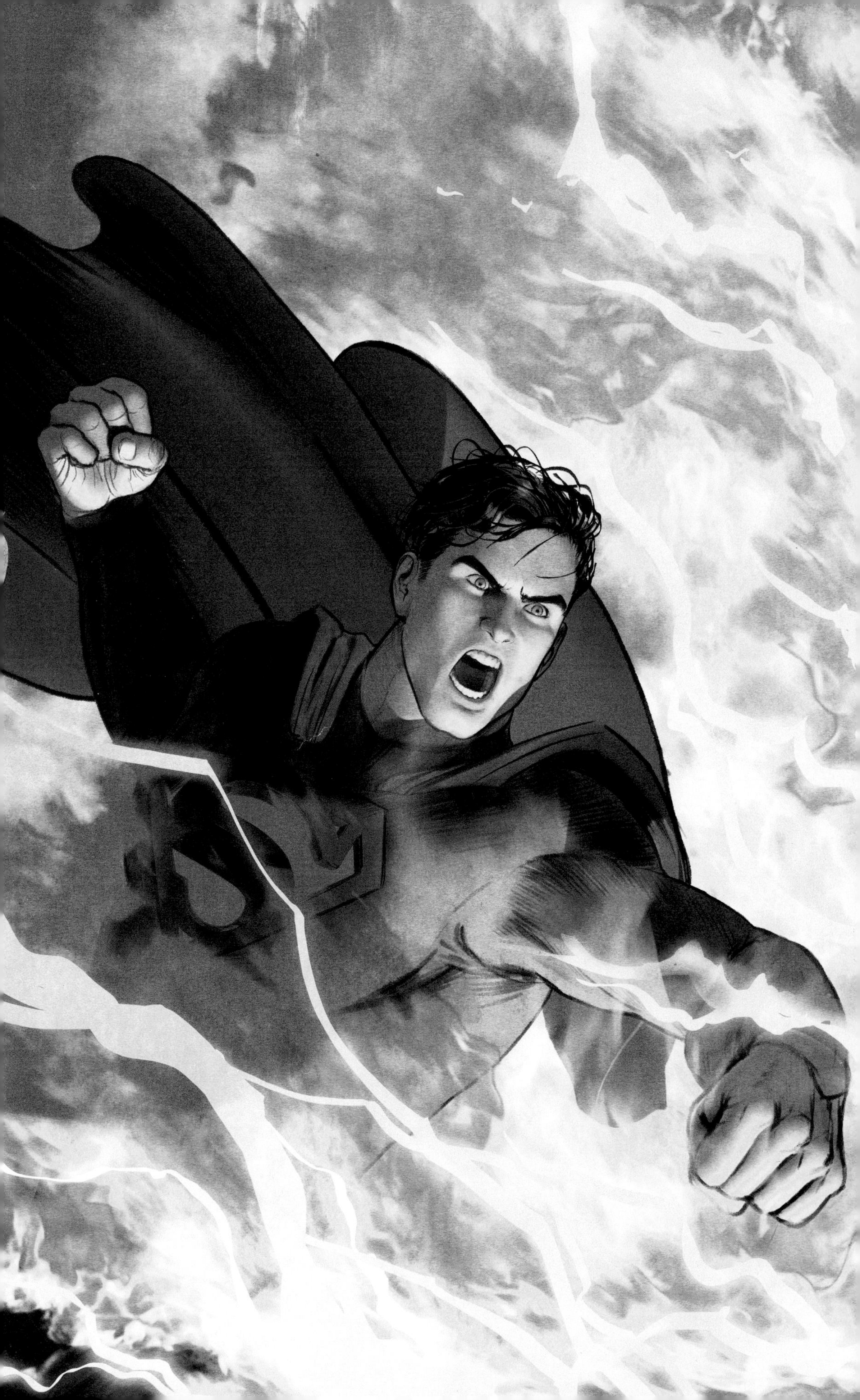

THE FINAL DAYS OF SUPERMAN PART 1: THIS MORTAL COIL

PETER J. TOMASI writer MIKEL JANÍN artist MIKEL JANÍN colorist ROB LEIGH letterer MIKEL JANÍN cover

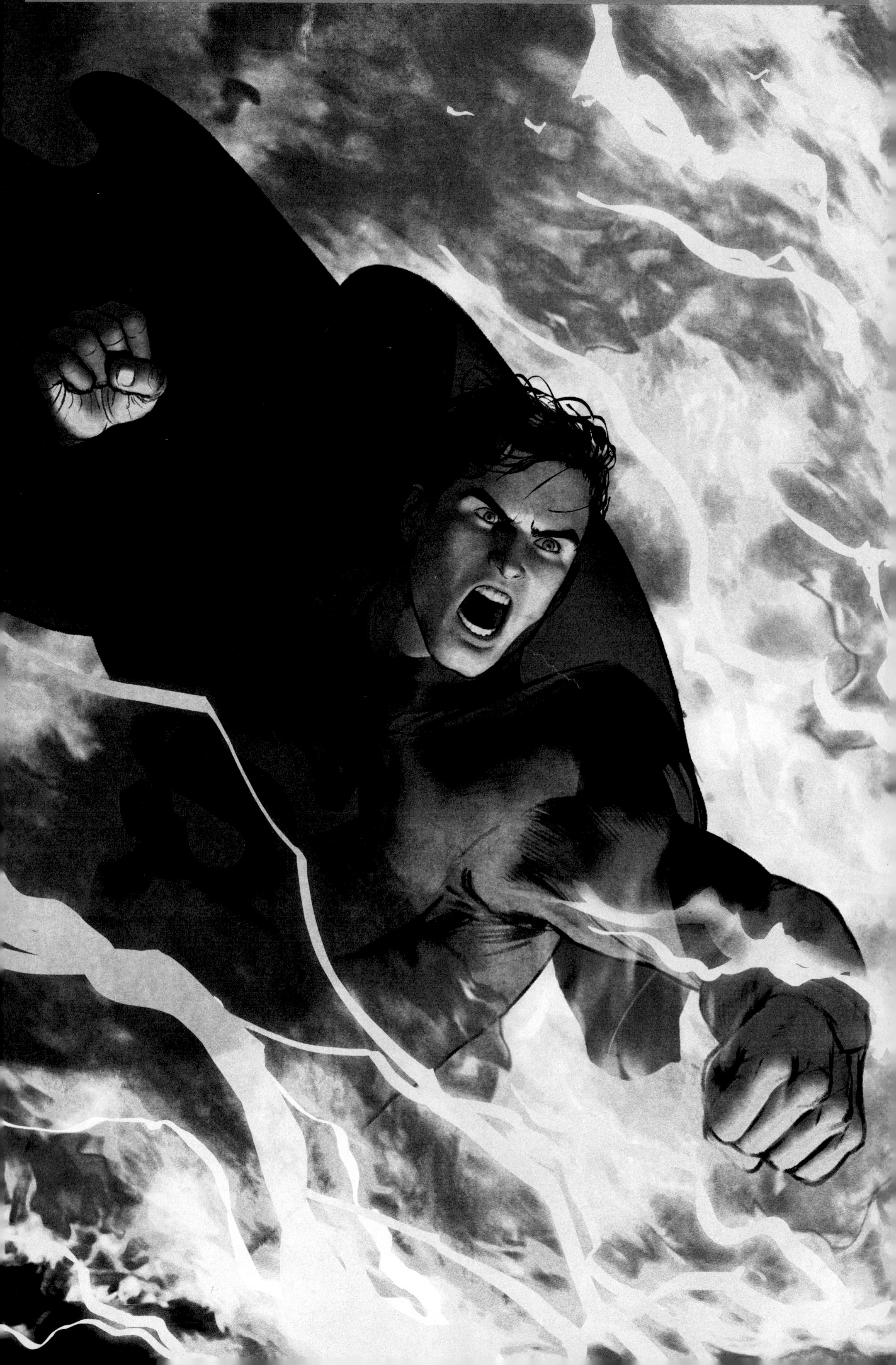

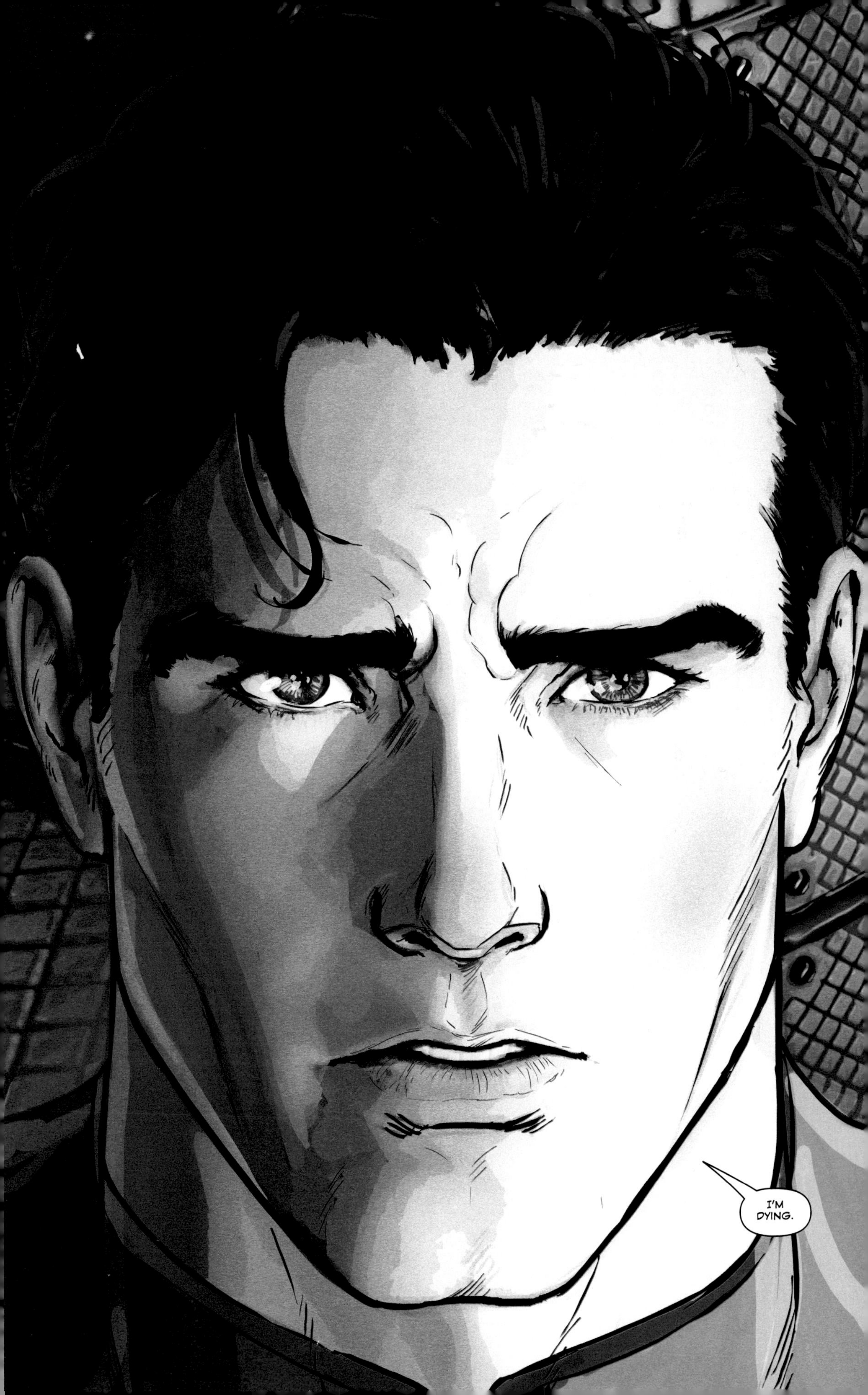
I'M DYING.

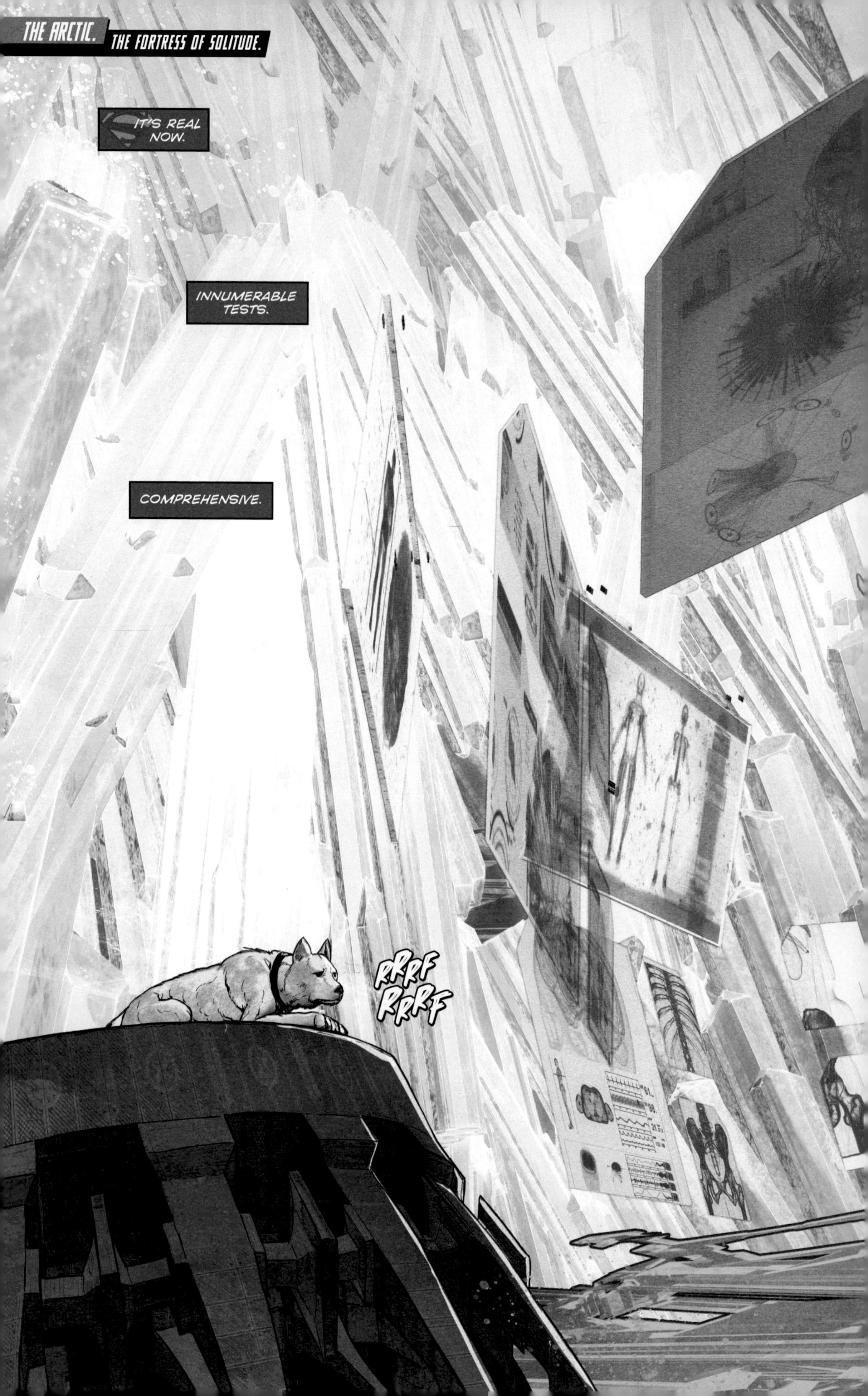
THE ARCTIC.
THE FORTRESS OF SOLITUDE.
IT'S REAL NOW.
INNUMERABLE TESTS.
COMPREHENSIVE.
RRRF RRRF

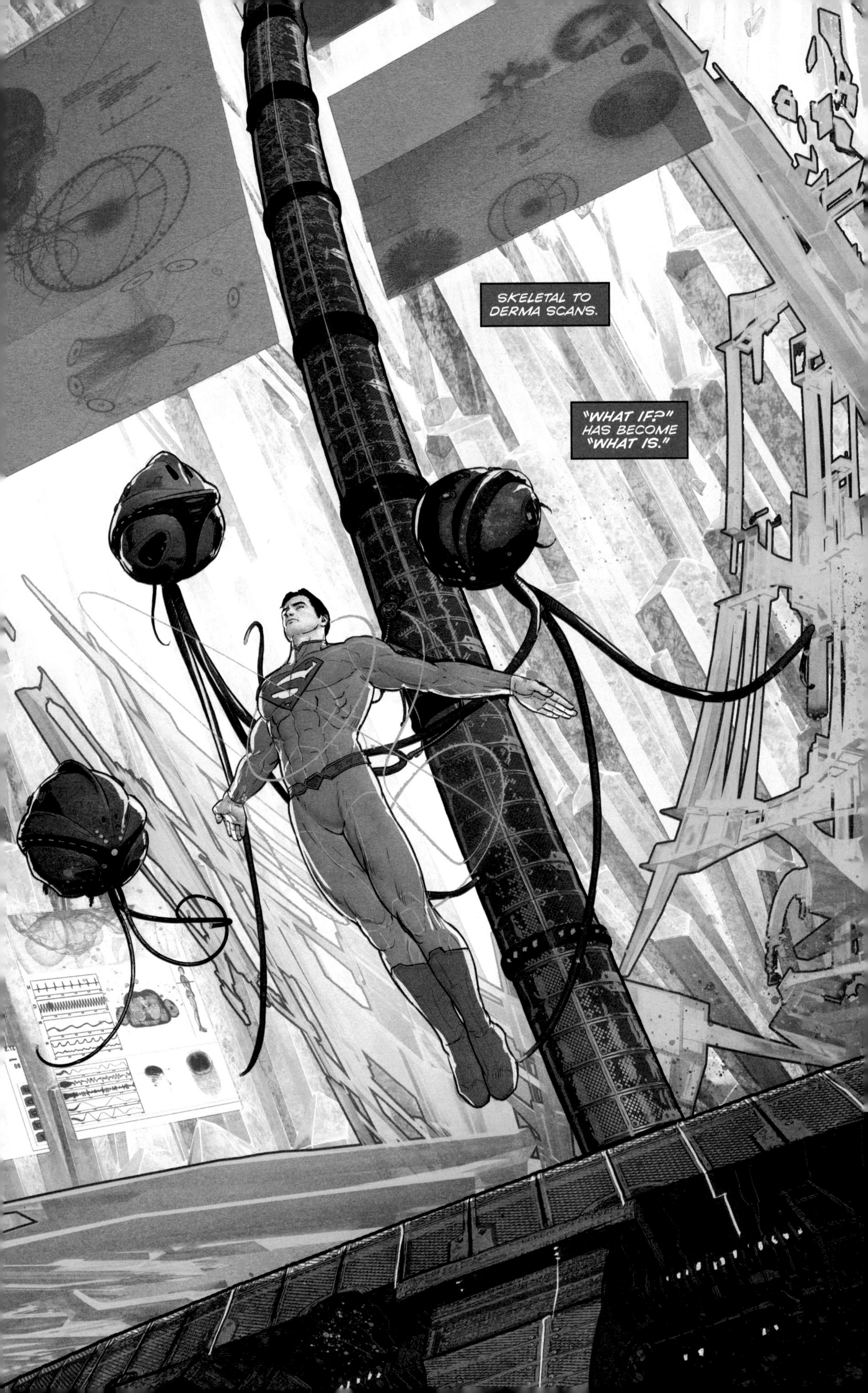
SKELETAL TO DERMA SCANS.
"WHAT IF?" HAS BECOME "WHAT IS."

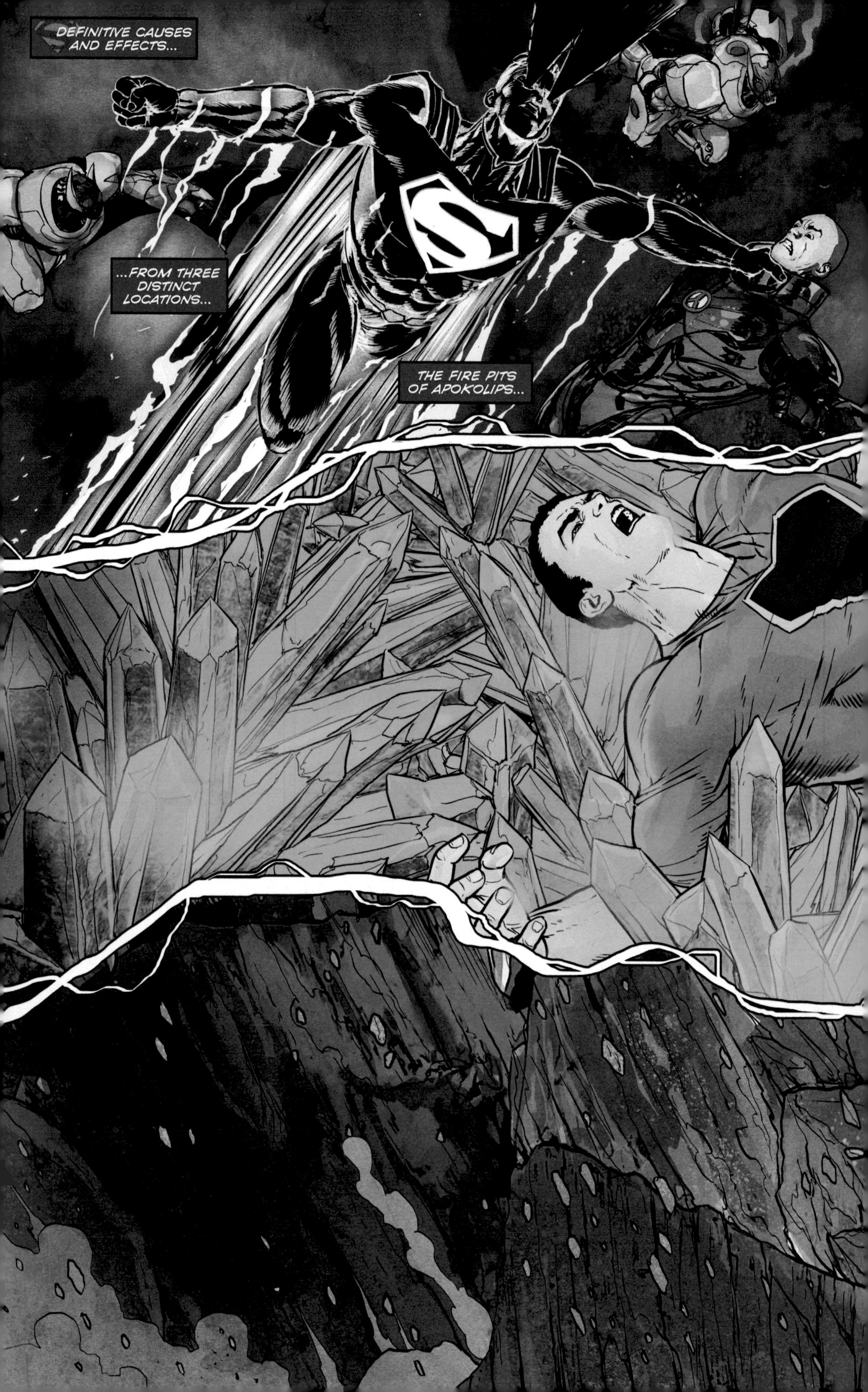
DEFINITIVE CAUSES AND EFFECTS...
...FROM THREE DISTINCT LOCATIONS...
THE FIRE PITS OF APOKOLIPS...

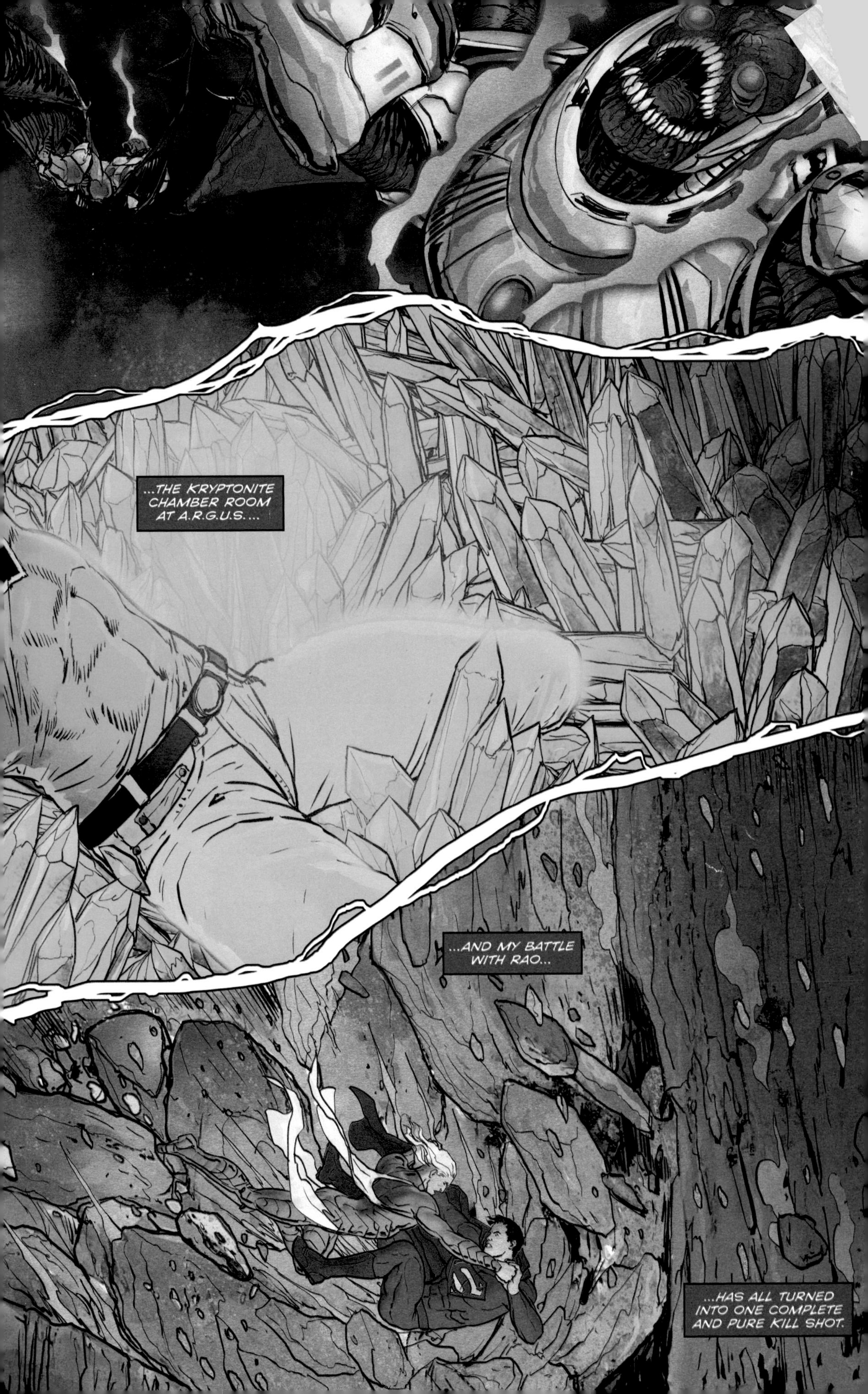
...THE KRYPTONITE CHAMBER ROOM AT A.R.G.U.S. ...
...AND MY BATTLE WITH RAO...
...HAS ALL TURNED INTO ONE COMPLETE AND PURE KILL SHOT.

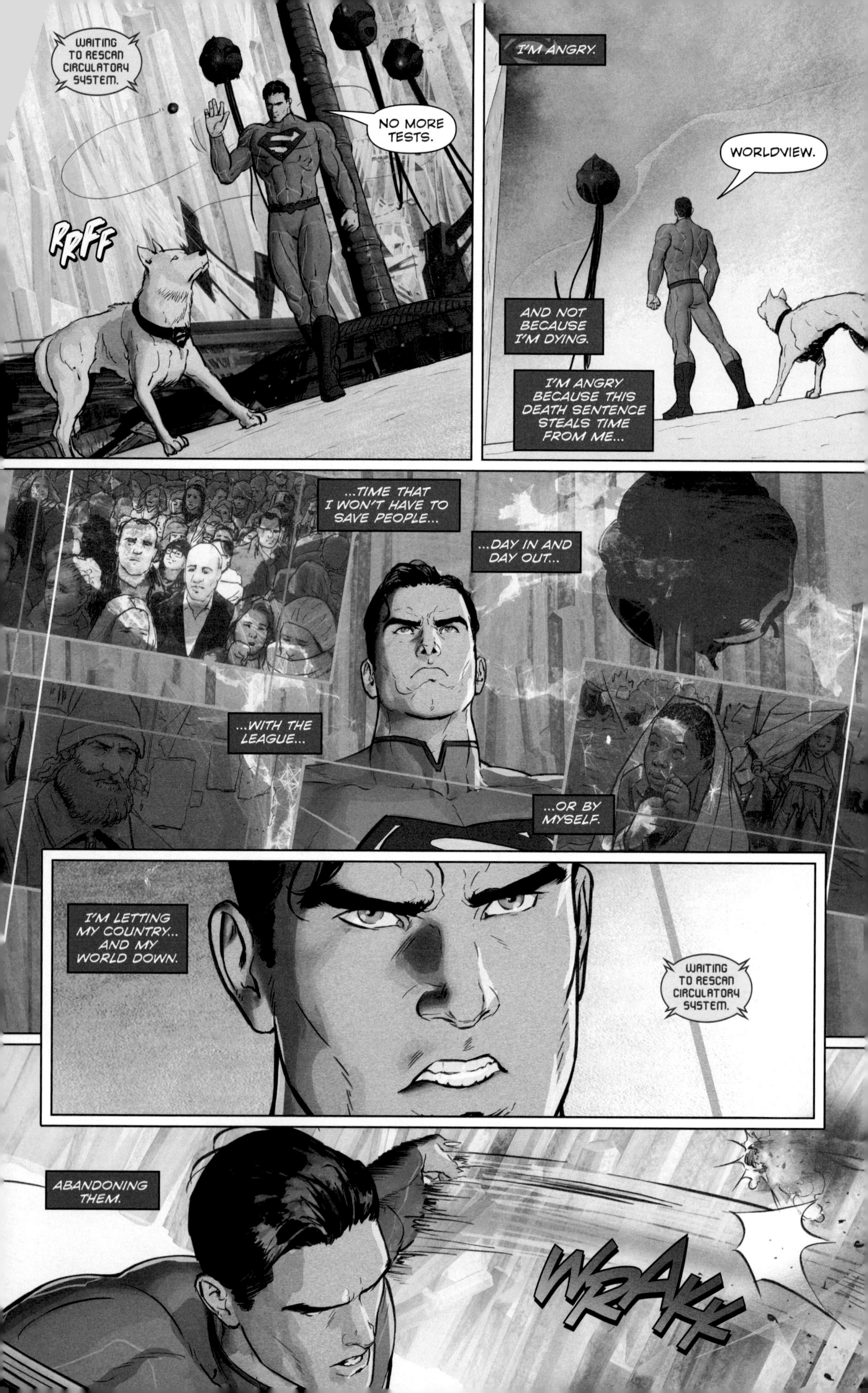
WAITING TO RESCAN CIRCULATORY SYSTEM.
NO MORE TESTS.
RRFF
I'M ANGRY.
WORLDVIEW.
AND NOT BECAUSE I'M DYING.
I'M ANGRY BECAUSE THIS DEATH SENTENCE STEALS TIME FROM ME...
...TIME THAT I WON'T HAVE TO SAVE PEOPLE...
...DAY IN AND DAY OUT...
...WITH THE LEAGUE...
...OR BY MYSELF.
I'M LETTING MY COUNTRY... AND MY WORLD DOWN.
WAITING TO RESCAN CIRCULATORY SYSTEM.
ABANDONING THEM.
WRAKK

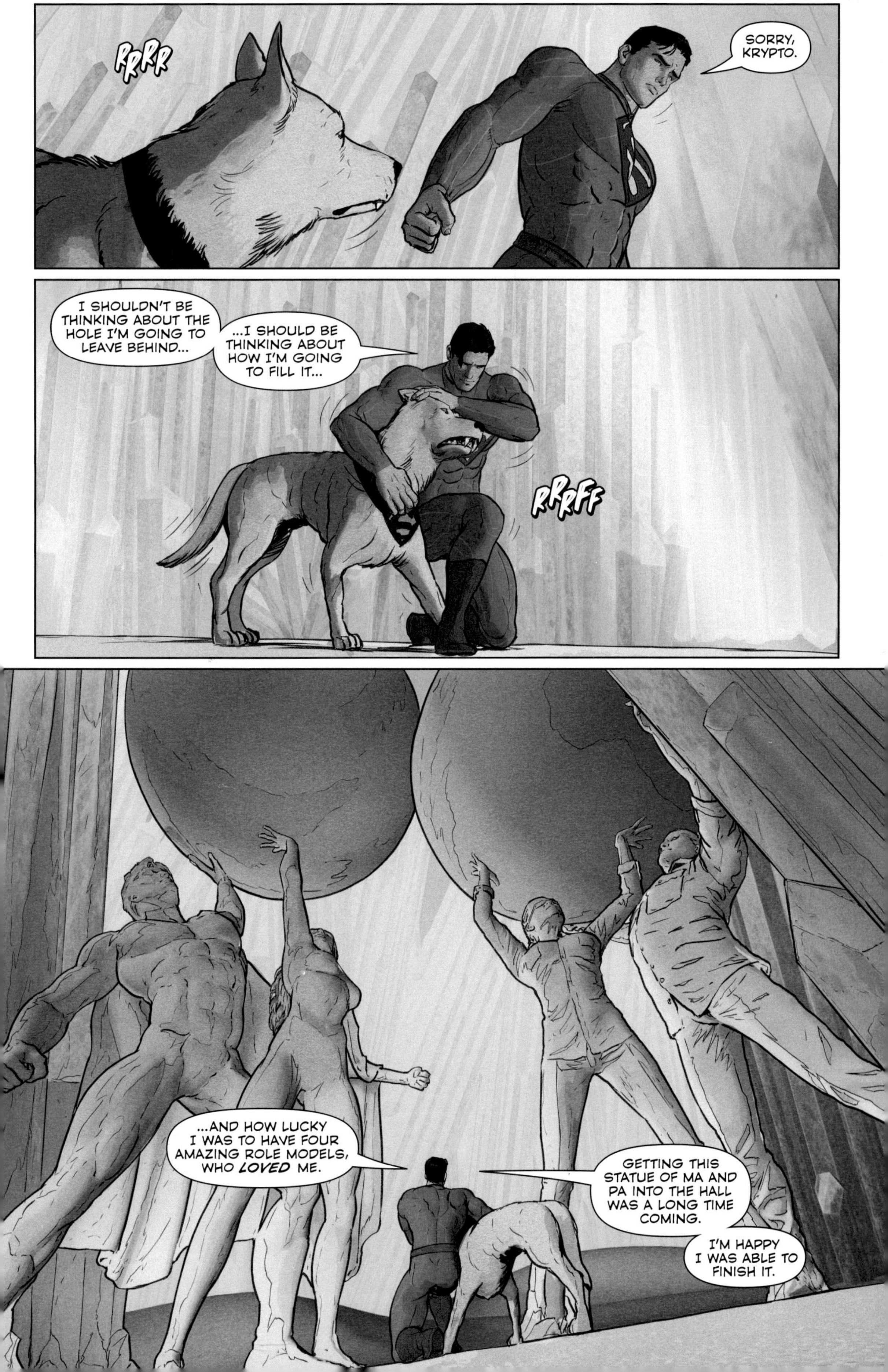
RRRR
SORRY, KRYPTO.
I SHOULDN'T BE THINKING ABOUT THE HOLE I'M GOING TO LEAVE BEHIND...
...I SHOULD BE THINKING ABOUT HOW I'M GOING TO FILL IT...
RRRFF
...AND HOW LUCKY I WAS TO HAVE FOUR AMAZING ROLE MODELS, WHO *LOVED* ME.
GETTING THIS STATUE OF MA AND PA INTO THE HALL WAS A LONG TIME COMING.
I'M HAPPY I WAS ABLE TO FINISH IT.

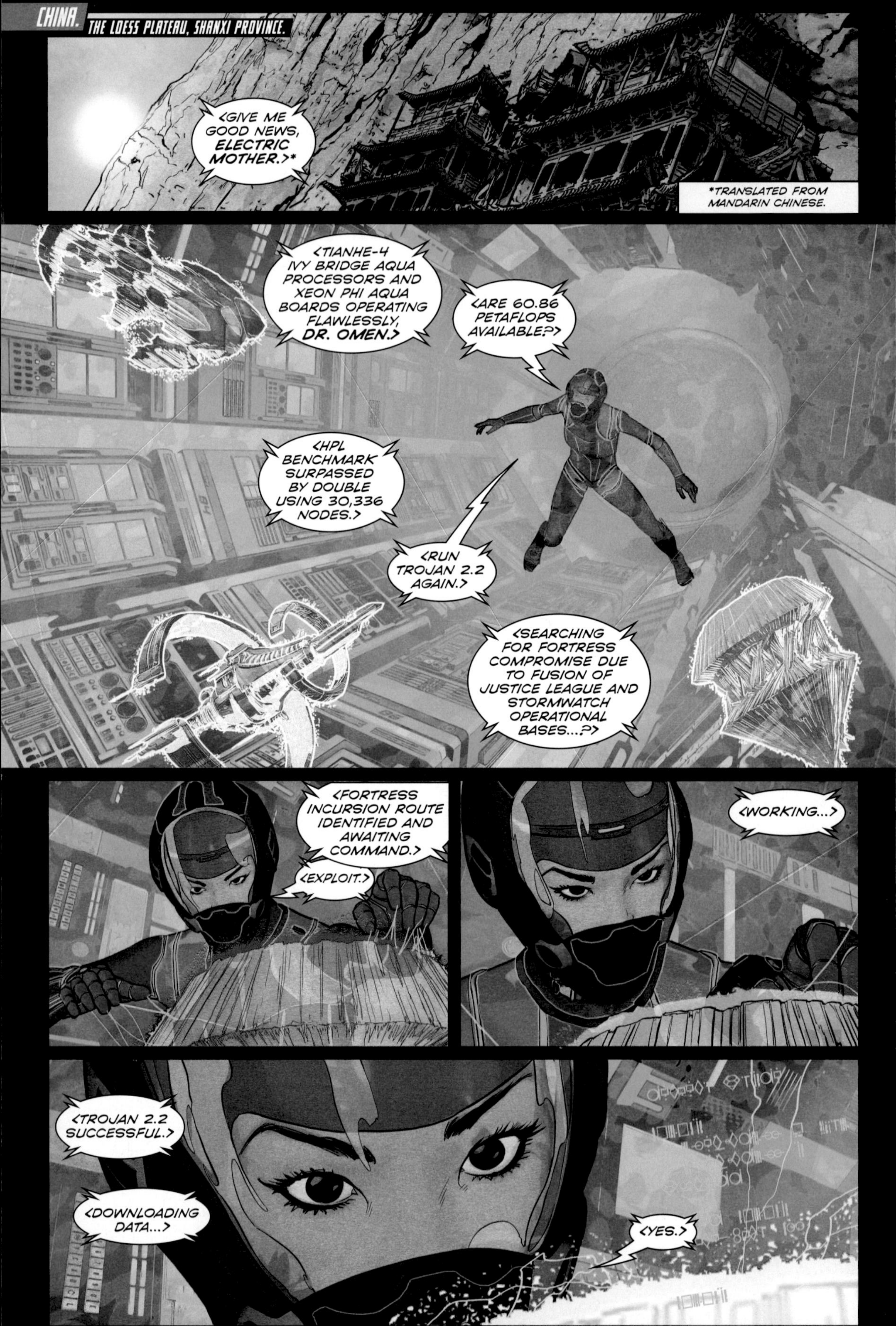
CHINA.
THE LOESS PLATEAU, SHANXI PROVINCE.
<GIVE ME GOOD NEWS, ELECTRIC MOTHER.>*
*TRANSLATED FROM MANDARIN CHINESE.
<TIANHE-4 IVY BRIDGE AQUA PROCESSORS AND XEON PHI AQUA BOARDS OPERATING FLAWLESSLY, DR. OMEN.>
<ARE 60.86 PETAFLOPS AVAILABLE?>
<HPL BENCHMARK SURPASSED BY DOUBLE USING 30,336 NODES.>
<RUN TROJAN 2.2 AGAIN.>
<SEARCHING FOR FORTRESS COMPROMISE DUE TO FUSION OF JUSTICE LEAGUE AND STORMWATCH OPERATIONAL BASES...?>
<FORTRESS INCURSION ROUTE IDENTIFIED AND AWAITING COMMAND.>
<EXPLOIT.>
<WORKING...>
<TROJAN 2.2 SUCCESSFUL.>
<DOWNLOADING DATA...>
<YES.>

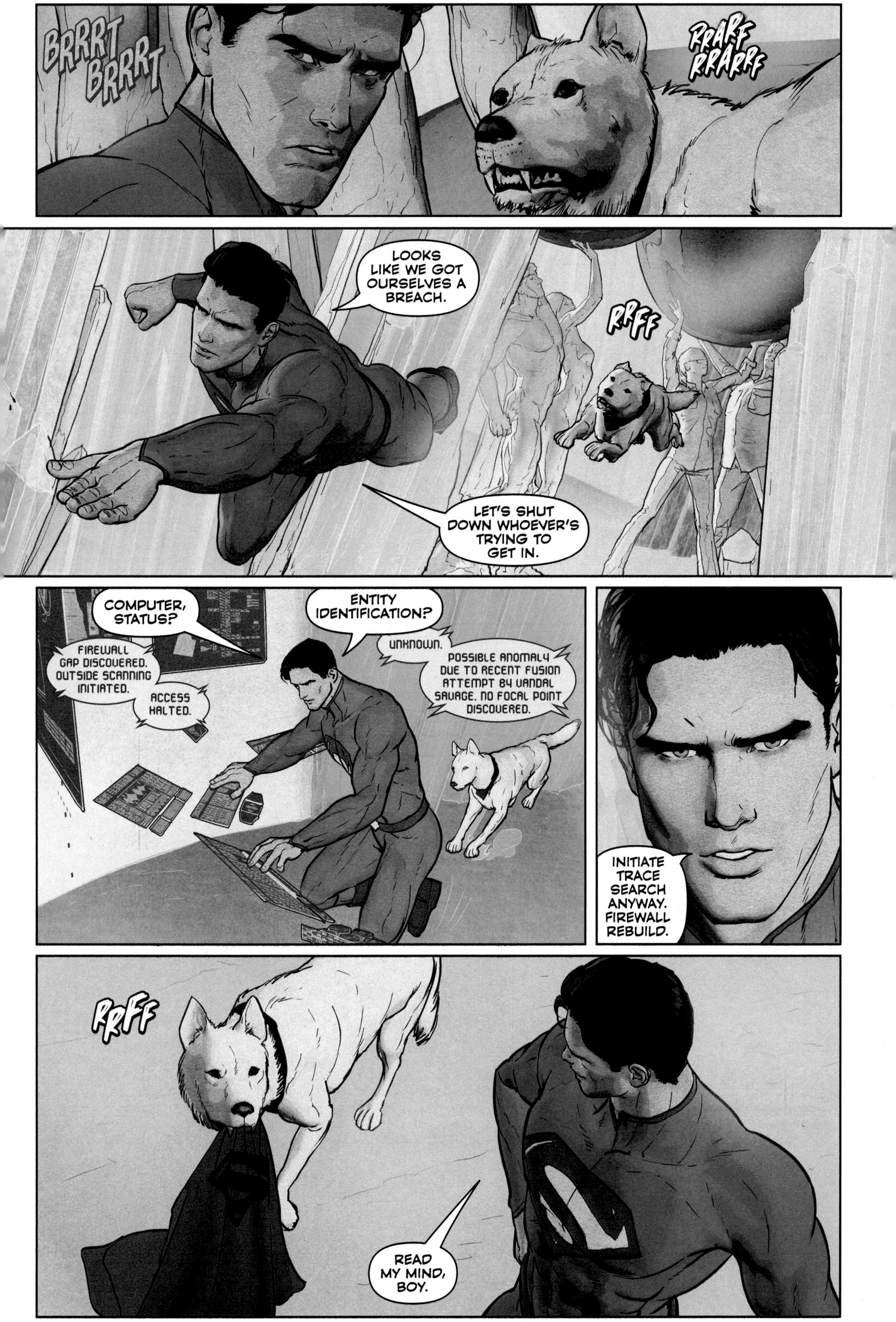
BRRRT BRRRT
RRARFF RRARFF
LOOKS LIKE WE GOT OURSELVES A BREACH.
RRFF
LET'S SHUT DOWN WHOEVER'S TRYING TO GET IN.
COMPUTER, STATUS?
FIREWALL GAP DISCOVERED. OUTSIDE SCANNING INITIATED.
ACCESS HALTED.
ENTITY IDENTIFICATION?
UNKNOWN.
POSSIBLE ANOMALY DUE TO RECENT FUSION ATTEMPT BY VANDAL SAVAGE. NO FOCAL POINT DISCOVERED.
INITIATE TRACE SEARCH ANYWAY. FIREWALL REBUILD.
RRFF
READ MY MIND, BOY.

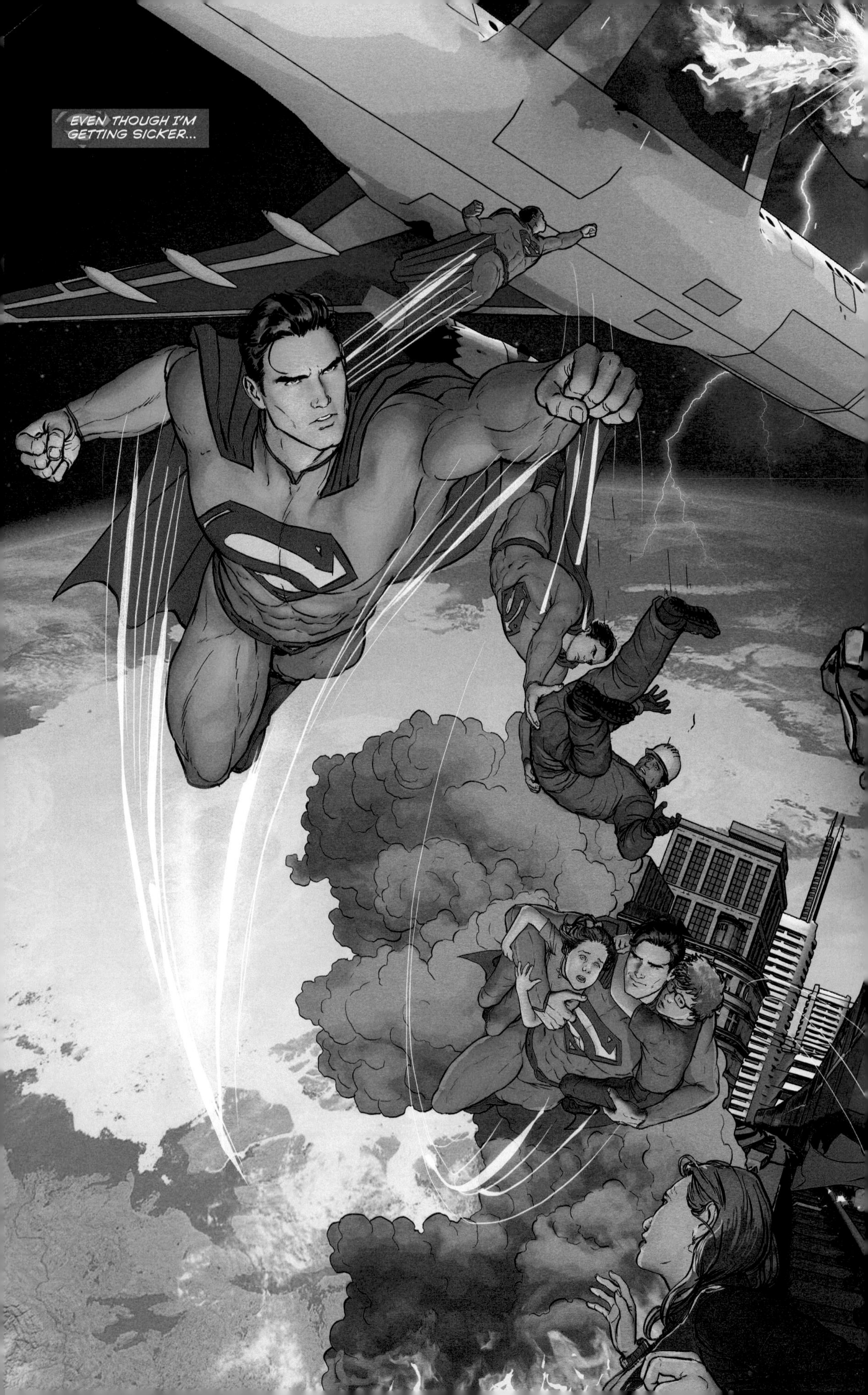
EVEN THOUGH I'M GETTING SICKER...

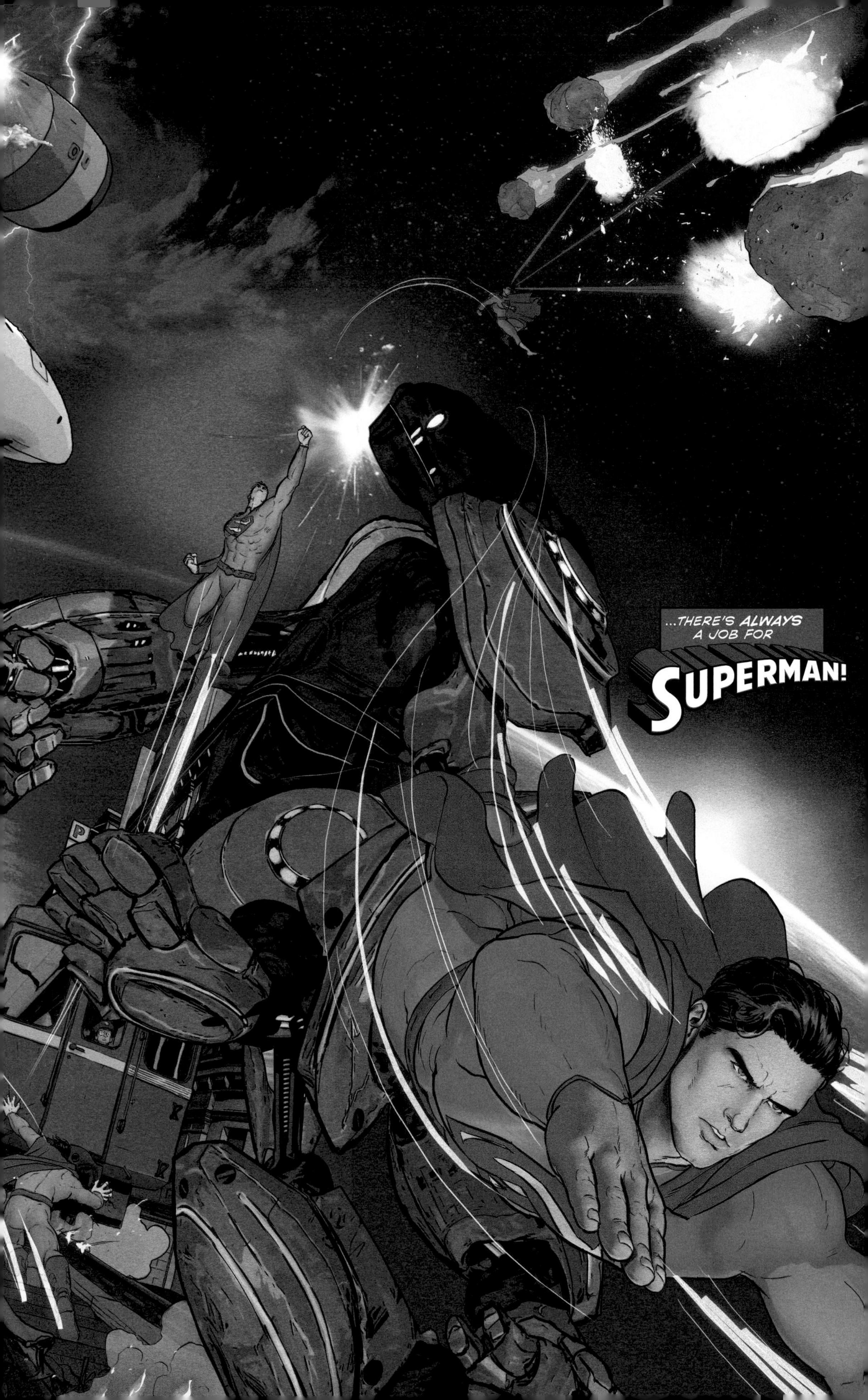
...THERE'S ALWAYS A JOB FOR
SUPERMAN!

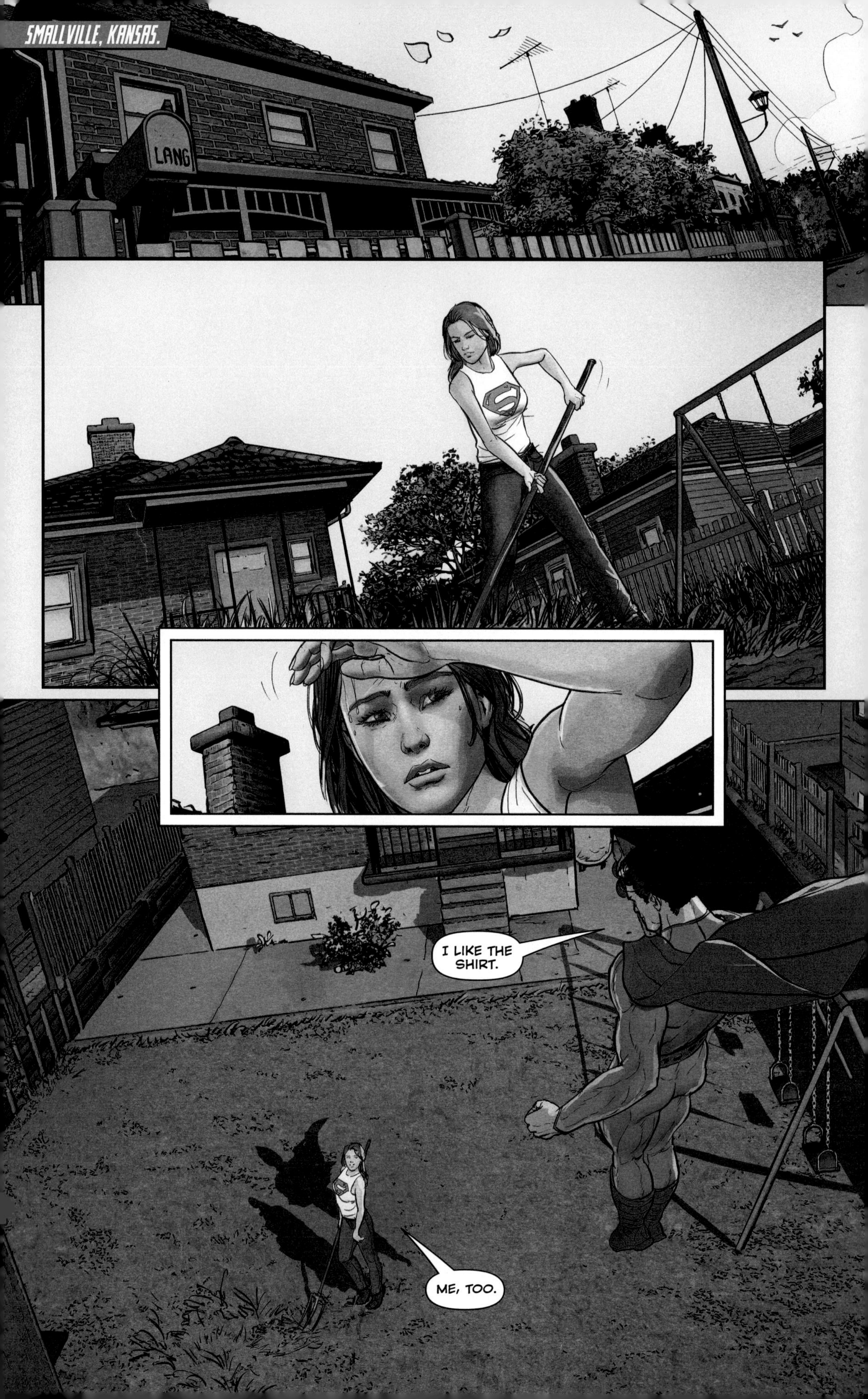
SMALLVILLE, KANSAS.
LANG
I LIKE THE SHIRT.
ME, TOO.

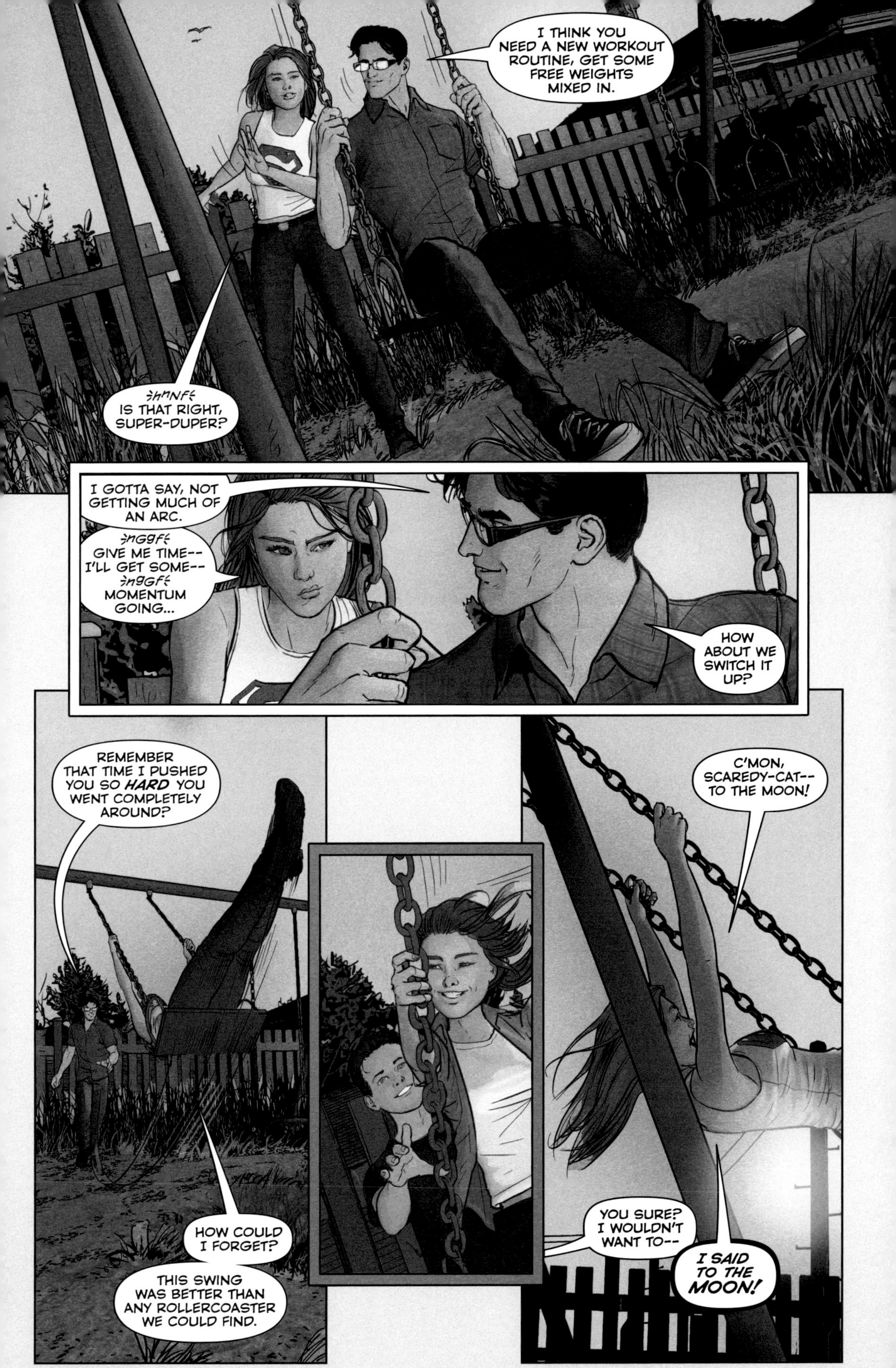
I THINK YOU NEED A NEW WORKOUT ROUTINE, GET SOME FREE WEIGHTS MIXED IN.
HNNF IS THAT RIGHT, SUPER-DUPER?
I GOTTA SAY, NOT GETTING MUCH OF AN ARC.
NGGF GIVE ME TIME-- I'LL GET SOME-- NGGF MOMENTUM GOING...
HOW ABOUT WE SWITCH IT UP?
REMEMBER THAT TIME I PUSHED YOU SO HARD YOU WENT COMPLETELY AROUND?
HOW COULD I FORGET?
THIS SWING WAS BETTER THAN ANY ROLLERCOASTER WE COULD FIND.
C'MON, SCAREDY-CAT-- TO THE MOON!
YOU SURE? I WOULDN'T WANT TO--
I SAID TO THE MOON!

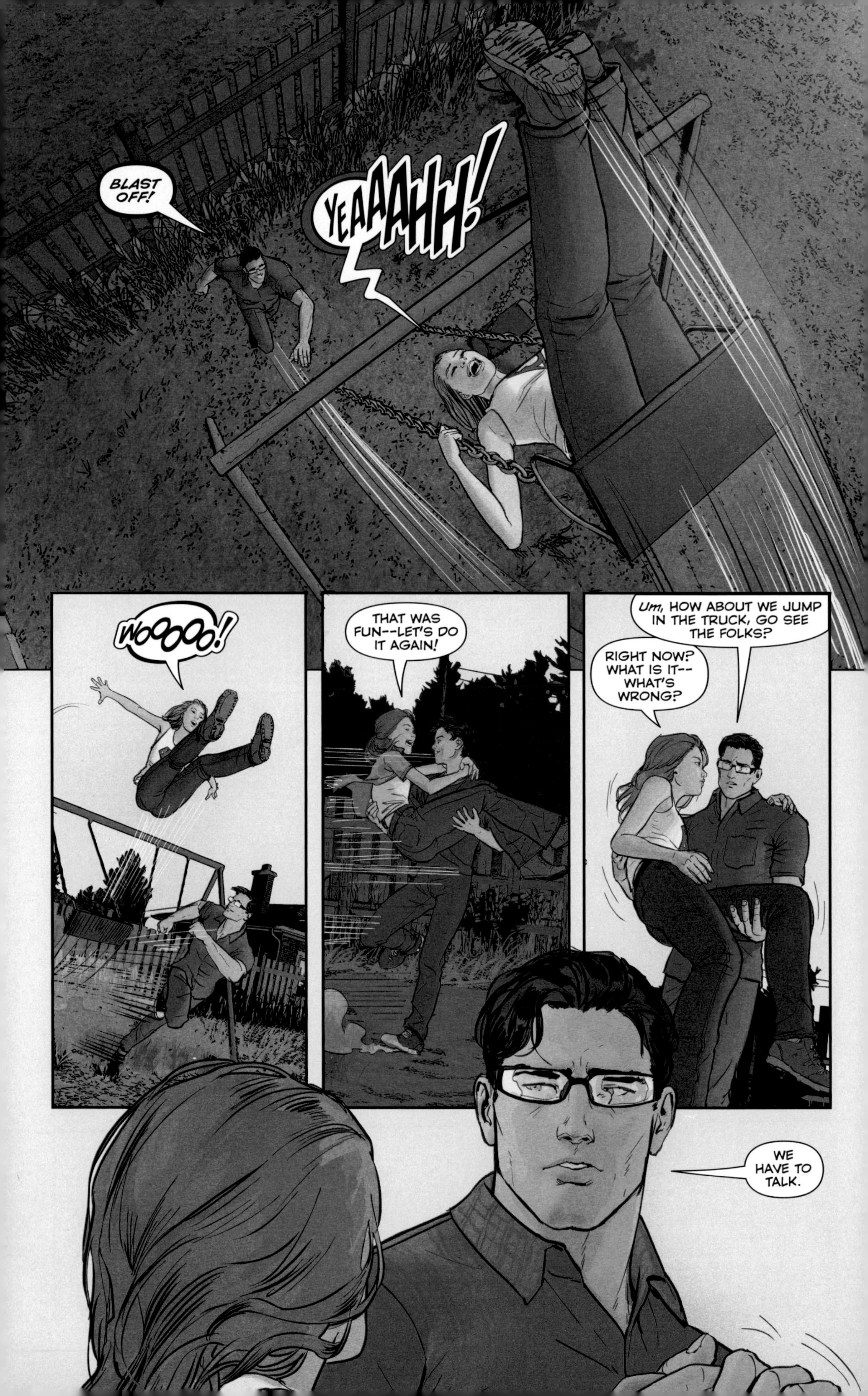
BLAST OFF!
YEAAAHH!
WOOOOO!
THAT WAS FUN--LET'S DO IT AGAIN!
Um, HOW ABOUT WE JUMP IN THE TRUCK, GO SEE THE FOLKS?
RIGHT NOW? WHAT IS IT--WHAT'S WRONG?
WE HAVE TO TALK.

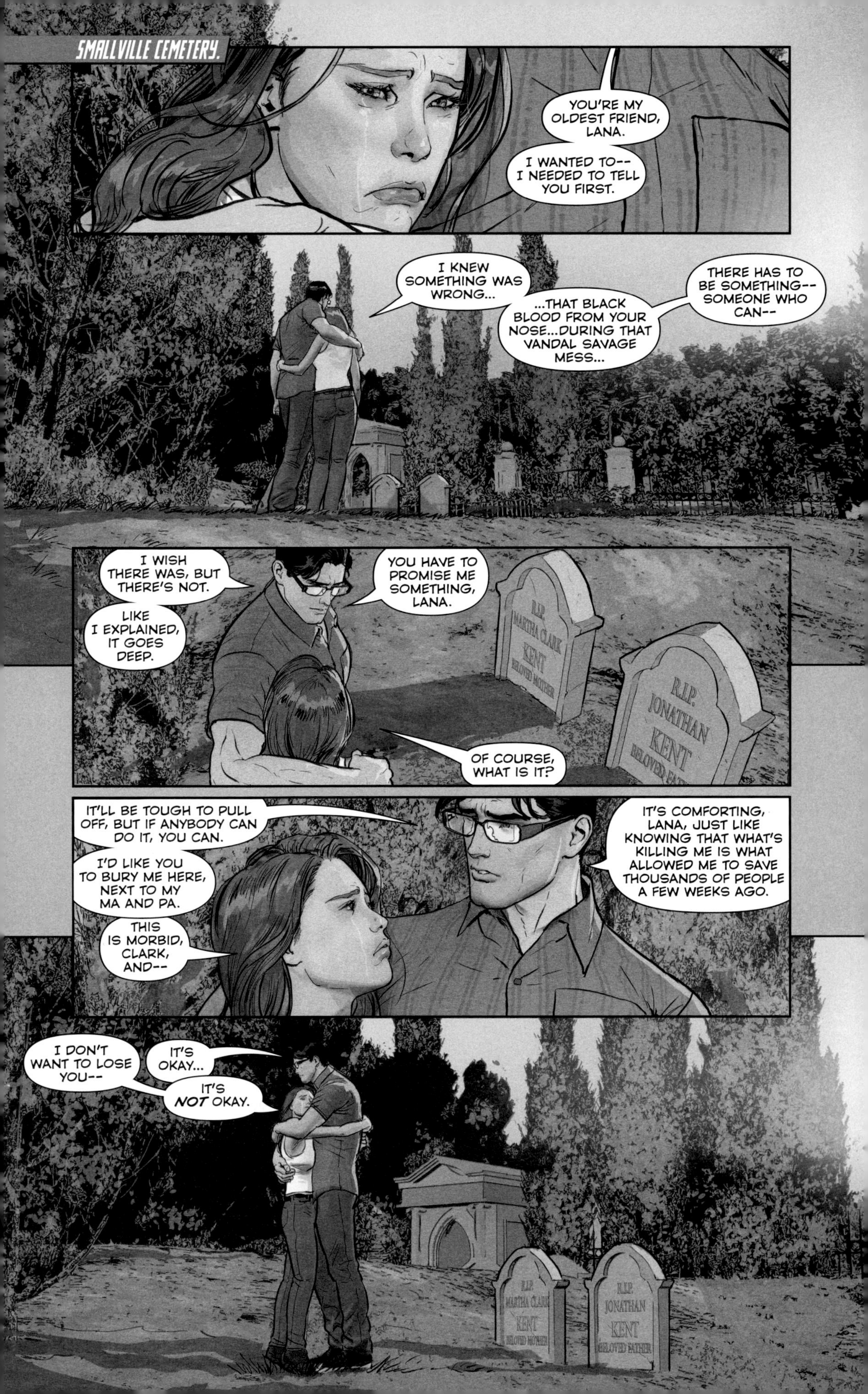
SMALLVILLE CEMETERY.
YOU'RE MY OLDEST FRIEND, LANA.
I WANTED TO-- I NEEDED TO TELL YOU FIRST.
I KNEW SOMETHING WAS WRONG...
...THAT BLACK BLOOD FROM YOUR NOSE...DURING THAT VANDAL SAVAGE MESS...
THERE HAS TO BE SOMETHING-- SOMEONE WHO CAN--
I WISH THERE WAS, BUT THERE'S NOT.
LIKE I EXPLAINED, IT GOES DEEP.
YOU HAVE TO PROMISE ME SOMETHING, LANA.
R.I.P. MARTHA CLARK KENT BELOVED MOTHER
R.I.P. JONATHAN KENT BELOVED FATHER
OF COURSE, WHAT IS IT?
IT'LL BE TOUGH TO PULL OFF, BUT IF ANYBODY CAN DO IT, YOU CAN.
I'D LIKE YOU TO BURY ME HERE, NEXT TO MY MA AND PA.
THIS IS MORBID, CLARK, AND--
IT'S COMFORTING, LANA, JUST LIKE KNOWING THAT WHAT'S KILLING ME IS WHAT ALLOWED ME TO SAVE THOUSANDS OF PEOPLE A FEW WEEKS AGO.
I DON'T WANT TO LOSE YOU--
IT'S OKAY...
IT'S NOT OKAY.
R.I.P. MARTHA CLARK KENT BELOVED MOTHER
R.I.P. JONATHAN KENT BELOVED FATHER

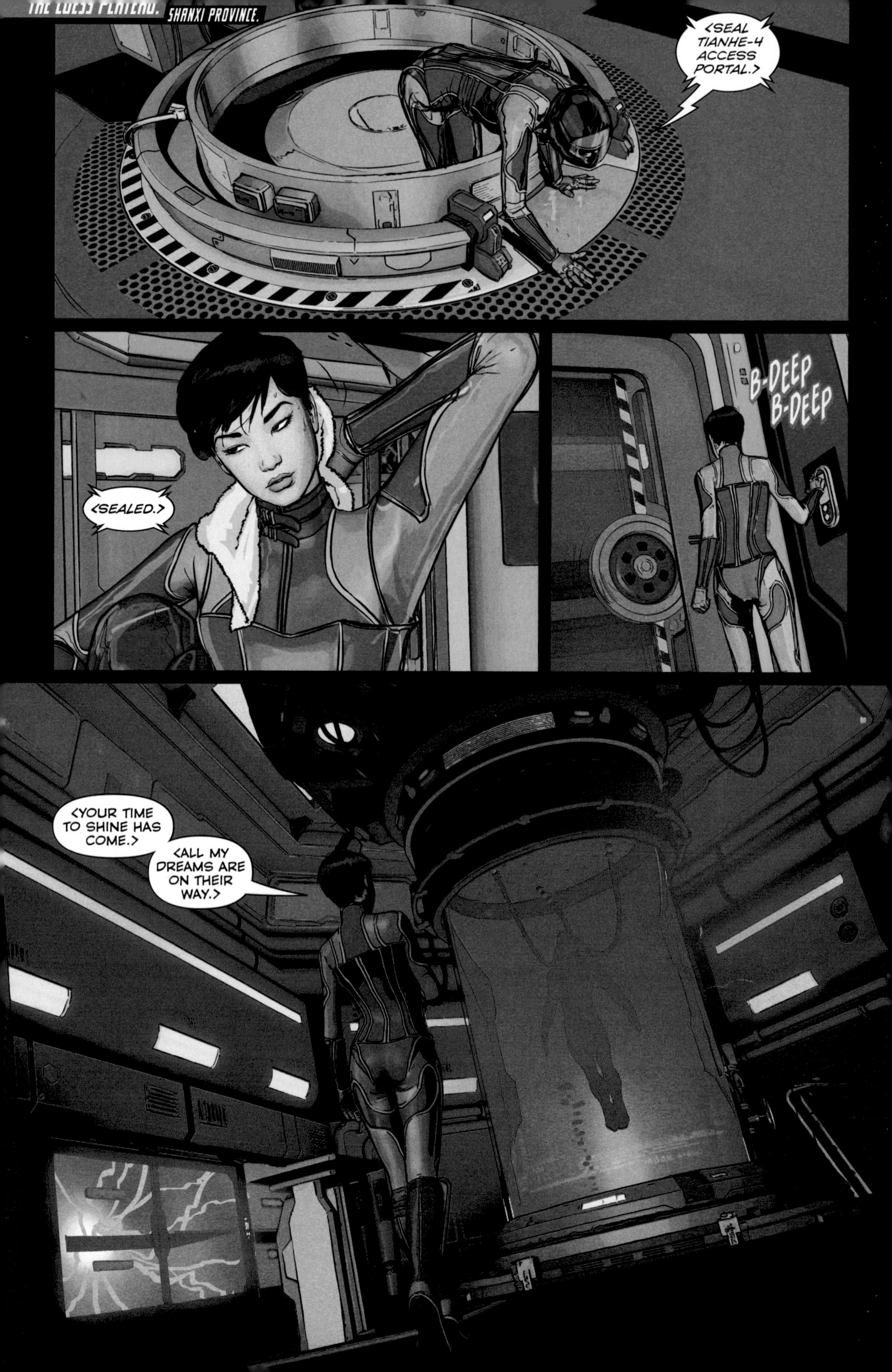
SHANXI PROVINCE.
<SEAL TIANHE-4 ACCESS PORTAL.>
<SEALED.>
B-DEEP
B-DEEP
<YOUR TIME TO SHINE HAS COME.>
<ALL MY DREAMS ARE ON THEIR WAY.>

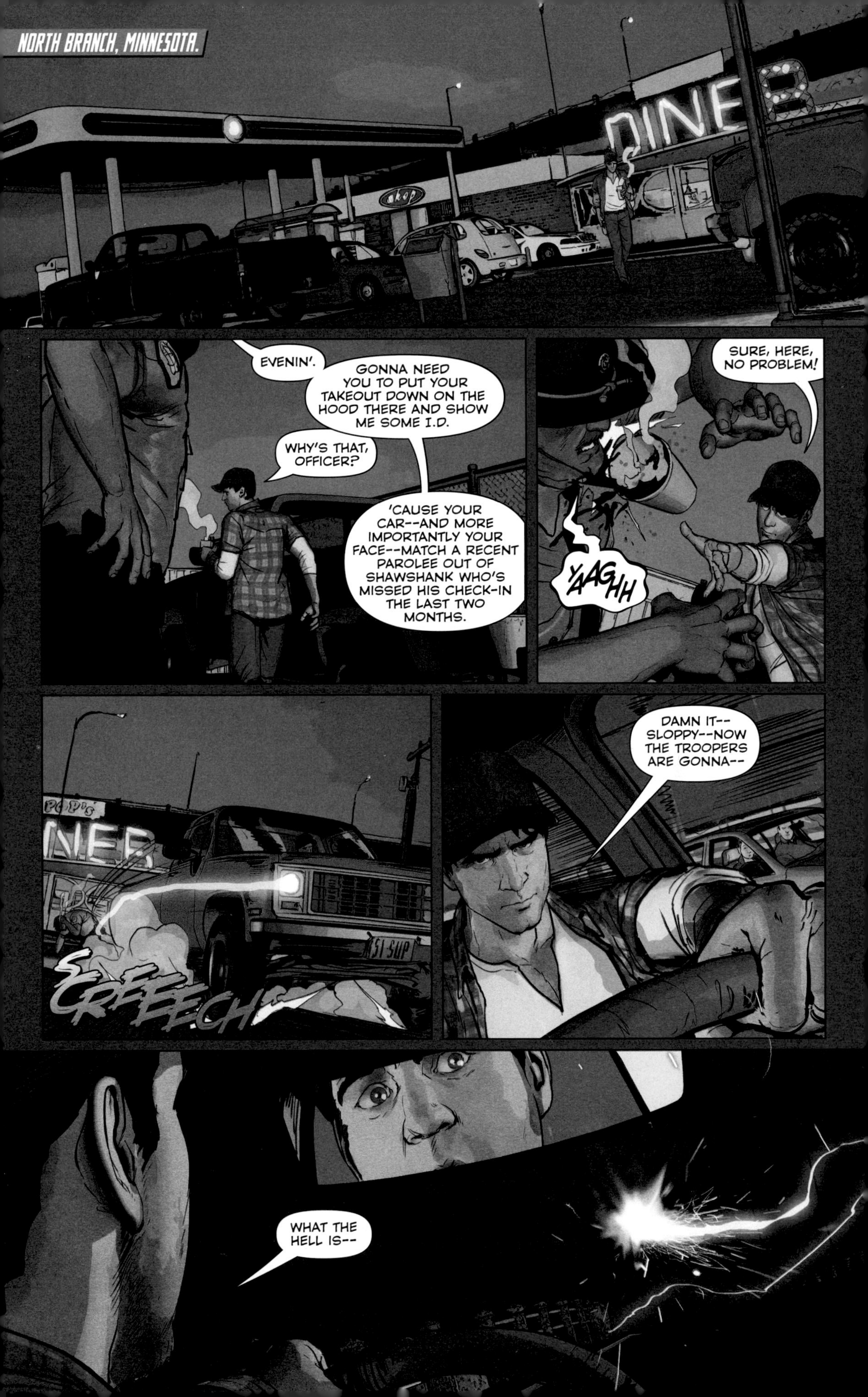
NORTH BRANCH, MINNESOTA.
EVENIN'.
GONNA NEED YOU TO PUT YOUR TAKEOUT DOWN ON THE HOOD THERE AND SHOW ME SOME I.D.
WHY'S THAT, OFFICER?
'CAUSE YOUR CAR--AND MORE IMPORTANTLY YOUR FACE--MATCH A RECENT PAROLEE OUT OF SHAWSHANK WHO'S MISSED HIS CHECK-IN THE LAST TWO MONTHS.
SURE, HERE, NO PROBLEM!
YAAGHH
SCREEECH
DAMN IT-- SLOPPY--NOW THE TROOPERS ARE GONNA--
WHAT THE HELL IS--

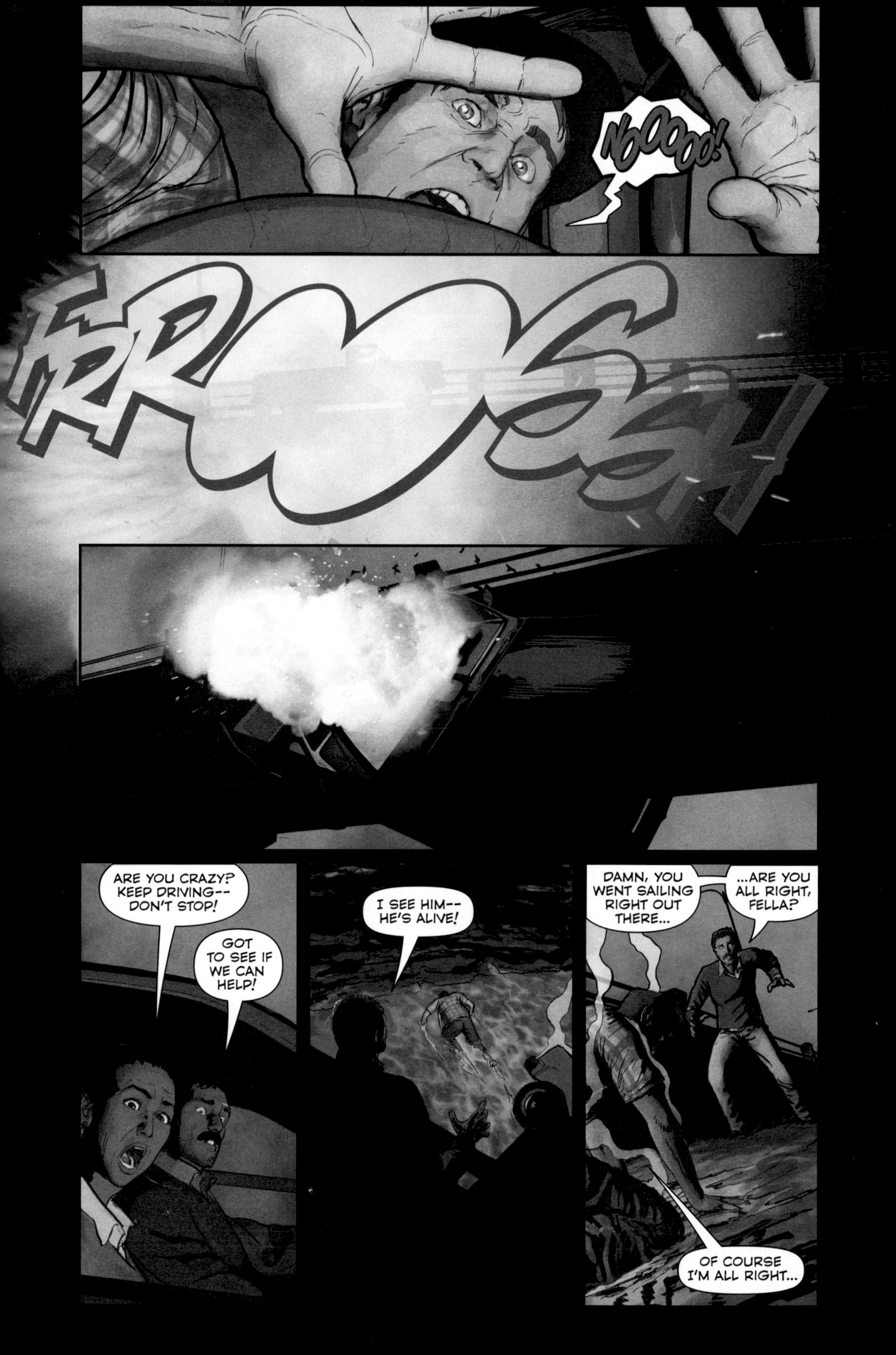
NOOOOO!
FRROOSSH
ARE YOU CRAZY? KEEP DRIVING-- DON'T STOP!
GOT TO SEE IF WE CAN HELP!
I SEE HIM-- HE'S ALIVE!
DAMN, YOU WENT SAILING RIGHT OUT THERE...
...ARE YOU ALL RIGHT, FELLA?
OF COURSE I'M ALL RIGHT...

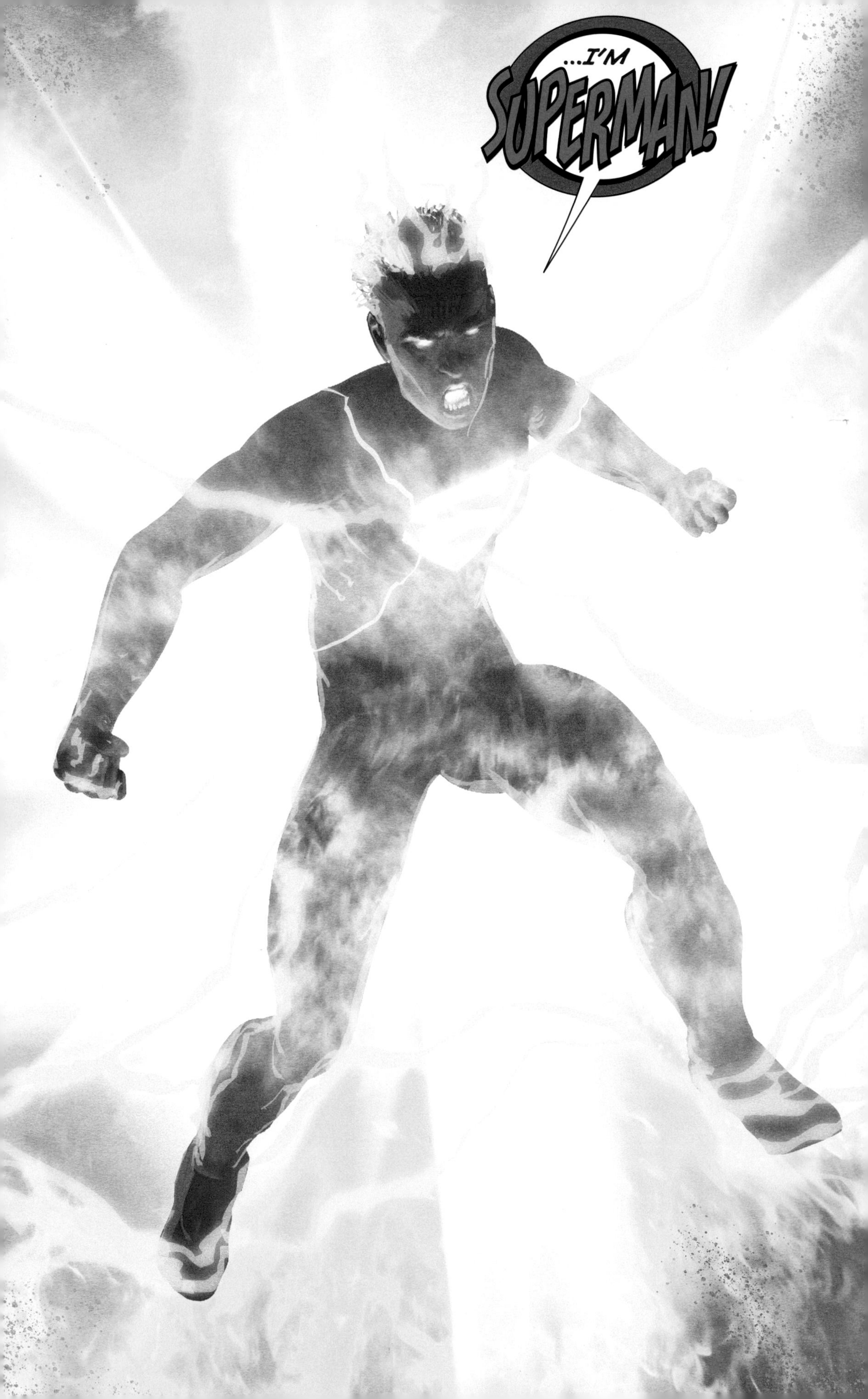
...I'M SUPERMAN!

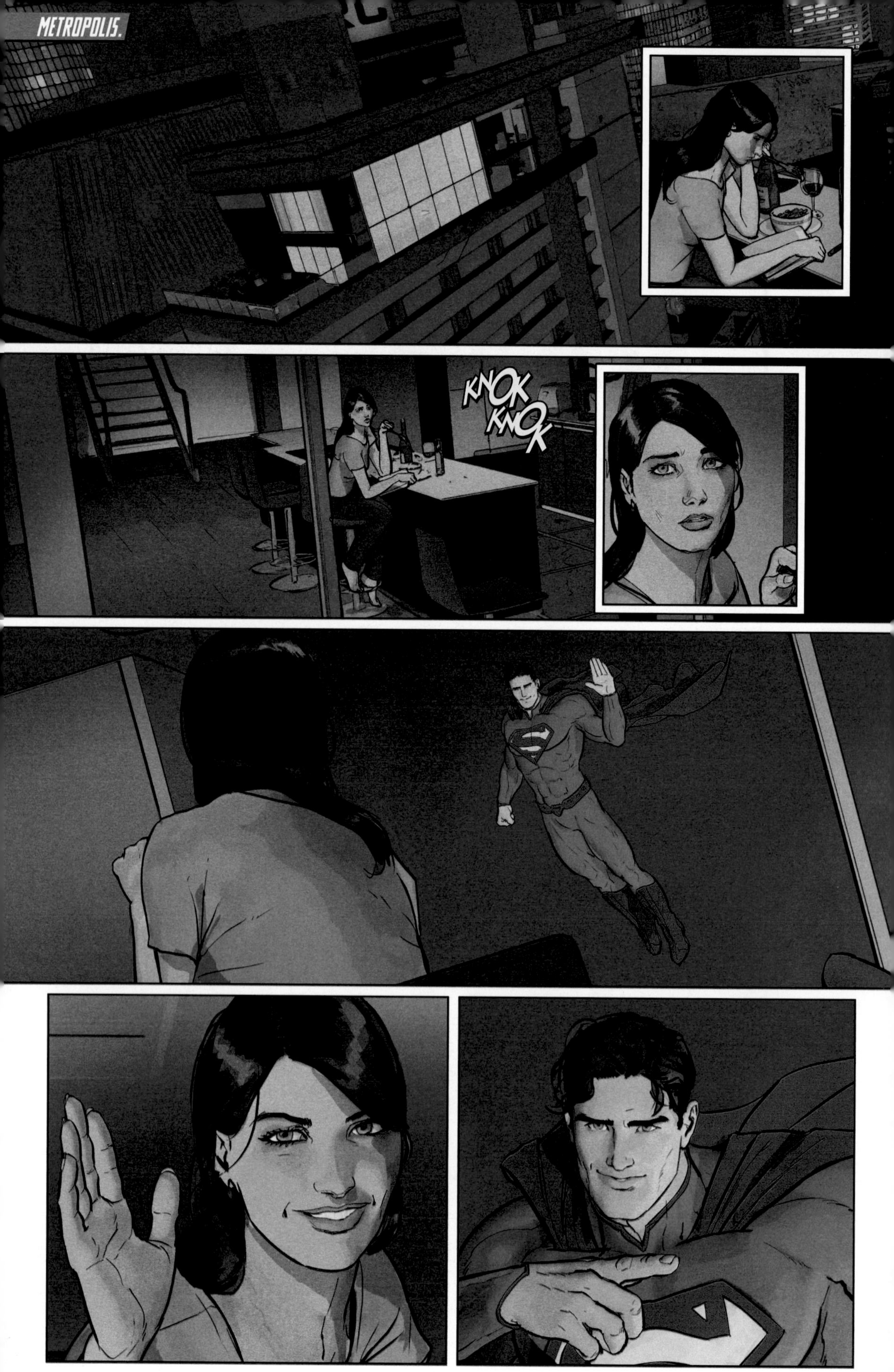
METROPOLIS.
KNOK KNOK

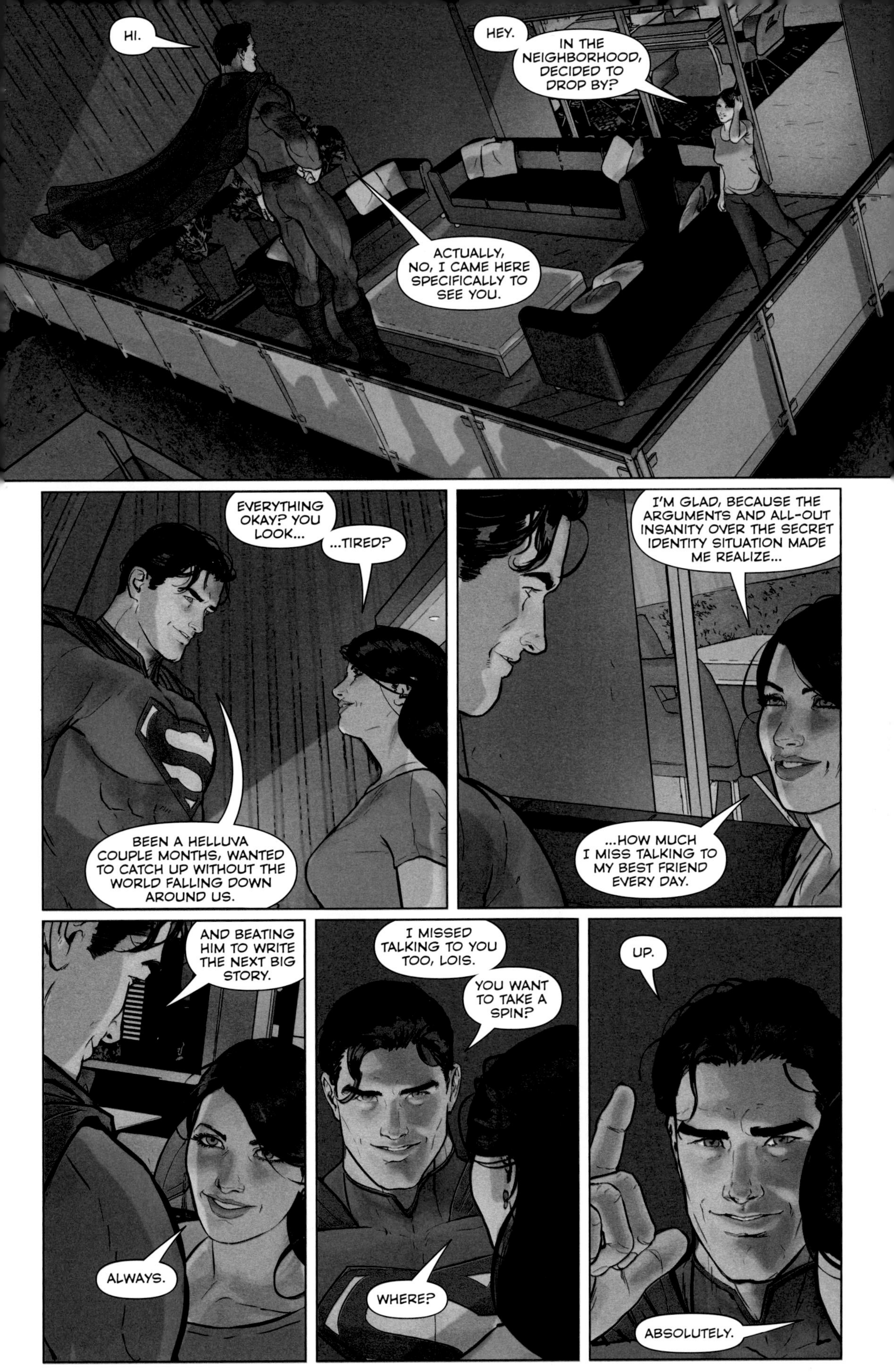
HI.
HEY.
IN THE NEIGHBORHOOD, DECIDED TO DROP BY?
ACTUALLY, NO, I CAME HERE SPECIFICALLY TO SEE YOU.
EVERYTHING OKAY? YOU LOOK...
...TIRED?
BEEN A HELLUVA COUPLE MONTHS, WANTED TO CATCH UP WITHOUT THE WORLD FALLING DOWN AROUND US.
I'M GLAD, BECAUSE THE ARGUMENTS AND ALL-OUT INSANITY OVER THE SECRET IDENTITY SITUATION MADE ME REALIZE...
...HOW MUCH I MISS TALKING TO MY BEST FRIEND EVERY DAY.
AND BEATING HIM TO WRITE THE NEXT BIG STORY.
ALWAYS.
I MISSED TALKING TO YOU TOO, LOIS.
YOU WANT TO TAKE A SPIN?
WHERE?
UP.
ABSOLUTELY.

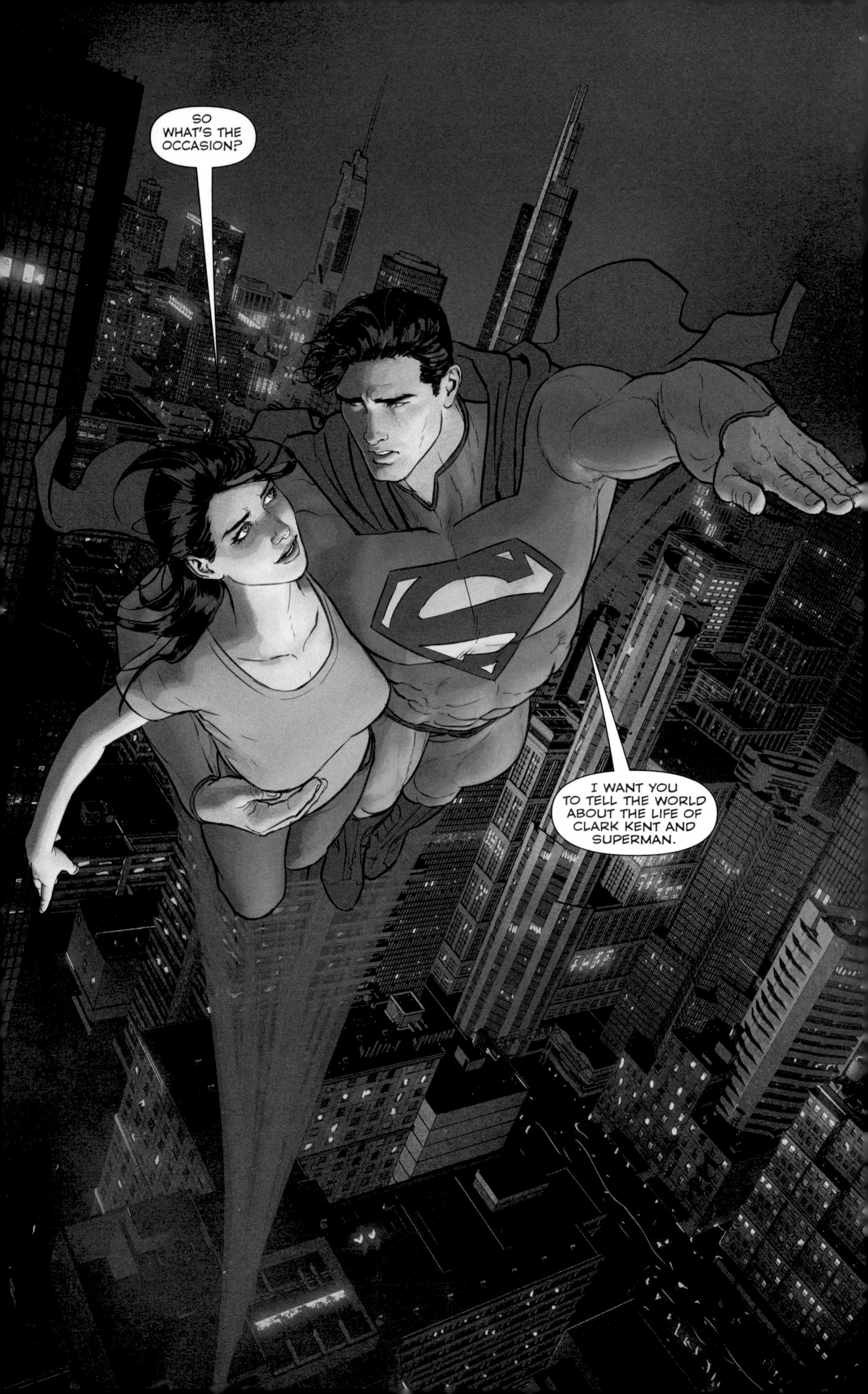
SO WHAT'S THE OCCASION?
I WANT YOU TO TELL THE WORLD ABOUT THE LIFE OF CLARK KENT AND SUPERMAN.

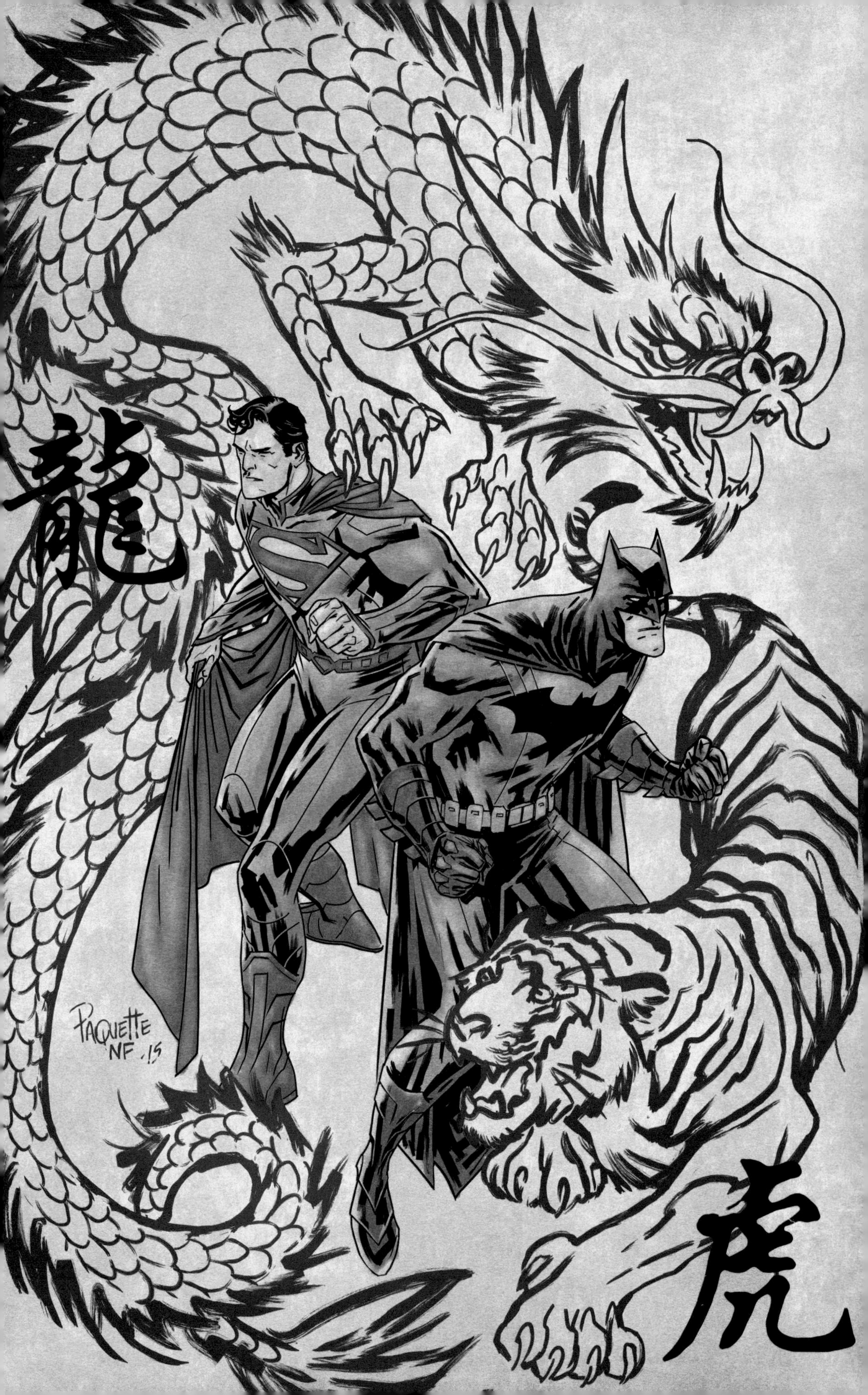
龍
PAQUETTE
NF '15
虎

THE FINAL DAYS OF SUPERMAN PART 2: DARK DISCOVERY

PETER J. TOMASI writer **DOUG MAHNKE** penciller **JAIME MENDOZA** inker **WIL QUINTANA** colorist **ROB LEIGH** letterer **YANICK PAQUETTE NATHAN FAIRBAIRN** cover

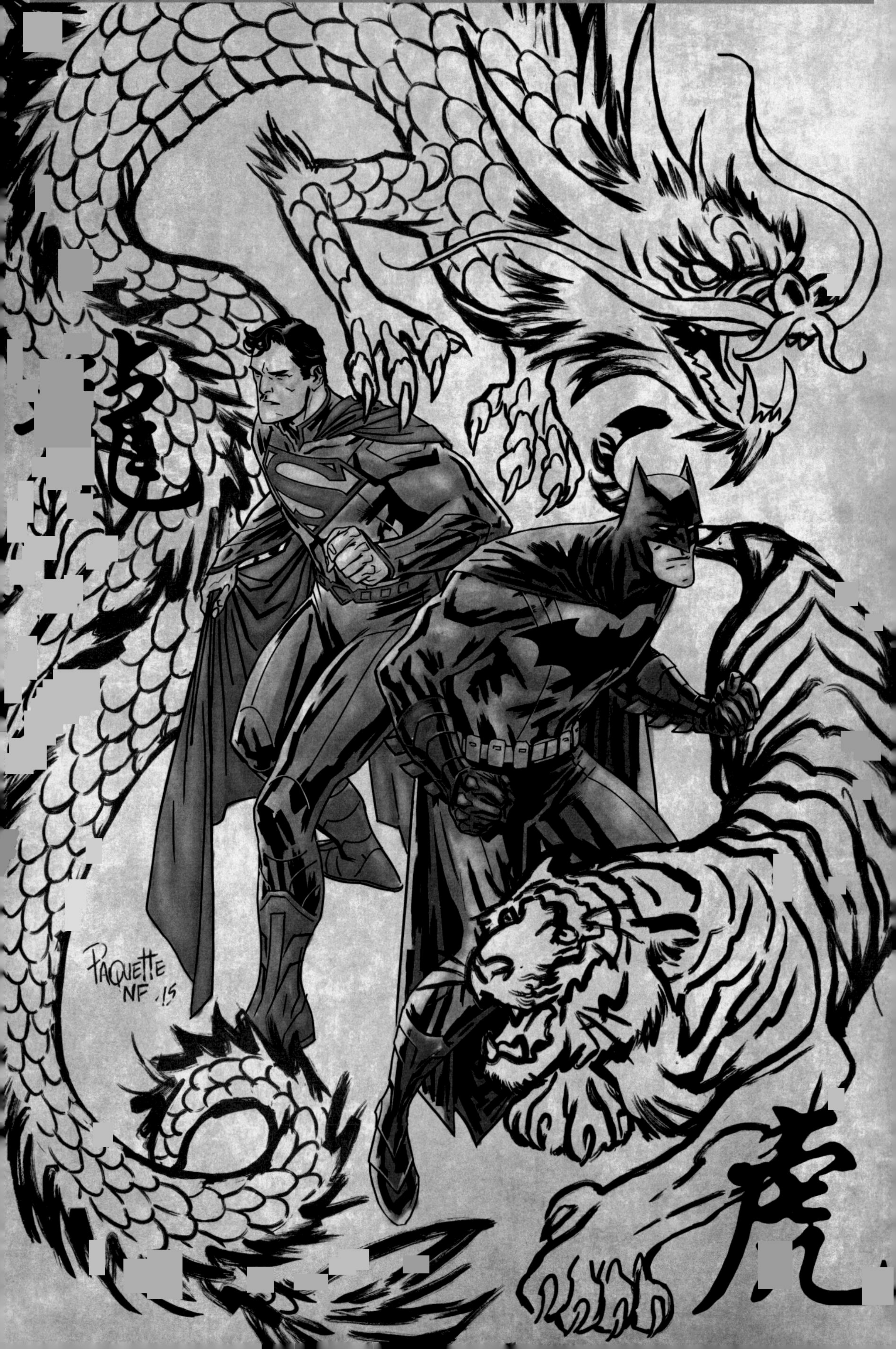
PAQUETTE
NF '15
虎

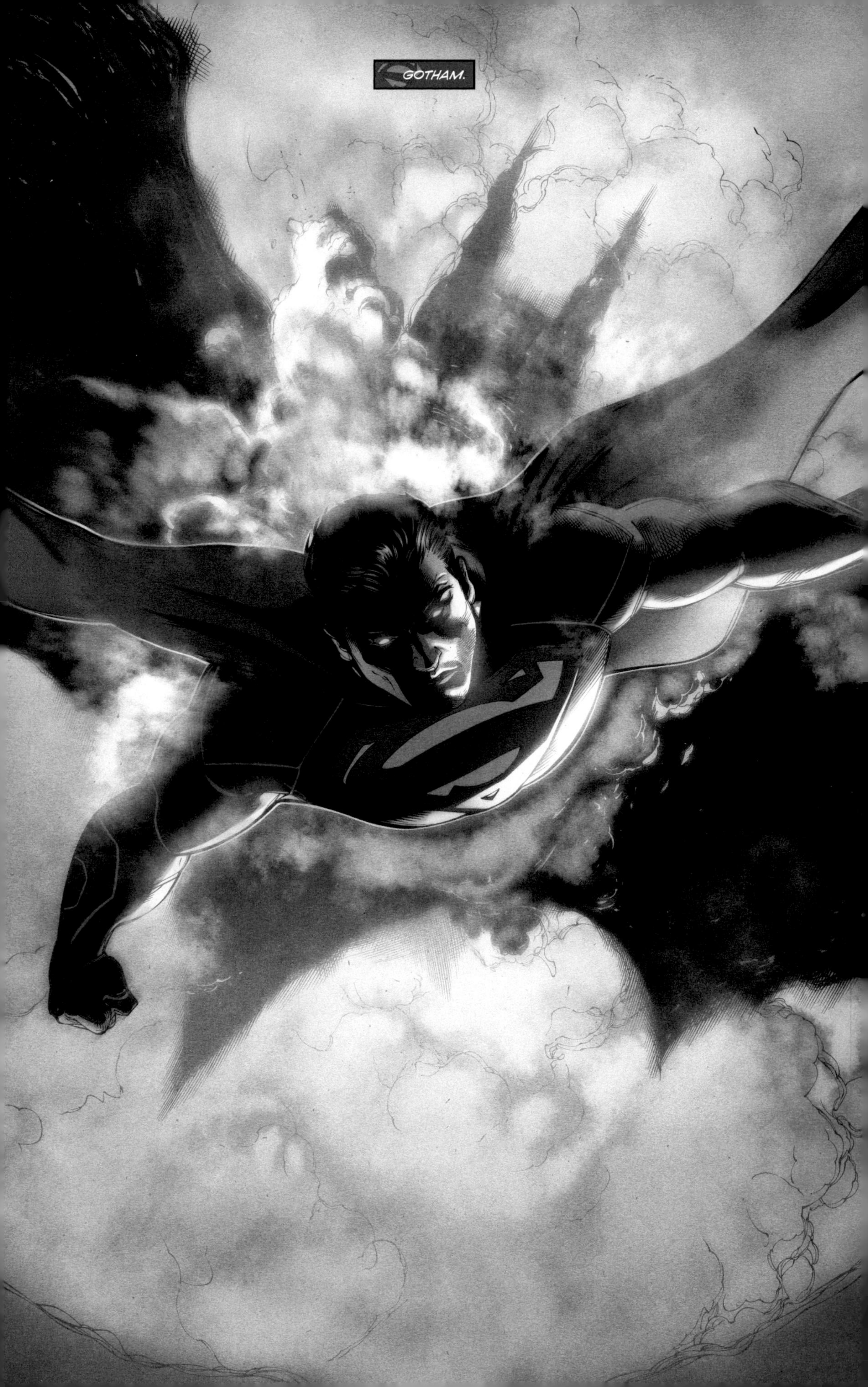
GOTHAM.

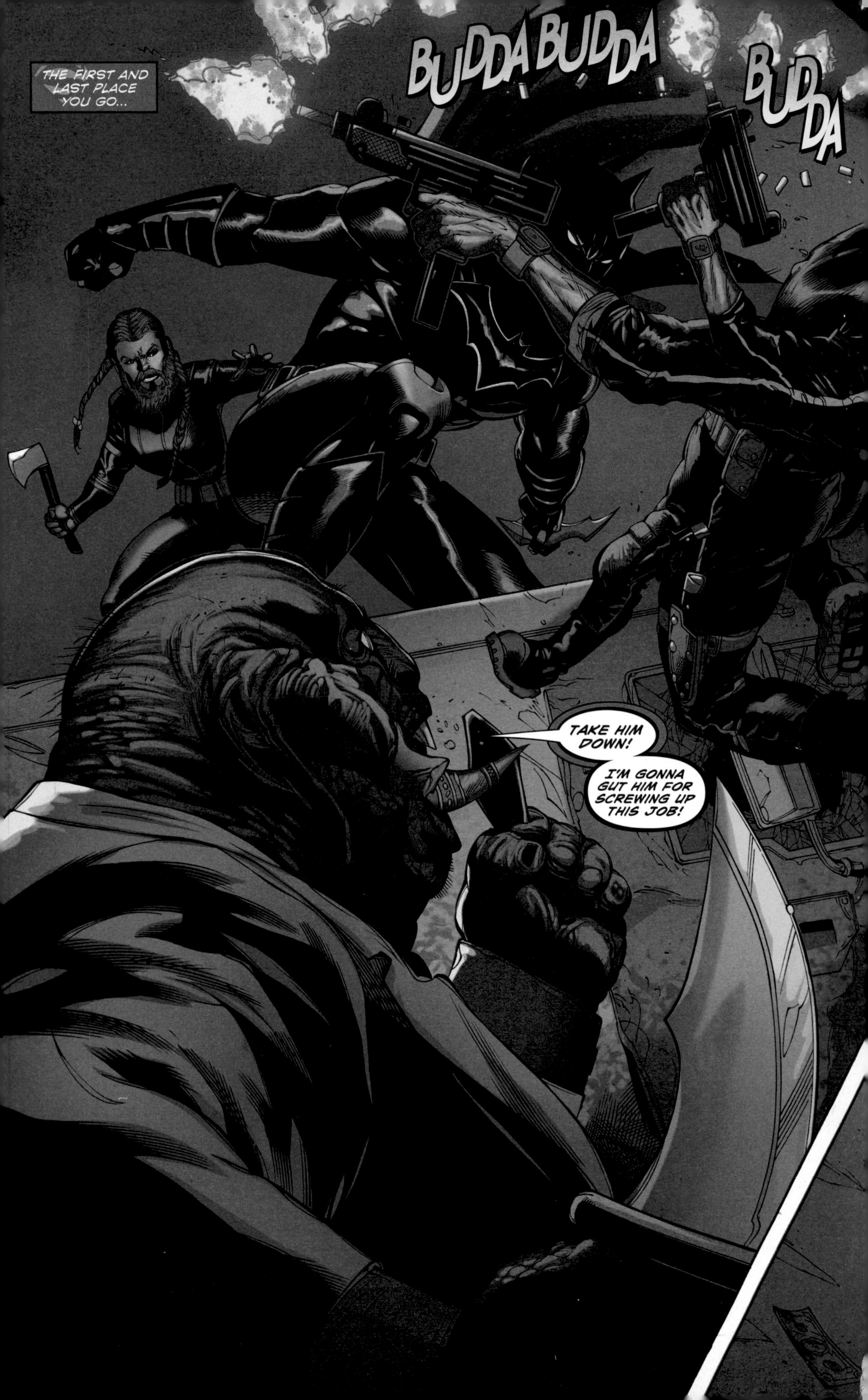
THE FIRST AND LAST PLACE YOU GO...
BUDDA BUDDA
BUDDA
TAKE HIM DOWN!
I'M GONNA GUT HIM FOR SCREWING UP THIS JOB!

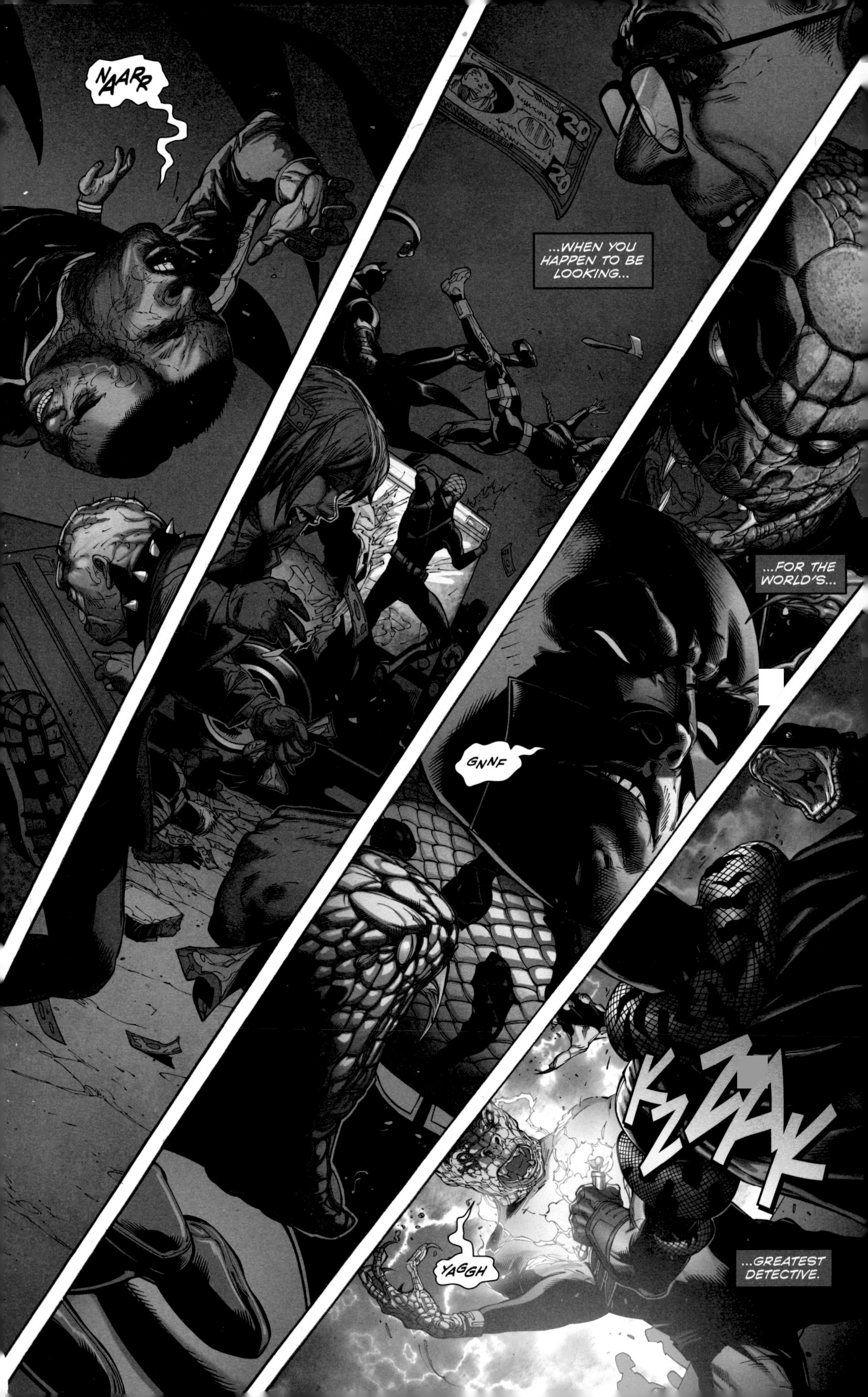
NAARR
...WHEN YOU HAPPEN TO BE LOOKING...
...FOR THE WORLD'S...
GNNF
KZZAK
YAGGH
...GREATEST DETECTIVE.

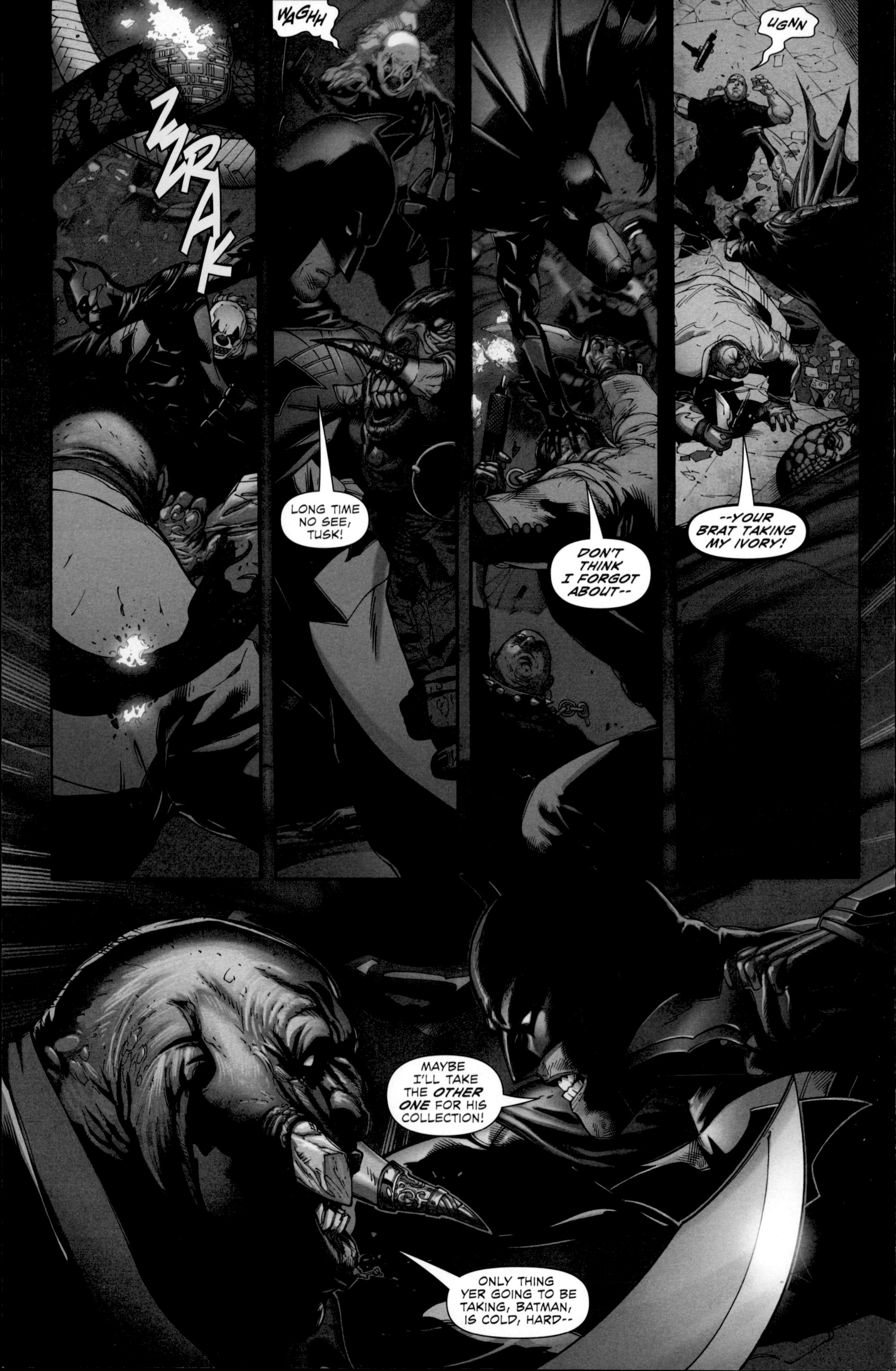
ZZRAK
WAGHH
LONG TIME NO SEE, TUSK!
DON'T THINK I FORGOT ABOUT--
UGNN
--YOUR BRAT TAKING MY IVORY!
MAYBE I'LL TAKE THE OTHER ONE FOR HIS COLLECTION!
ONLY THING YER GOING TO BE TAKING, BATMAN, IS COLD, HARD--

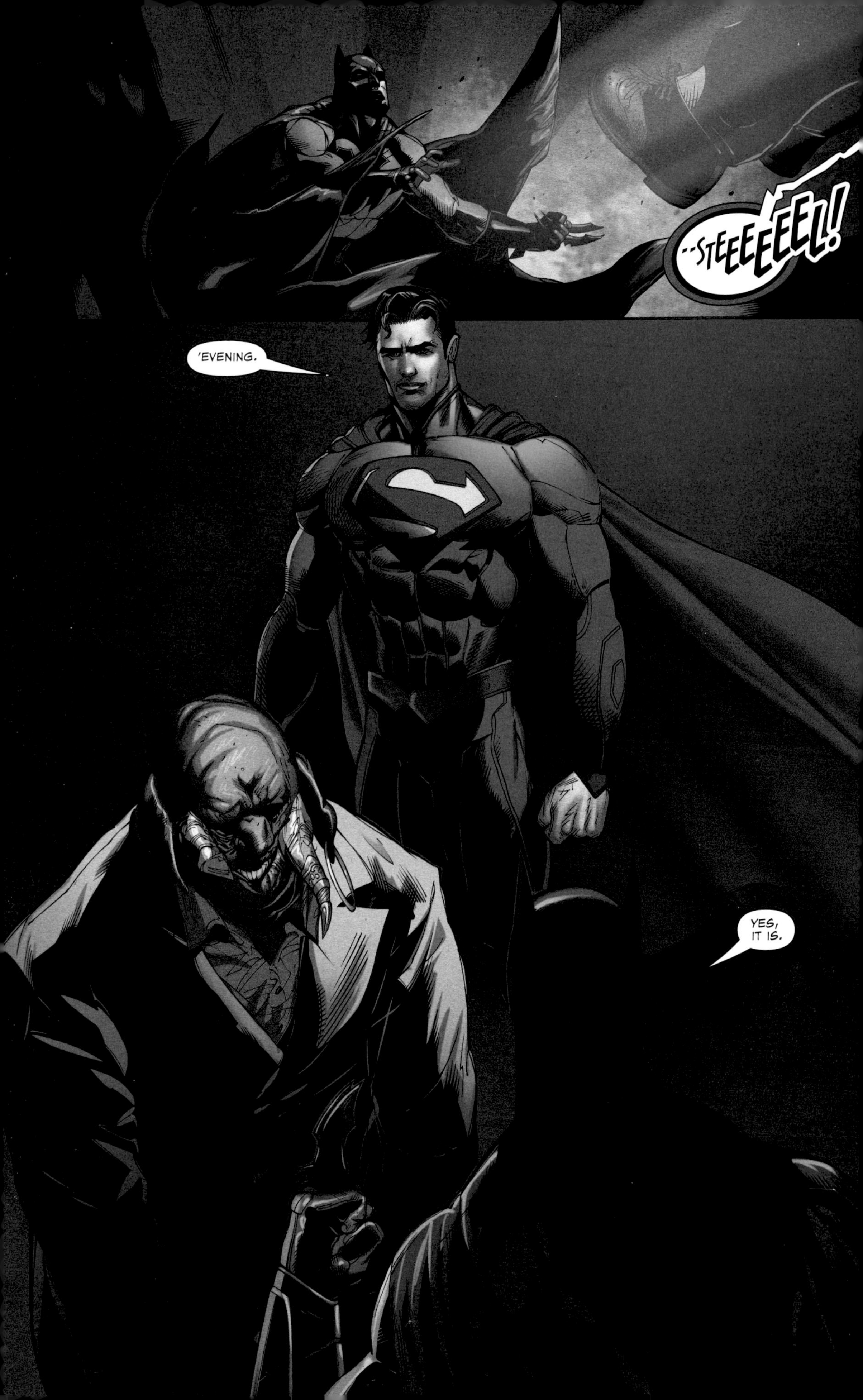
--STEEEEEEL!!
'EVENING.
YES, IT IS.

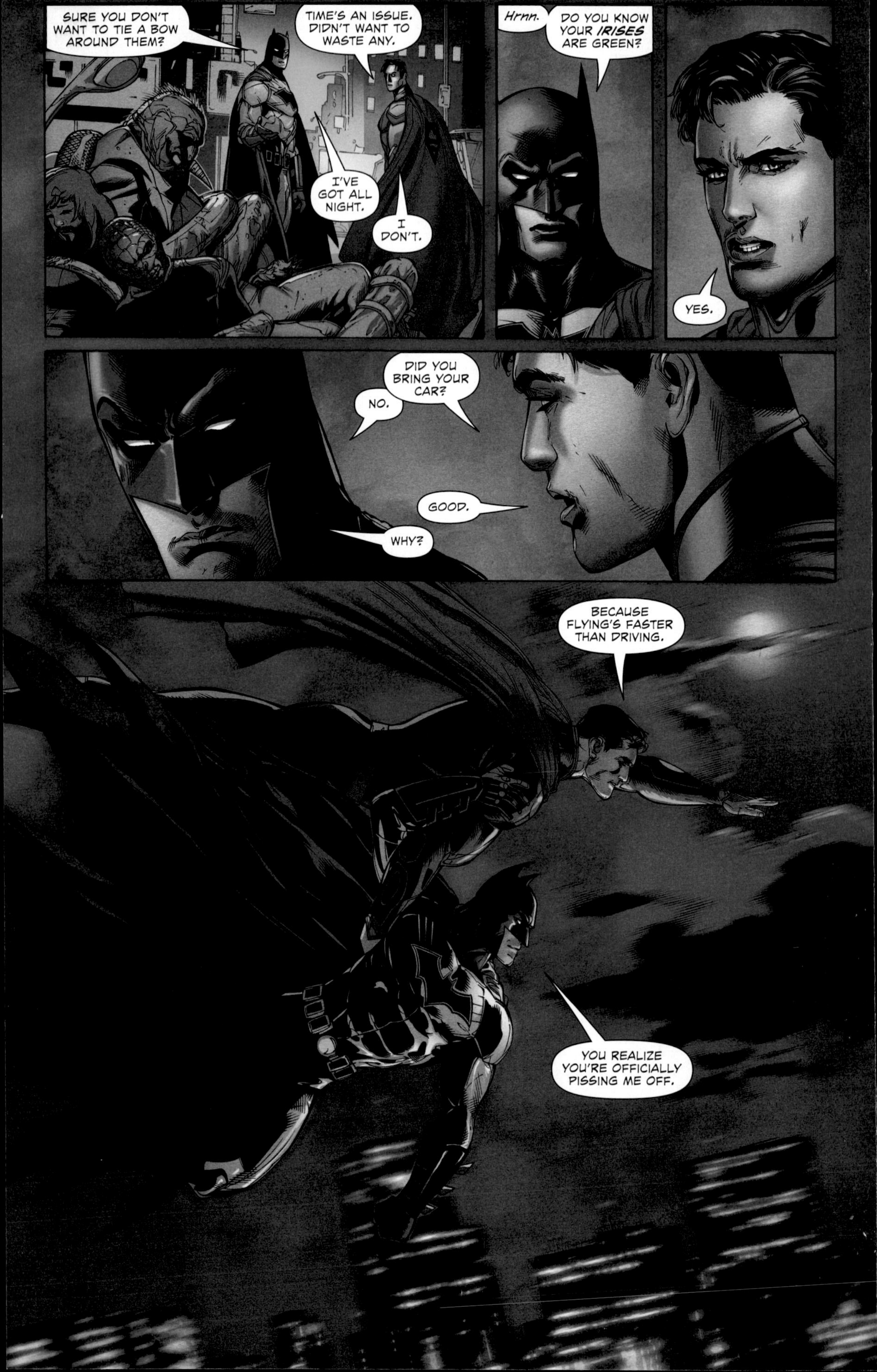
SURE YOU DON'T WANT TO TIE A BOW AROUND THEM?
TIME'S AN ISSUE. DIDN'T WANT TO WASTE ANY.
I'VE GOT ALL NIGHT.
I DON'T.
Hrnn.
DO YOU KNOW YOUR IRISES ARE GREEN?
YES.
DID YOU BRING YOUR CAR?
NO.
GOOD.
WHY?
BECAUSE FLYING'S FASTER THAN DRIVING.
YOU REALIZE YOU'RE OFFICIALLY PISSING ME OFF.

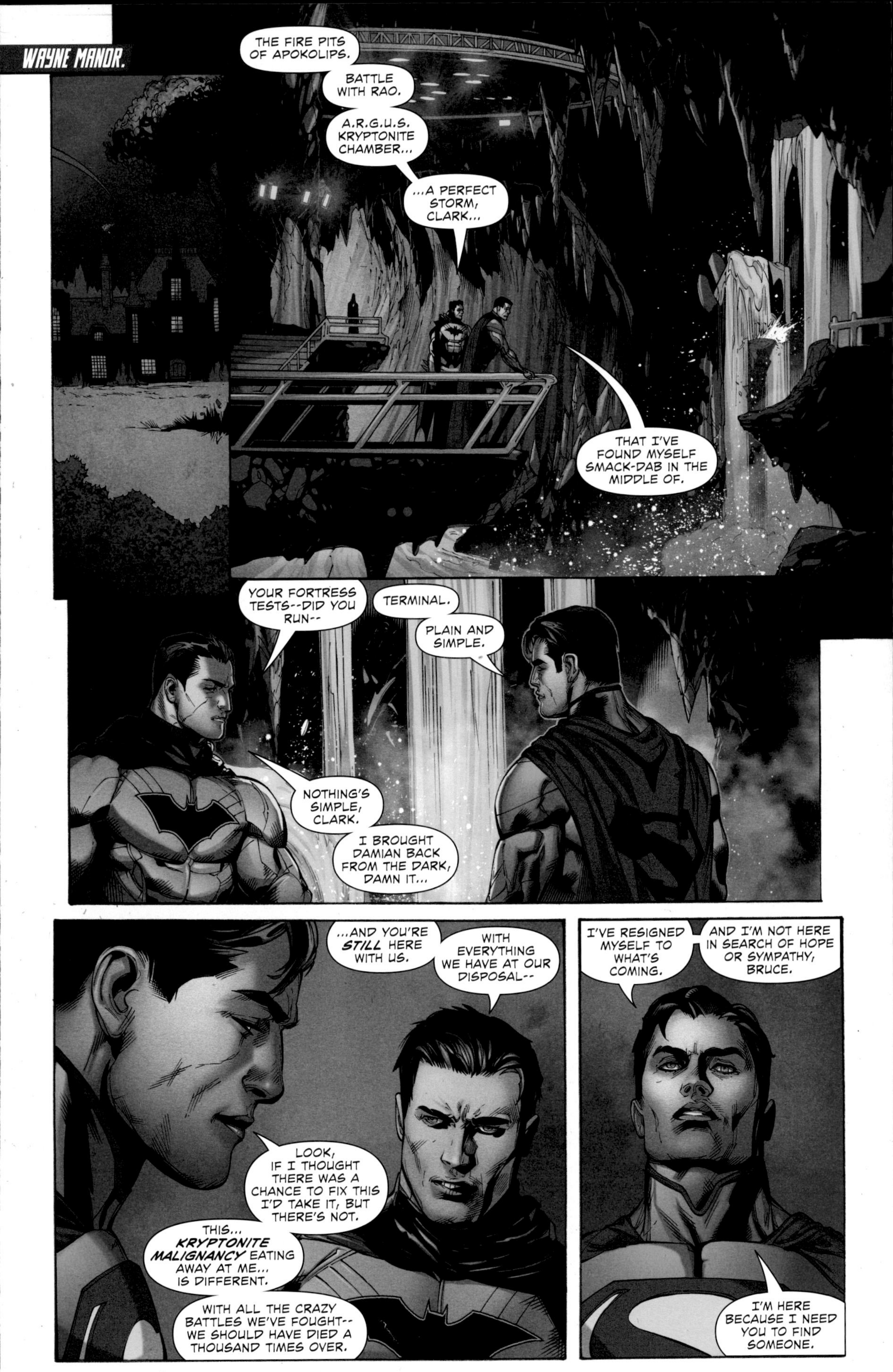
WAYNE MANOR.
THE FIRE PITS OF APOKOLIPS.
BATTLE WITH RAO.
A.R.G.U.S. KRYPTONITE CHAMBER...
...A PERFECT STORM, CLARK...
THAT I'VE FOUND MYSELF SMACK-DAB IN THE MIDDLE OF.
YOUR FORTRESS TESTS--DID YOU RUN--
TERMINAL.
PLAIN AND SIMPLE.
NOTHING'S SIMPLE, CLARK.
I BROUGHT DAMIAN BACK FROM THE DARK, DAMN IT...
...AND YOU'RE STILL HERE WITH US.
WITH EVERYTHING WE HAVE AT OUR DISPOSAL--
LOOK, IF I THOUGHT THERE WAS A CHANCE TO FIX THIS I'D TAKE IT, BUT THERE'S NOT.
THIS... KRYPTONITE MALIGNANCY EATING AWAY AT ME... IS DIFFERENT.
WITH ALL THE CRAZY BATTLES WE'VE FOUGHT--WE SHOULD HAVE DIED A THOUSAND TIMES OVER.
I'VE RESIGNED MYSELF TO WHAT'S COMING.
AND I'M NOT HERE IN SEARCH OF HOPE OR SYMPATHY, BRUCE.
I'M HERE BECAUSE I NEED YOU TO FIND SOMEONE.

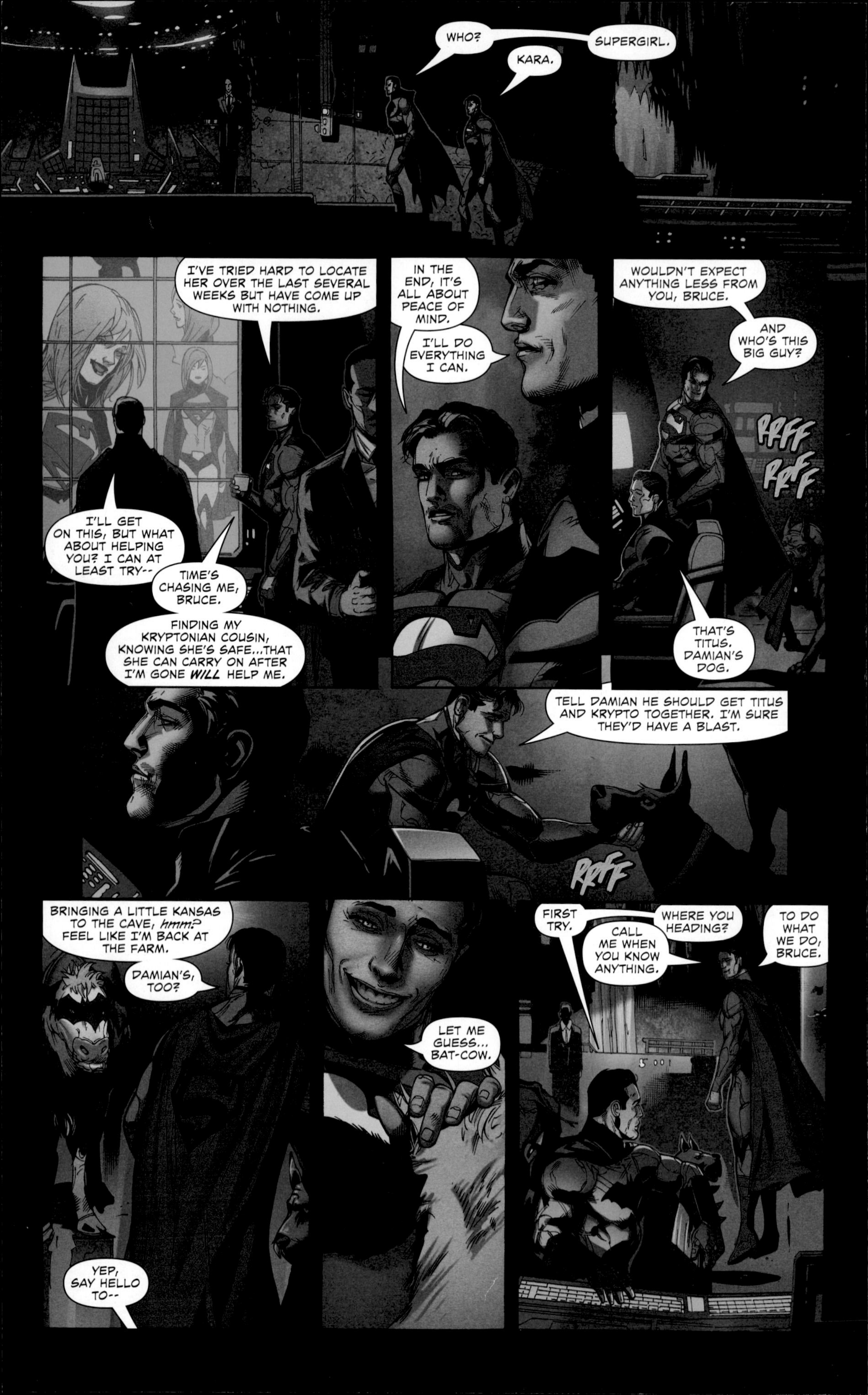
WHO?
SUPERGIRL.
KARA.
I'VE TRIED HARD TO LOCATE HER OVER THE LAST SEVERAL WEEKS BUT HAVE COME UP WITH NOTHING.
I'LL GET ON THIS, BUT WHAT ABOUT HELPING YOU? I CAN AT LEAST TRY--
TIME'S CHASING ME, BRUCE.
FINDING MY KRYPTONIAN COUSIN, KNOWING SHE'S SAFE...THAT SHE CAN CARRY ON AFTER I'M GONE ***WILL*** HELP ME.
IN THE END, IT'S ALL ABOUT PEACE OF MIND.
I'LL DO EVERYTHING I CAN.
WOULDN'T EXPECT ANYTHING LESS FROM YOU, BRUCE.
AND WHO'S THIS BIG GUY?
RRFF RRFF
THAT'S TITUS. DAMIAN'S DOG.
TELL DAMIAN HE SHOULD GET TITUS AND KRYPTO TOGETHER. I'M SURE THEY'D HAVE A BLAST.
RRFF
BRINGING A LITTLE KANSAS TO THE CAVE, *hmm?* FEEL LIKE I'M BACK AT THE FARM.
DAMIAN'S, TOO?
YEP, SAY HELLO TO--
LET ME GUESS... BAT-COW.
FIRST TRY.
WHERE YOU HEADING?
CALL ME WHEN YOU KNOW ANYTHING.
TO DO WHAT WE DO, BRUCE.

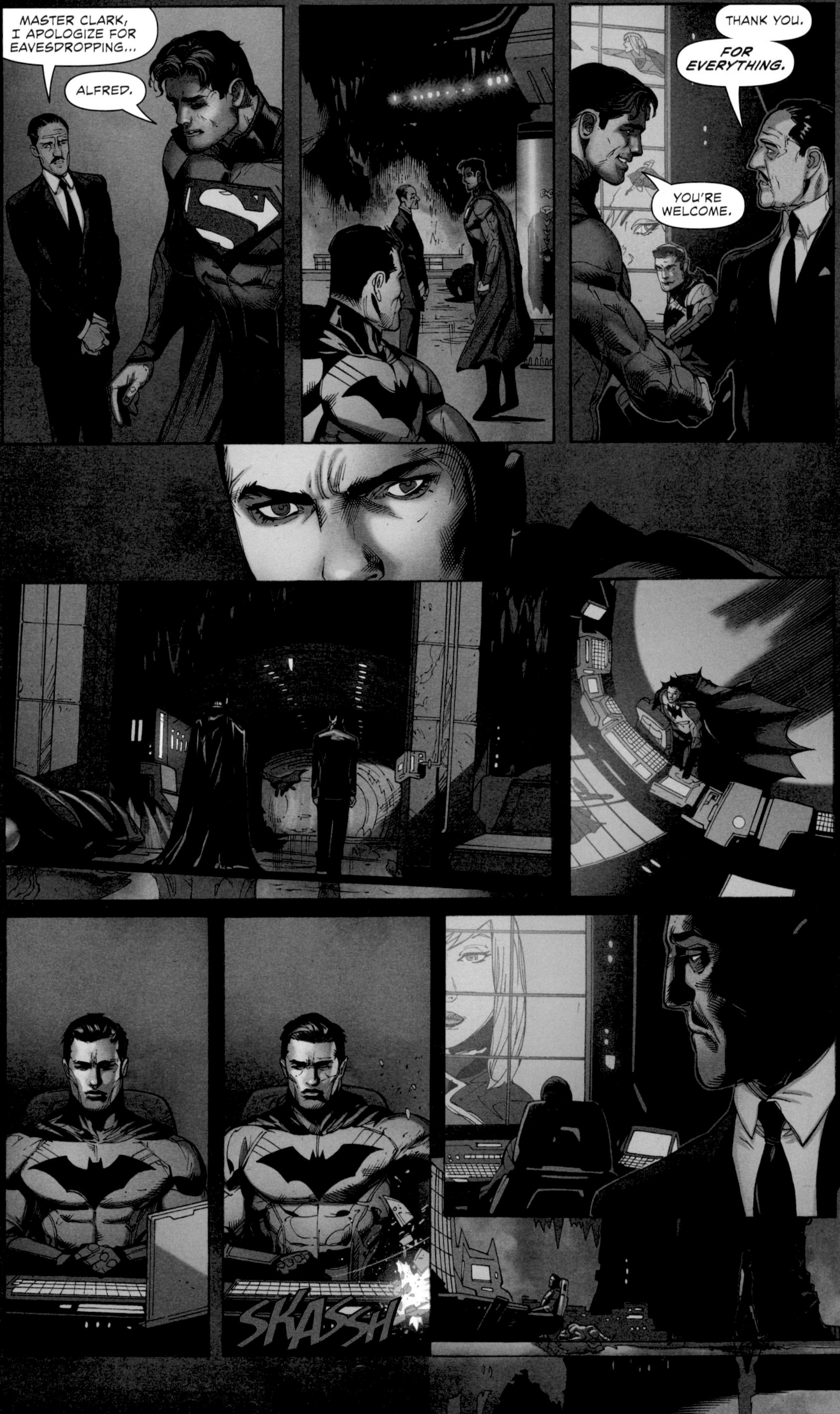
MASTER CLARK, I APOLOGIZE FOR EAVESDROPPING...
ALFRED.
THANK YOU.
FOR EVERYTHING.
YOU'RE WELCOME.
SKASSH

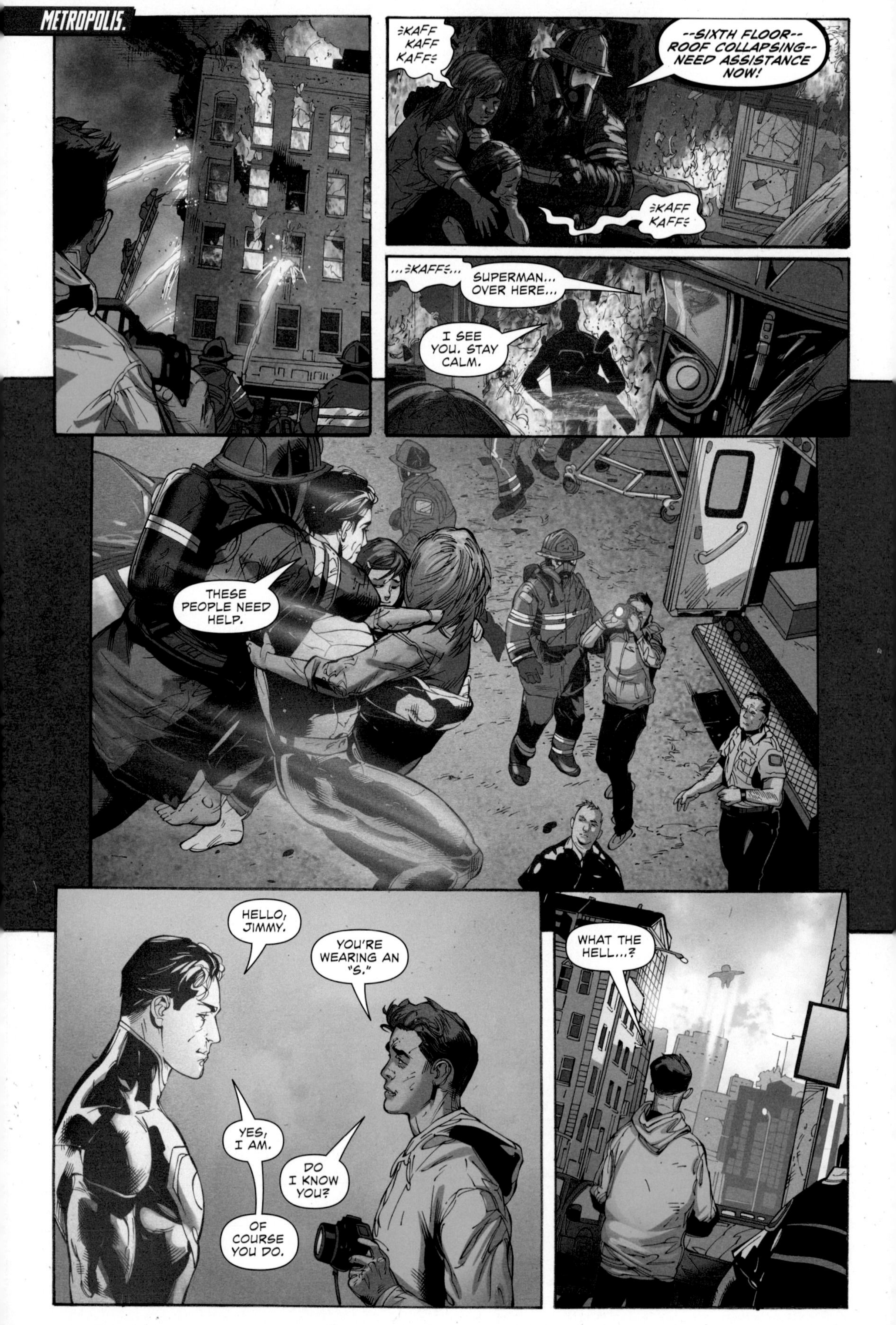
METROPOLIS.
KAFF KAFF KAFF
--SIXTH FLOOR-- ROOF COLLAPSING-- NEED ASSISTANCE NOW!
KAFF KAFF
...KAFF...
SUPERMAN... OVER HERE...
I SEE YOU. STAY CALM.
THESE PEOPLE NEED HELP.
HELLO, JIMMY.
YOU'RE WEARING AN "S."
YES, I AM.
DO I KNOW YOU?
OF COURSE YOU DO.
WHAT THE HELL...?

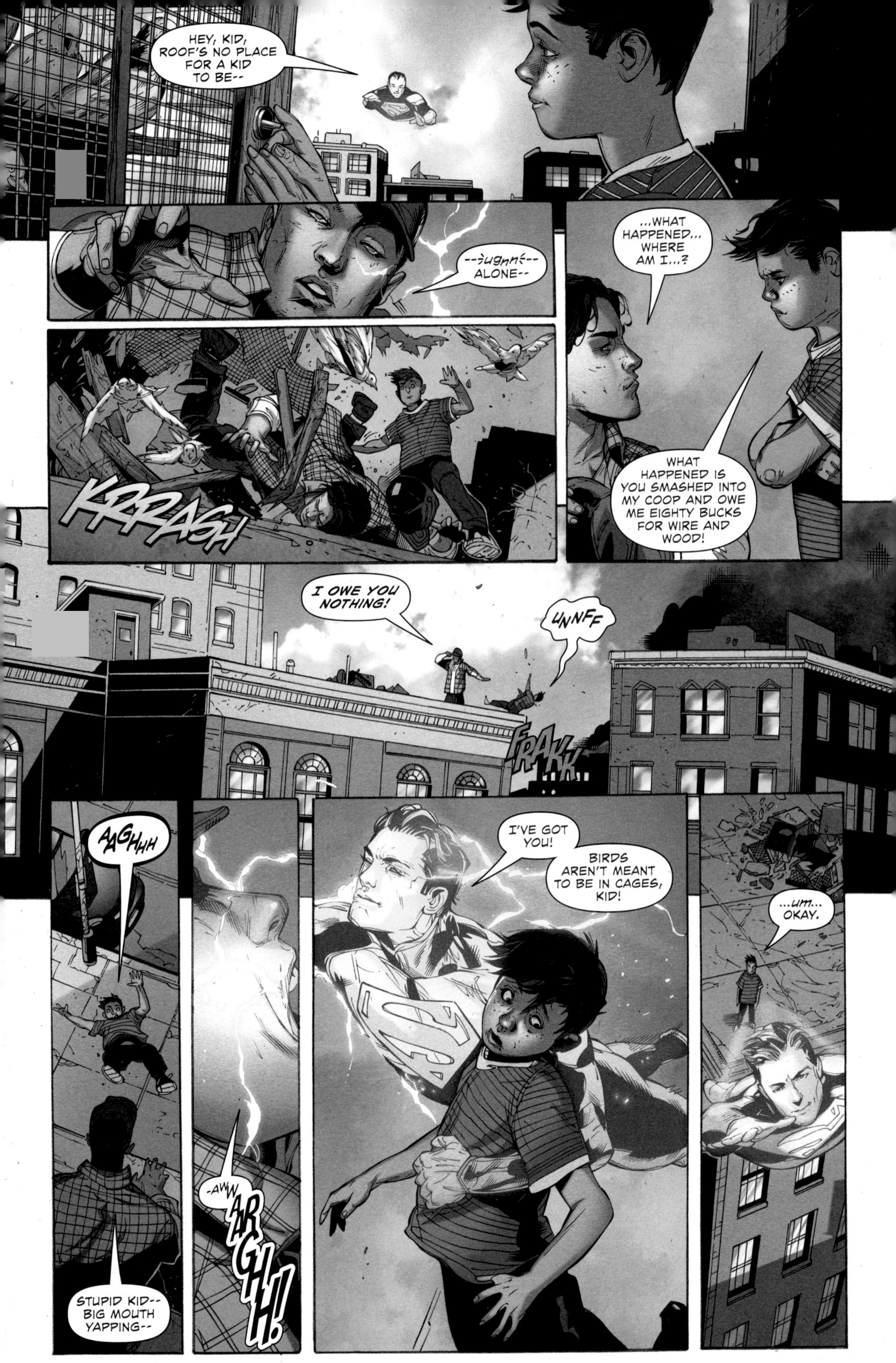
HEY, KID, ROOF'S NO PLACE FOR A KID TO BE--
--ugnn--
ALONE--
KRRASH
...WHAT HAPPENED... WHERE AM I...?
WHAT HAPPENED IS YOU SMASHED INTO MY COOP AND OWE ME EIGHTY BUCKS FOR WIRE AND WOOD!
I OWE YOU NOTHING!
UNNFF
FRAKK
AAGHHH
STUPID KID-- BIG MOUTH YAPPING--
-AWWARGHH!
I'VE GOT YOU!
BIRDS AREN'T MEANT TO BE IN CAGES, KID!
...UM... OKAY.

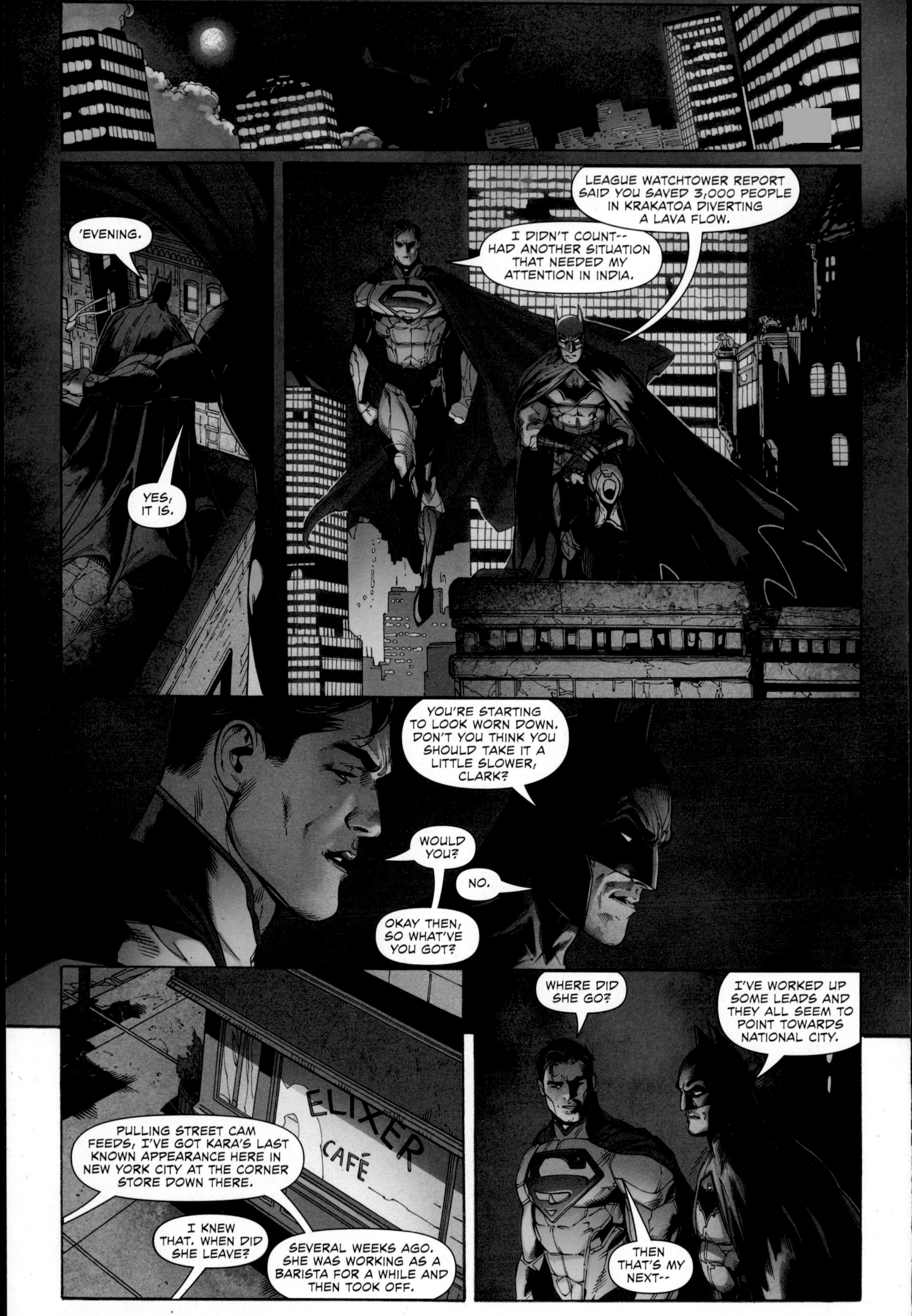
'EVENING.
YES, IT IS.
LEAGUE WATCHTOWER REPORT SAID YOU SAVED 3,000 PEOPLE IN KRAKATOA DIVERTING A LAVA FLOW.
I DIDN'T COUNT-- HAD ANOTHER SITUATION THAT NEEDED MY ATTENTION IN INDIA.
YOU'RE STARTING TO LOOK WORN DOWN. DON'T YOU THINK YOU SHOULD TAKE IT A LITTLE SLOWER, CLARK?
WOULD YOU?
NO.
OKAY THEN, SO WHAT'VE YOU GOT?
PULLING STREET CAM FEEDS, I'VE GOT KARA'S LAST KNOWN APPEARANCE HERE IN NEW YORK CITY AT THE CORNER STORE DOWN THERE.
ELIXER
CAFÉ
I KNEW THAT. WHEN DID SHE LEAVE?
SEVERAL WEEKS AGO. SHE WAS WORKING AS A BARISTA FOR A WHILE AND THEN TOOK OFF.
WHERE DID SHE GO?
I'VE WORKED UP SOME LEADS AND THEY ALL SEEM TO POINT TOWARDS NATIONAL CITY.
THEN THAT'S MY NEXT--

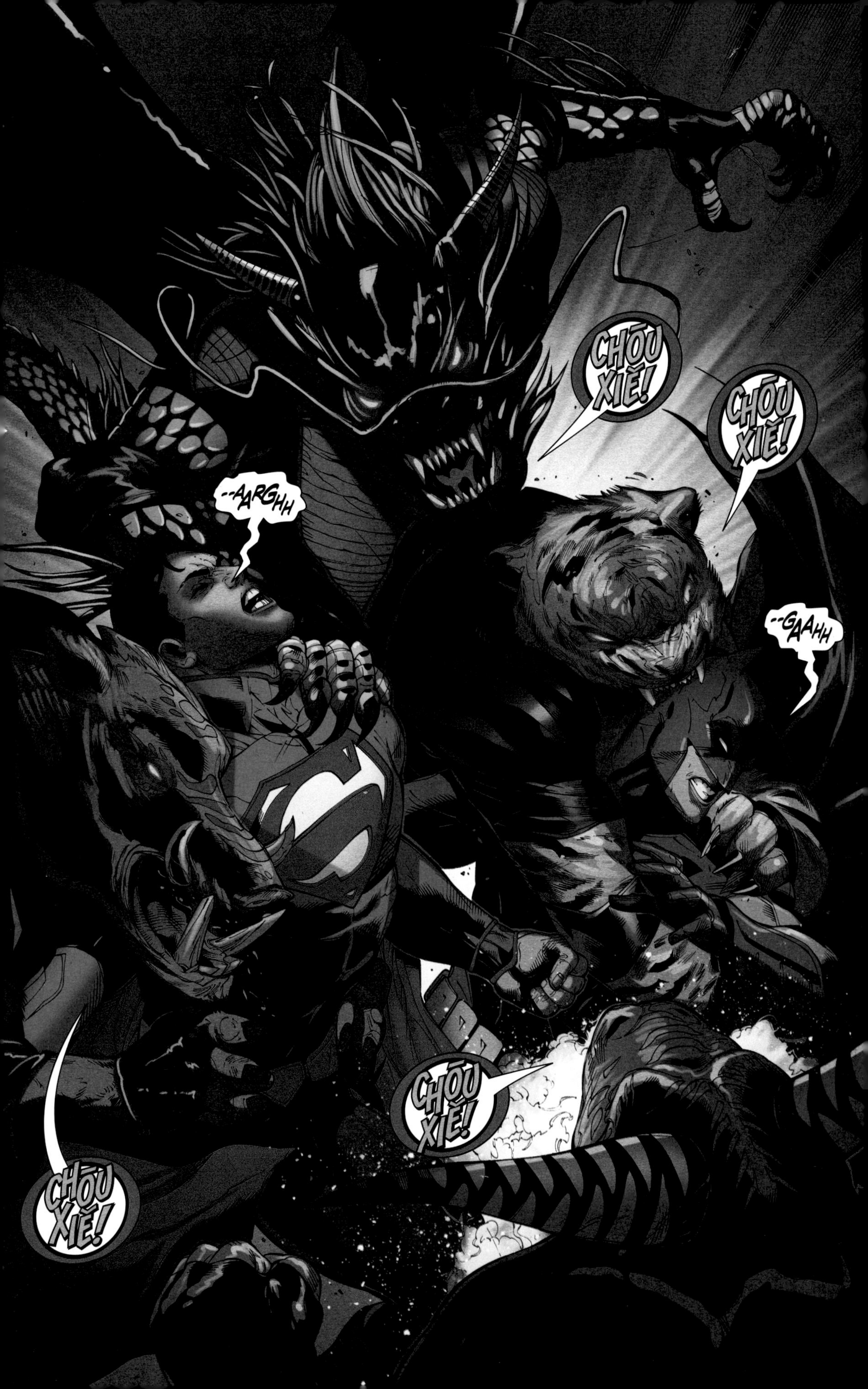
CHŌU XIĚ!
CHŌU XIĚ!
--AARGHH
--GAAHH
CHŌU XIĚ!
CHŌU XIĚ!

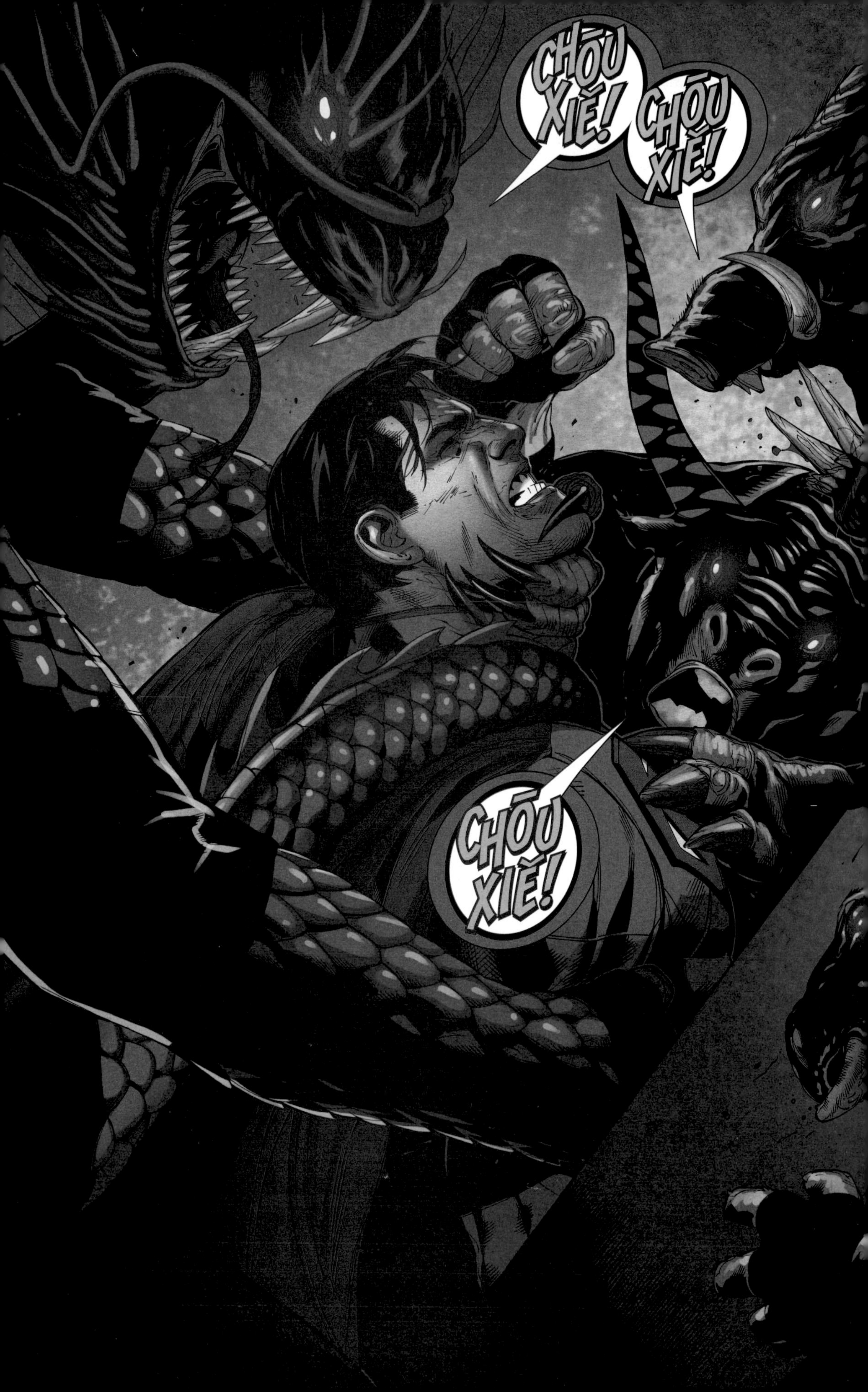

CHŌU XIĔ!
CHŌU XIĔ!
CHŌU XIĔ!

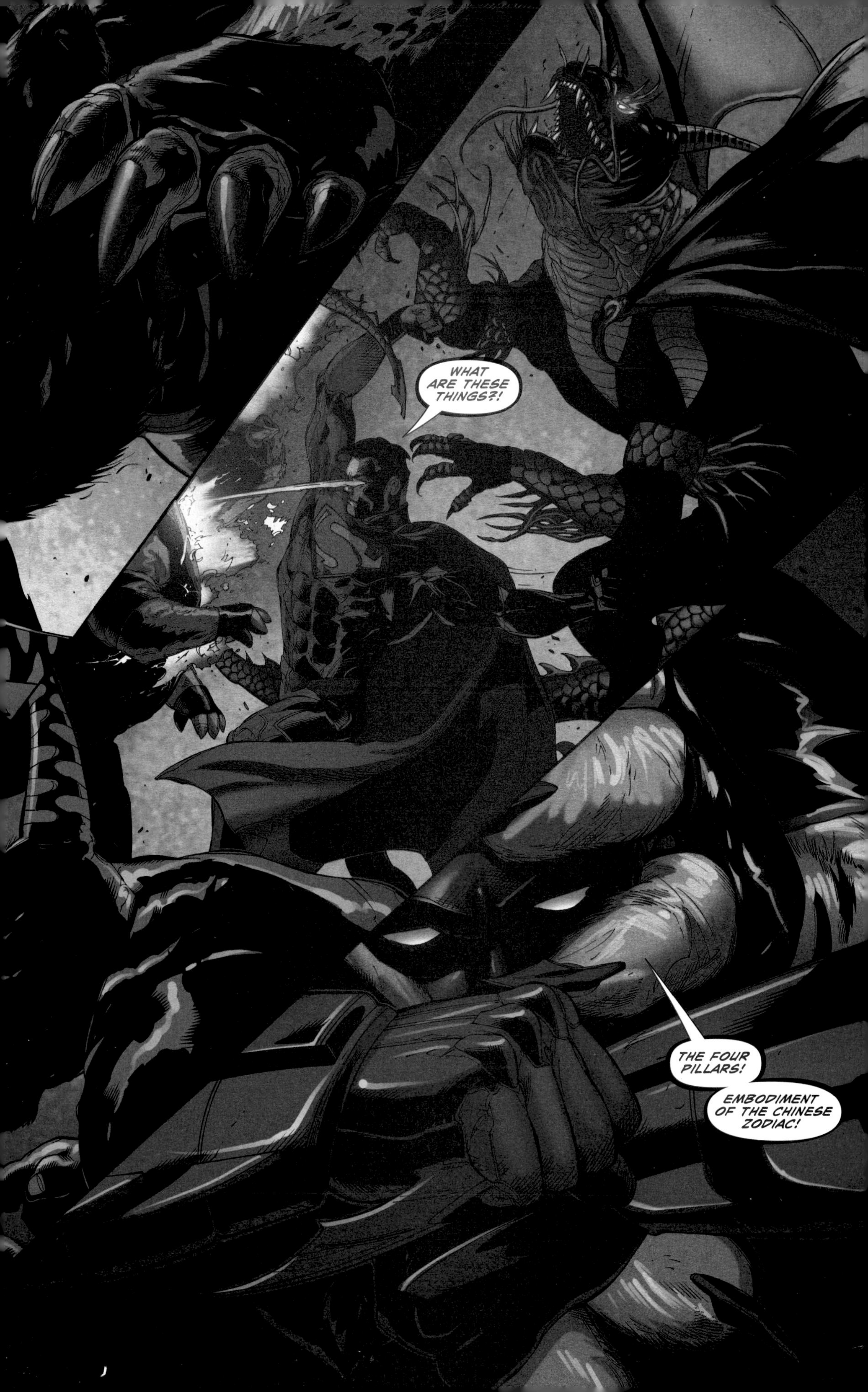
WHAT ARE THESE THINGS?!
THE FOUR PILLARS!
EMBODIMENT OF THE CHINESE ZODIAC!

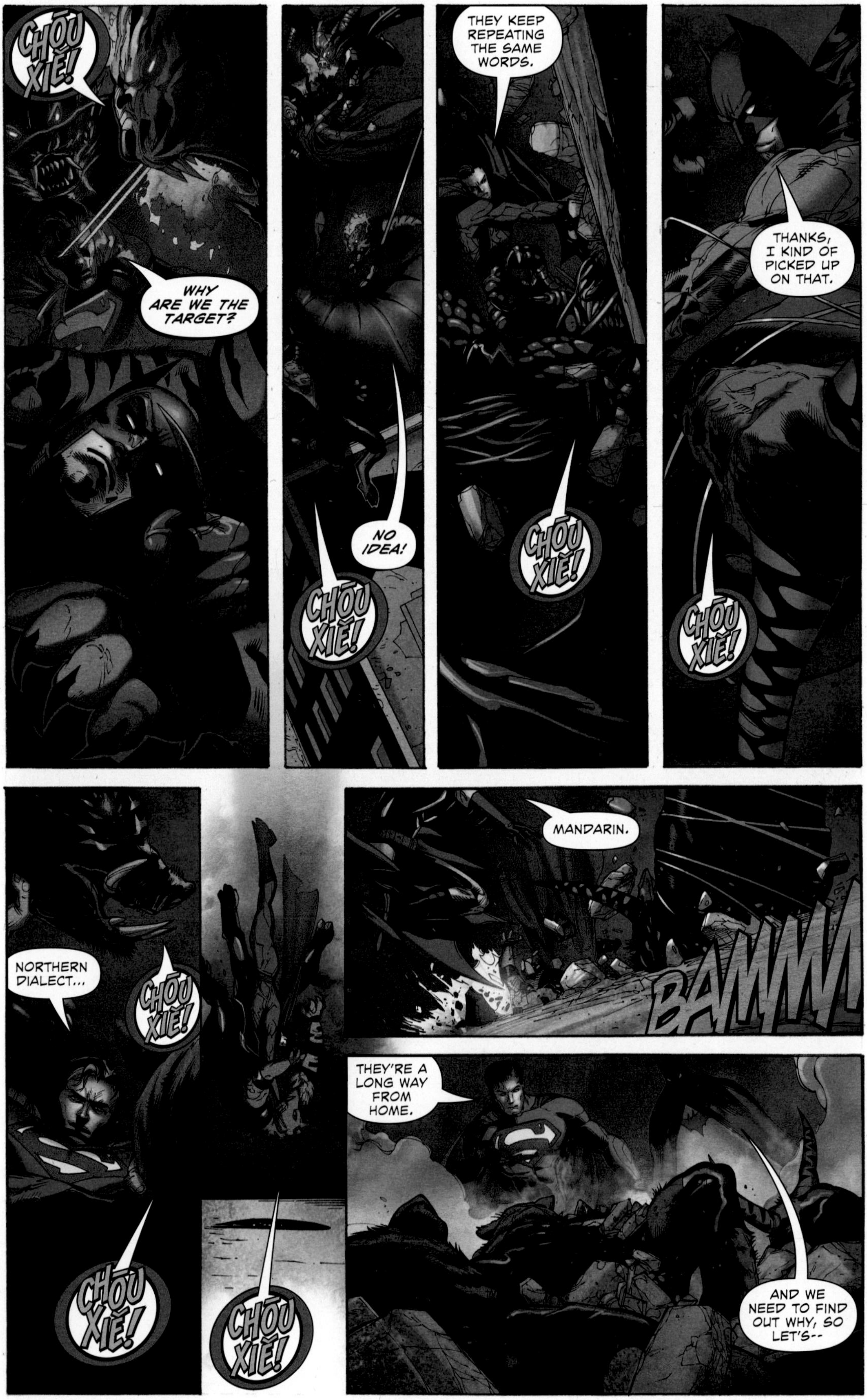

CHŌU XIĒ!
WHY ARE WE THE TARGET?
CHŌU XIĒ!
NO IDEA!
THEY KEEP REPEATING THE SAME WORDS.
CHŌU XIĒ!
THANKS, I KIND OF PICKED UP ON THAT.
CHŌU XIĒ!
NORTHERN DIALECT...
CHŌU XIĒ!
CHŌU XIĒ!
CHŌU XIĒ!
MANDARIN.
BAMM
THEY'RE A LONG WAY FROM HOME.
AND WE NEED TO FIND OUT WHY, SO LET'S--

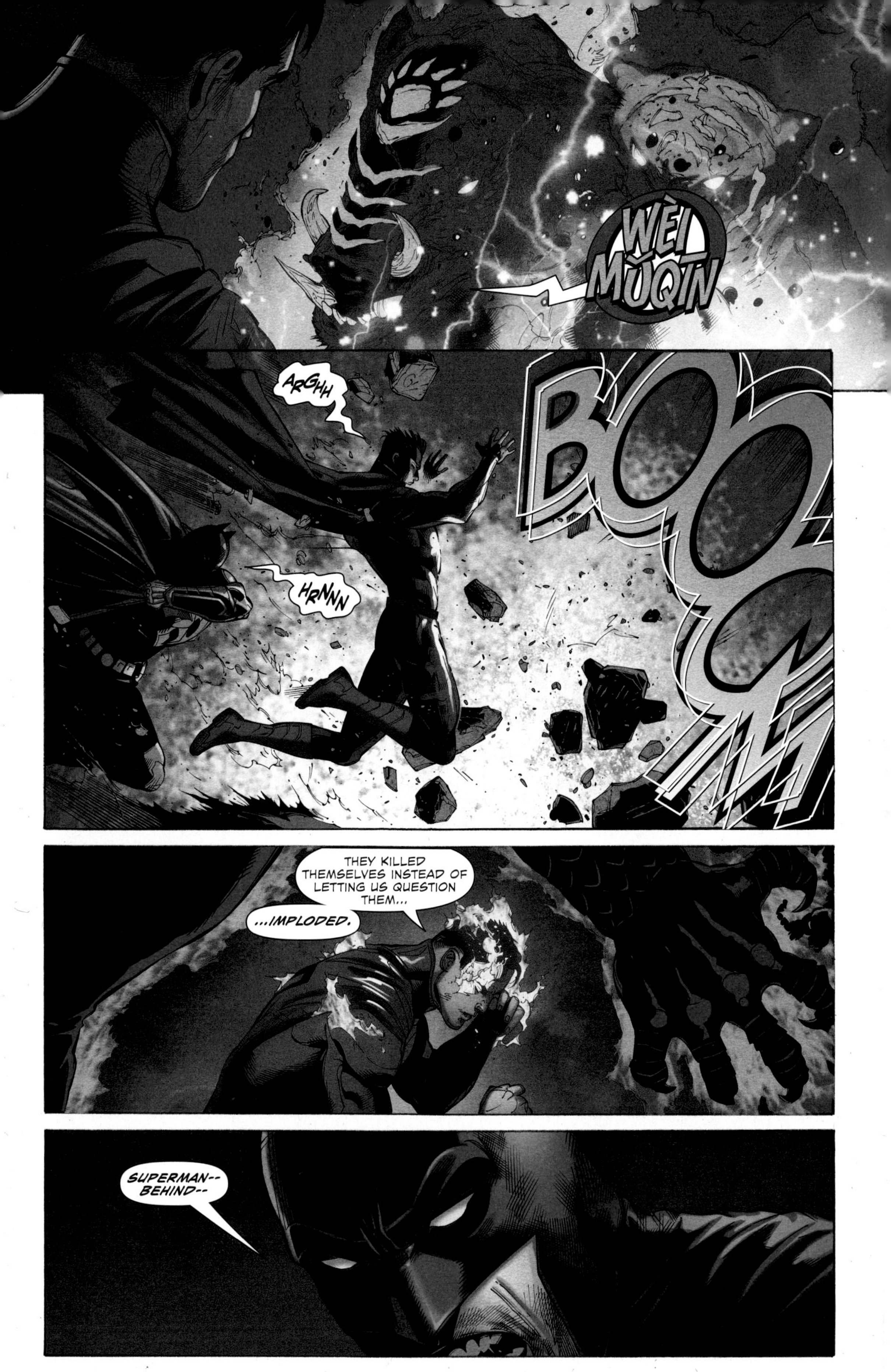
WÈI MÙQÍN
ARGHH
HRNNN
BOOM
THEY KILLED THEMSELVES INSTEAD OF LETTING US QUESTION THEM...
...IMPLODED.
SUPERMAN-- BEHIND--

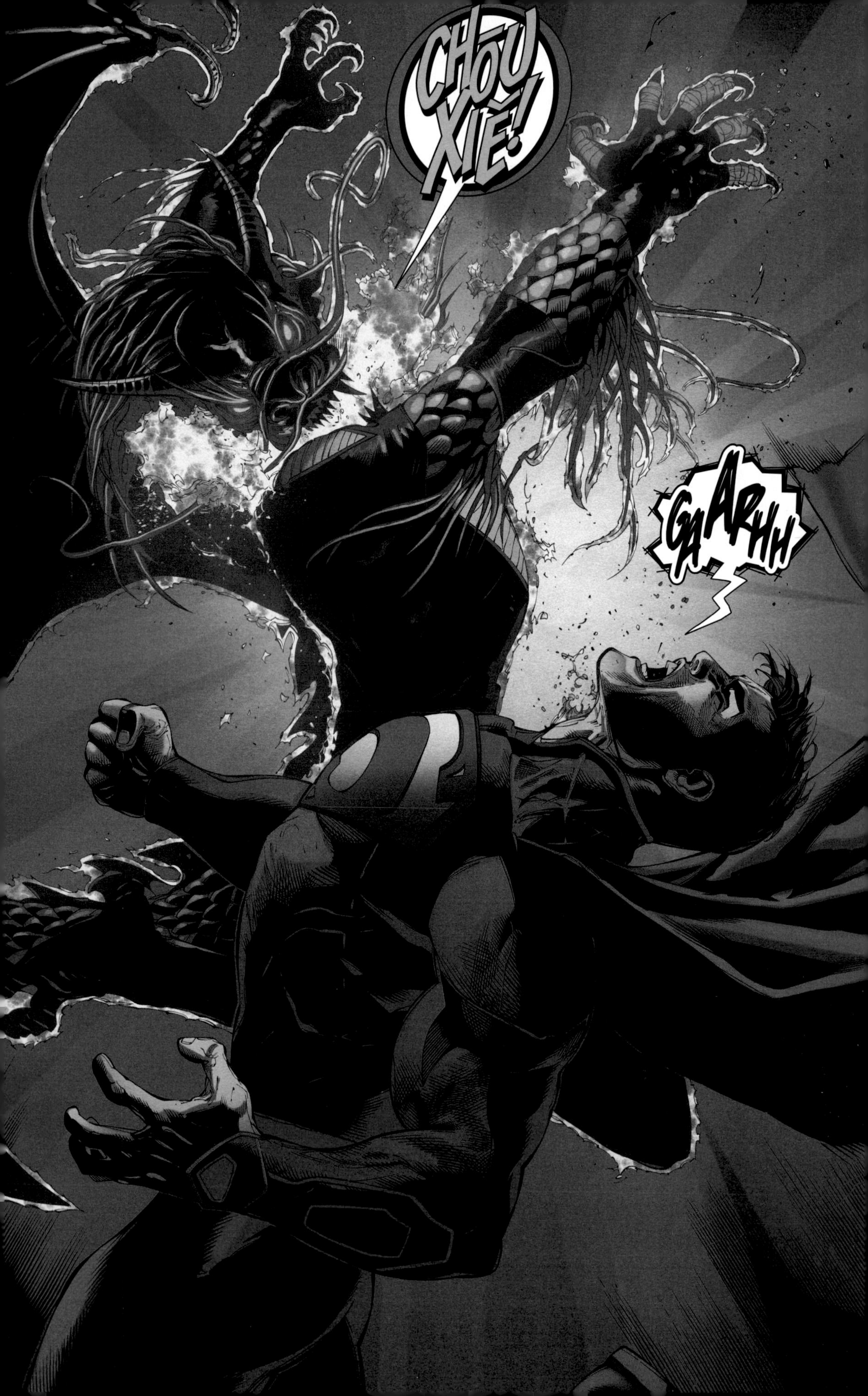
CHŌU XIĚ!
GAARHH

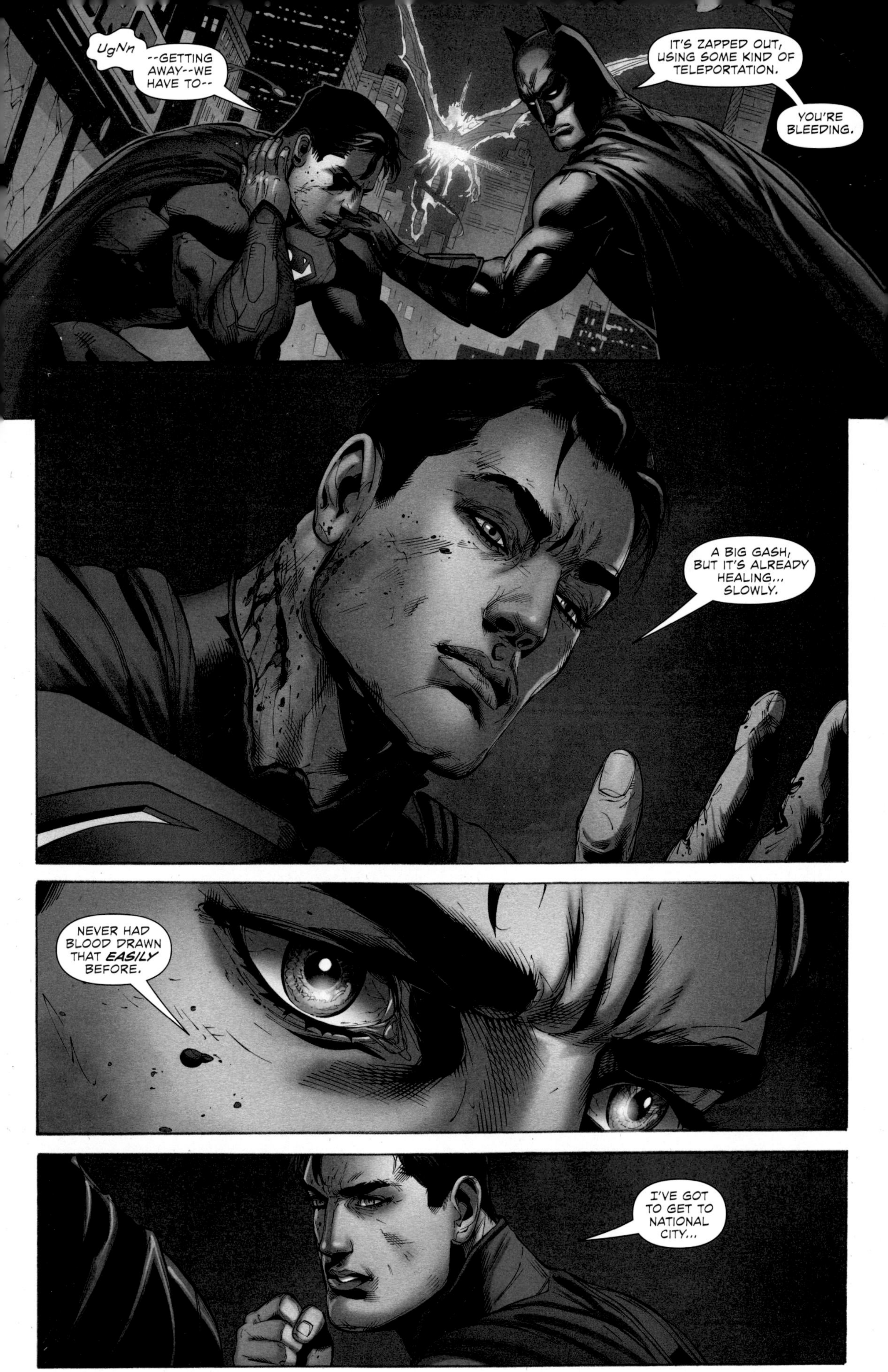
UgNn
--GETTING AWAY--WE HAVE TO--
IT'S ZAPPED OUT, USING SOME KIND OF TELEPORTATION.
YOU'RE BLEEDING.
A BIG GASH, BUT IT'S ALREADY HEALING... SLOWLY.
NEVER HAD BLOOD DRAWN THAT *EASILY* BEFORE.
I'VE GOT TO GET TO NATIONAL CITY...

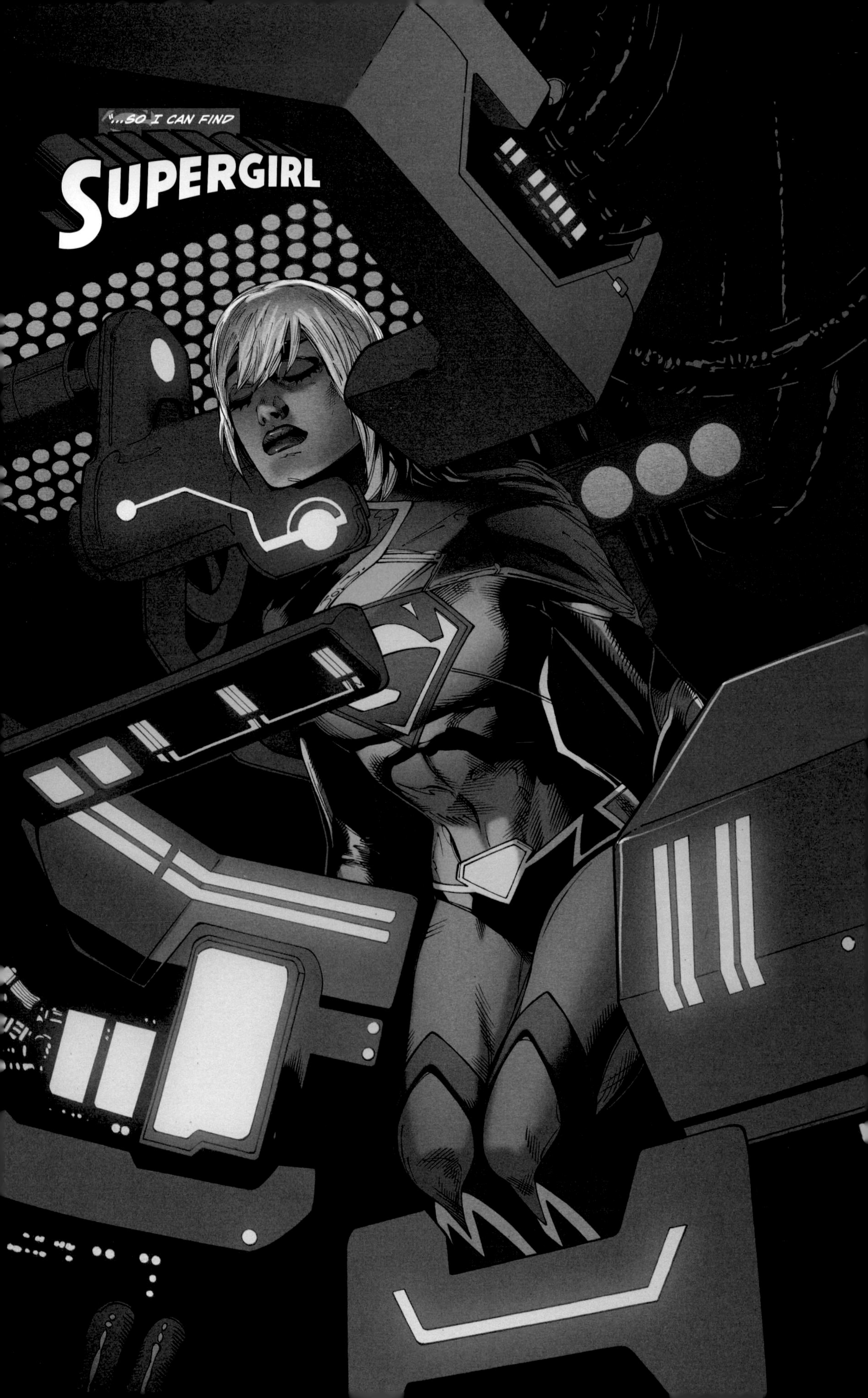
"...SO I CAN FIND
SUPERGIRL

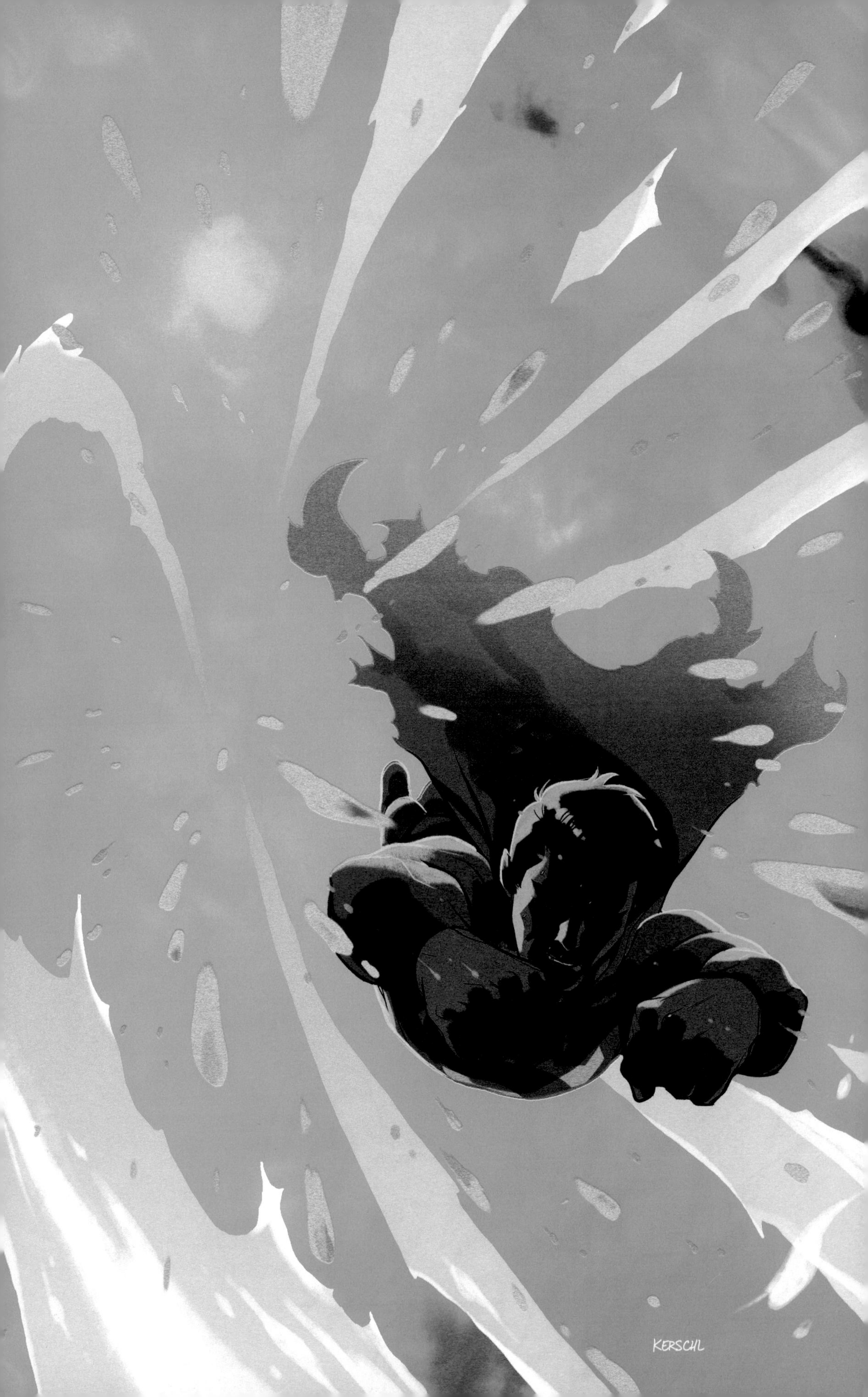
KERSCHL

THE FINAL DAYS OF SUPERMAN PART 3: DAZED AND CONFUSED

PETER J. TOMASI writer PAUL PELLETIER penciller SANDRA HOPE ARCHER inker TOMEU MOREY colorist ROB LEIGH letterer KARL KERSCHL cover

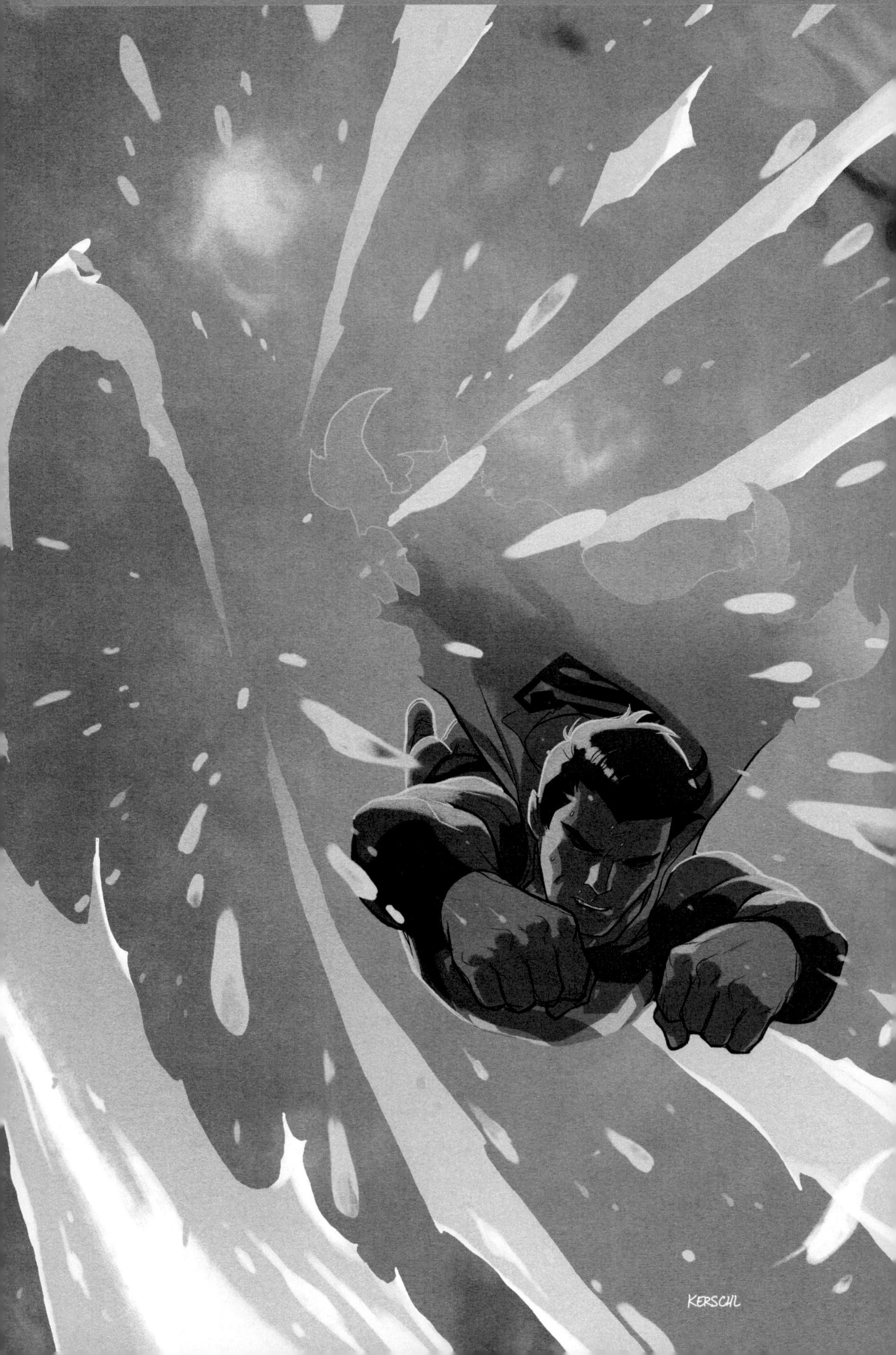
KERSCHL

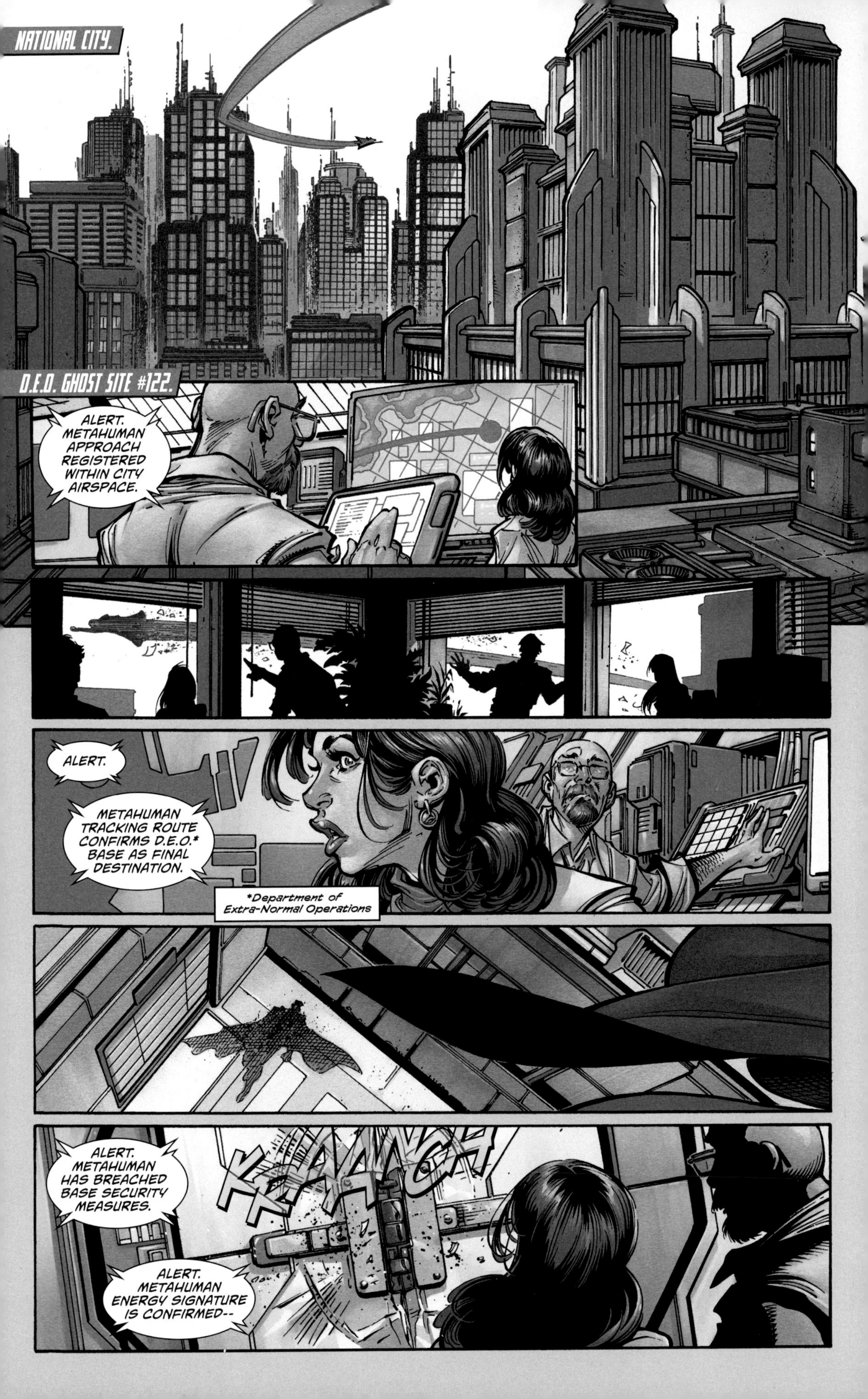
NATIONAL CITY.
D.E.O. GHOST SITE #122.
ALERT. METAHUMAN APPROACH REGISTERED WITHIN CITY AIRSPACE.
ALERT.
METAHUMAN TRACKING ROUTE CONFIRMS D.E.O.* BASE AS FINAL DESTINATION.
*Department of Extra-Normal Operations
KRAAACH
ALERT. METAHUMAN HAS BREACHED BASE SECURITY MEASURES.
ALERT. METAHUMAN ENERGY SIGNATURE IS CONFIRMED--

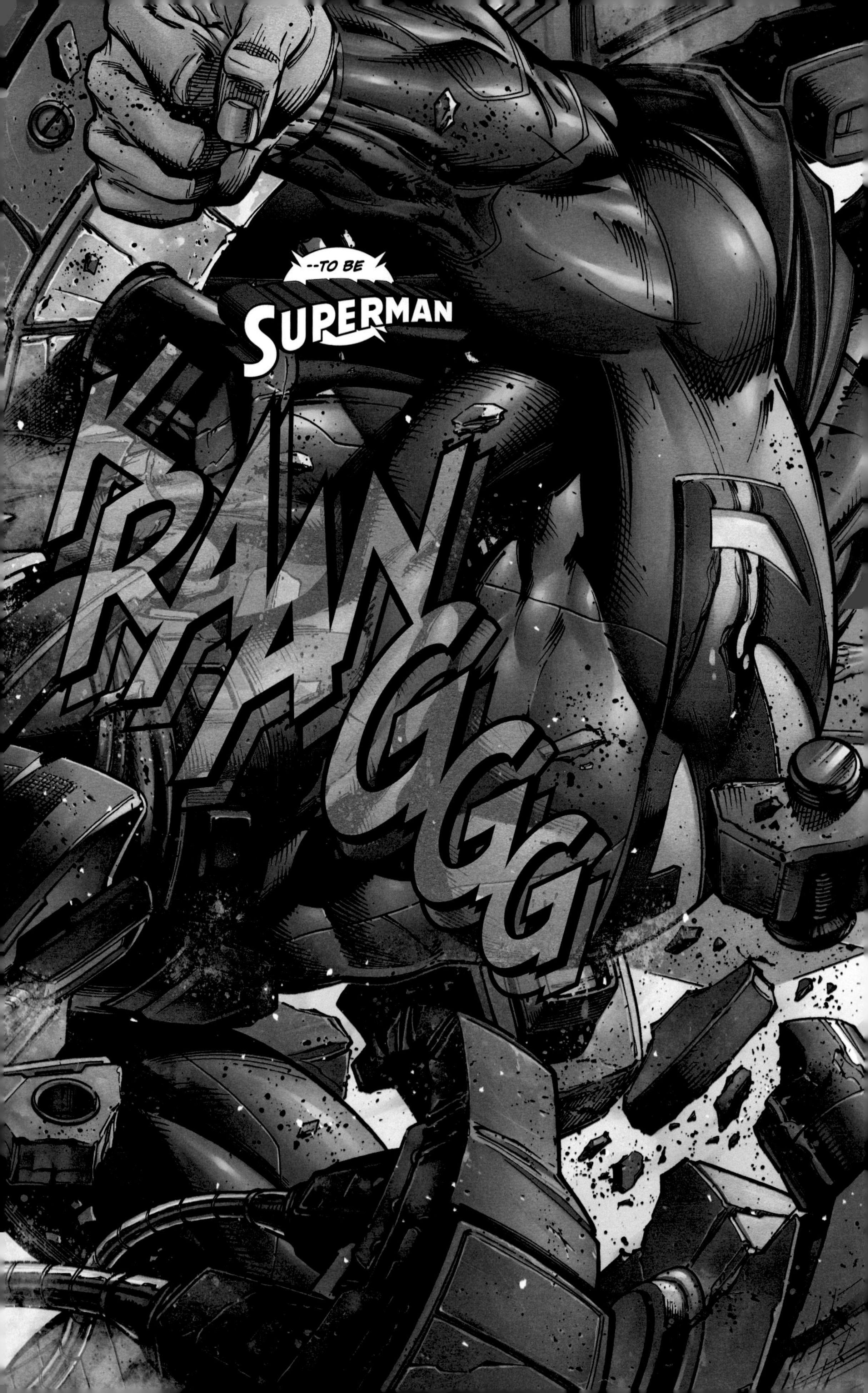
--TO BE
SUPERMAN

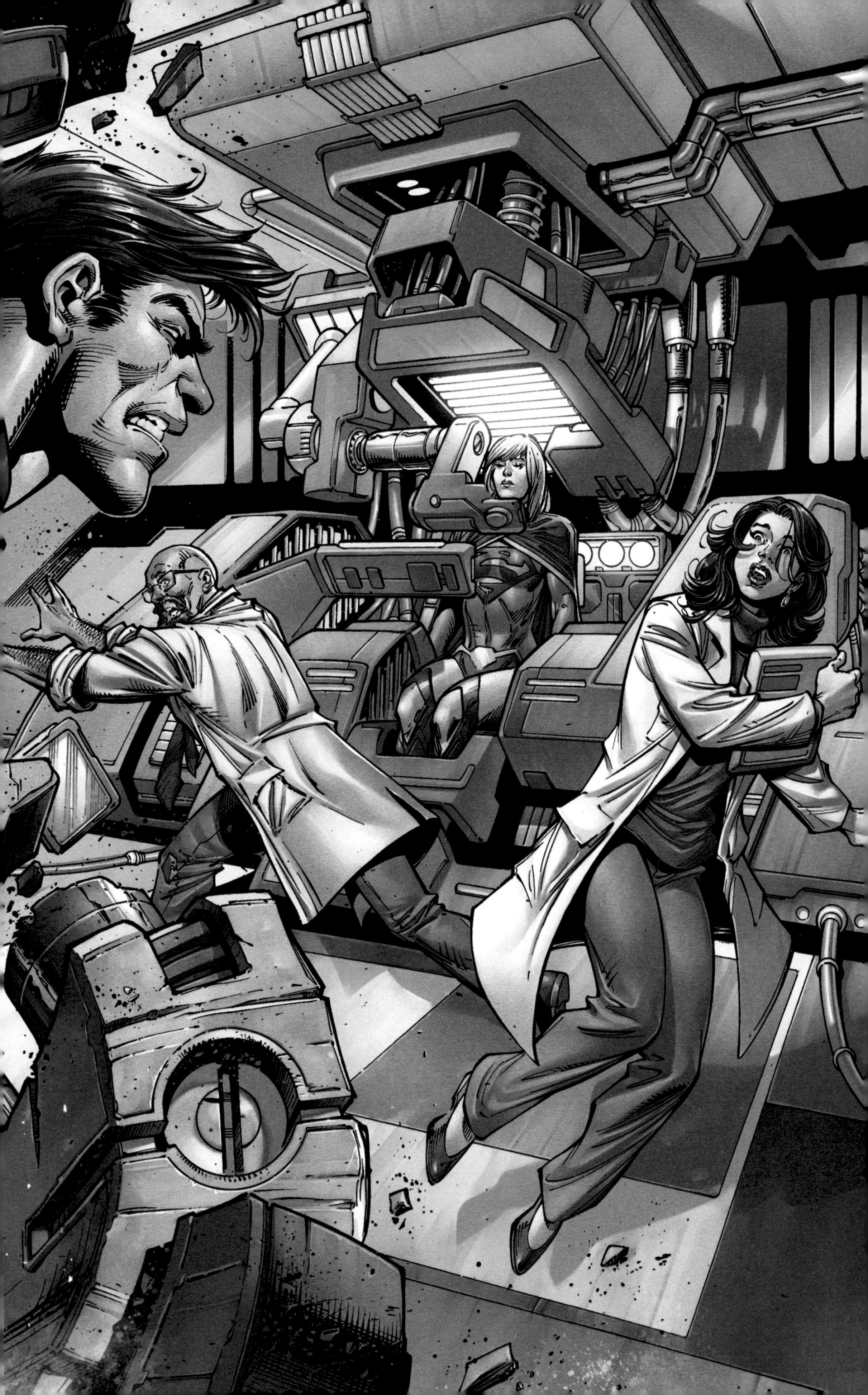

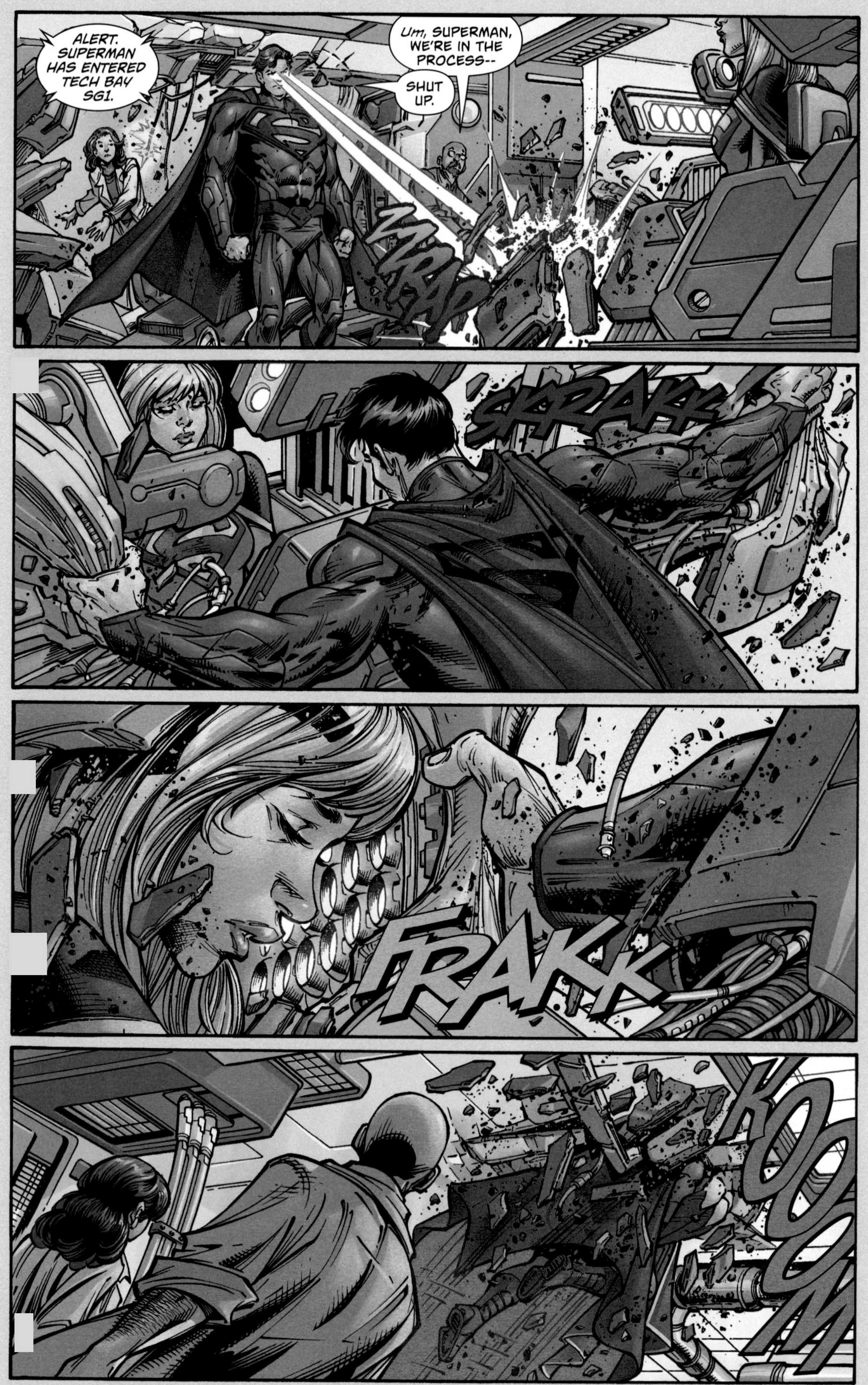
ALERT. SUPERMAN HAS ENTERED TECH BAY SG1.
Um, SUPERMAN, WE'RE IN THE PROCESS--
SHUT UP.
ZZZRAP!
SKRAKK
FRAKK
KOOOM

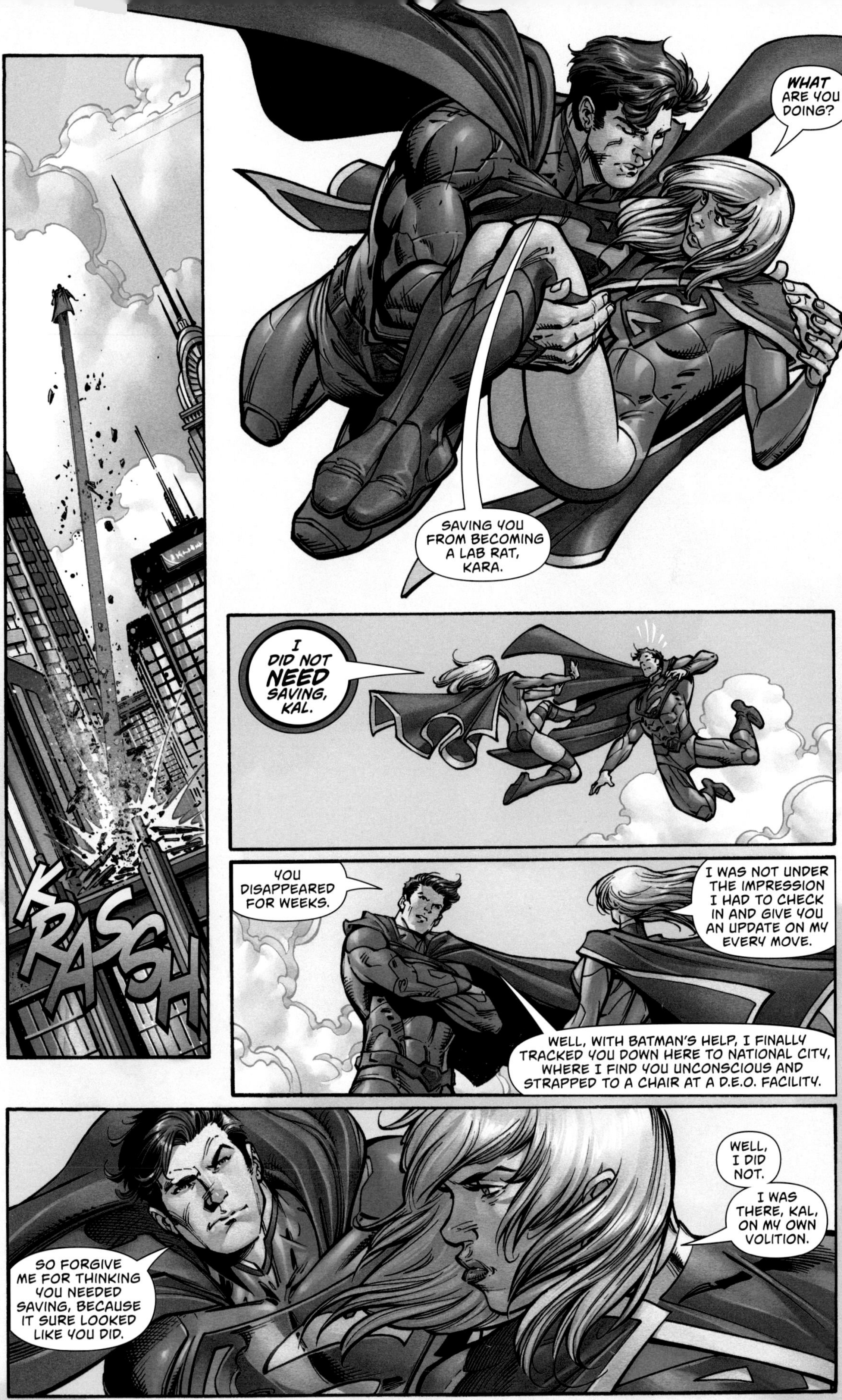
WHAT ARE YOU DOING?
SAVING YOU FROM BECOMING A LAB RAT, KARA.
KRASH
I DID NOT NEED SAVING, KAL.
YOU DISAPPEARED FOR WEEKS.
I WAS NOT UNDER THE IMPRESSION I HAD TO CHECK IN AND GIVE YOU AN UPDATE ON MY EVERY MOVE.
WELL, WITH BATMAN'S HELP, I FINALLY TRACKED YOU DOWN HERE TO NATIONAL CITY, WHERE I FIND YOU UNCONSCIOUS AND STRAPPED TO A CHAIR AT A D.E.O. FACILITY.
SO FORGIVE ME FOR THINKING YOU NEEDED SAVING, BECAUSE IT SURE LOOKED LIKE YOU DID.
WELL, I DID NOT.
I WAS THERE, KAL, ON MY OWN VOLITION.

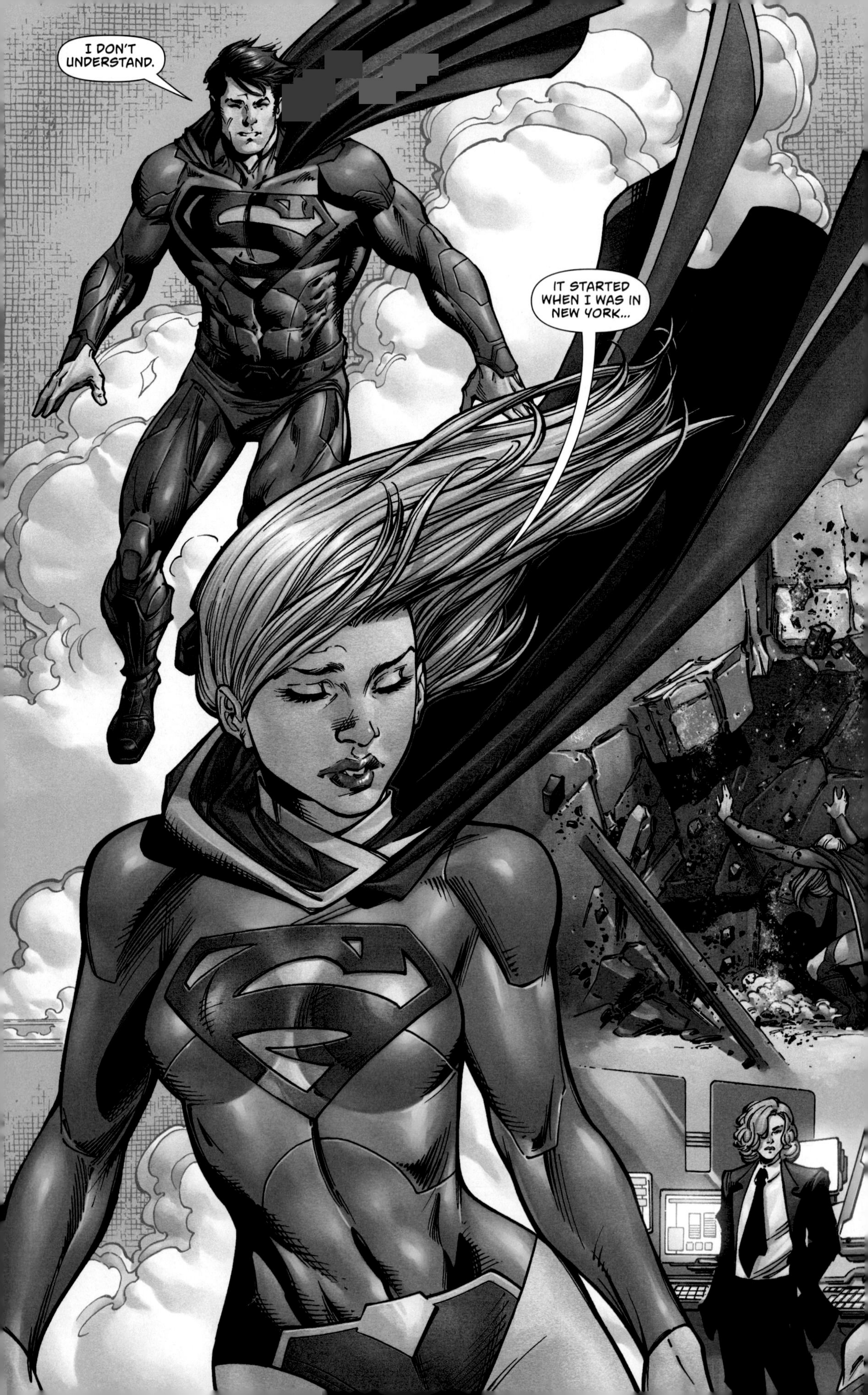
I DON'T UNDERSTAND.
IT STARTED WHEN I WAS IN NEW YORK...

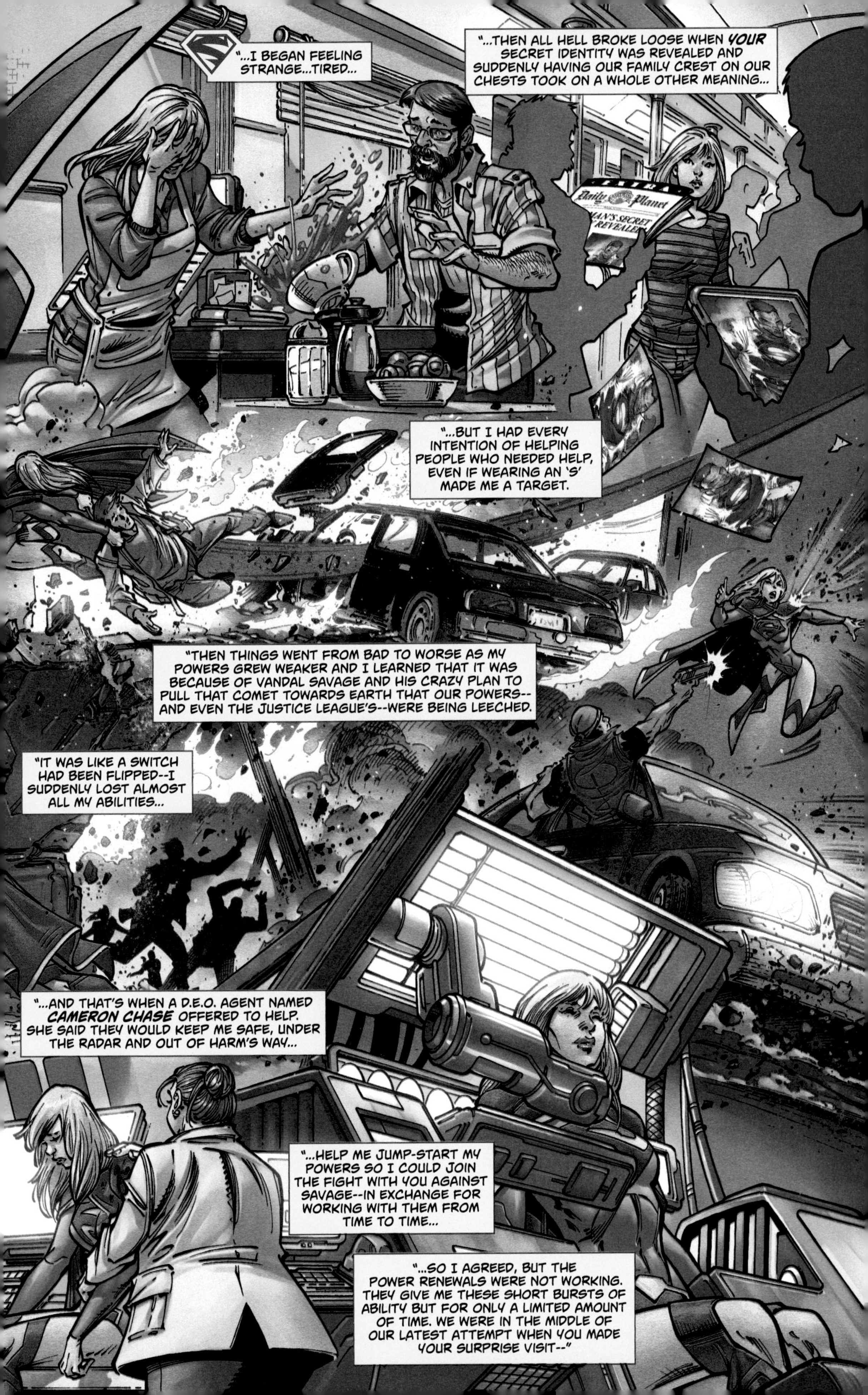
"...I BEGAN FEELING STRANGE...TIRED...
"...THEN ALL HELL BROKE LOOSE WHEN *YOUR* SECRET IDENTITY WAS REVEALED AND SUDDENLY HAVING OUR FAMILY CREST ON OUR CHESTS TOOK ON A WHOLE OTHER MEANING...
Daily Planet
"...BUT I HAD EVERY INTENTION OF HELPING PEOPLE WHO NEEDED HELP, EVEN IF WEARING AN 'S' MADE ME A TARGET.
"THEN THINGS WENT FROM BAD TO WORSE AS MY POWERS GREW WEAKER AND I LEARNED THAT IT WAS BECAUSE OF VANDAL SAVAGE AND HIS CRAZY PLAN TO PULL THAT COMET TOWARDS EARTH THAT OUR POWERS--AND EVEN THE JUSTICE LEAGUE'S--WERE BEING LEECHED.
"IT WAS LIKE A SWITCH HAD BEEN FLIPPED--I SUDDENLY LOST ALMOST ALL MY ABILITIES...
"...AND THAT'S WHEN A D.E.O. AGENT NAMED *CAMERON CHASE* OFFERED TO HELP. SHE SAID THEY WOULD KEEP ME SAFE, UNDER THE RADAR AND OUT OF HARM'S WAY...
"...HELP ME JUMP-START MY POWERS SO I COULD JOIN THE FIGHT WITH YOU AGAINST SAVAGE--IN EXCHANGE FOR WORKING WITH THEM FROM TIME TO TIME...
"...SO I AGREED, BUT THE POWER RENEWALS WERE NOT WORKING. THEY GIVE ME THESE SHORT BURSTS OF ABILITY BUT FOR ONLY A LIMITED AMOUNT OF TIME. WE WERE IN THE MIDDLE OF OUR LATEST ATTEMPT WHEN YOU MADE YOUR SURPRISE VISIT--"

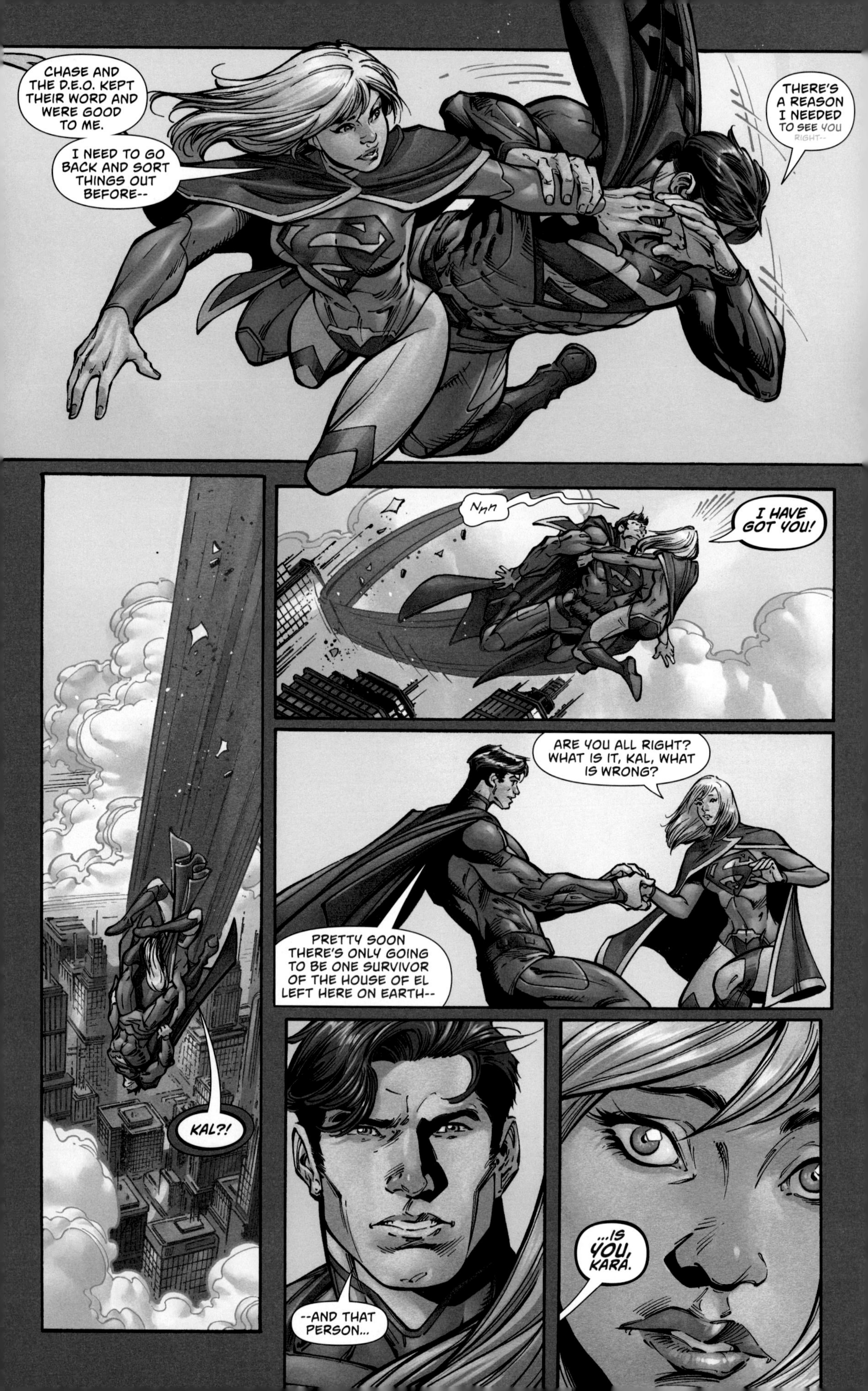
CHASE AND THE D.E.O. KEPT THEIR WORD AND WERE GOOD TO ME.
I NEED TO GO BACK AND SORT THINGS OUT BEFORE--
THERE'S A REASON I NEEDED TO SEE YOU RIGHT--
KAL?!
Nnn
I HAVE GOT YOU!
ARE YOU ALL RIGHT? WHAT IS IT, KAL, WHAT IS WRONG?
PRETTY SOON THERE'S ONLY GOING TO BE ONE SURVIVOR OF THE HOUSE OF EL LEFT HERE ON EARTH--
--AND THAT PERSON...
...IS YOU, KARA.

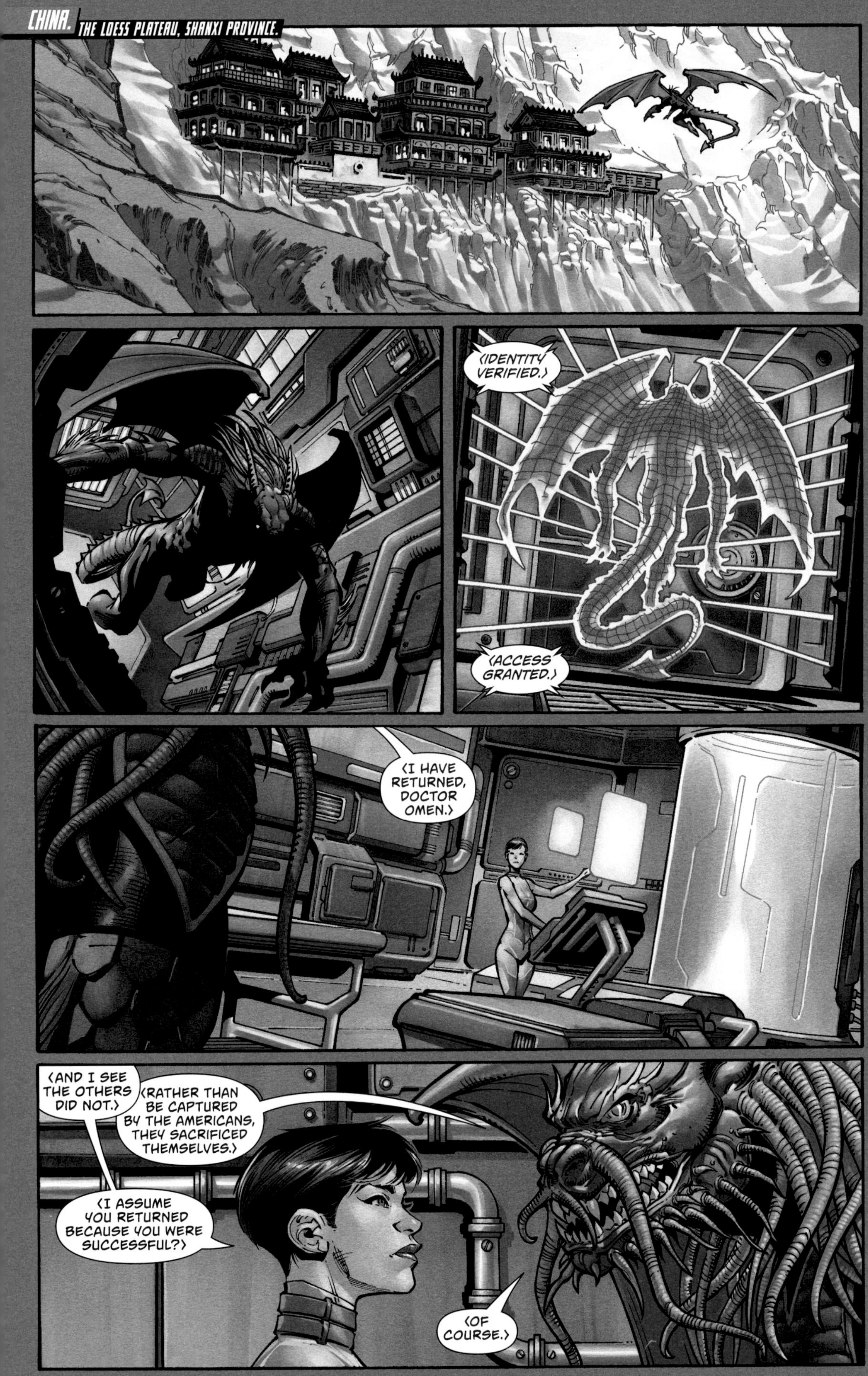

CHINA. THE LOESS PLATEAU, SHANXI PROVINCE.
‹IDENTITY VERIFIED.›
‹ACCESS GRANTED.›
‹I HAVE RETURNED, DOCTOR OMEN.›
‹AND I SEE THE OTHERS DID NOT.›
‹RATHER THAN BE CAPTURED BY THE AMERICANS, THEY SACRIFICED THEMSELVES.›
‹I ASSUME YOU RETURNED BECAUSE YOU WERE SUCCESSFUL?›
‹OF COURSE.›

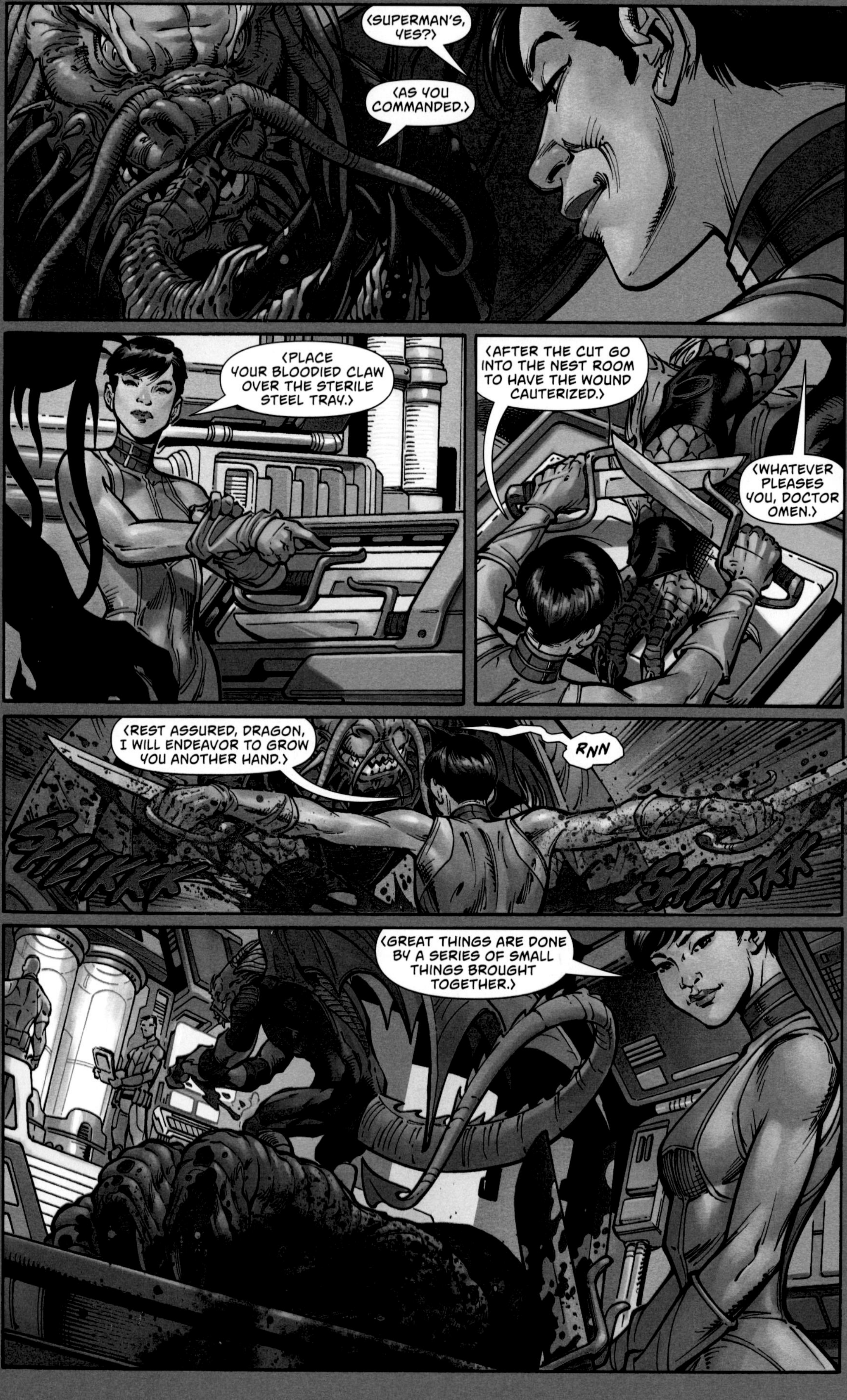
‹SUPERMAN'S, YES?›
‹AS YOU COMMANDED.›
‹PLACE YOUR BLOODIED CLAW OVER THE STERILE STEEL TRAY.›
‹AFTER THE CUT GO INTO THE NEST ROOM TO HAVE THE WOUND CAUTERIZED.›
‹WHATEVER PLEASES YOU, DOCTOR OMEN.›
‹REST ASSURED, DRAGON, I WILL ENDEAVOR TO GROW YOU ANOTHER HAND.›
RNN
SHLIKKK
SHLIKKK
‹GREAT THINGS ARE DONE BY A SERIES OF SMALL THINGS BROUGHT TOGETHER.›

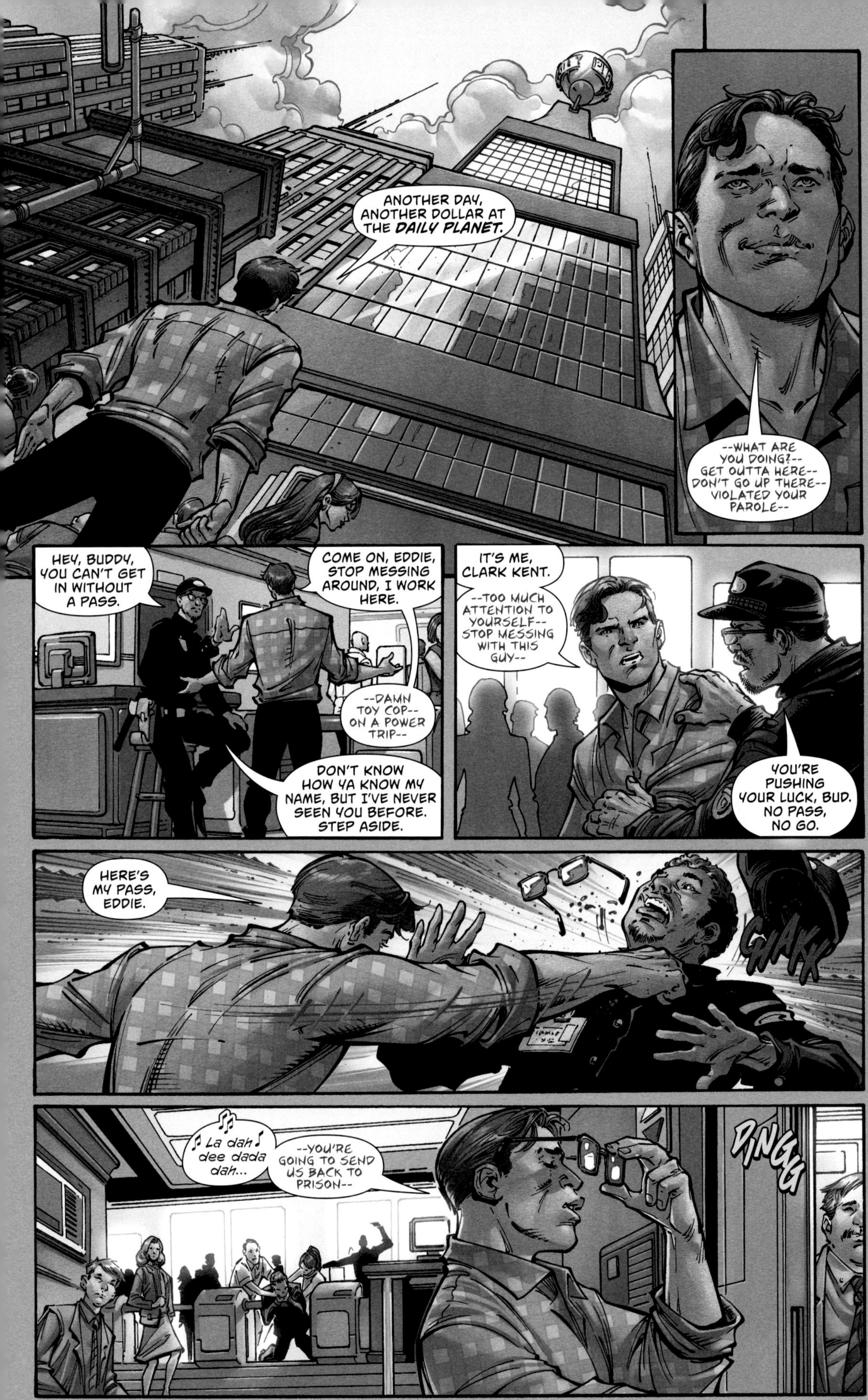
ANOTHER DAY, ANOTHER DOLLAR AT THE DAILY PLANET.
--WHAT ARE YOU DOING?-- GET OUTTA HERE-- DON'T GO UP THERE-- VIOLATED YOUR PAROLE--
HEY, BUDDY, YOU CAN'T GET IN WITHOUT A PASS.
COME ON, EDDIE, STOP MESSING AROUND, I WORK HERE.
--DAMN TOY COP-- ON A POWER TRIP--
DON'T KNOW HOW YA KNOW MY NAME, BUT I'VE NEVER SEEN YOU BEFORE. STEP ASIDE.
IT'S ME, CLARK KENT.
--TOO MUCH ATTENTION TO YOURSELF-- STOP MESSING WITH THIS GUY--
YOU'RE PUSHING YOUR LUCK, BUD. NO PASS, NO GO.
HERE'S MY PASS, EDDIE.
GWAK
♪ La dah ♪ dee dada dah...
--YOU'RE GOING TO SEND US BACK TO PRISON--
DINGG

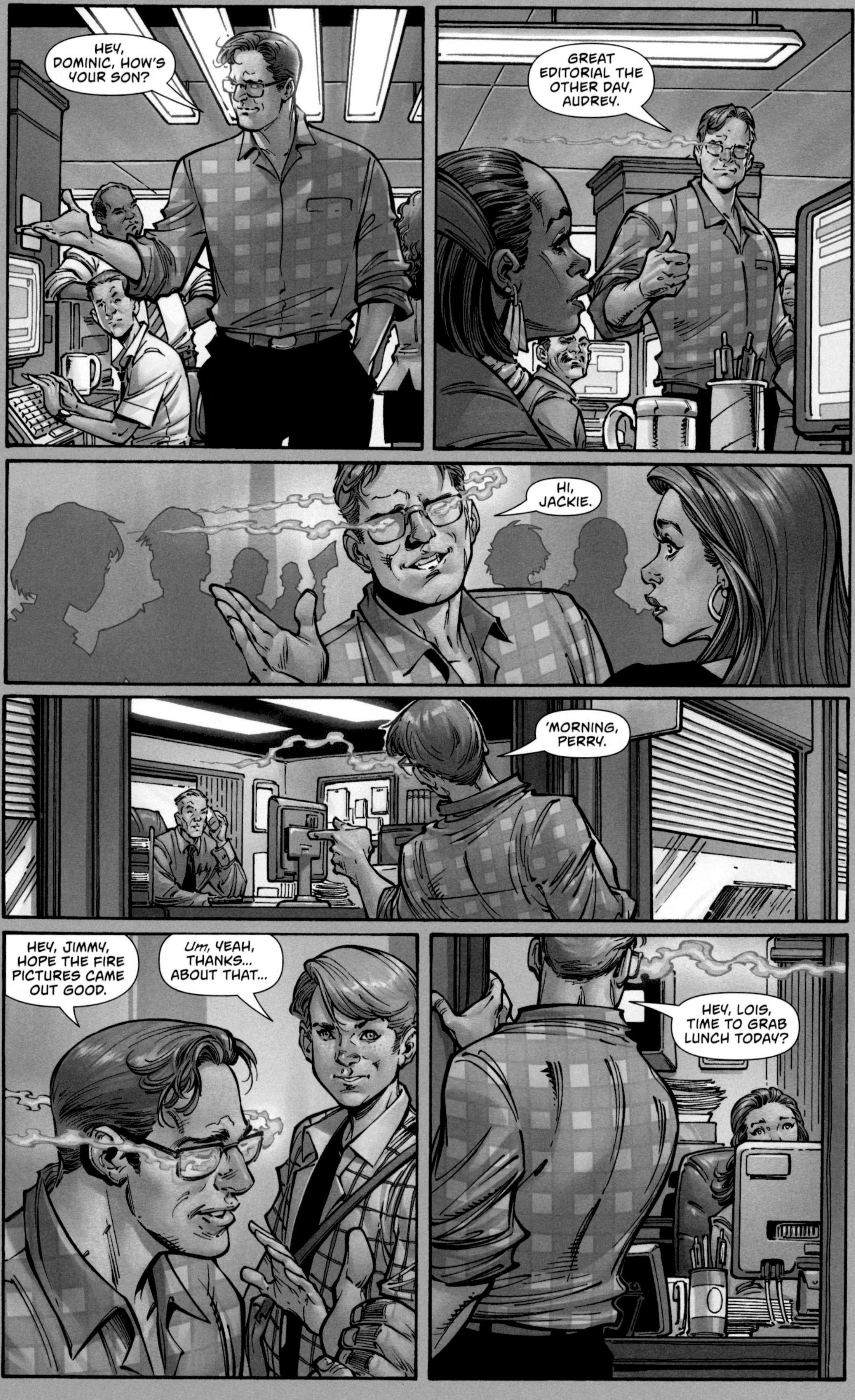
HEY, DOMINIC, HOW'S YOUR SON?
GREAT EDITORIAL THE OTHER DAY, AUDREY.
HI, JACKIE.
'MORNING, PERRY.
HEY, JIMMY, HOPE THE FIRE PICTURES CAME OUT GOOD.
UM, YEAH, THANKS... ABOUT THAT...
HEY, LOIS, TIME TO GRAB LUNCH TODAY?

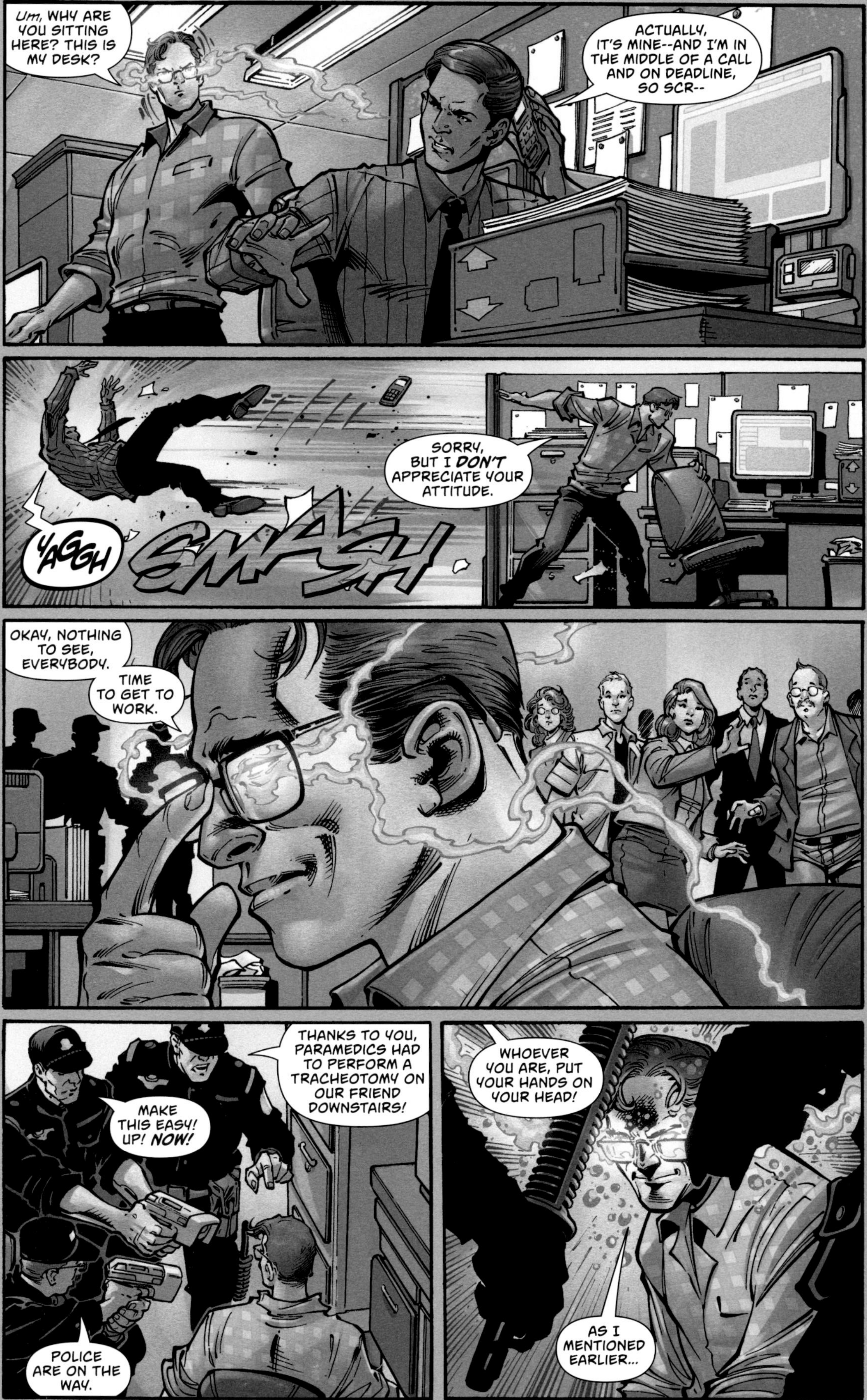

Um, WHY ARE YOU SITTING HERE? THIS IS MY DESK?
ACTUALLY, IT'S MINE--AND I'M IN THE MIDDLE OF A CALL AND ON DEADLINE, SO SCR--
YAGGH
SMASH
SORRY, BUT I DON'T APPRECIATE YOUR ATTITUDE.
OKAY, NOTHING TO SEE, EVERYBODY.
TIME TO GET TO WORK.
MAKE THIS EASY! UP! NOW!
THANKS TO YOU, PARAMEDICS HAD TO PERFORM A TRACHEOTOMY ON OUR FRIEND DOWNSTAIRS!
POLICE ARE ON THE WAY.
WHOEVER YOU ARE, PUT YOUR HANDS ON YOUR HEAD!
AS I MENTIONED EARLIER...

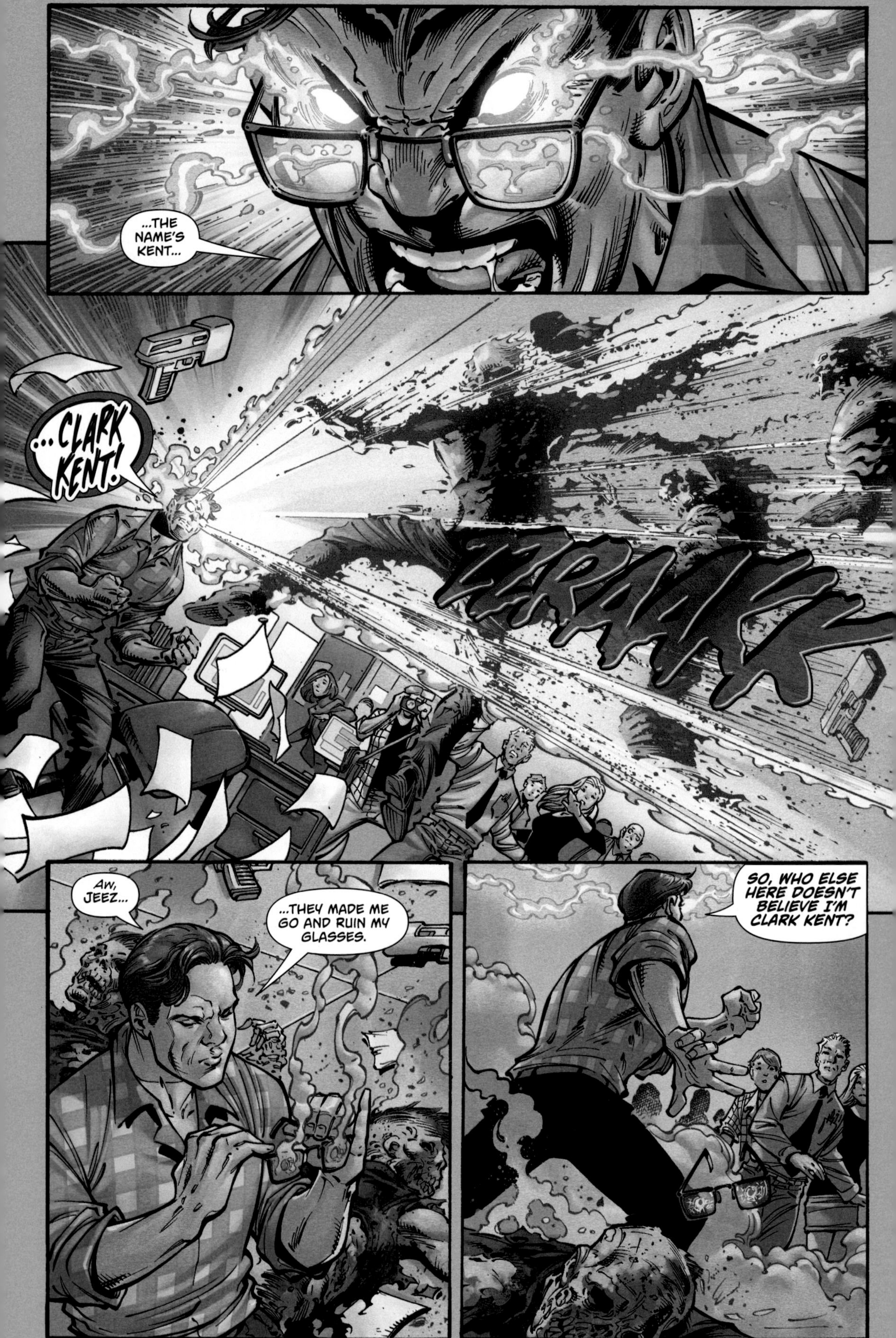
...THE NAME'S KENT...
...CLARK KENT!
ZZRAAKK
AW, JEEZ...
...THEY MADE ME GO AND RUIN MY GLASSES.
SO, WHO ELSE HERE DOESN'T BELIEVE I'M CLARK KENT?

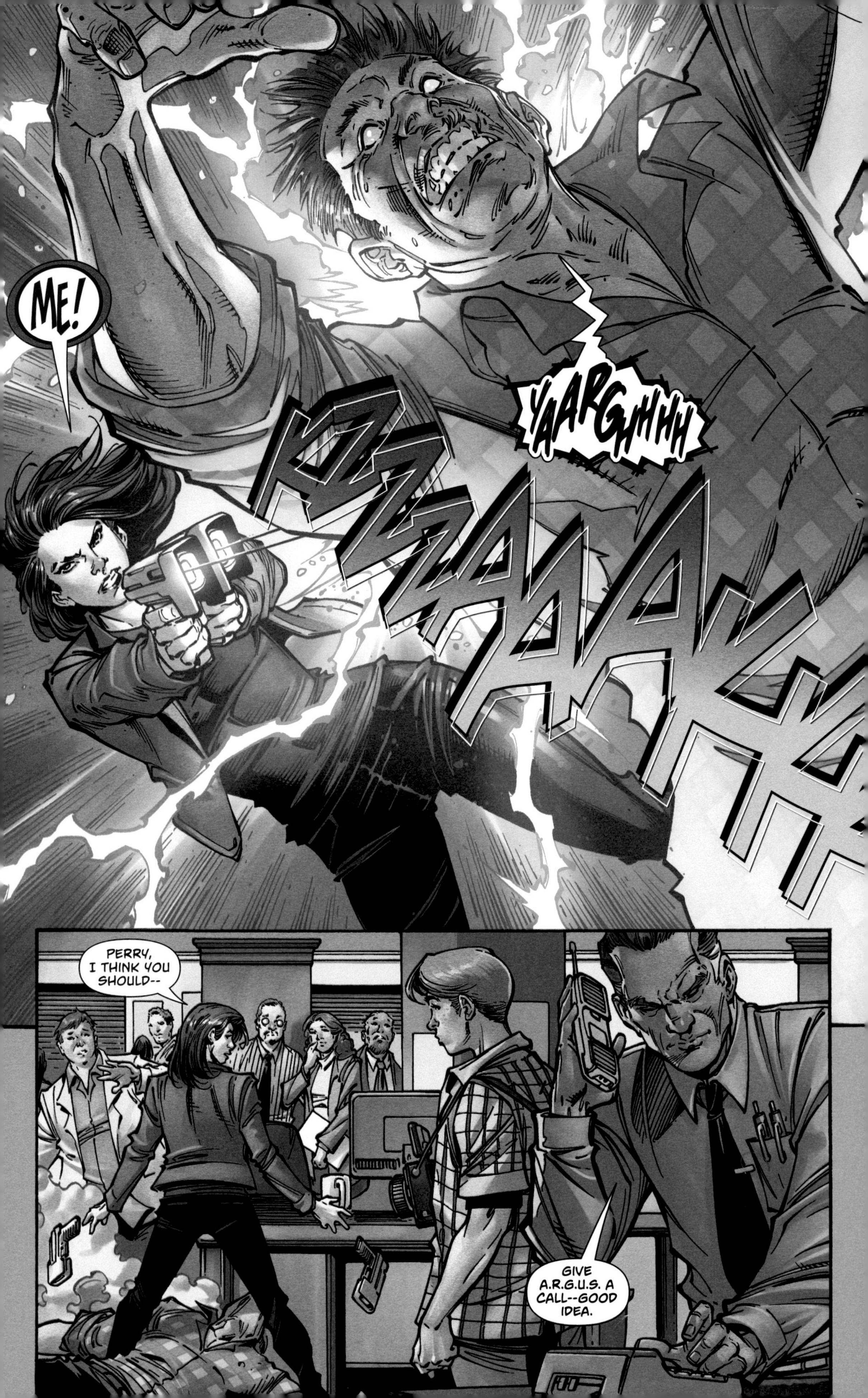
ME!
YAARGHHHH
KZZZAAAAAAAAZZZT
PERRY, I THINK YOU SHOULD--
GIVE A.R.G.U.S. A CALL--GOOD IDEA.

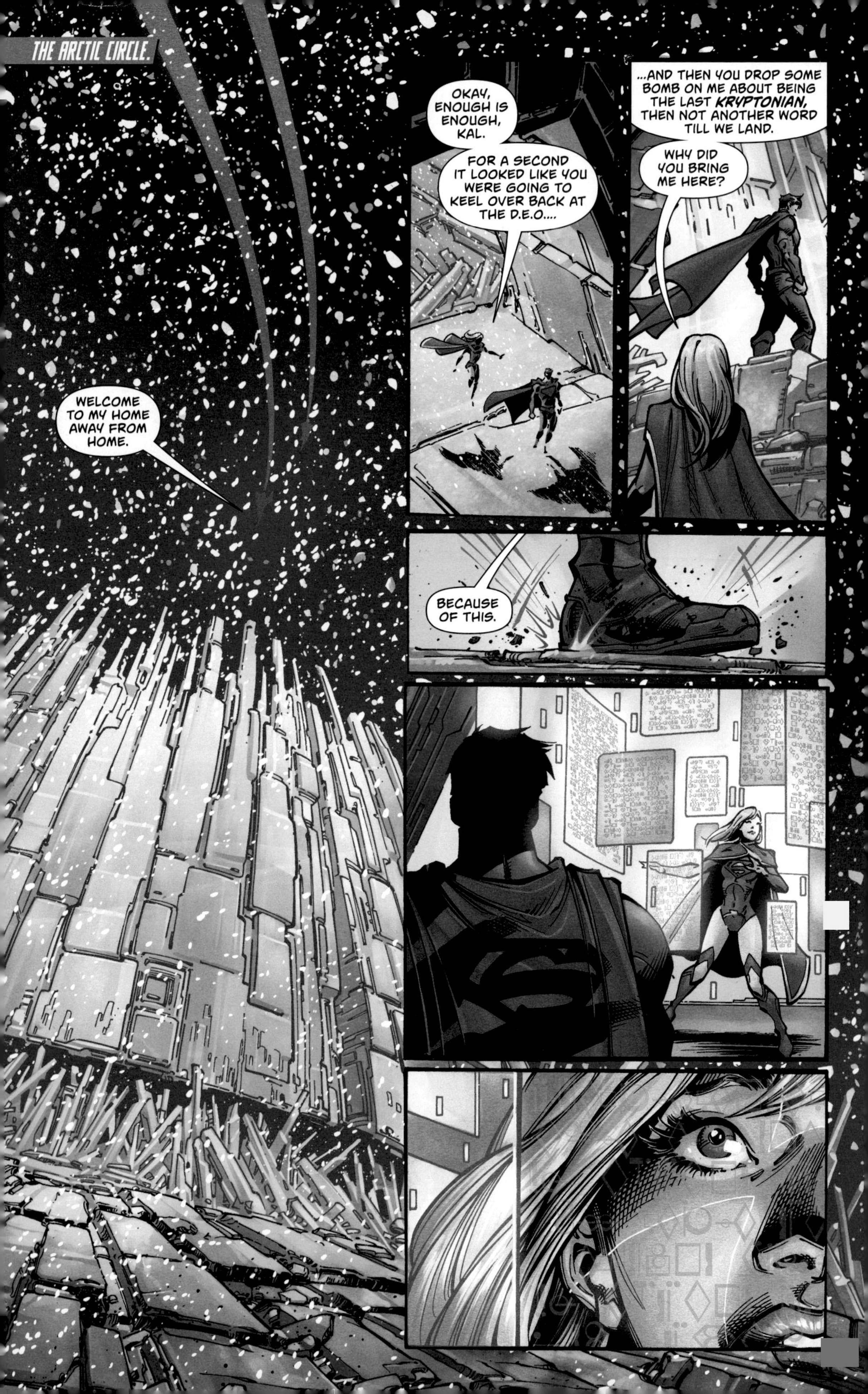

THE ARCTIC CIRCLE.
WELCOME TO MY HOME AWAY FROM HOME.
OKAY, ENOUGH IS ENOUGH, KAL.
FOR A SECOND IT LOOKED LIKE YOU WERE GOING TO KEEL OVER BACK AT THE D.E.O....
...AND THEN YOU DROP SOME BOMB ON ME ABOUT BEING THE LAST KRYPTONIAN, THEN NOT ANOTHER WORD TILL WE LAND.
WHY DID YOU BRING ME HERE?
BECAUSE OF THIS.

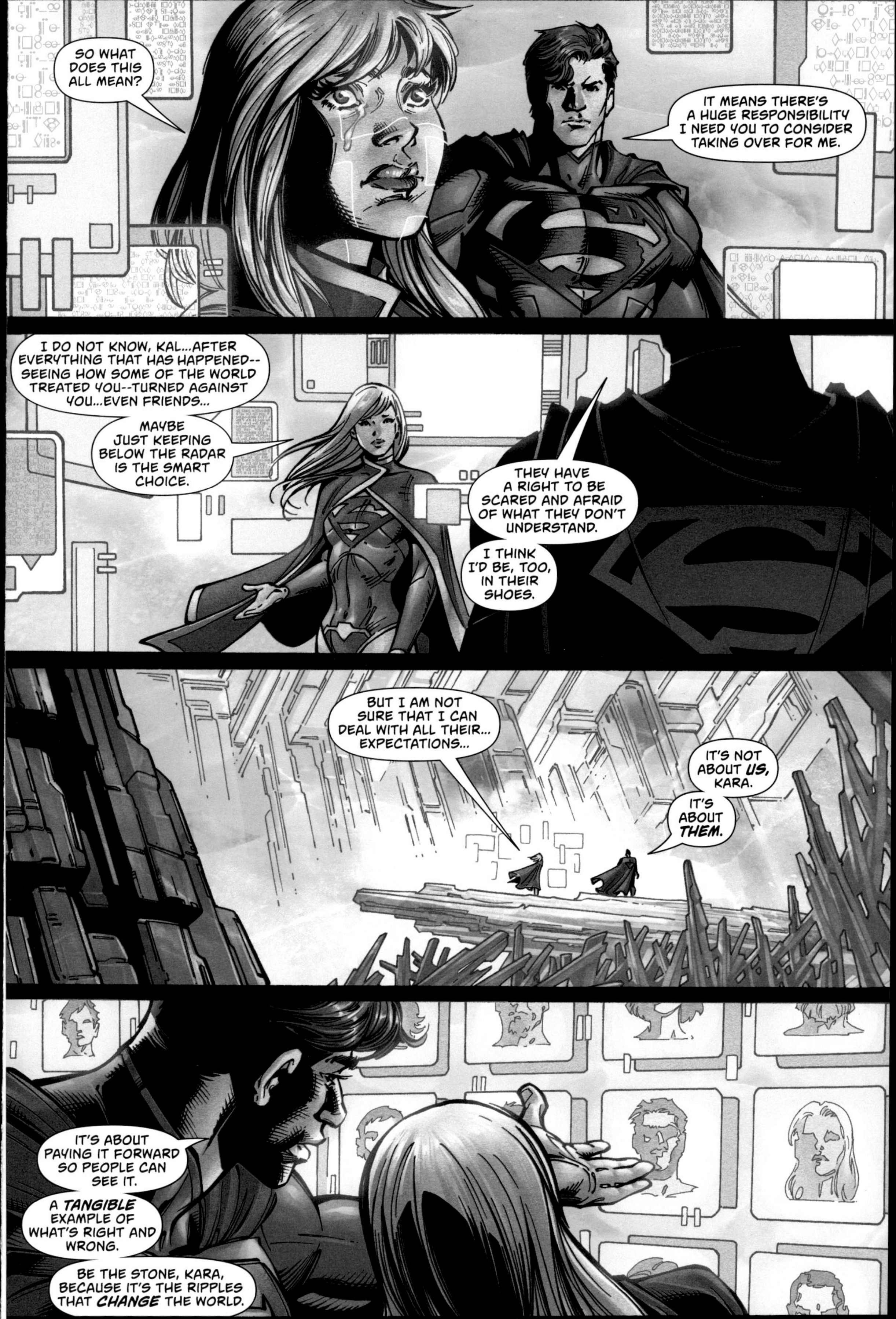
SO WHAT DOES THIS ALL MEAN?
IT MEANS THERE'S A HUGE RESPONSIBILITY I NEED YOU TO CONSIDER TAKING OVER FOR ME.
I DO NOT KNOW, KAL...AFTER EVERYTHING THAT HAS HAPPENED--SEEING HOW SOME OF THE WORLD TREATED YOU--TURNED AGAINST YOU...EVEN FRIENDS...
MAYBE JUST KEEPING BELOW THE RADAR IS THE SMART CHOICE.
THEY HAVE A RIGHT TO BE SCARED AND AFRAID OF WHAT THEY DON'T UNDERSTAND.
I THINK I'D BE, TOO, IN THEIR SHOES.
BUT I AM NOT SURE THAT I CAN DEAL WITH ALL THEIR... EXPECTATIONS...
IT'S NOT ABOUT *US*, KARA.
IT'S ABOUT *THEM*.
IT'S ABOUT PAYING IT FORWARD SO PEOPLE CAN SEE IT.
A *TANGIBLE* EXAMPLE OF WHAT'S RIGHT AND WRONG.
BE THE STONE, KARA, BECAUSE IT'S THE RIPPLES THAT *CHANGE* THE WORLD.

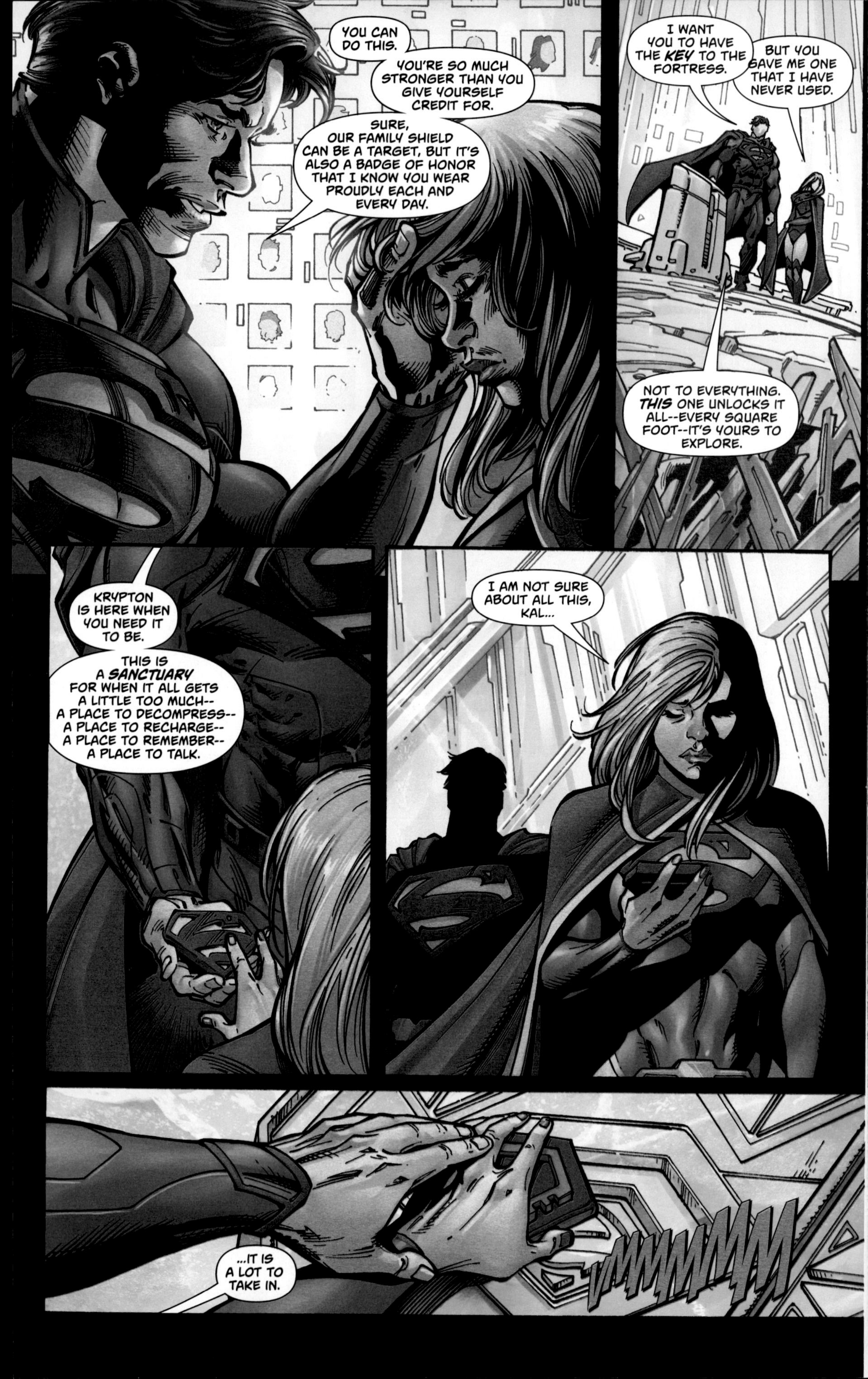
YOU CAN DO THIS.
YOU'RE SO MUCH STRONGER THAN YOU GIVE YOURSELF CREDIT FOR.
SURE, OUR FAMILY SHIELD CAN BE A TARGET, BUT IT'S ALSO A BADGE OF HONOR THAT I KNOW YOU WEAR PROUDLY EACH AND EVERY DAY.
I WANT YOU TO HAVE THE KEY TO THE FORTRESS.
BUT YOU GAVE ME ONE THAT I HAVE NEVER USED.
NOT TO EVERYTHING. THIS ONE UNLOCKS IT ALL--EVERY SQUARE FOOT--IT'S YOURS TO EXPLORE.
KRYPTON IS HERE WHEN YOU NEED IT TO BE.
THIS IS A SANCTUARY FOR WHEN IT ALL GETS A LITTLE TOO MUCH--A PLACE TO DECOMPRESS--A PLACE TO RECHARGE--A PLACE TO REMEMBER--A PLACE TO TALK.
I AM NOT SURE ABOUT ALL THIS, KAL...
...IT IS A LOT TO TAKE IN.
VMMMMM

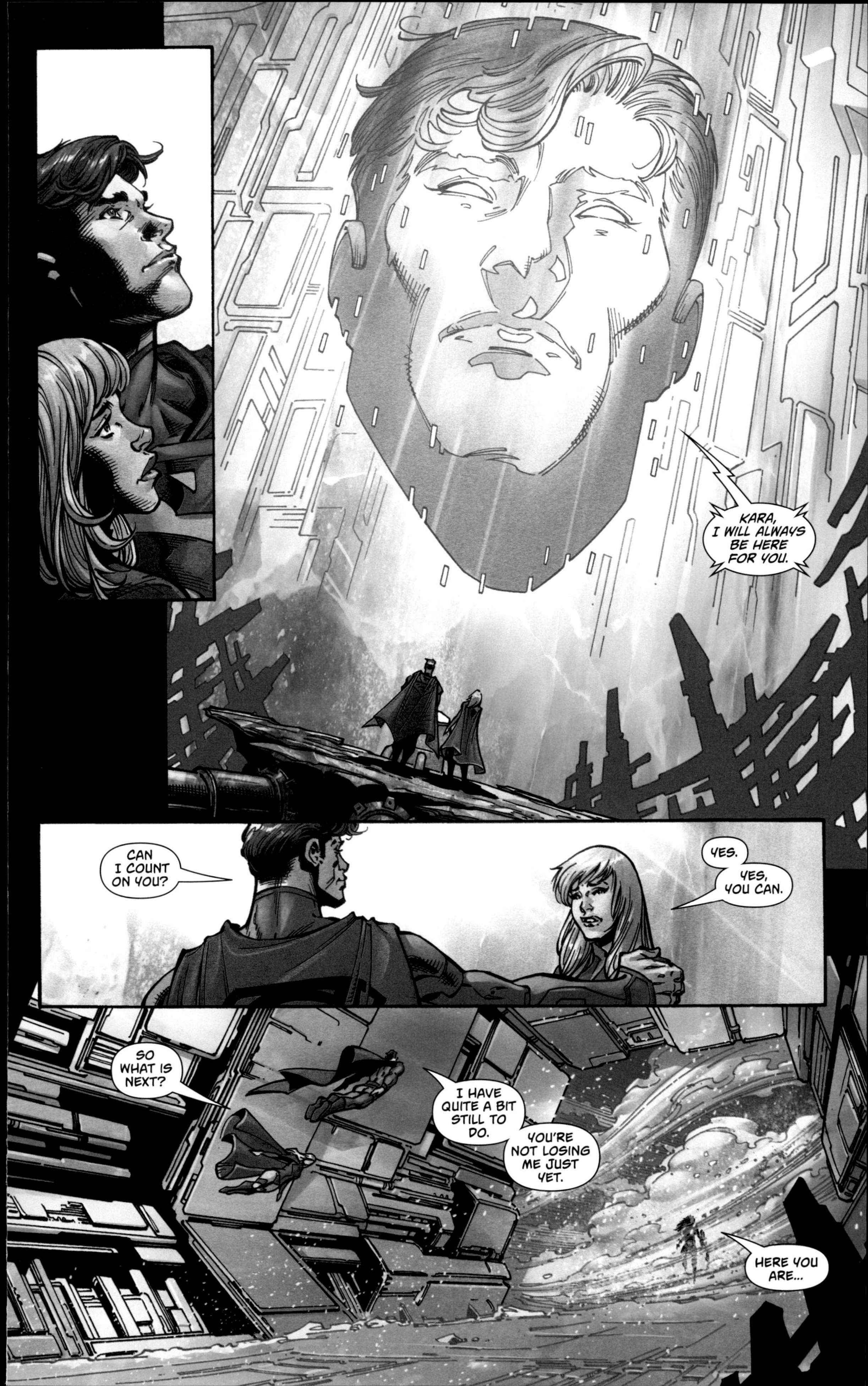
KARA, I WILL ALWAYS BE HERE FOR YOU.
CAN I COUNT ON YOU?
YES.
YES, YOU CAN.
SO WHAT IS NEXT?
I HAVE QUITE A BIT STILL TO DO.
YOU'RE NOT LOSING ME JUST YET.
HERE YOU ARE...

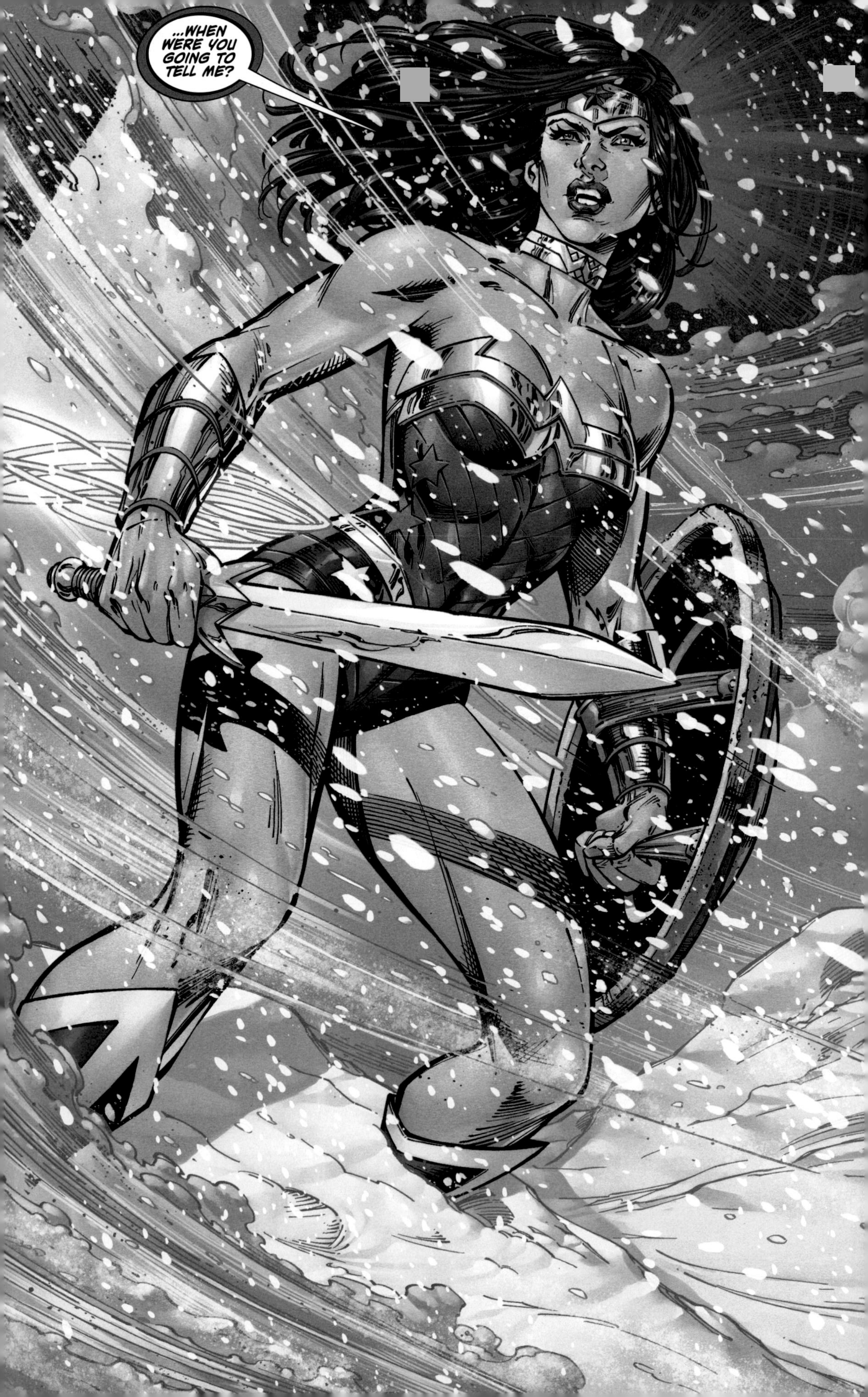
...WHEN WERE YOU GOING TO TELL ME?

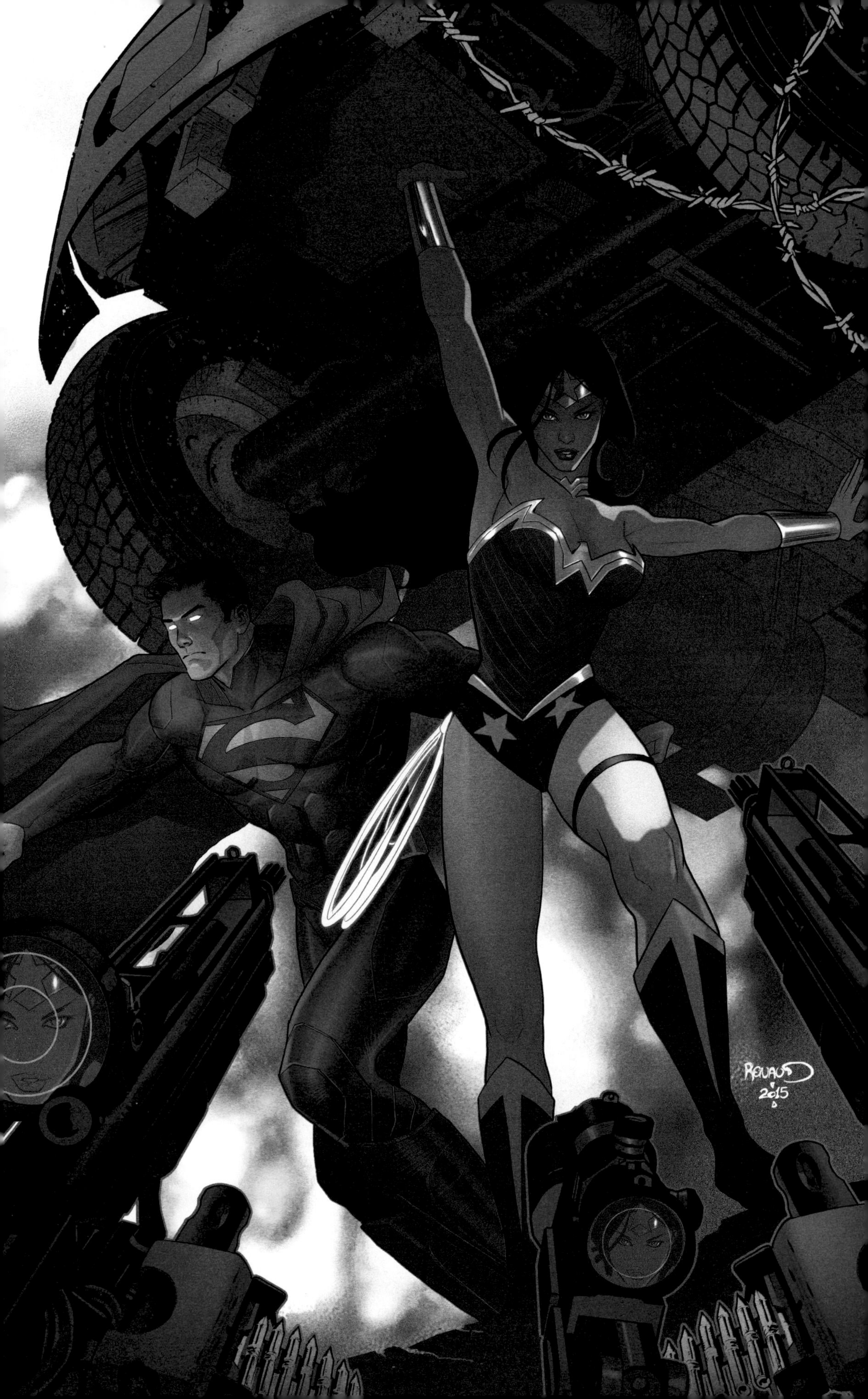
RENAUD
2015

THE FINAL DAYS OF SUPERMAN PART 4: LAST KISS

PETER J. TOMASI writer **ED BENES** artist **SANDRA HOPE ARCHER** inker **ALEX SINCLAIR** colorist **ROB LEIGH** letterer **PAUL RENAUD** cover

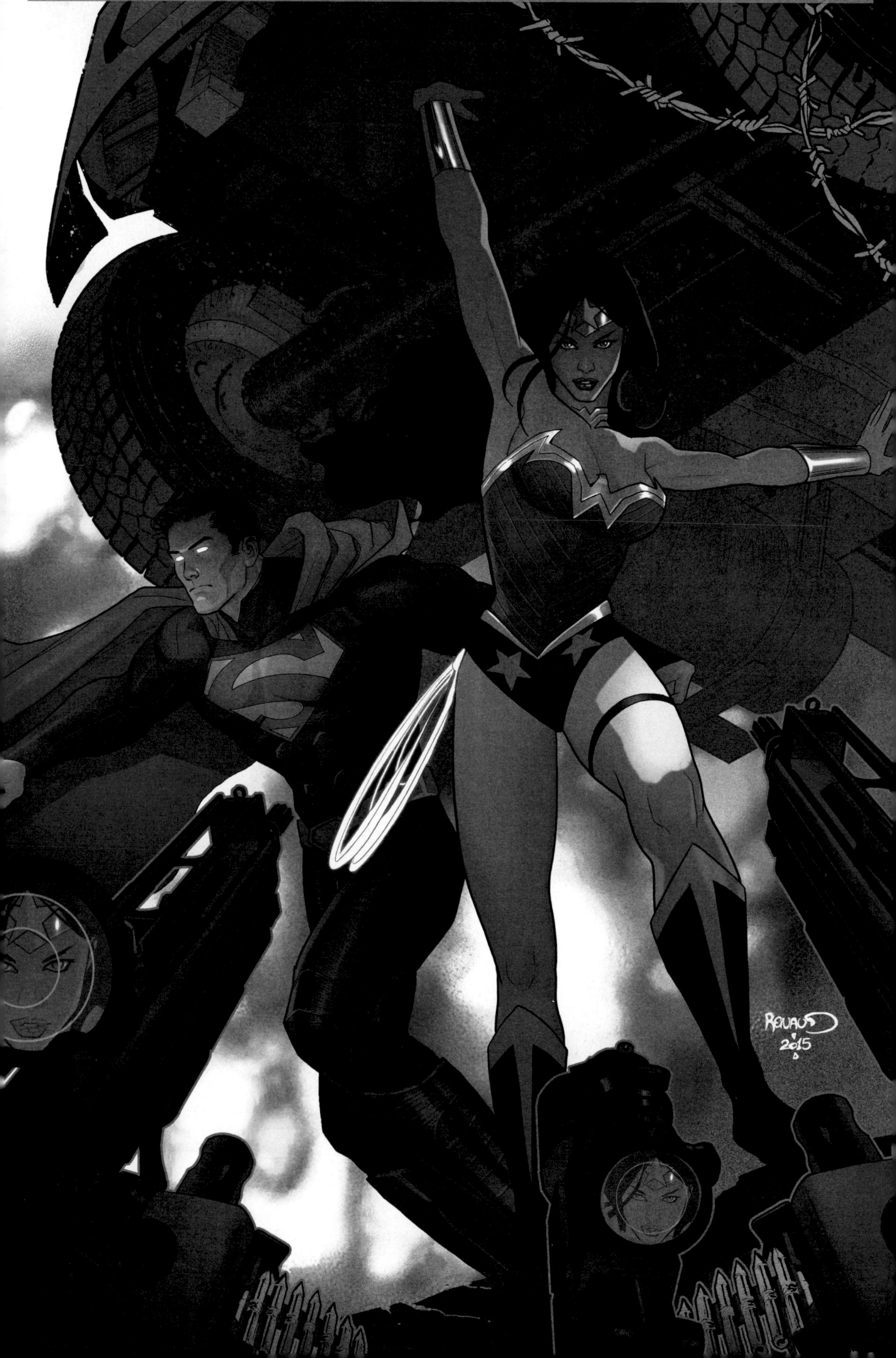
RENAUD 2015

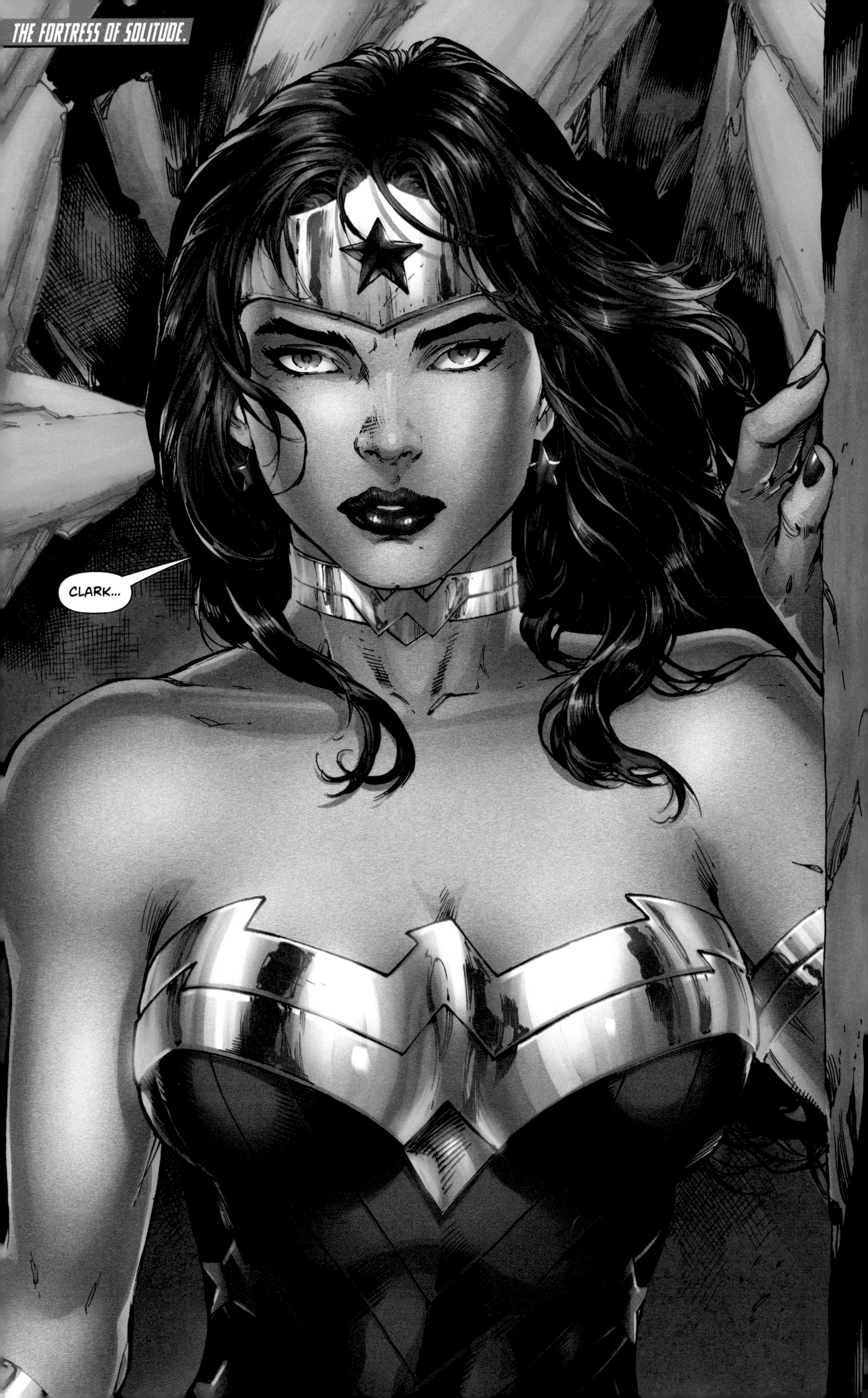
THE FORTRESS OF SOLITUDE.
CLARK...

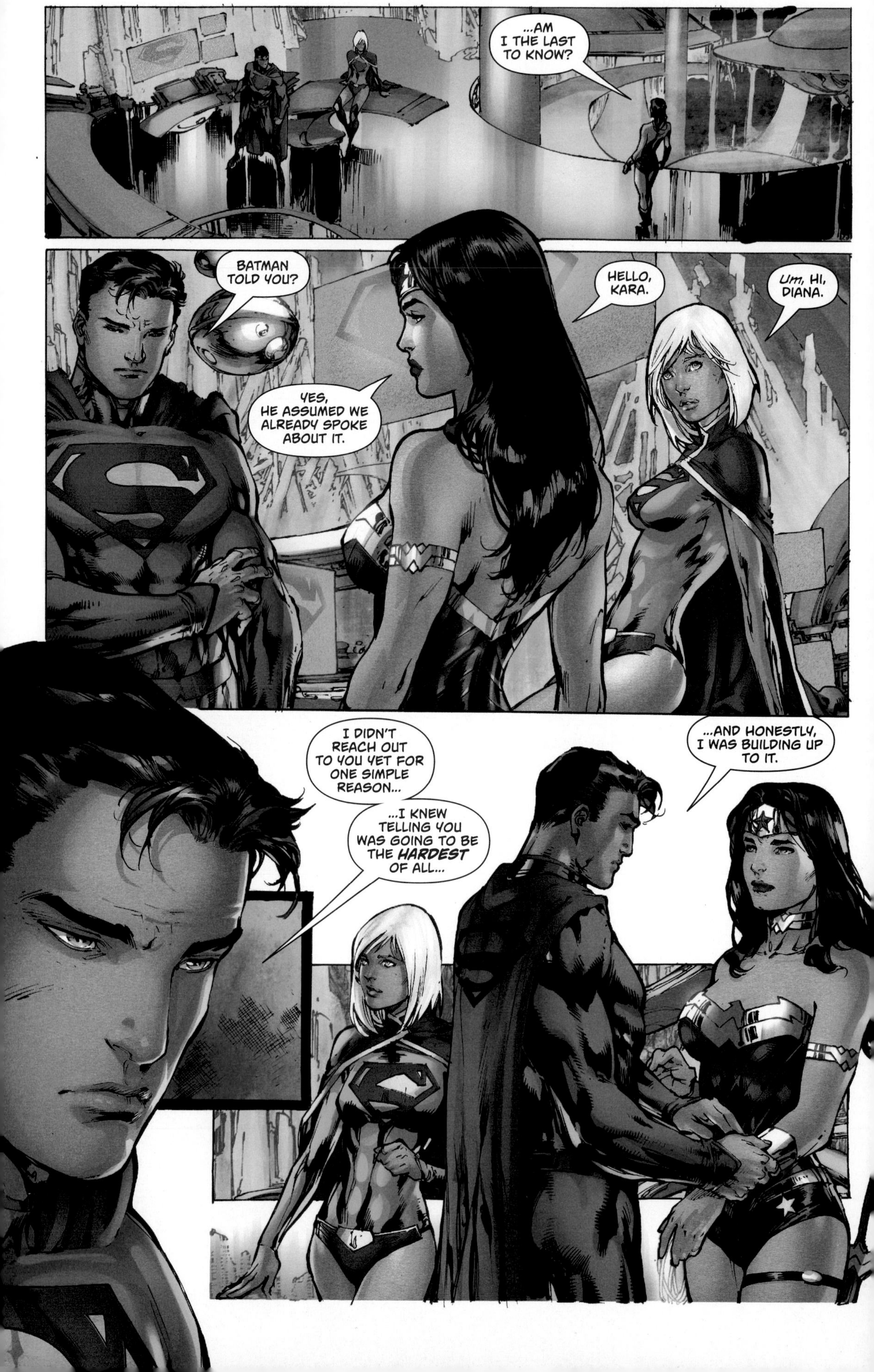
...AM I THE LAST TO KNOW?
BATMAN TOLD YOU?
YES, HE ASSUMED WE ALREADY SPOKE ABOUT IT.
HELLO, KARA.
Um, HI, DIANA.
I DIDN'T REACH OUT TO YOU YET FOR ONE SIMPLE REASON...
...I KNEW TELLING YOU WAS GOING TO BE THE HARDEST OF ALL...
...AND HONESTLY, I WAS BUILDING UP TO IT.

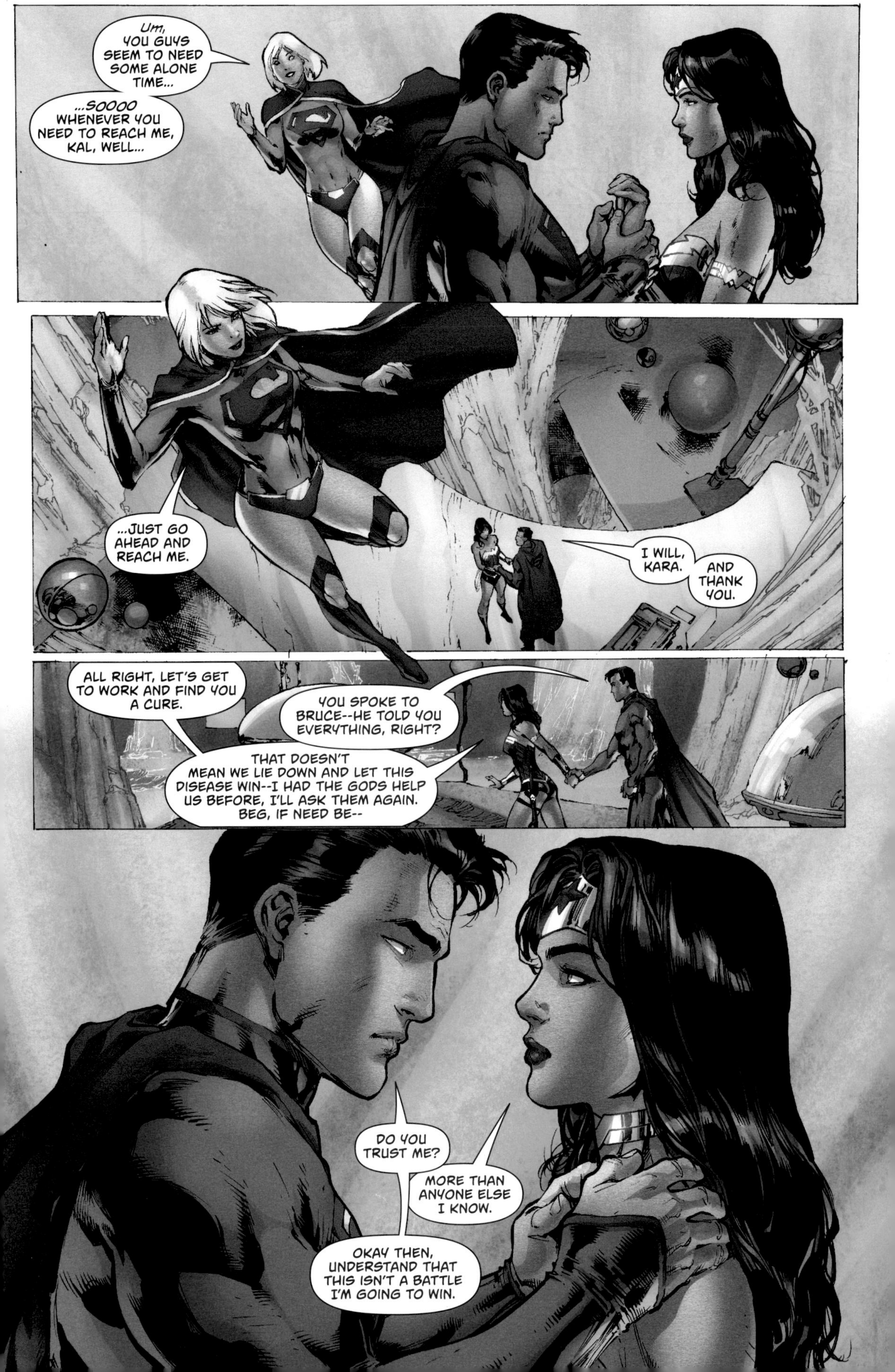

UM, YOU GUYS SEEM TO NEED SOME ALONE TIME...
...SOOOO WHENEVER YOU NEED TO REACH ME, KAL, WELL...
...JUST GO AHEAD AND REACH ME.
I WILL, KARA.
AND THANK YOU.
ALL RIGHT, LET'S GET TO WORK AND FIND YOU A CURE.
YOU SPOKE TO BRUCE--HE TOLD YOU EVERYTHING, RIGHT?
THAT DOESN'T MEAN WE LIE DOWN AND LET THIS DISEASE WIN--I HAD THE GODS HELP US BEFORE, I'LL ASK THEM AGAIN. BEG, IF NEED BE--
DO YOU TRUST ME?
MORE THAN ANYONE ELSE I KNOW.
OKAY THEN, UNDERSTAND THAT THIS ISN'T A BATTLE I'M GOING TO WIN.

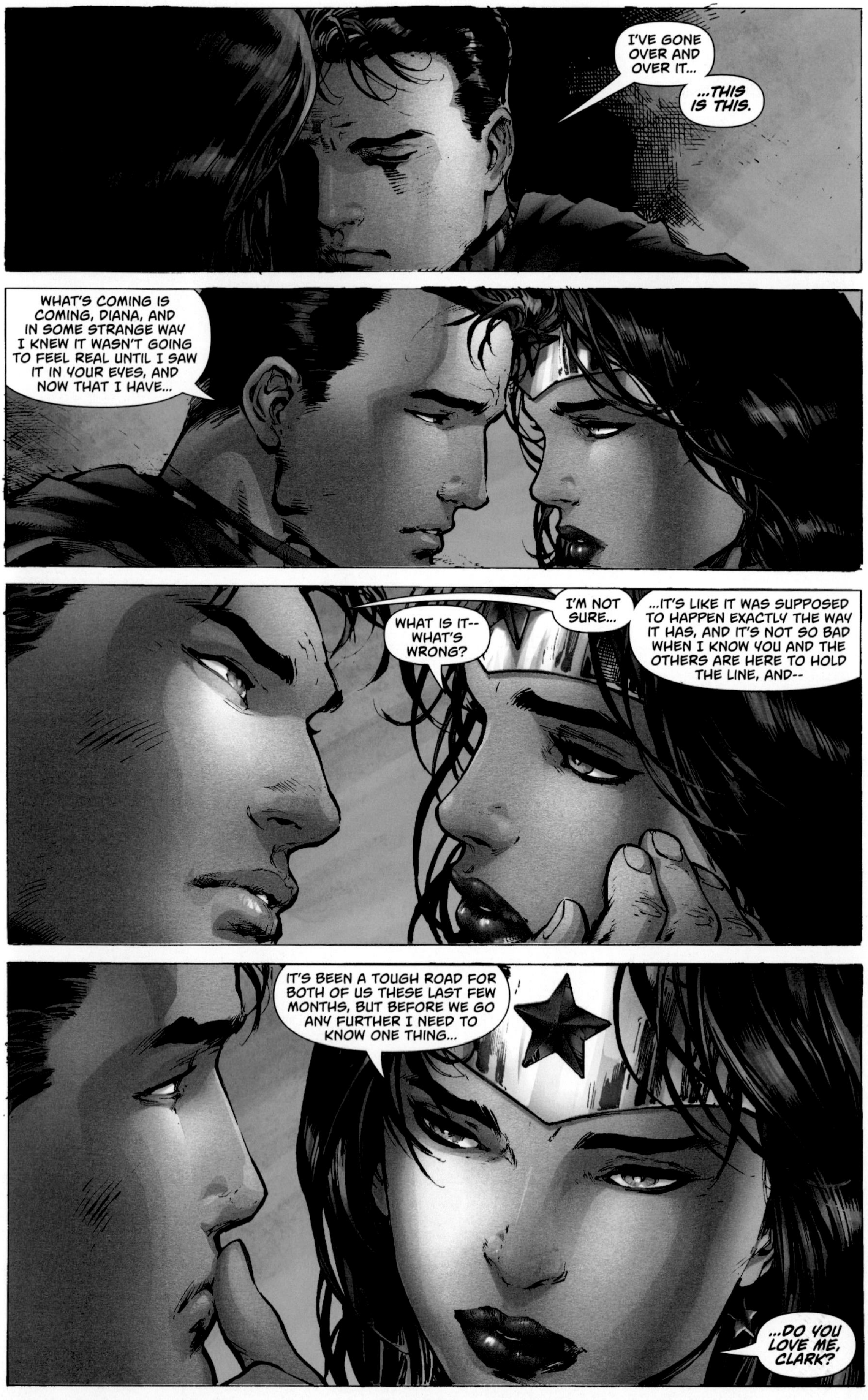
I'VE GONE OVER AND OVER IT...
...THIS IS THIS.
WHAT'S COMING IS COMING, DIANA, AND IN SOME STRANGE WAY I KNEW IT WASN'T GOING TO FEEL REAL UNTIL I SAW IT IN YOUR EYES, AND NOW THAT I HAVE...
WHAT IS IT-- WHAT'S WRONG?
I'M NOT SURE...
...IT'S LIKE IT WAS SUPPOSED TO HAPPEN EXACTLY THE WAY IT HAS, AND IT'S NOT SO BAD WHEN I KNOW YOU AND THE OTHERS ARE HERE TO HOLD THE LINE, AND--
IT'S BEEN A TOUGH ROAD FOR BOTH OF US THESE LAST FEW MONTHS, BUT BEFORE WE GO ANY FURTHER I NEED TO KNOW ONE THING...
...DO YOU LOVE ME, CLARK?

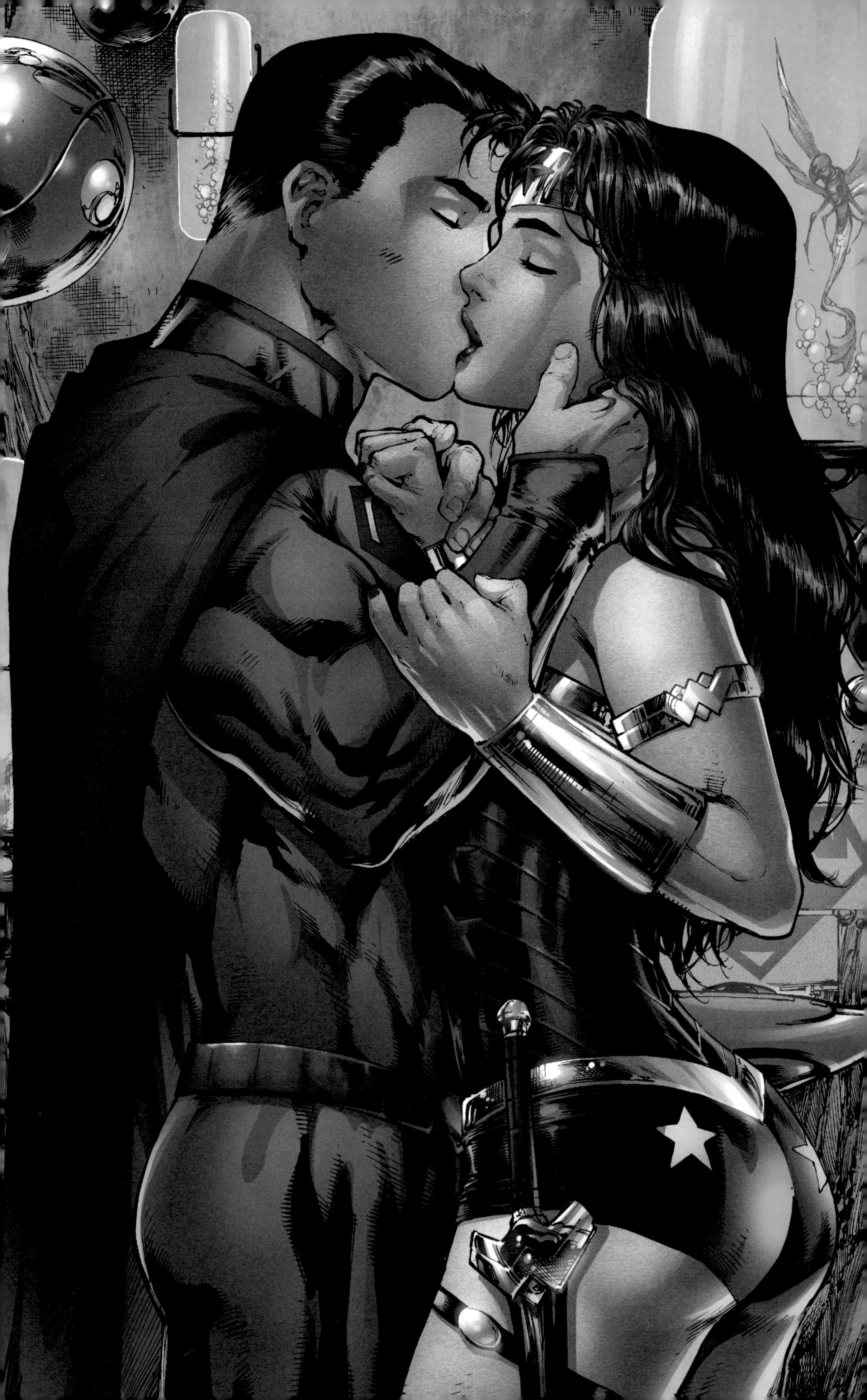

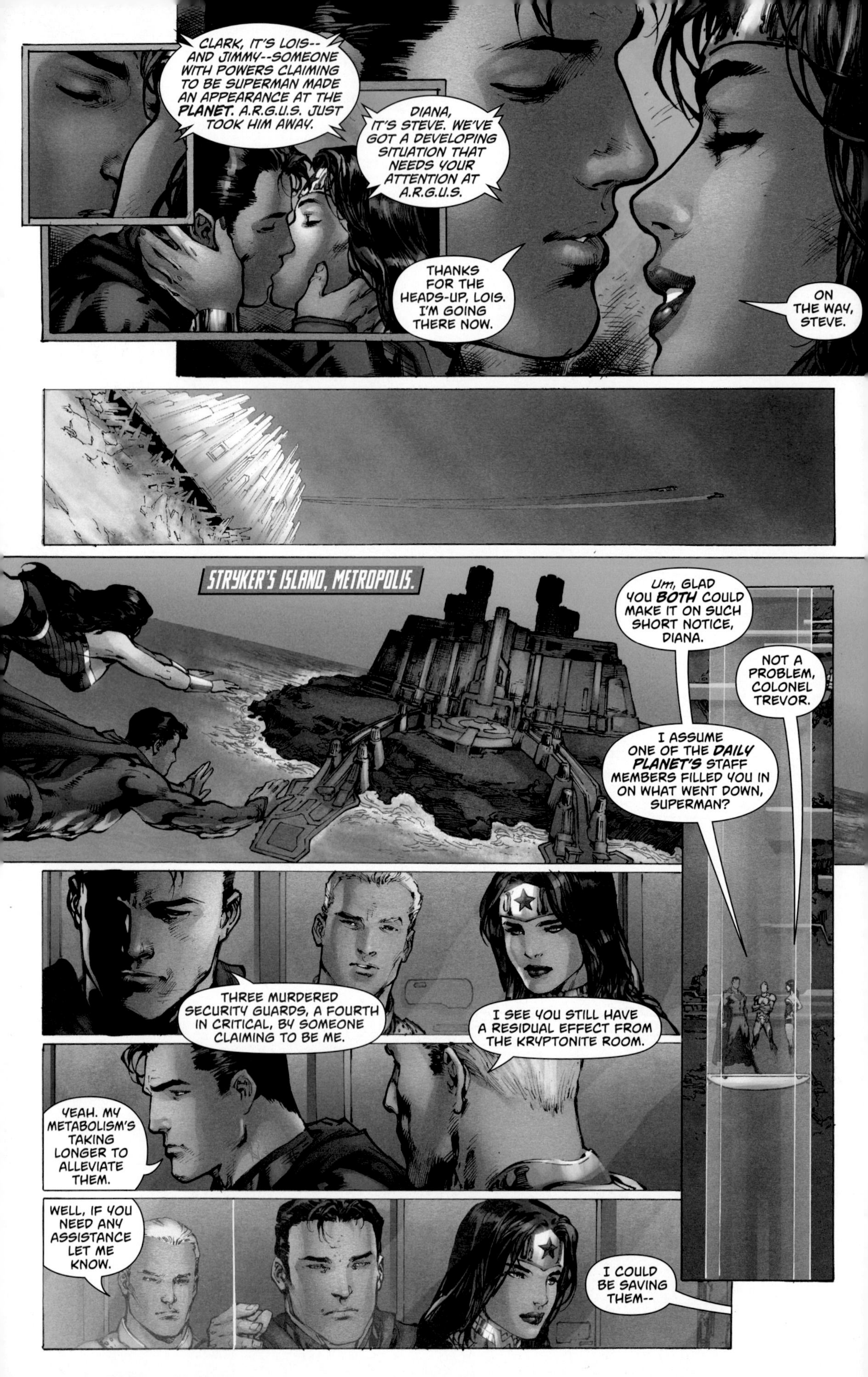
CLARK, IT'S LOIS--AND JIMMY--SOMEONE WITH POWERS CLAIMING TO BE SUPERMAN MADE AN APPEARANCE AT THE PLANET. A.R.G.U.S. JUST TOOK HIM AWAY.
DIANA, IT'S STEVE. WE'VE GOT A DEVELOPING SITUATION THAT NEEDS YOUR ATTENTION AT A.R.G.U.S.
THANKS FOR THE HEADS-UP, LOIS. I'M GOING THERE NOW.
ON THE WAY, STEVE.
STRYKER'S ISLAND, METROPOLIS.
UM, GLAD YOU BOTH COULD MAKE IT ON SUCH SHORT NOTICE, DIANA.
NOT A PROBLEM, COLONEL TREVOR.
I ASSUME ONE OF THE DAILY PLANET'S STAFF MEMBERS FILLED YOU IN ON WHAT WENT DOWN, SUPERMAN?
THREE MURDERED SECURITY GUARDS, A FOURTH IN CRITICAL, BY SOMEONE CLAIMING TO BE ME.
I SEE YOU STILL HAVE A RESIDUAL EFFECT FROM THE KRYPTONITE ROOM.
YEAH. MY METABOLISM'S TAKING LONGER TO ALLEVIATE THEM.
WELL, IF YOU NEED ANY ASSISTANCE LET ME KNOW.
I COULD BE SAVING THEM--

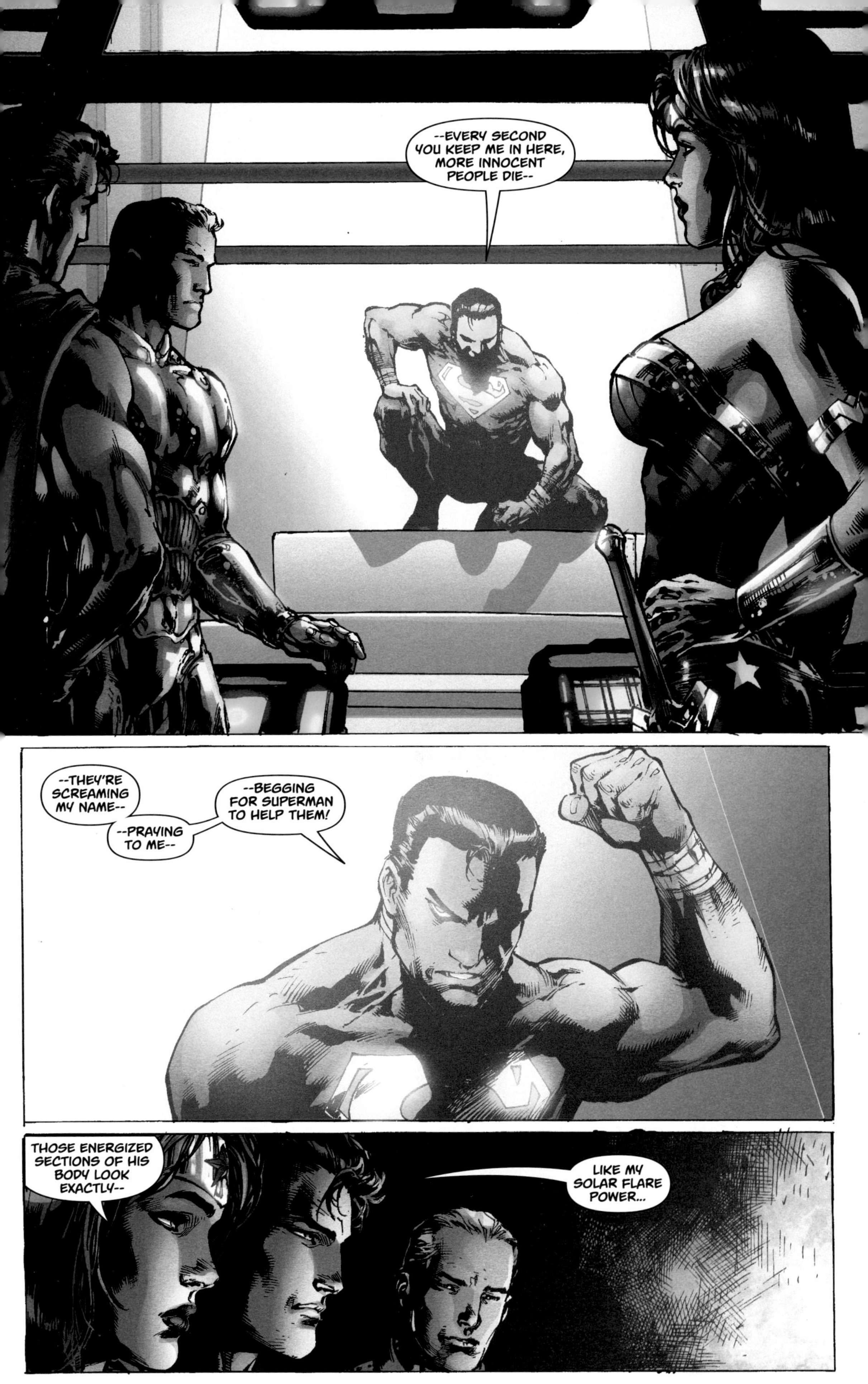
--EVERY SECOND YOU KEEP ME IN HERE, MORE INNOCENT PEOPLE DIE--
--THEY'RE SCREAMING MY NAME--
--PRAYING TO ME--
--BEGGING FOR SUPERMAN TO HELP THEM!
THOSE ENERGIZED SECTIONS OF HIS BODY LOOK EXACTLY--
LIKE MY SOLAR FLARE POWER...

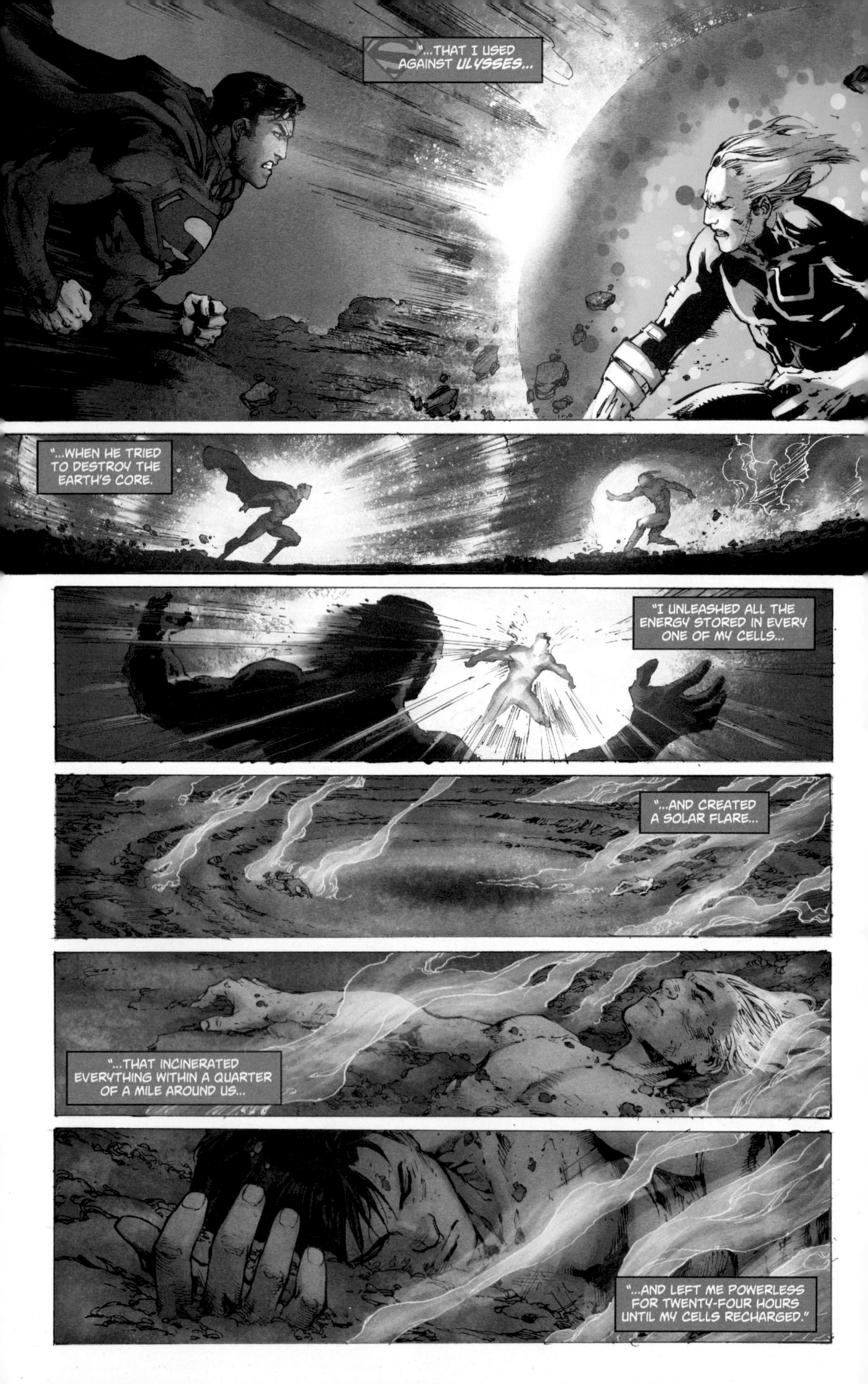
"...THAT I USED AGAINST ULYSSES...
"...WHEN HE TRIED TO DESTROY THE EARTH'S CORE.
"I UNLEASHED ALL THE ENERGY STORED IN EVERY ONE OF MY CELLS...
"...AND CREATED A SOLAR FLARE...
"...THAT INCINERATED EVERYTHING WITHIN A QUARTER OF A MILE AROUND US...
"...AND LEFT ME POWERLESS FOR TWENTY-FOUR HOURS UNTIL MY CELLS RECHARGED."

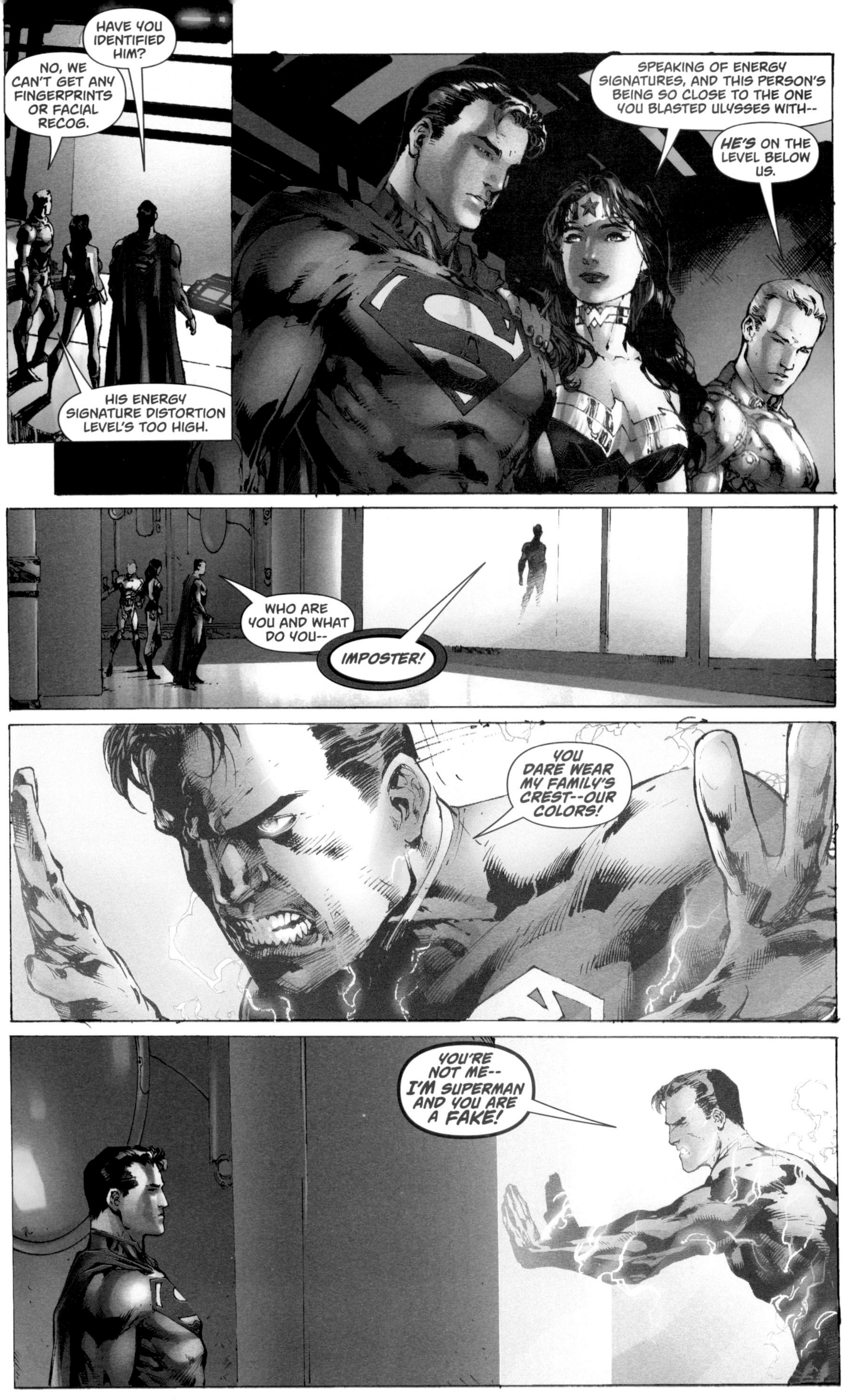
HAVE YOU IDENTIFIED HIM?
NO, WE CAN'T GET ANY FINGERPRINTS OR FACIAL RECOG.
HIS ENERGY SIGNATURE DISTORTION LEVEL'S TOO HIGH.
SPEAKING OF ENERGY SIGNATURES, AND THIS PERSON'S BEING SO CLOSE TO THE ONE YOU BLASTED ULYSSES WITH--
HE'S ON THE LEVEL BELOW US.
WHO ARE YOU AND WHAT DO YOU--
IMPOSTER!
YOU DARE WEAR MY FAMILY'S CREST--OUR COLORS!
YOU'RE NOT ME-- I'M SUPERMAN AND YOU ARE A FAKE!

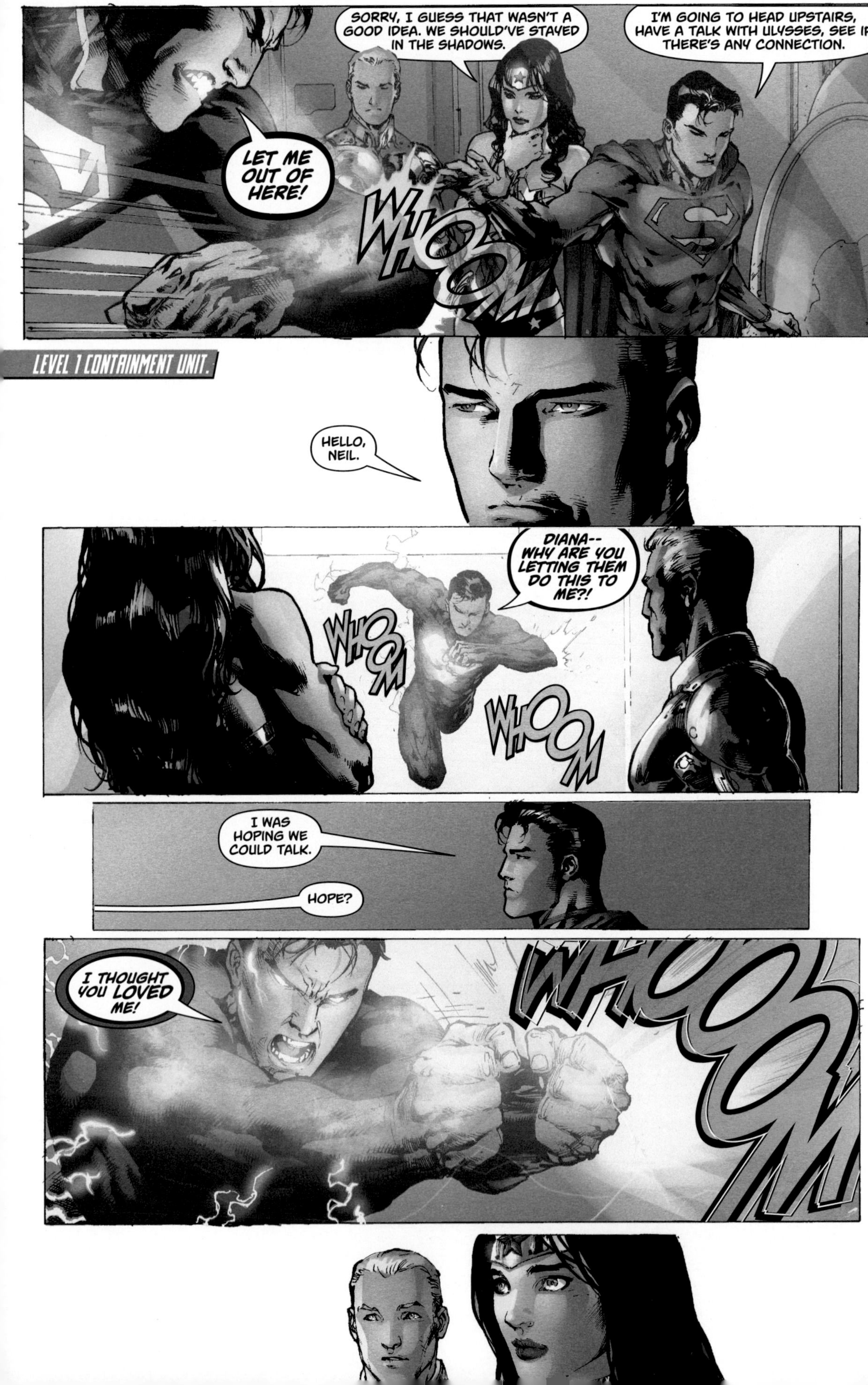

SORRY, I GUESS THAT WASN'T A GOOD IDEA. WE SHOULD'VE STAYED IN THE SHADOWS.
I'M GOING TO HEAD UPSTAIRS, HAVE A TALK WITH ULYSSES, SEE IF THERE'S ANY CONNECTION.
LET ME OUT OF HERE!
WHOOOM
LEVEL 1 CONTAINMENT UNIT.
HELLO, NEIL.
DIANA-- WHY ARE YOU LETTING THEM DO THIS TO ME?!
WHOOM
WHOOM
I WAS HOPING WE COULD TALK.
HOPE?
I THOUGHT YOU LOVED ME!

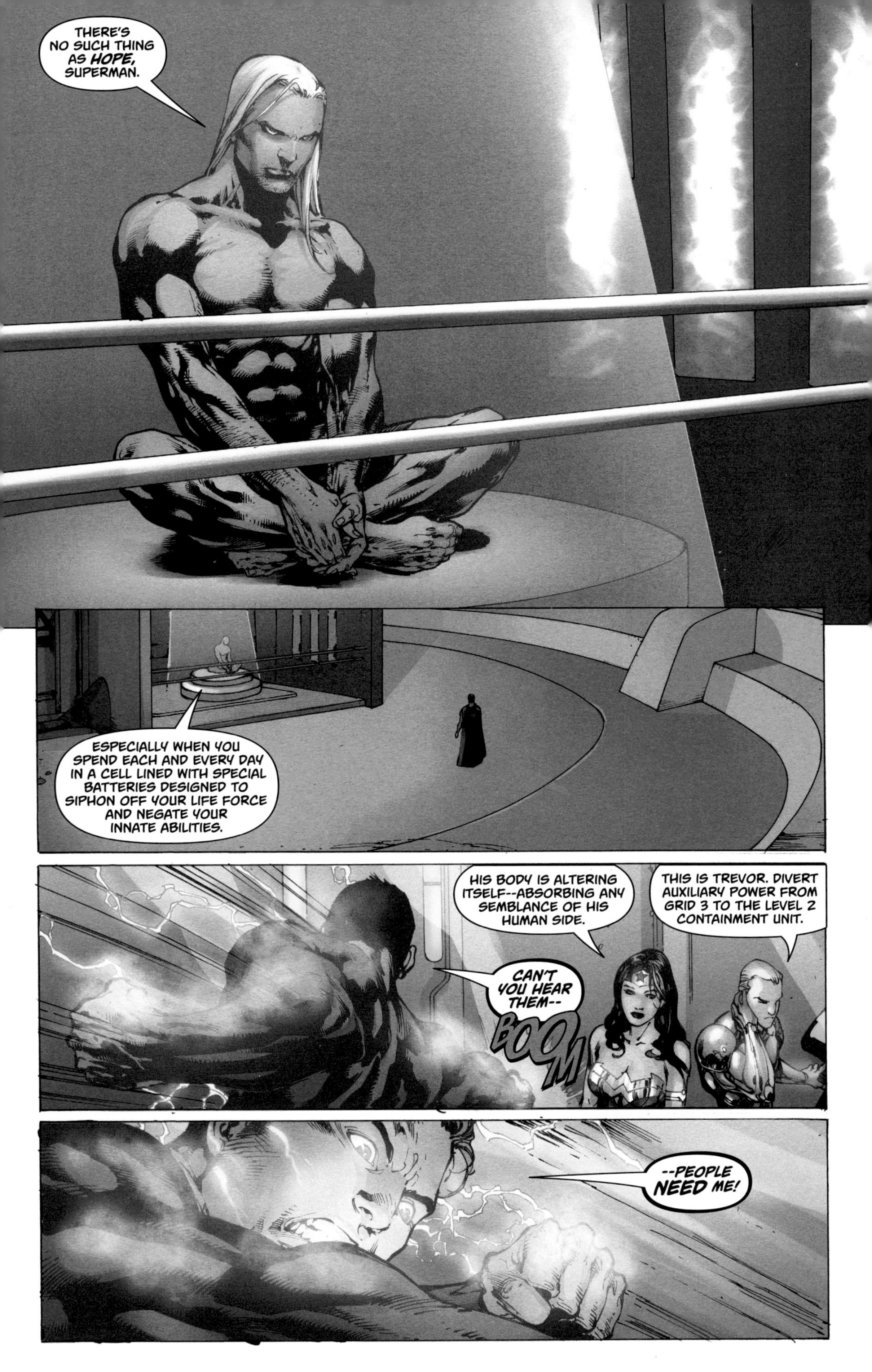
THERE'S NO SUCH THING AS HOPE, SUPERMAN.
ESPECIALLY WHEN YOU SPEND EACH AND EVERY DAY IN A CELL LINED WITH SPECIAL BATTERIES DESIGNED TO SIPHON OFF YOUR LIFE FORCE AND NEGATE YOUR INNATE ABILITIES.
CAN'T YOU HEAR THEM--
HIS BODY IS ALTERING ITSELF--ABSORBING ANY SEMBLANCE OF HIS HUMAN SIDE.
THIS IS TREVOR. DIVERT AUXILIARY POWER FROM GRID 3 TO THE LEVEL 2 CONTAINMENT UNIT.
BOOM
--PEOPLE NEED ME!

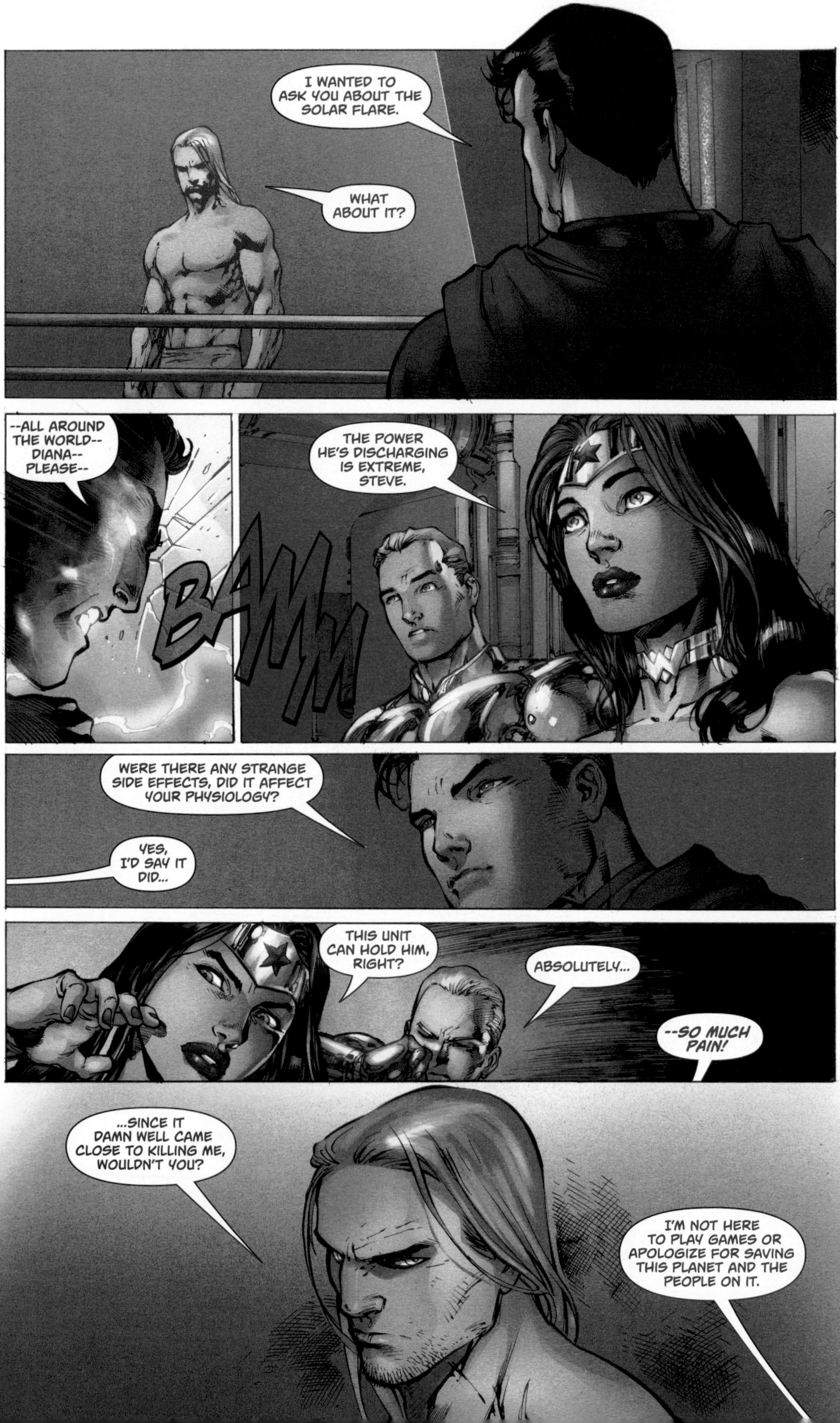
I WANTED TO ASK YOU ABOUT THE SOLAR FLARE.
WHAT ABOUT IT?
--ALL AROUND THE WORLD-- DIANA-- PLEASE--
THE POWER HE'S DISCHARGING IS EXTREME, STEVE.
BAMM
WERE THERE ANY STRANGE SIDE EFFECTS, DID IT AFFECT YOUR PHYSIOLOGY?
YES, I'D SAY IT DID...
THIS UNIT CAN HOLD HIM, RIGHT?
ABSOLUTELY...
--SO MUCH PAIN!
...SINCE IT DAMN WELL CAME CLOSE TO KILLING ME, WOULDN'T YOU?
I'M NOT HERE TO PLAY GAMES OR APOLOGIZE FOR SAVING THIS PLANET AND THE PEOPLE ON IT.

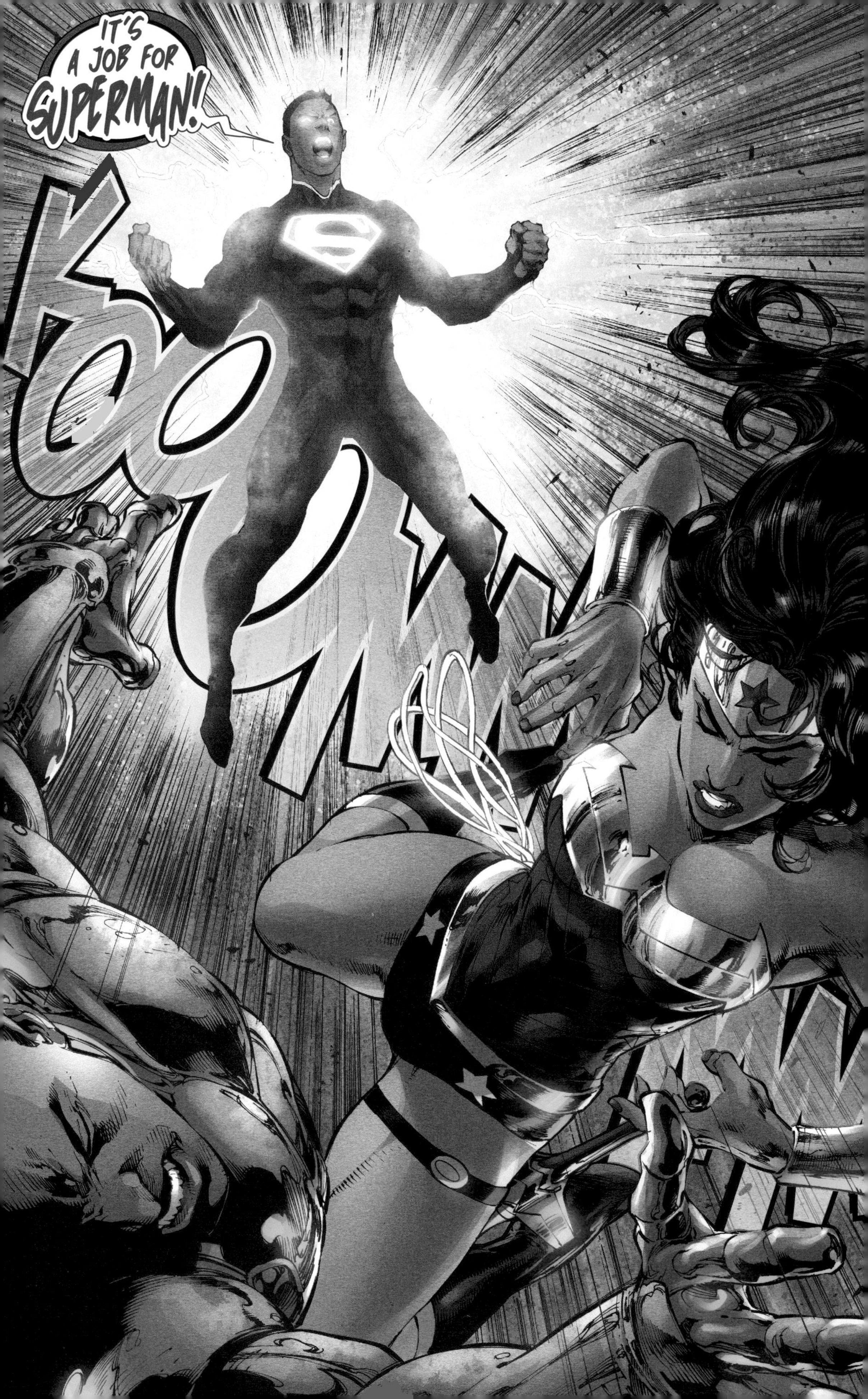
IT'S A JOB FOR SUPERMAN!!

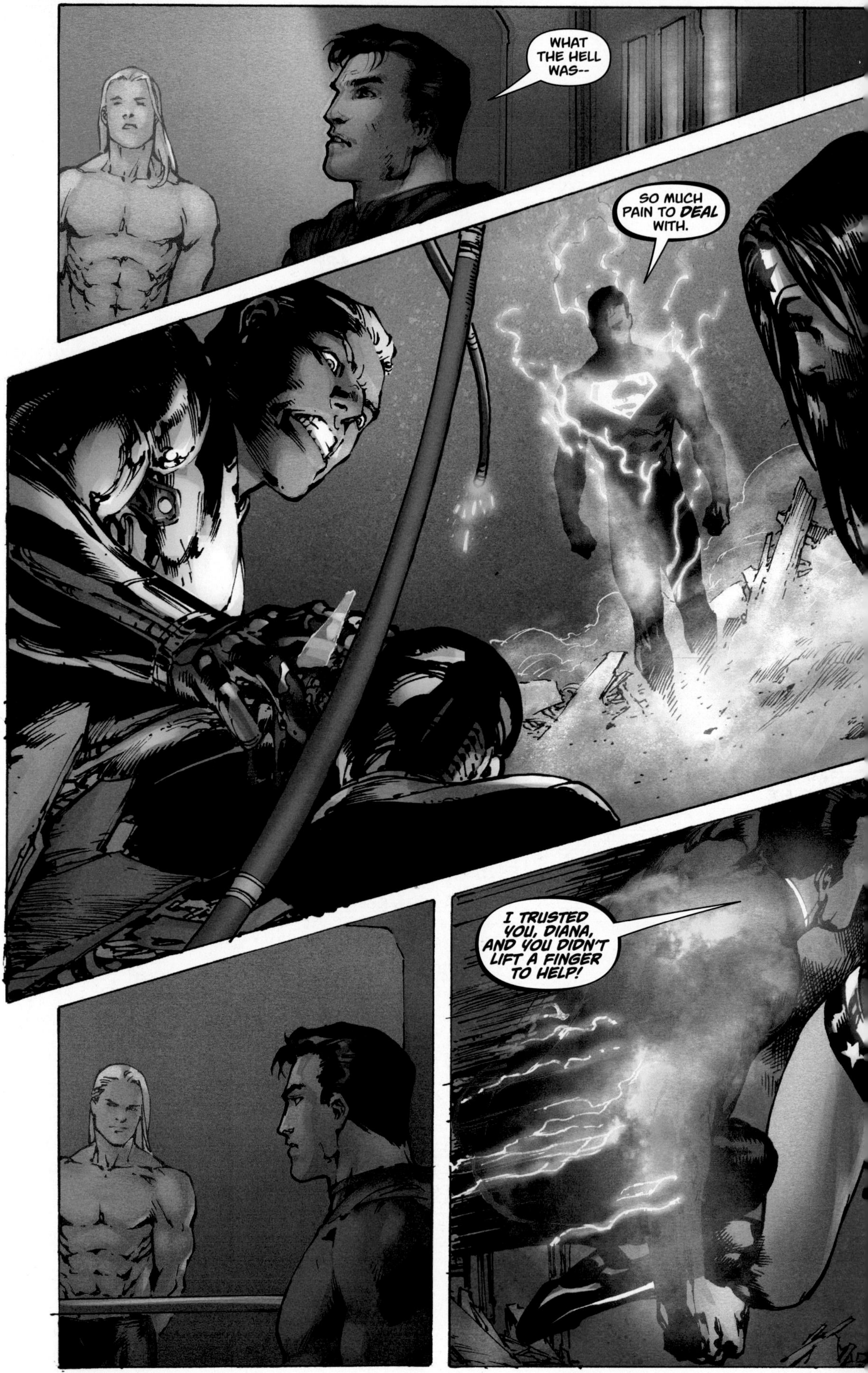
WHAT THE HELL WAS--
SO MUCH PAIN TO DEAL WITH.
I TRUSTED YOU, DIANA, AND YOU DIDN'T LIFT A FINGER TO HELP!

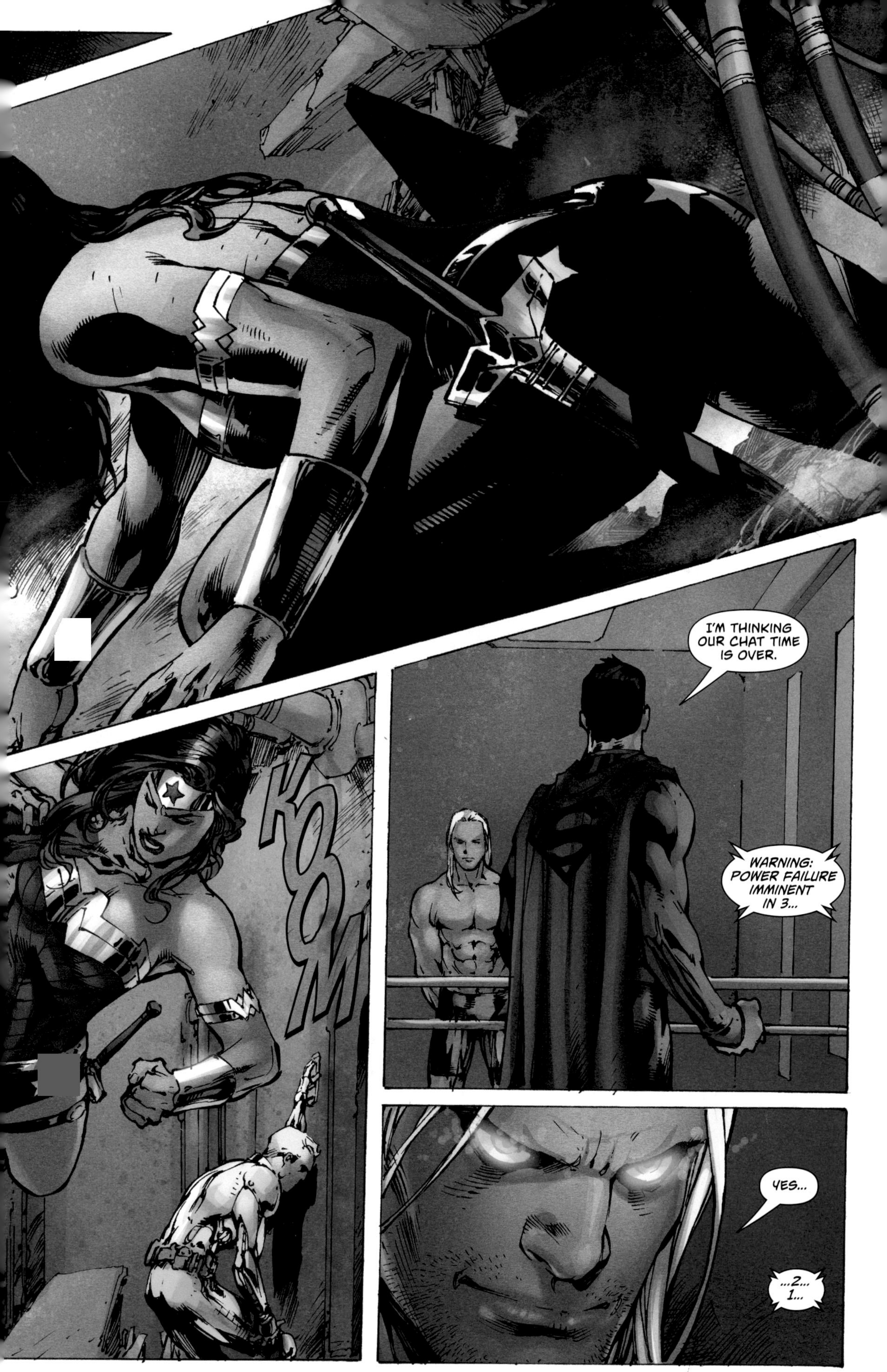
KOOM
I'M THINKING OUR CHAT TIME IS OVER.
WARNING: POWER FAILURE IMMINENT IN 3...
YES...
...2... 1...

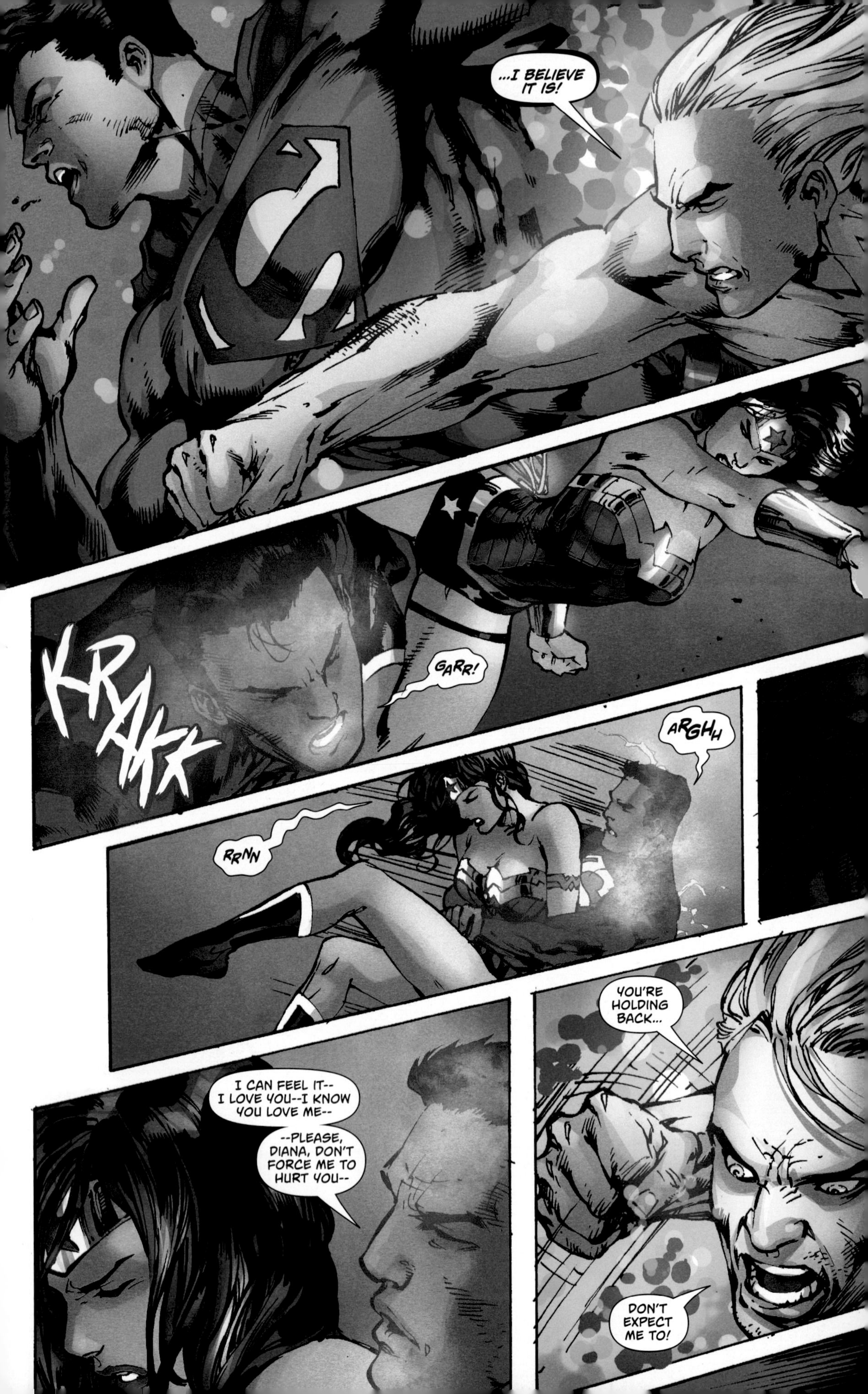
...I BELIEVE IT IS!
KRAKK
GARR!
ARGHH
RRNN
YOU'RE HOLDING BACK...
DON'T EXPECT ME TO!
I CAN FEEL IT-- I LOVE YOU--I KNOW YOU LOVE ME--
--PLEASE, DIANA, DON'T FORCE ME TO HURT YOU--

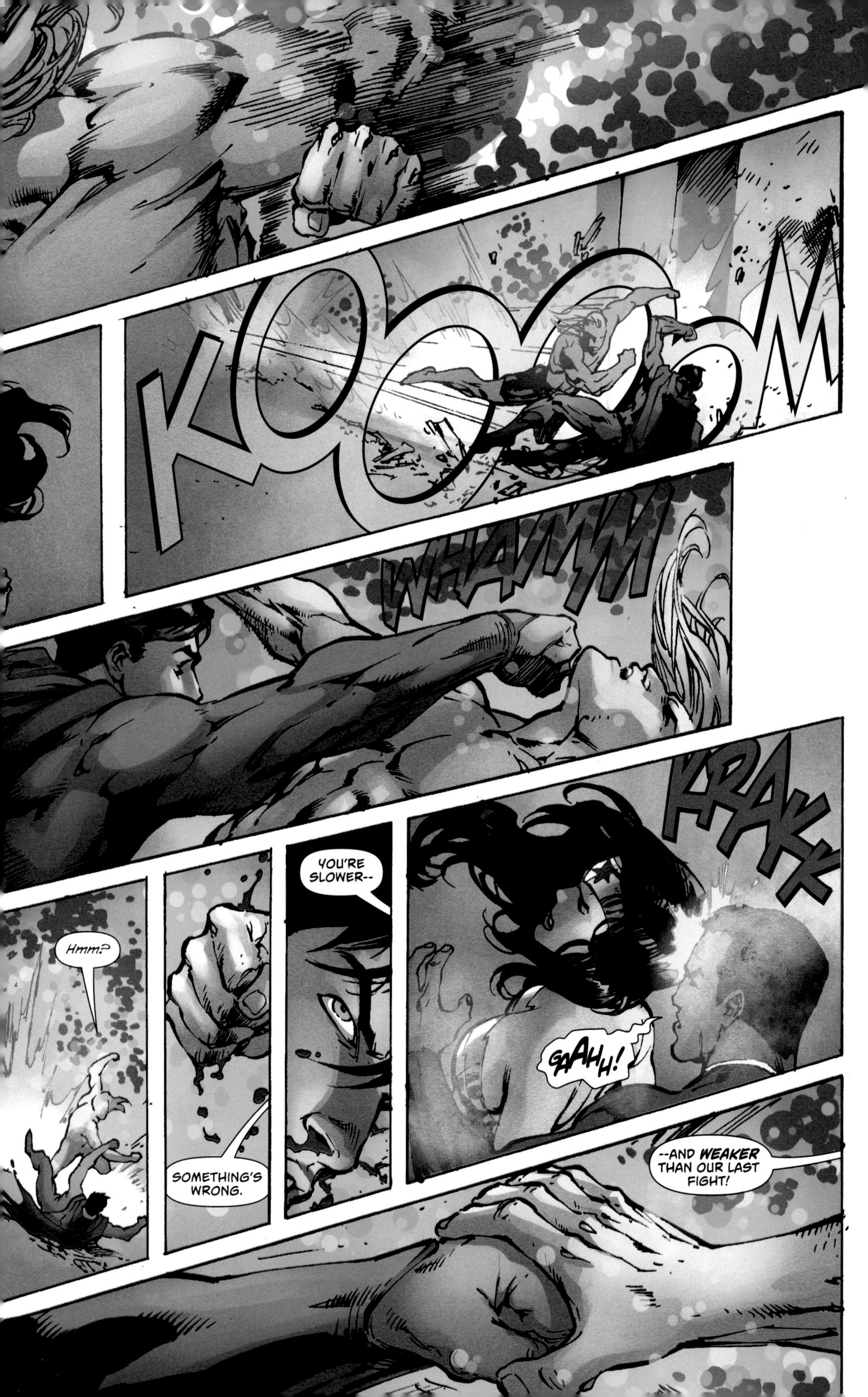
KOOOOOM
WHAMM
KRAKK
Hmm?
SOMETHING'S WRONG.
YOU'RE SLOWER--
GAAHH!
--AND **WEAKER** THAN OUR LAST FIGHT!

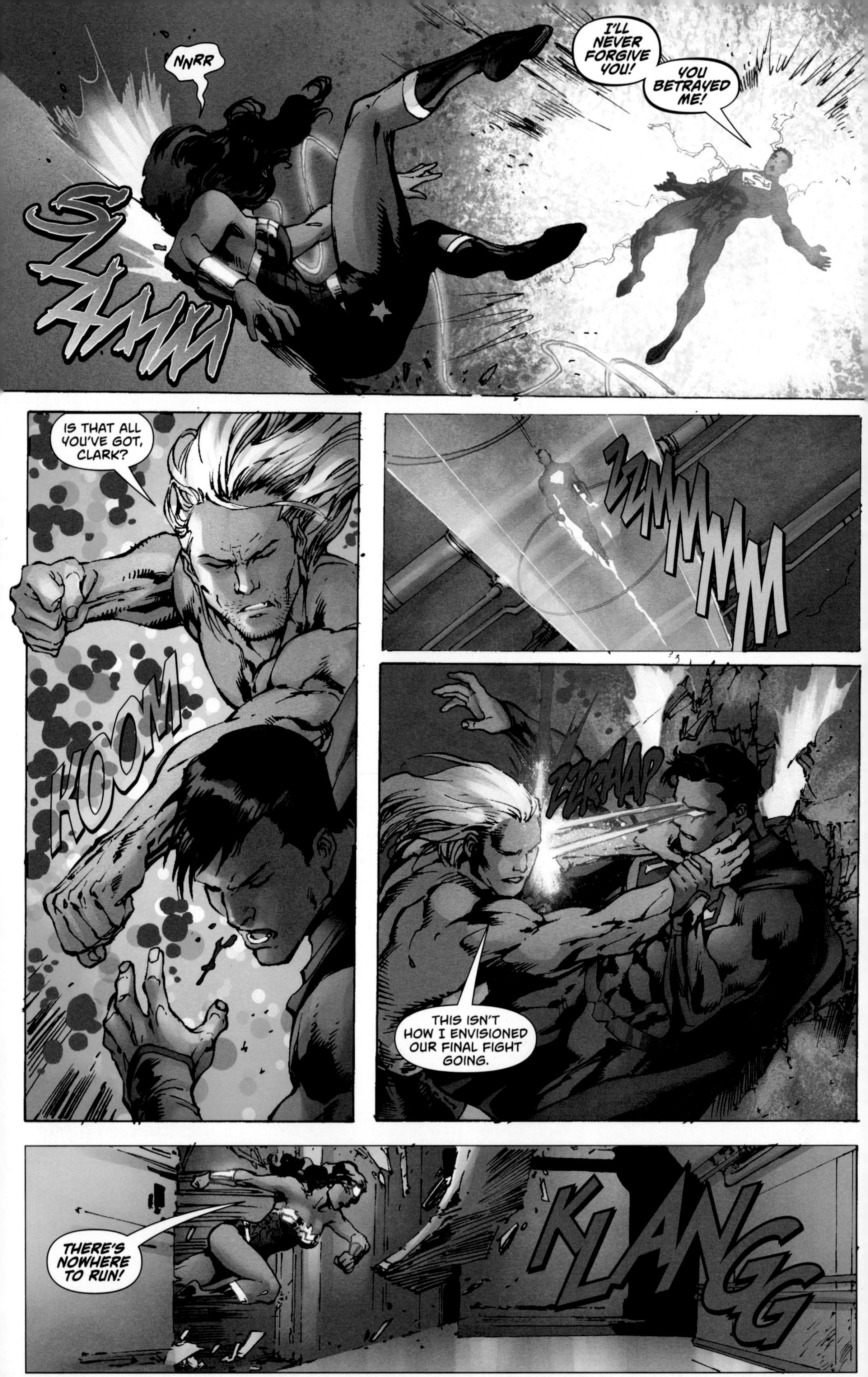
NNRR
SZAMM
I'LL NEVER FORGIVE YOU!
YOU BETRAYED ME!
IS THAT ALL YOU'VE GOT, CLARK?
KOOM
ZZMMMMM
ZZRAAAP
THIS ISN'T HOW I ENVISIONED OUR FINAL FIGHT GOING.
THERE'S NOWHERE TO RUN!
KLANGG

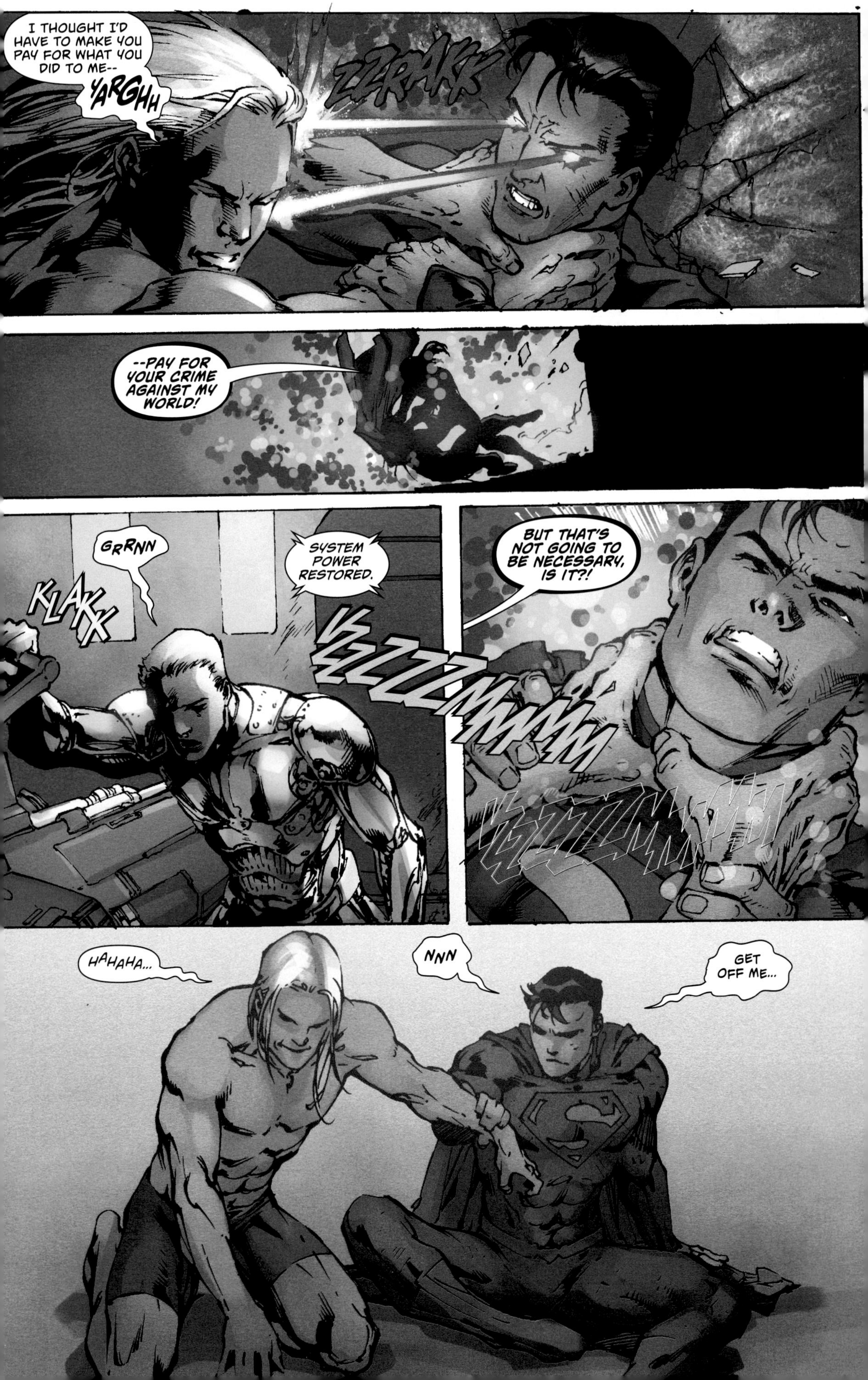
I THOUGHT I'D HAVE TO MAKE YOU PAY FOR WHAT YOU DID TO ME--
YARGHH
ZZRAKK
--PAY FOR YOUR CRIME AGAINST MY WORLD!
GRRNN
KLAKK
SYSTEM POWER RESTORED.
VZZZZMMMM
BUT THAT'S NOT GOING TO BE NECESSARY, IS IT?!
VZZZZMMMMM
HAHAHA...
NNN
GET OFF ME...

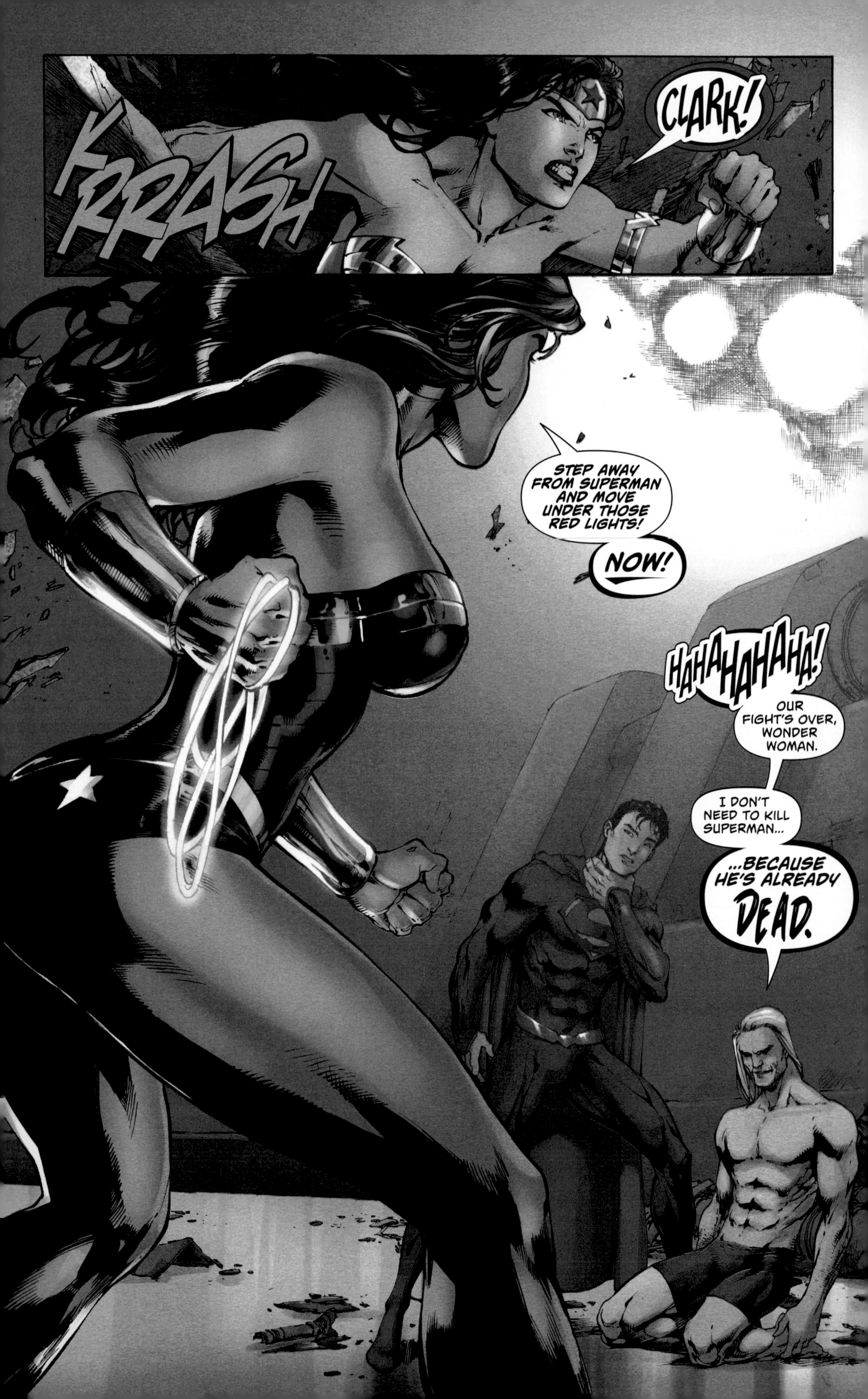

KRRASH
CLARK!
STEP AWAY FROM SUPERMAN AND MOVE UNDER THOSE RED LIGHTS!
NOW!
HAHAHAHAHA!
OUR FIGHT'S OVER, WONDER WOMAN.
I DON'T NEED TO KILL SUPERMAN...
...BECAUSE HE'S ALREADY DEAD.

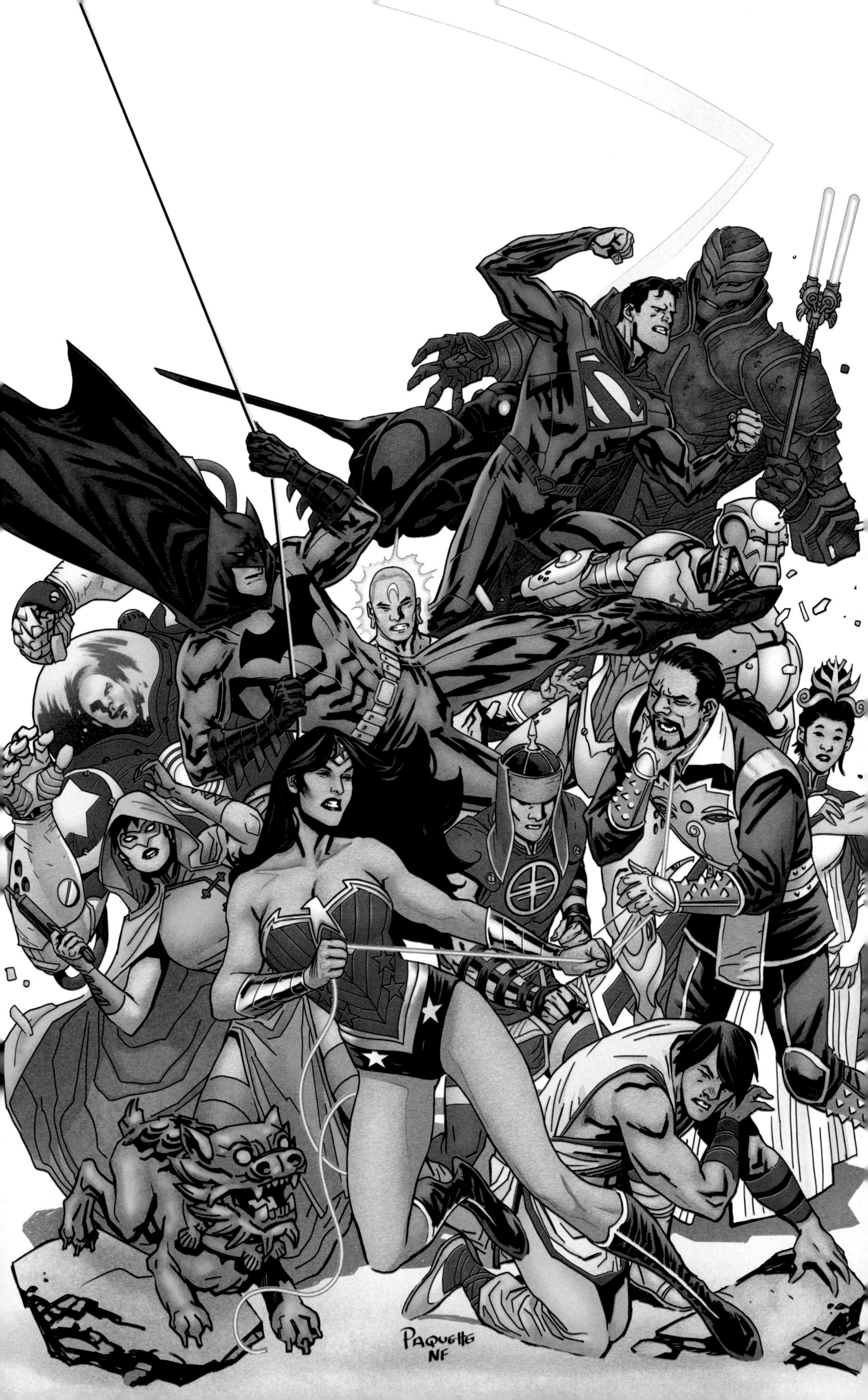
PAQUETTE
NF

THE FINAL DAYS OF SUPERMAN PART 5: OMEN OF DEATH

PETER J. TOMASI writer **DOUG MAHNKE** penciller **JAIME MENDOZA CHRISTIAN ALAMY JOHN LIVESAY TOM NGUYEN** inkers
WIL QUINTANA colorist **ROB LEIGH** letterer **YANICK PAQUETTE NATHAN FAIRBAIRN** cover

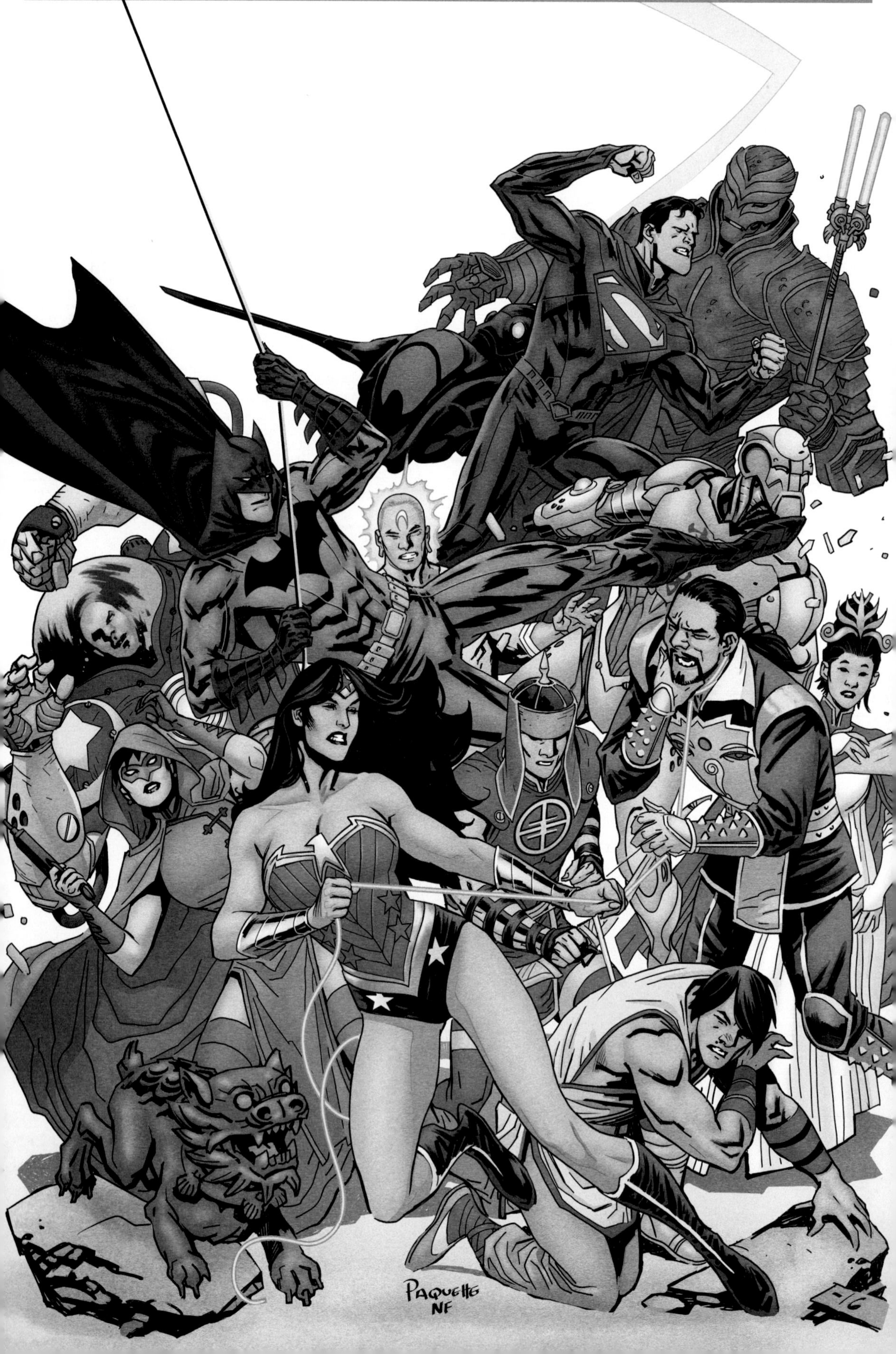

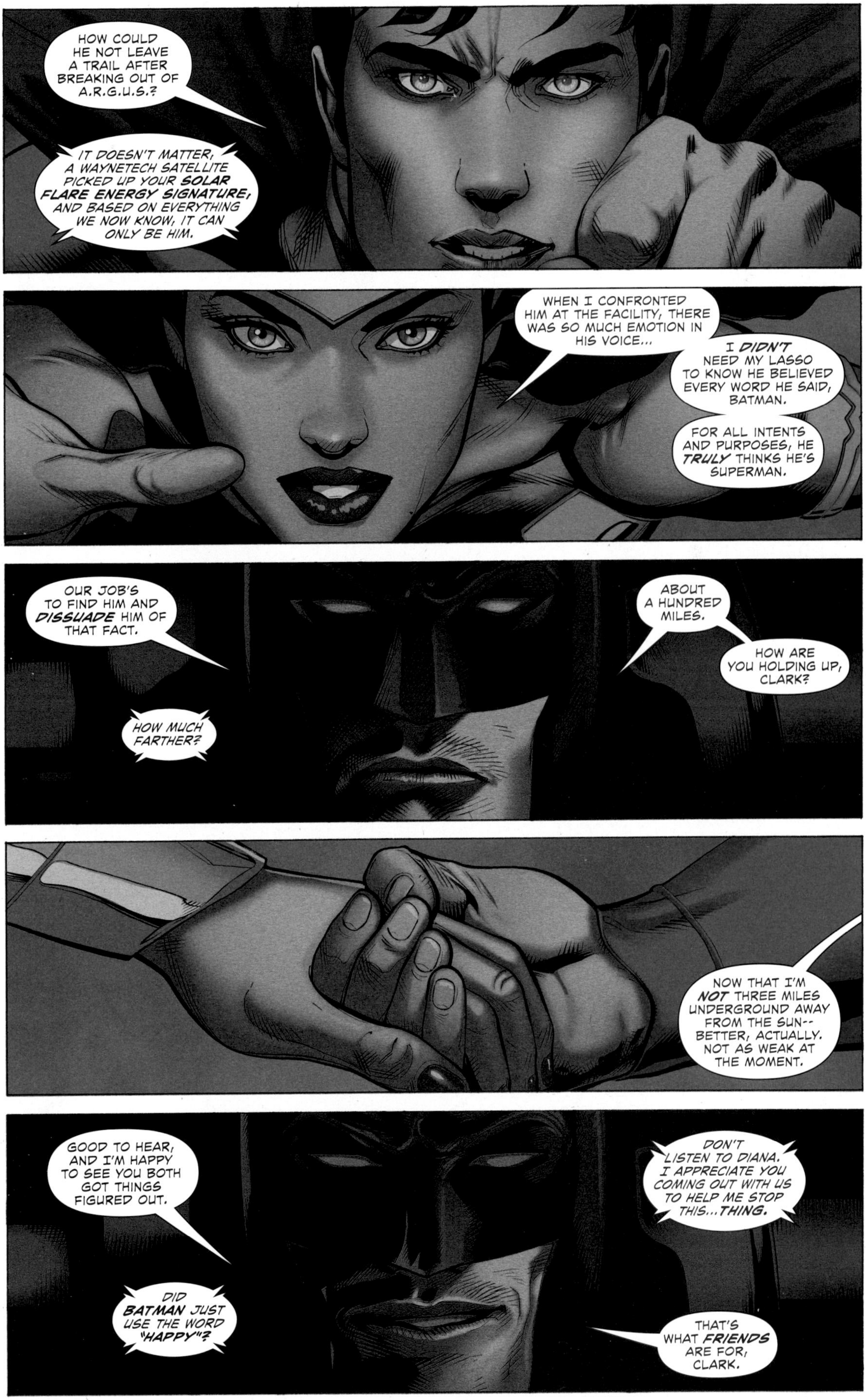
HOW COULD HE NOT LEAVE A TRAIL AFTER BREAKING OUT OF A.R.G.U.S.?
IT DOESN'T MATTER, A WAYNETECH SATELLITE PICKED UP YOUR SOLAR FLARE ENERGY SIGNATURE, AND BASED ON EVERYTHING WE NOW KNOW, IT CAN ONLY BE HIM.
WHEN I CONFRONTED HIM AT THE FACILITY, THERE WAS SO MUCH EMOTION IN HIS VOICE...
I DIDN'T NEED MY LASSO TO KNOW HE BELIEVED EVERY WORD HE SAID, BATMAN.
FOR ALL INTENTS AND PURPOSES, HE TRULY THINKS HE'S SUPERMAN.
OUR JOB'S TO FIND HIM AND DISSUADE HIM OF THAT FACT.
HOW MUCH FARTHER?
ABOUT A HUNDRED MILES.
HOW ARE YOU HOLDING UP, CLARK?
NOW THAT I'M NOT THREE MILES UNDERGROUND AWAY FROM THE SUN-- BETTER, ACTUALLY. NOT AS WEAK AT THE MOMENT.
GOOD TO HEAR, AND I'M HAPPY TO SEE YOU BOTH GOT THINGS FIGURED OUT.
DID BATMAN JUST USE THE WORD "HAPPY"?
DON'T LISTEN TO DIANA. I APPRECIATE YOU COMING OUT WITH US TO HELP ME STOP THIS...THING.
THAT'S WHAT FRIENDS ARE FOR, CLARK.

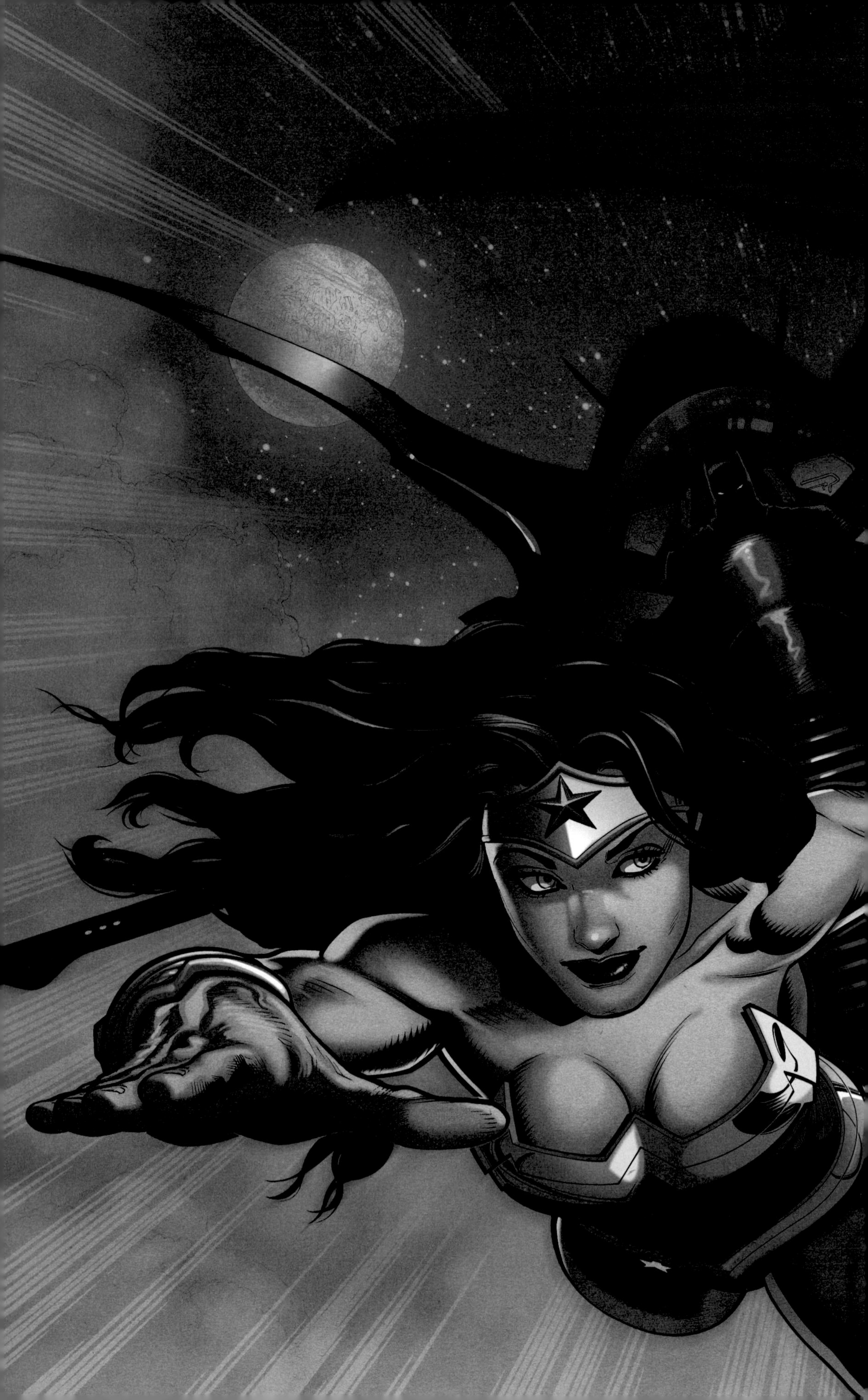

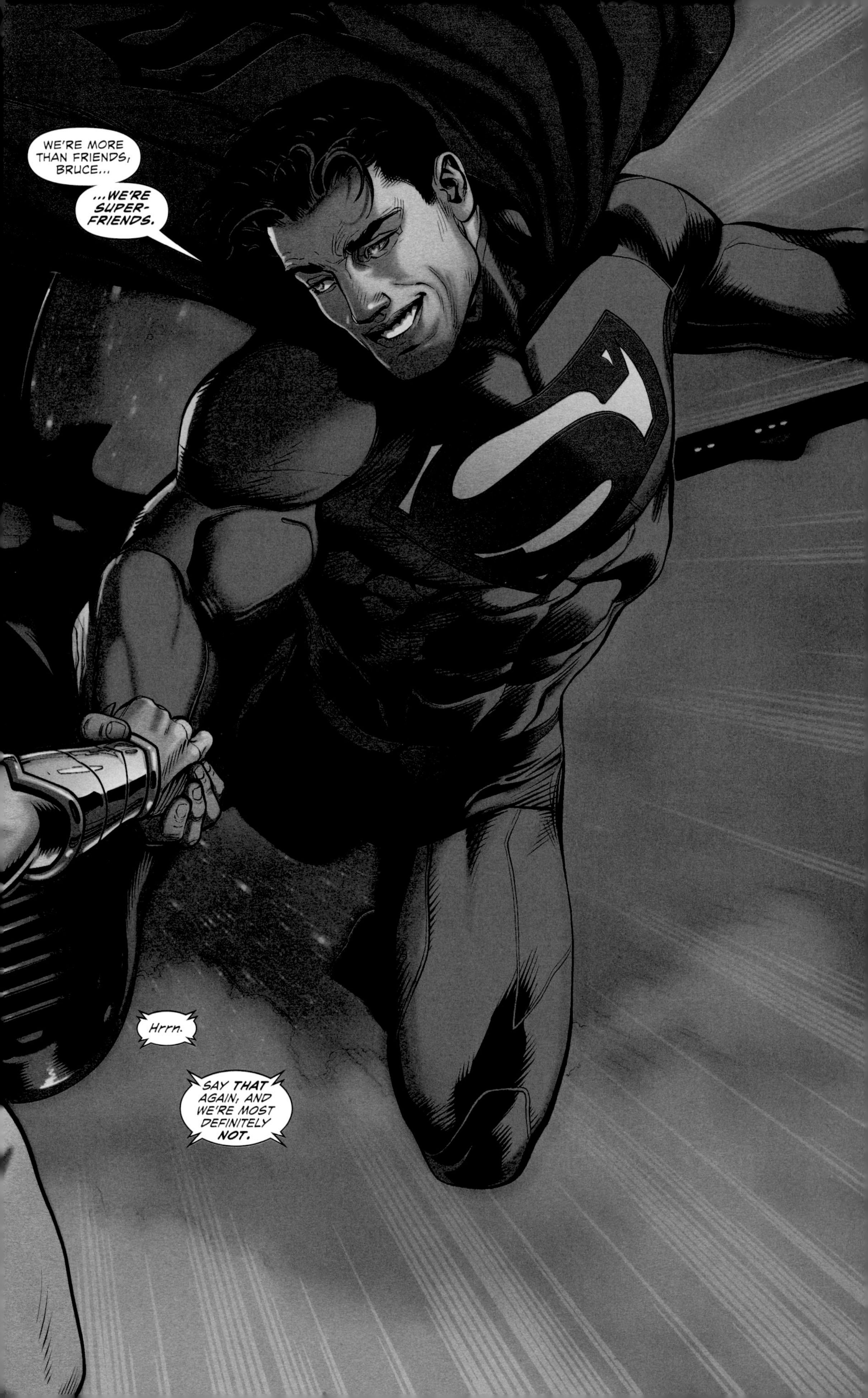
WE'RE MORE THAN FRIENDS, BRUCE...
...WE'RE SUPER-FRIENDS.
Hrrn.
SAY THAT AGAIN, AND WE'RE MOST DEFINITELY NOT.

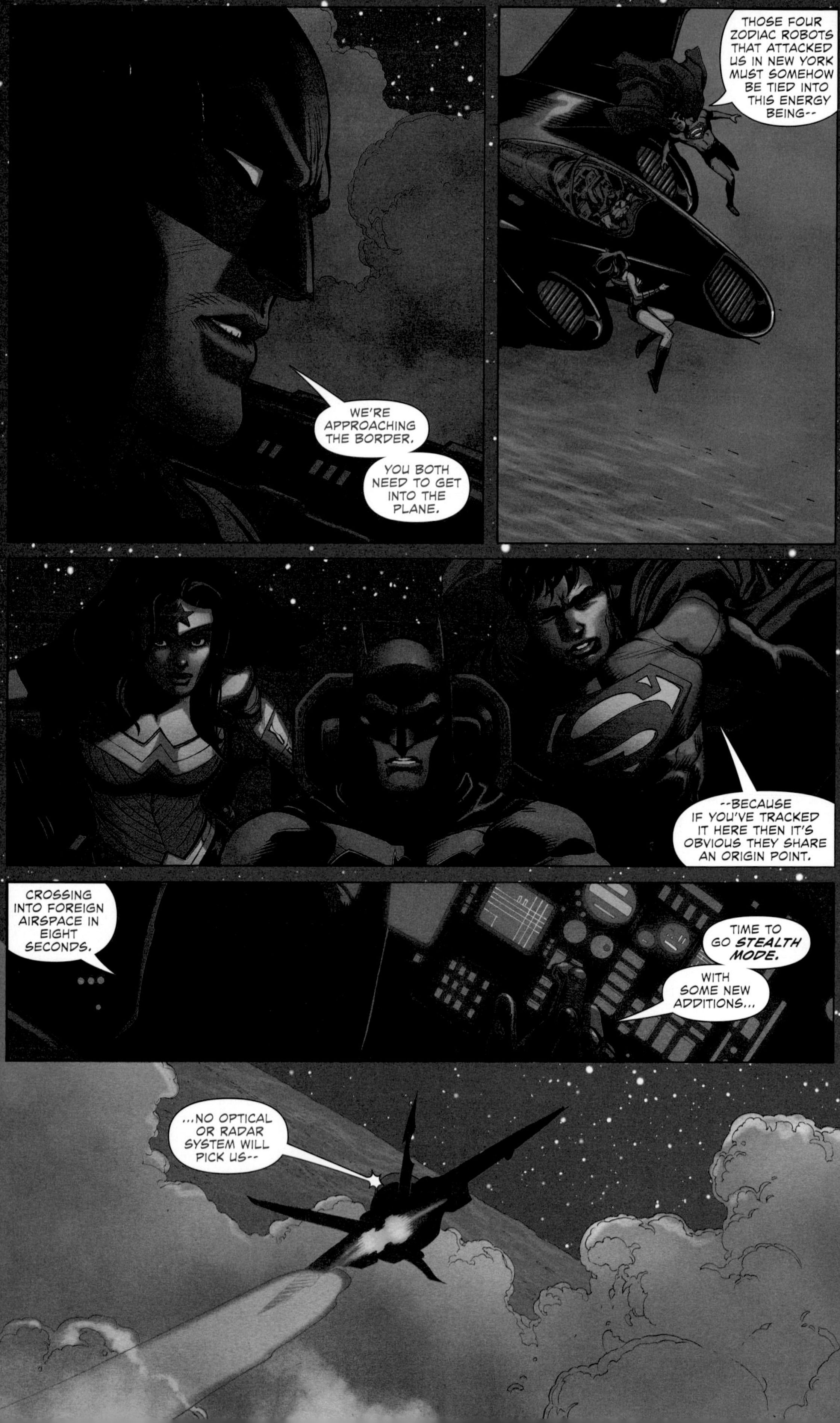
WE'RE APPROACHING THE BORDER.
YOU BOTH NEED TO GET INTO THE PLANE.
THOSE FOUR ZODIAC ROBOTS THAT ATTACKED US IN NEW YORK MUST SOMEHOW BE TIED INTO THIS ENERGY BEING--
--BECAUSE IF YOU'VE TRACKED IT HERE THEN IT'S OBVIOUS THEY SHARE AN ORIGIN POINT.
CROSSING INTO FOREIGN AIRSPACE IN EIGHT SECONDS.
TIME TO GO STEALTH MODE.
WITH SOME NEW ADDITIONS...
...NO OPTICAL OR RADAR SYSTEM WILL PICK US--

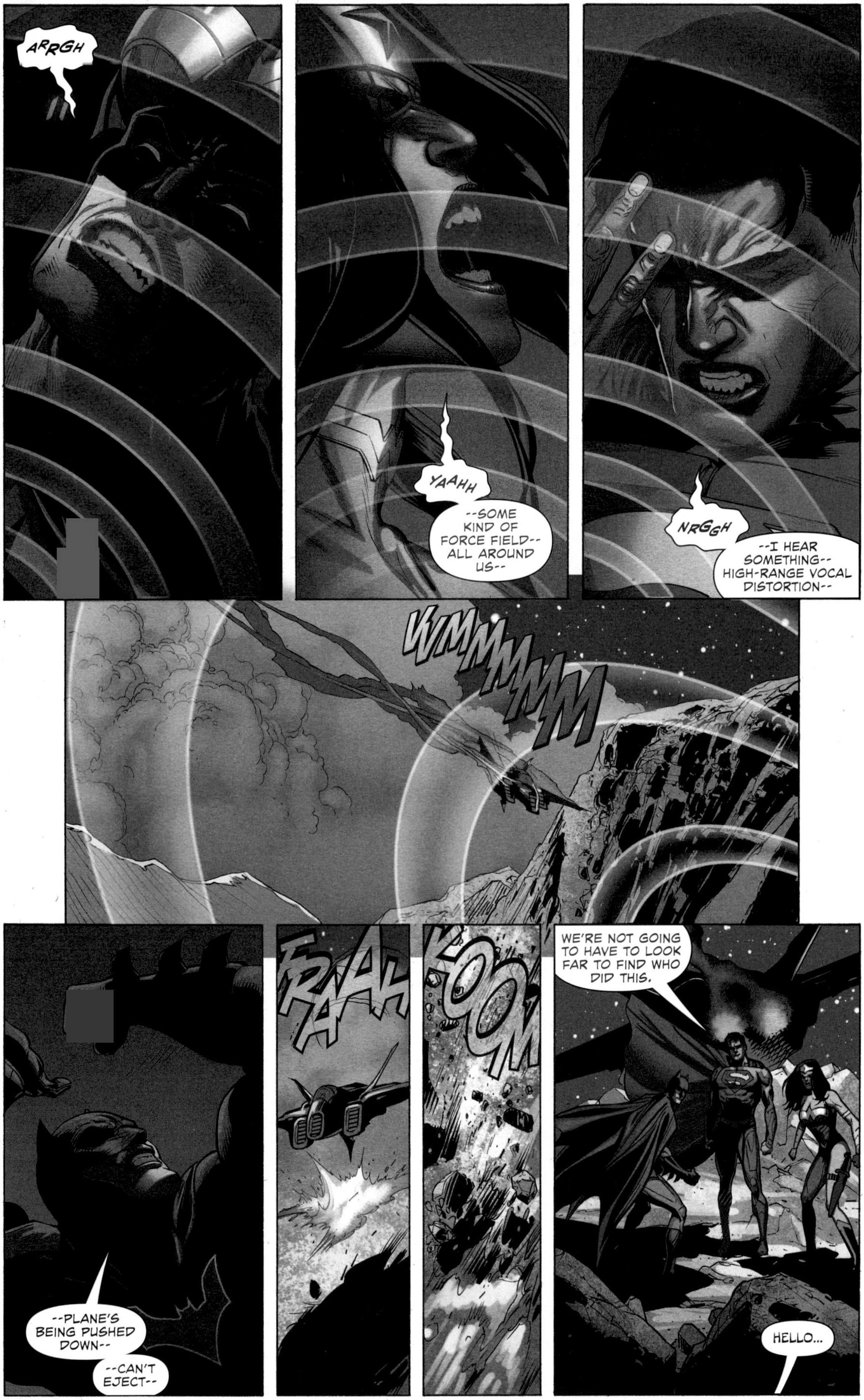
ARRGH
YAAHH
--SOME KIND OF FORCE FIELD--ALL AROUND US--
NRGGH
--I HEAR SOMETHING--HIGH-RANGE VOCAL DISTORTION--
VVMMMMMM
--PLANE'S BEING PUSHED DOWN--
--CAN'T EJECT--
FRAAK
KOOM
WE'RE NOT GOING TO HAVE TO LOOK FAR TO FIND WHO DID THIS.
HELLO...

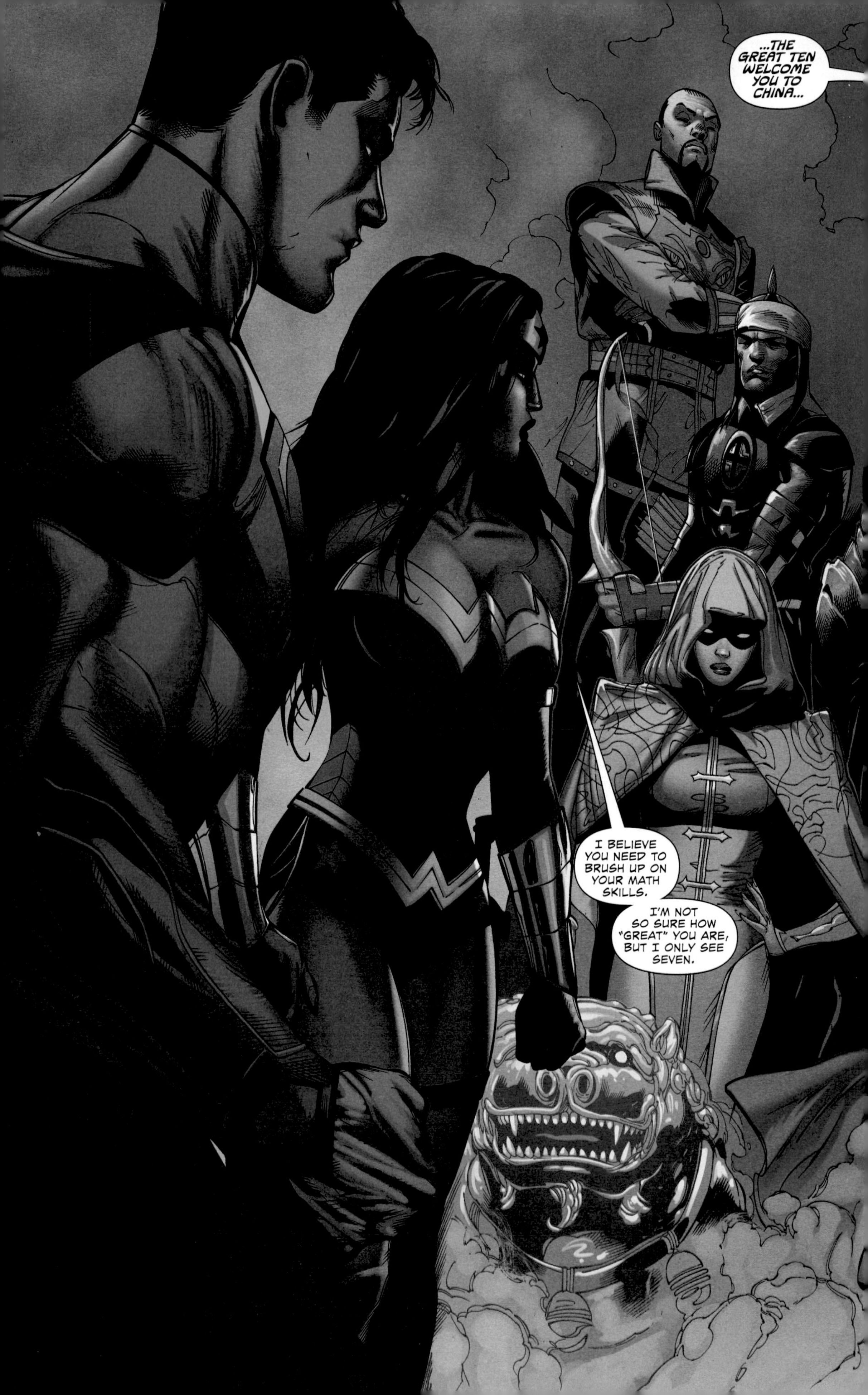
...THE GREAT TEN WELCOME YOU TO CHINA...
I BELIEVE YOU NEED TO BRUSH UP ON YOUR MATH SKILLS.
I'M NOT SO SURE HOW "GREAT" YOU ARE, BUT I ONLY SEE SEVEN.

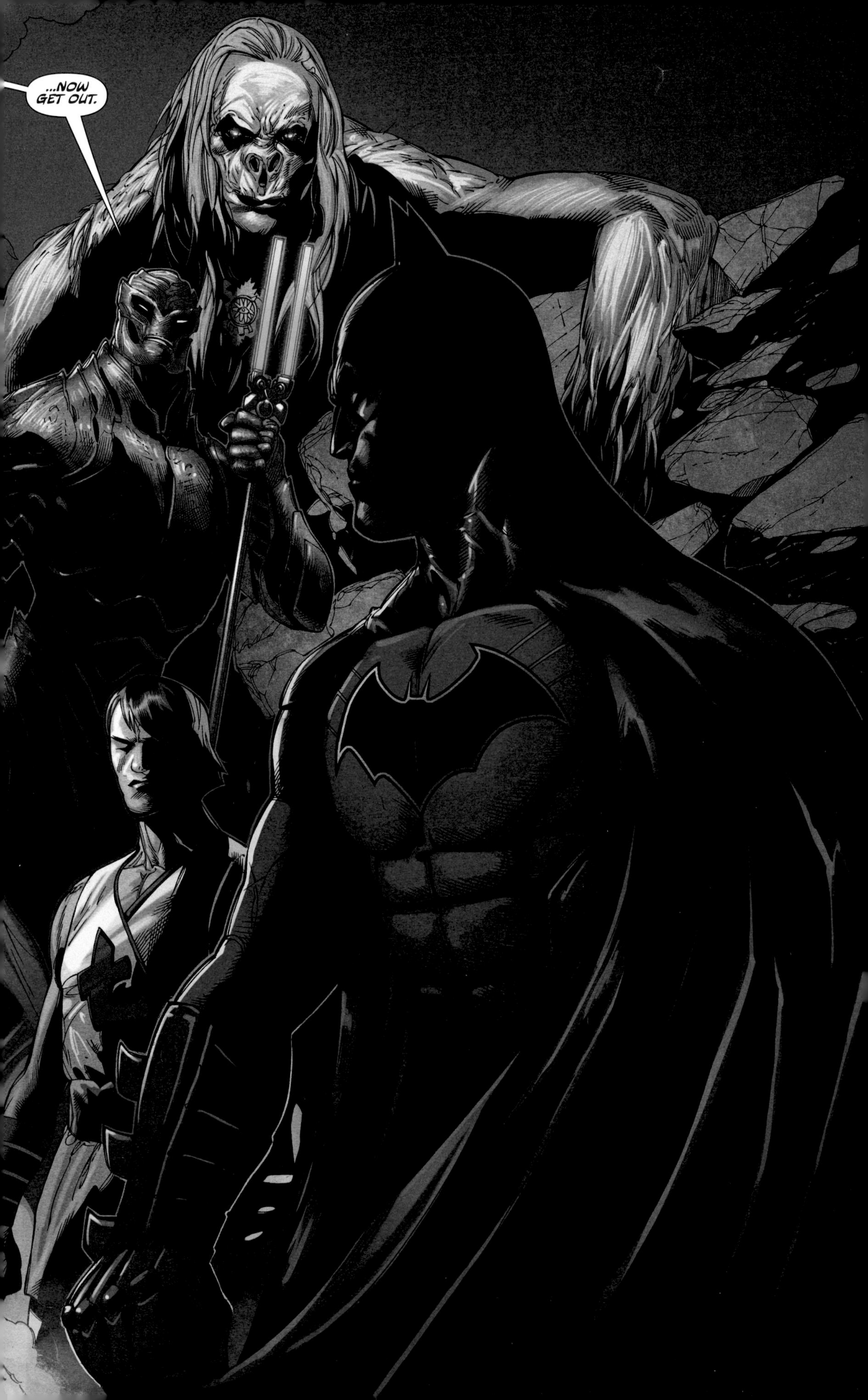
...NOW GET OUT.

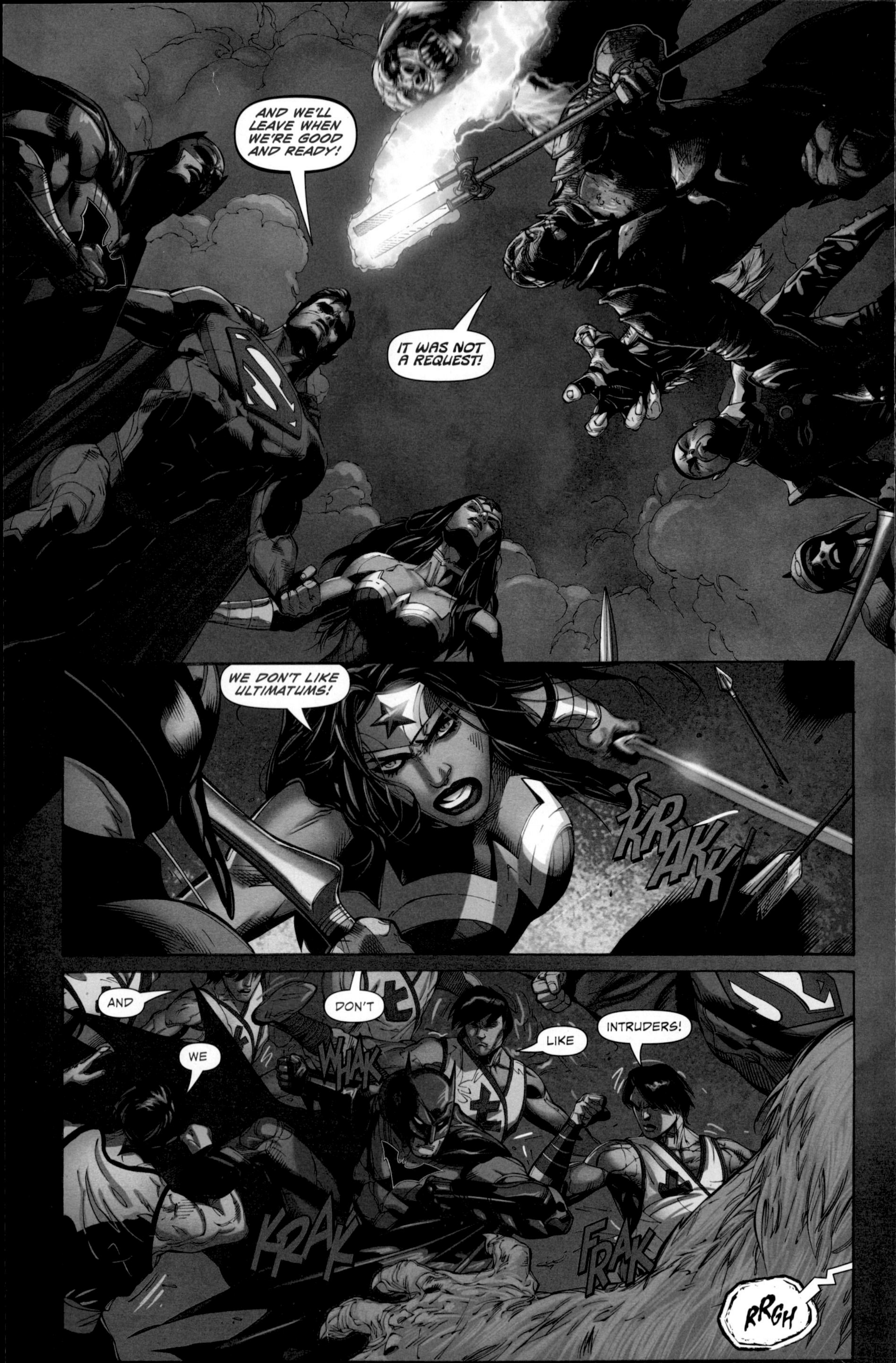
AND WE'LL LEAVE WHEN WE'RE GOOD AND READY!
IT WAS NOT A REQUEST!
WE DON'T LIKE ULTIMATUMS!
KRAKK
AND
WE
DON'T
WHAK
LIKE
INTRUDERS!
KRAK
FRAK
RRGH

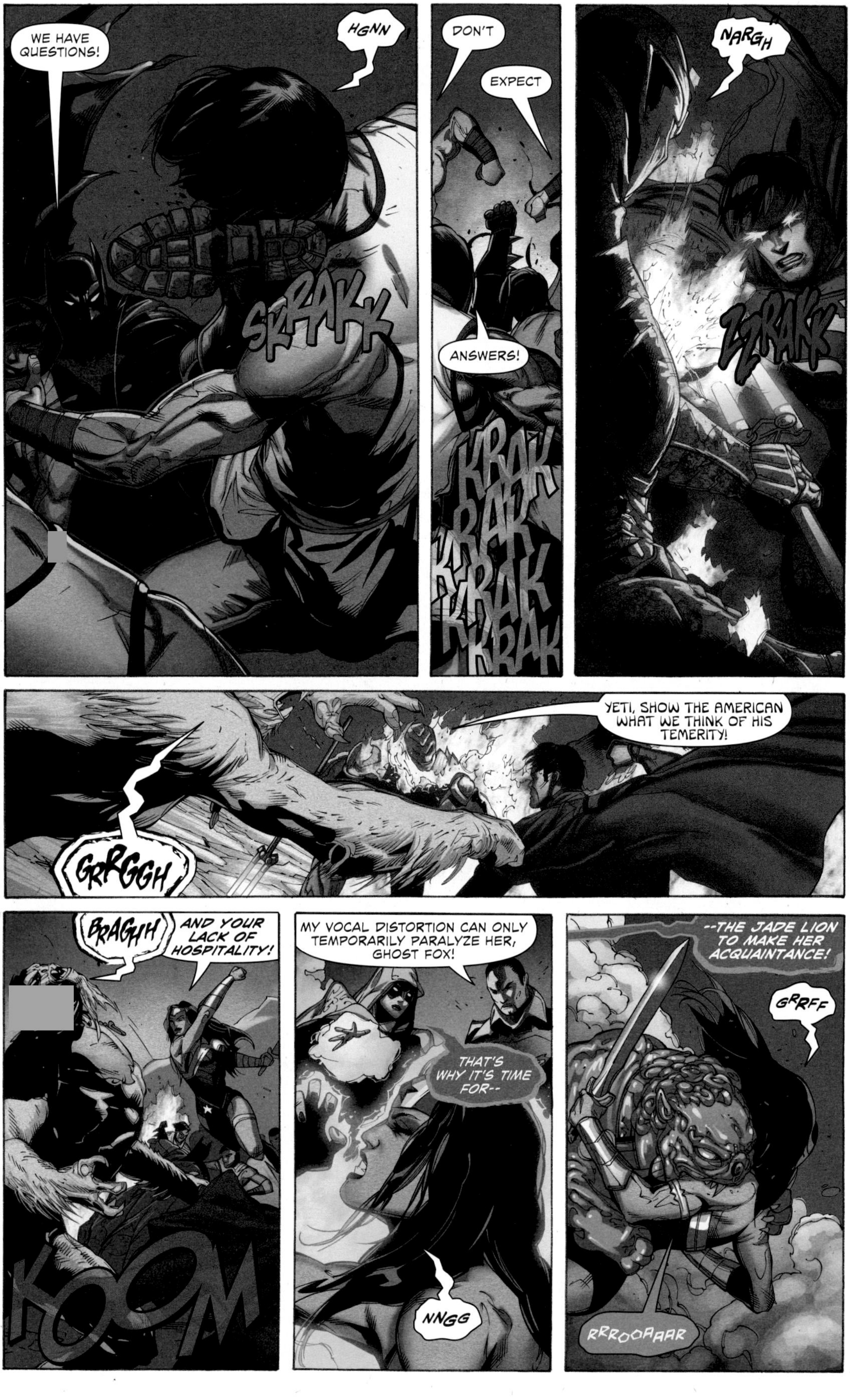

WE HAVE QUESTIONS!
HGNN
SKRAKK
DON'T
EXPECT
ANSWERS!
KRAK
NARGH
ZZRAKK
YETI, SHOW THE AMERICAN WHAT WE THINK OF HIS TEMERITY!
GRRGGH
BRAGHH
AND YOUR LACK OF HOSPITALITY!
KOOM
MY VOCAL DISTORTION CAN ONLY TEMPORARILY PARALYZE HER, GHOST FOX!
THAT'S WHY IT'S TIME FOR--
NNGG
--THE JADE LION TO MAKE HER ACQUAINTANCE!
GRRFF
RRROOAAAR

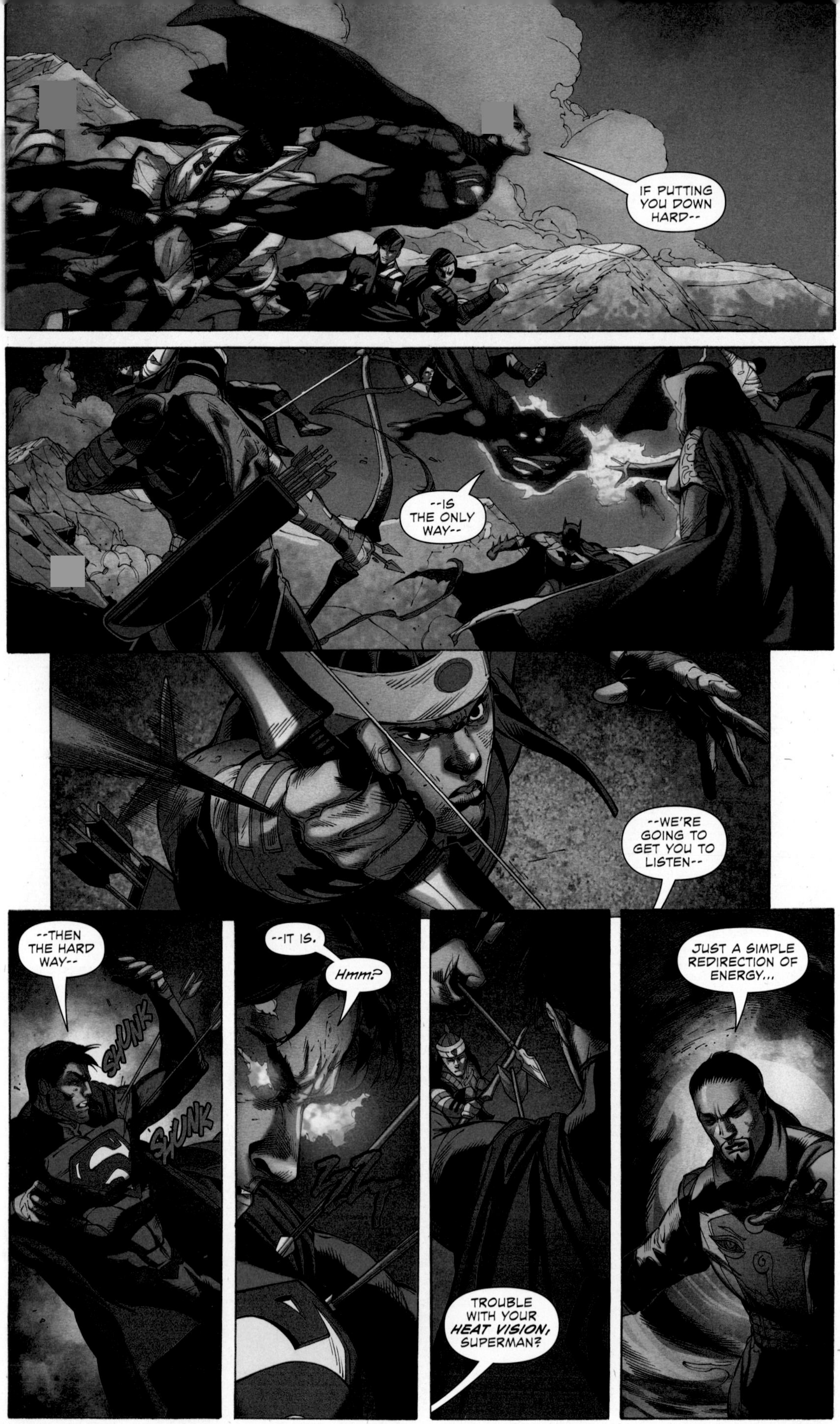

IF PUTTING YOU DOWN HARD--
--IS THE ONLY WAY--
--WE'RE GOING TO GET YOU TO LISTEN--
--THEN THE HARD WAY--
SHUNK
SHUNK
--IT IS.
Hmm?
TROUBLE WITH YOUR HEAT VISION, SUPERMAN?
JUST A SIMPLE REDIRECTION OF ENERGY...

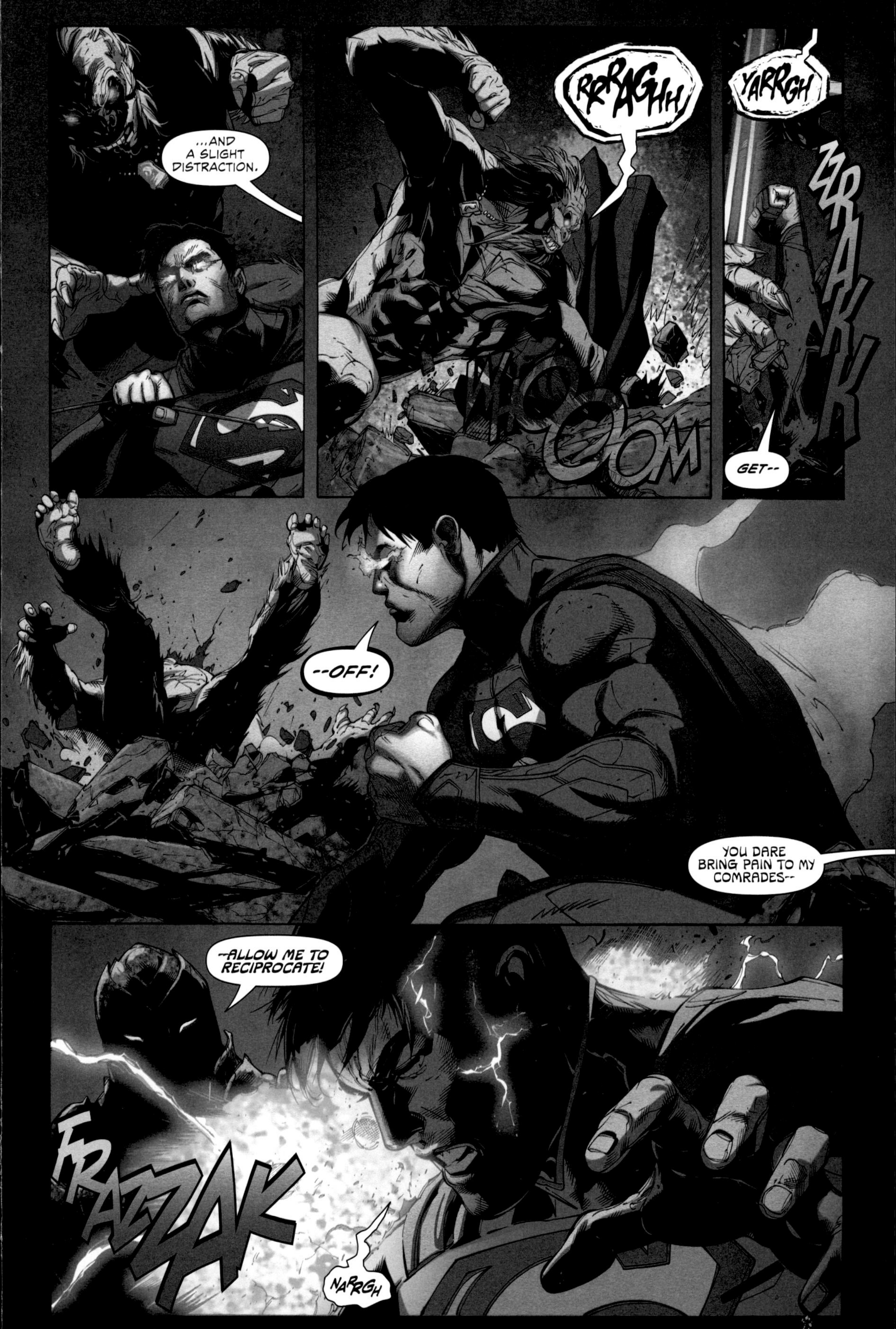
...AND A SLIGHT DISTRACTION.
RRRAGHH
WHOOOOM
YARRGH
ZZRAKK
GET--
--OFF!
YOU DARE BRING PAIN TO MY COMRADES--
--ALLOW ME TO RECIPROCATE!
FRAZZAK
NARRGH

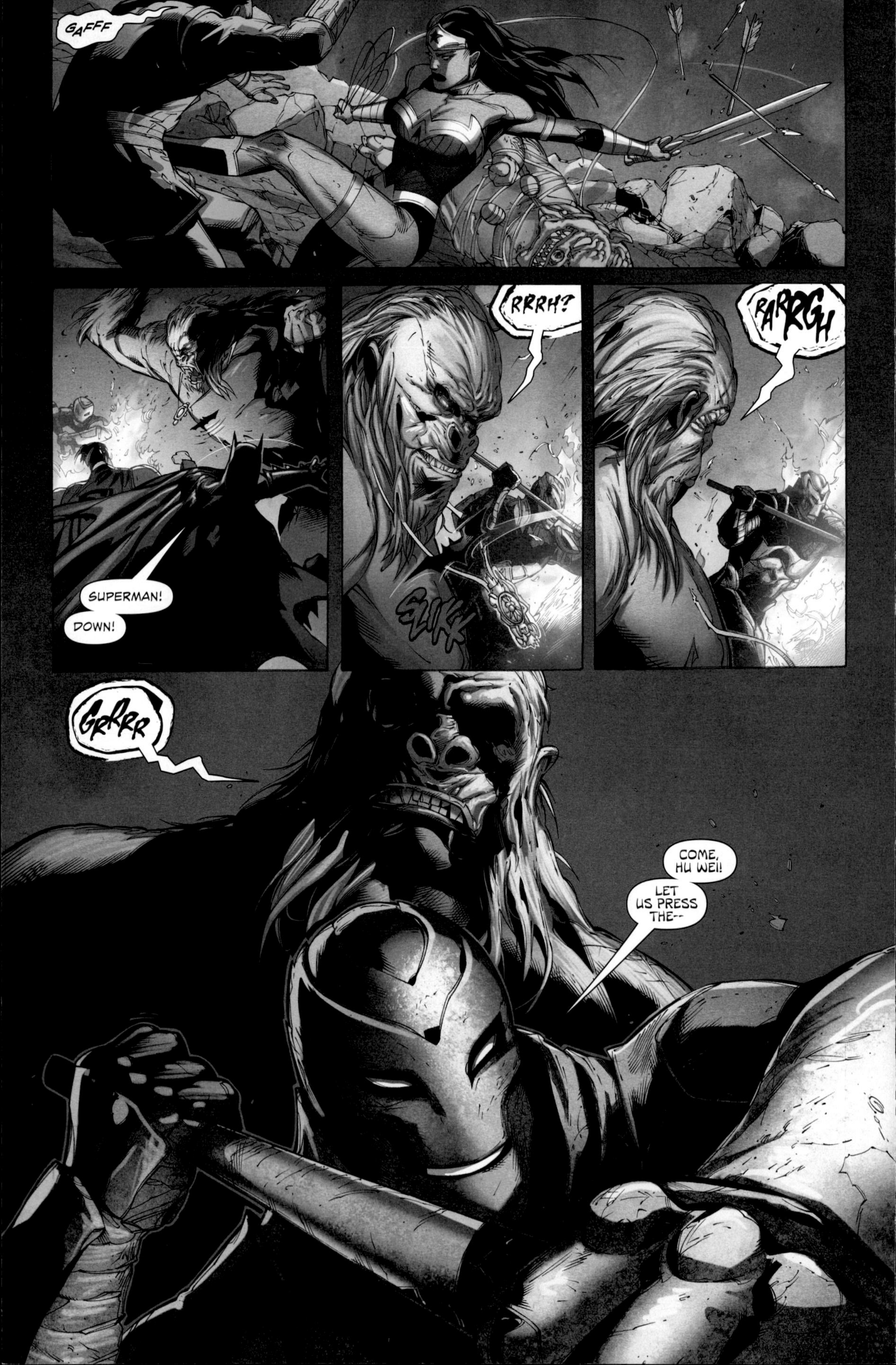
GAFFF
SUPERMAN!
DOWN!
RRRH?
SLIK
RARRGH
GRRRR
COME, HU WEI!
LET US PRESS THE--

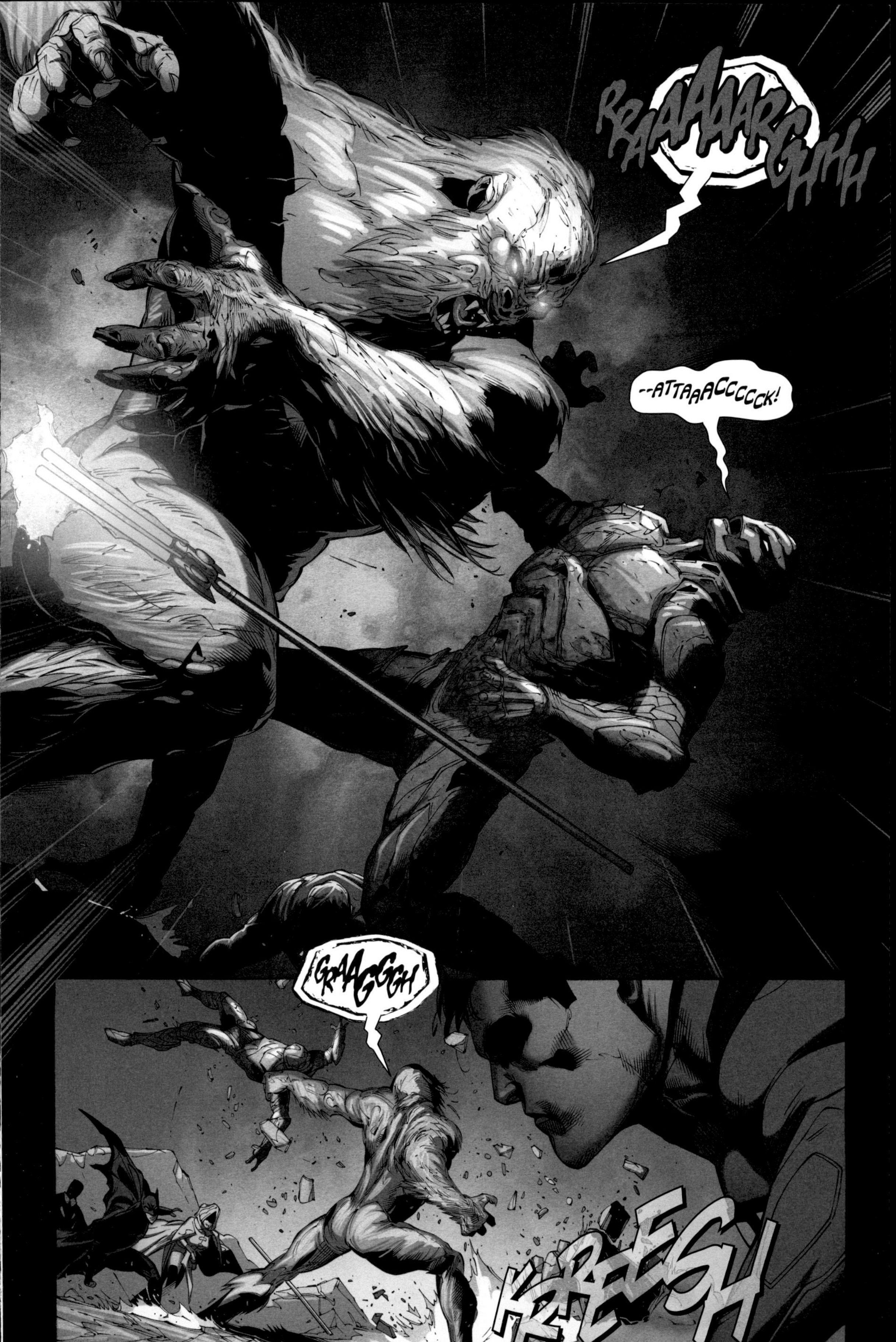
RRAAAAARGHHH
--ATTAAACCCCCK!
GRAAGGGH
KREESH

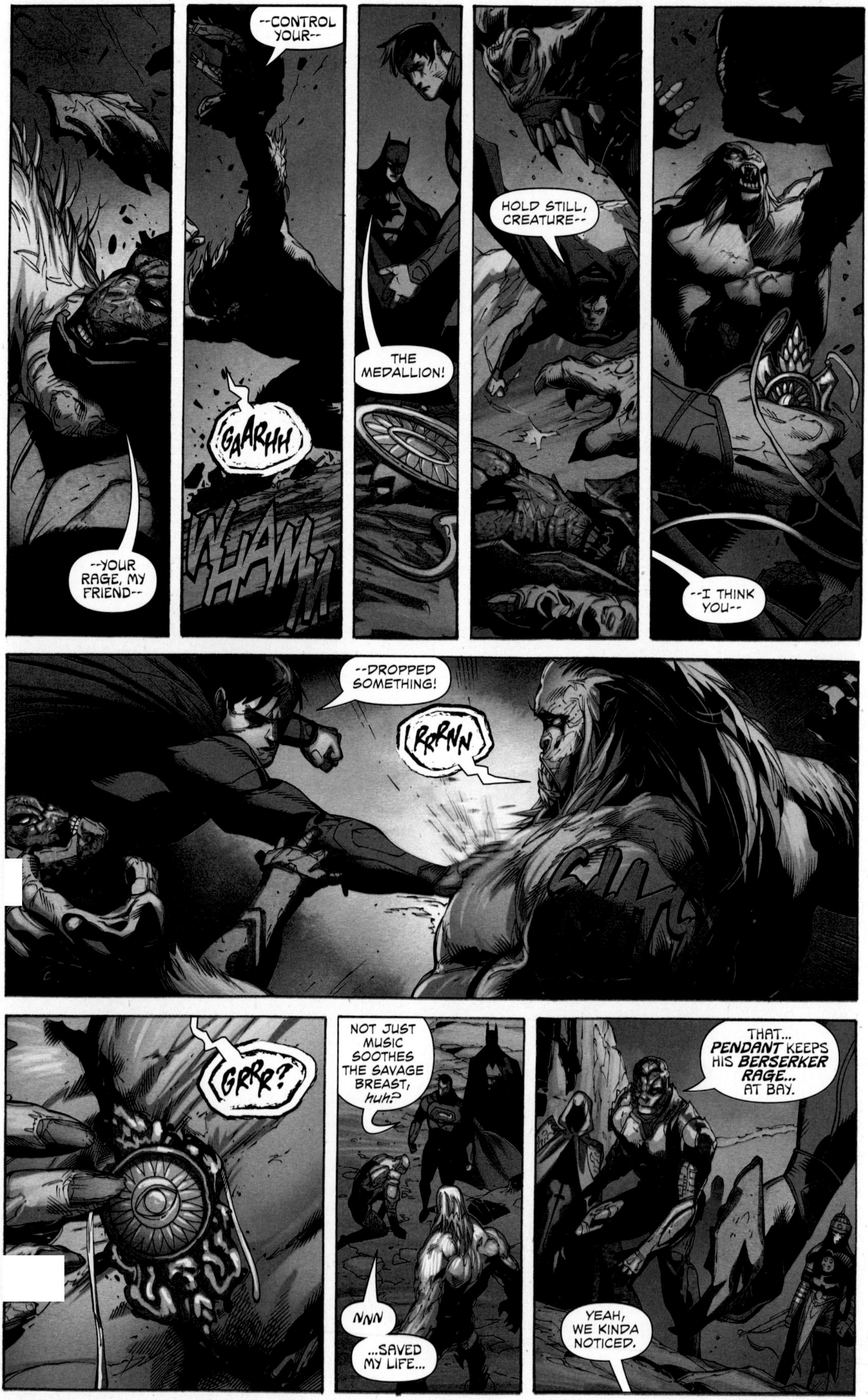
--YOUR RAGE, MY FRIEND--
--CONTROL YOUR--
GAARHH
WHAM
THE MEDALLION!
HOLD STILL, CREATURE--
--I THINK YOU--
--DROPPED SOMETHING!
RRRNN
GRRR?
NOT JUST MUSIC SOOTHES THE SAVAGE BREAST, *huh?*
NNN
...SAVED MY LIFE...
THAT... ***PENDANT*** KEEPS HIS ***BERSERKER RAGE...*** AT BAY.
YEAH, WE KINDA NOTICED.

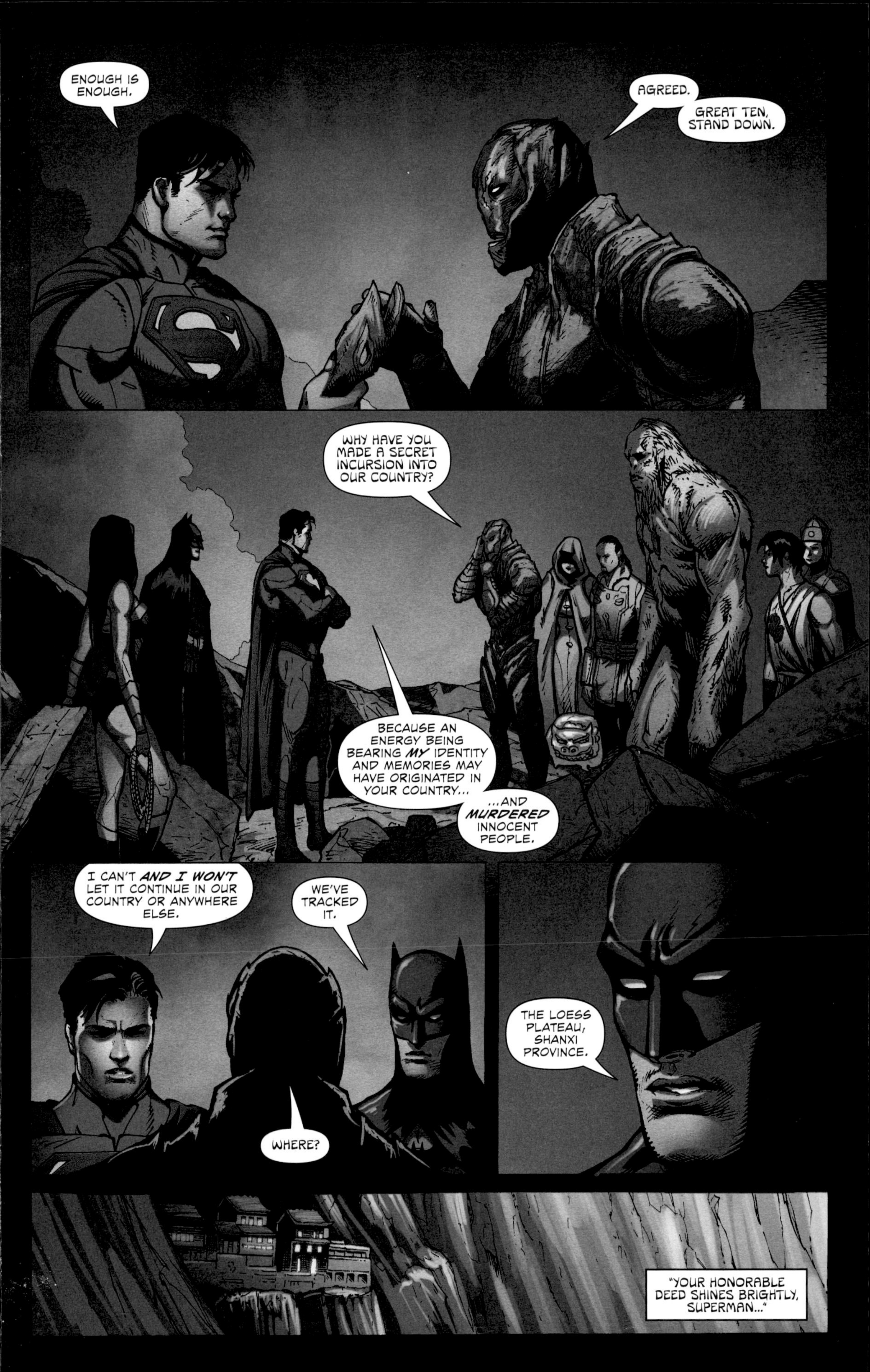
ENOUGH IS ENOUGH.
AGREED.
GREAT TEN, STAND DOWN.
WHY HAVE YOU MADE A SECRET INCURSION INTO OUR COUNTRY?
BECAUSE AN ENERGY BEING BEARING *MY* IDENTITY AND MEMORIES MAY HAVE ORIGINATED IN YOUR COUNTRY...
...AND *MURDERED* INNOCENT PEOPLE.
I CAN'T *AND I WON'T* LET IT CONTINUE IN OUR COUNTRY OR ANYWHERE ELSE.
WE'VE TRACKED IT.
WHERE?
THE LOESS PLATEAU, SHANXI PROVINCE.
"YOUR HONORABLE DEED SHINES BRIGHTLY, SUPERMAN..."

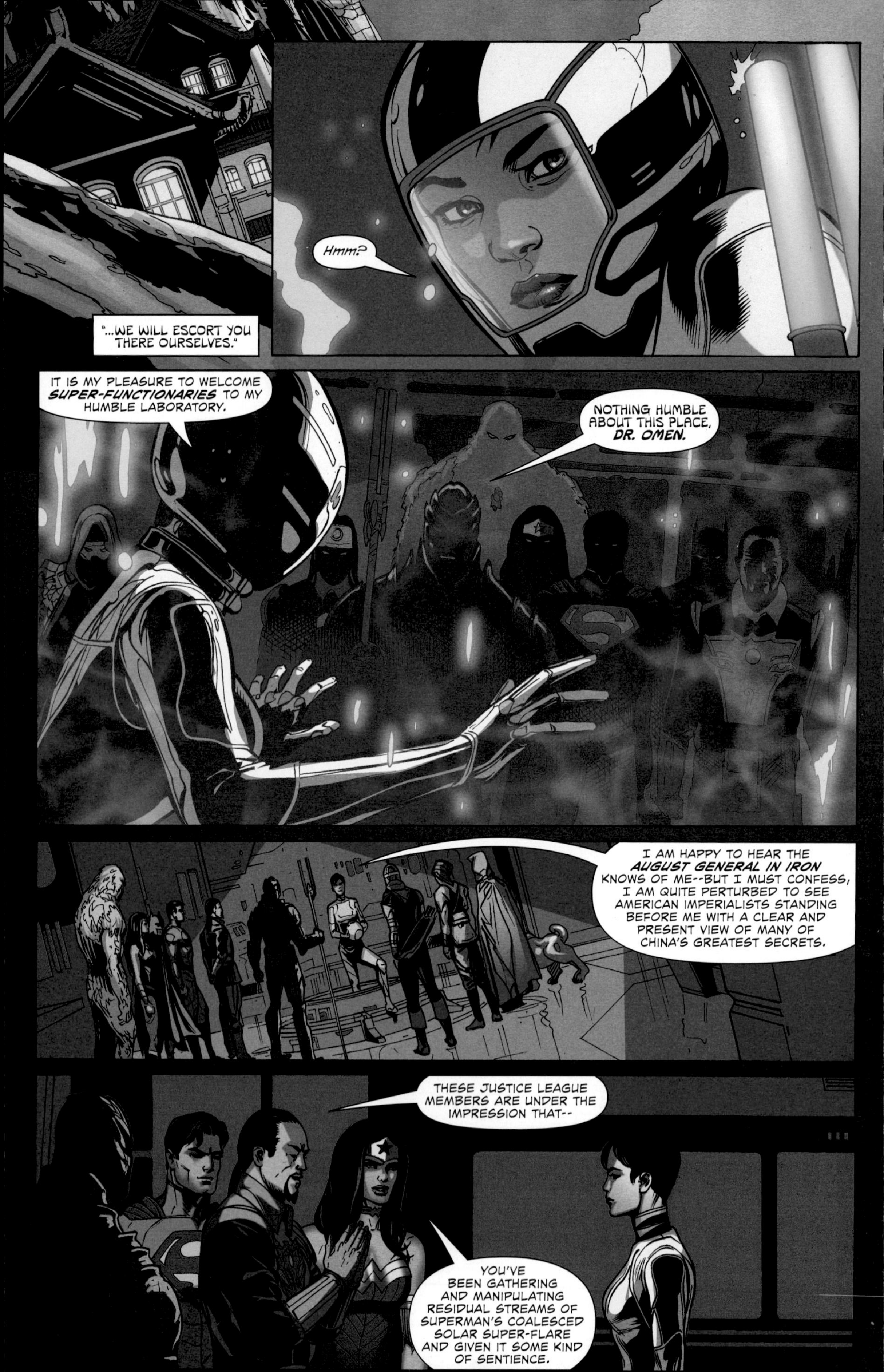
Hmm?
"...WE WILL ESCORT YOU THERE OURSELVES."
IT IS MY PLEASURE TO WELCOME SUPER-FUNCTIONARIES TO MY HUMBLE LABORATORY.
NOTHING HUMBLE ABOUT THIS PLACE, DR. OMEN.
I AM HAPPY TO HEAR THE AUGUST GENERAL IN IRON KNOWS OF ME--BUT I MUST CONFESS, I AM QUITE PERTURBED TO SEE AMERICAN IMPERIALISTS STANDING BEFORE ME WITH A CLEAR AND PRESENT VIEW OF MANY OF CHINA'S GREATEST SECRETS.
THESE JUSTICE LEAGUE MEMBERS ARE UNDER THE IMPRESSION THAT--
YOU'VE BEEN GATHERING AND MANIPULATING RESIDUAL STREAMS OF SUPERMAN'S COALESCED SOLAR SUPER-FLARE AND GIVEN IT SOME KIND OF SENTIENCE.

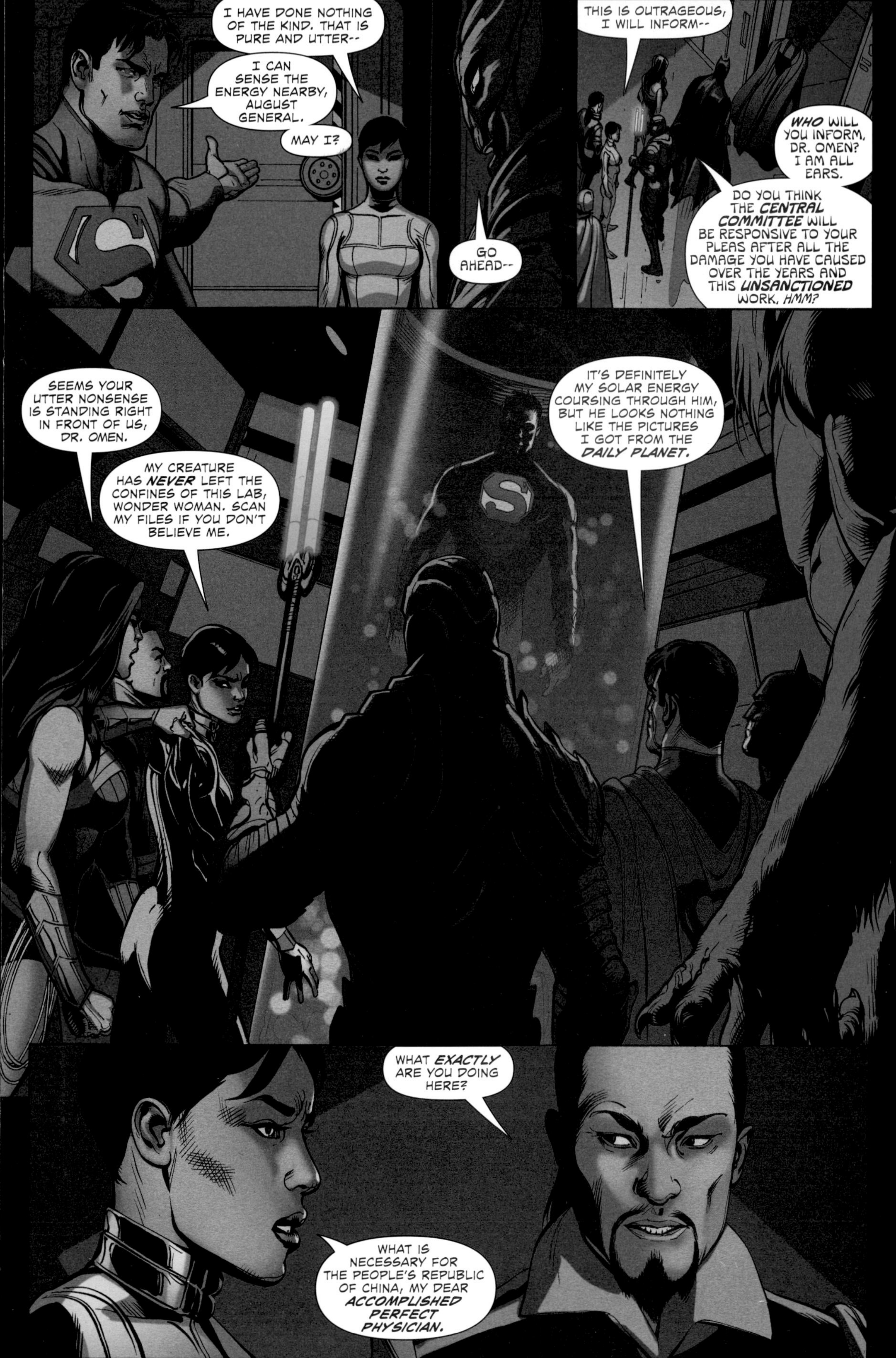
I HAVE DONE NOTHING OF THE KIND. THAT IS PURE AND UTTER--
I CAN SENSE THE ENERGY NEARBY, AUGUST GENERAL.
MAY I?
GO AHEAD--
THIS IS OUTRAGEOUS, I WILL INFORM--
WHO WILL YOU INFORM, DR. OMEN? I AM ALL EARS.
DO YOU THINK THE CENTRAL COMMITTEE WILL BE RESPONSIVE TO YOUR PLEAS AFTER ALL THE DAMAGE YOU HAVE CAUSED OVER THE YEARS AND THIS UNSANCTIONED WORK, HMM?
SEEMS YOUR UTTER NONSENSE IS STANDING RIGHT IN FRONT OF US, DR. OMEN.
MY CREATURE HAS NEVER LEFT THE CONFINES OF THIS LAB, WONDER WOMAN. SCAN MY FILES IF YOU DON'T BELIEVE ME.
IT'S DEFINITELY MY SOLAR ENERGY COURSING THROUGH HIM, BUT HE LOOKS NOTHING LIKE THE PICTURES I GOT FROM THE DAILY PLANET.
WHAT EXACTLY ARE YOU DOING HERE?
WHAT IS NECESSARY FOR THE PEOPLE'S REPUBLIC OF CHINA, MY DEAR ACCOMPLISHED PERFECT PHYSICIAN.

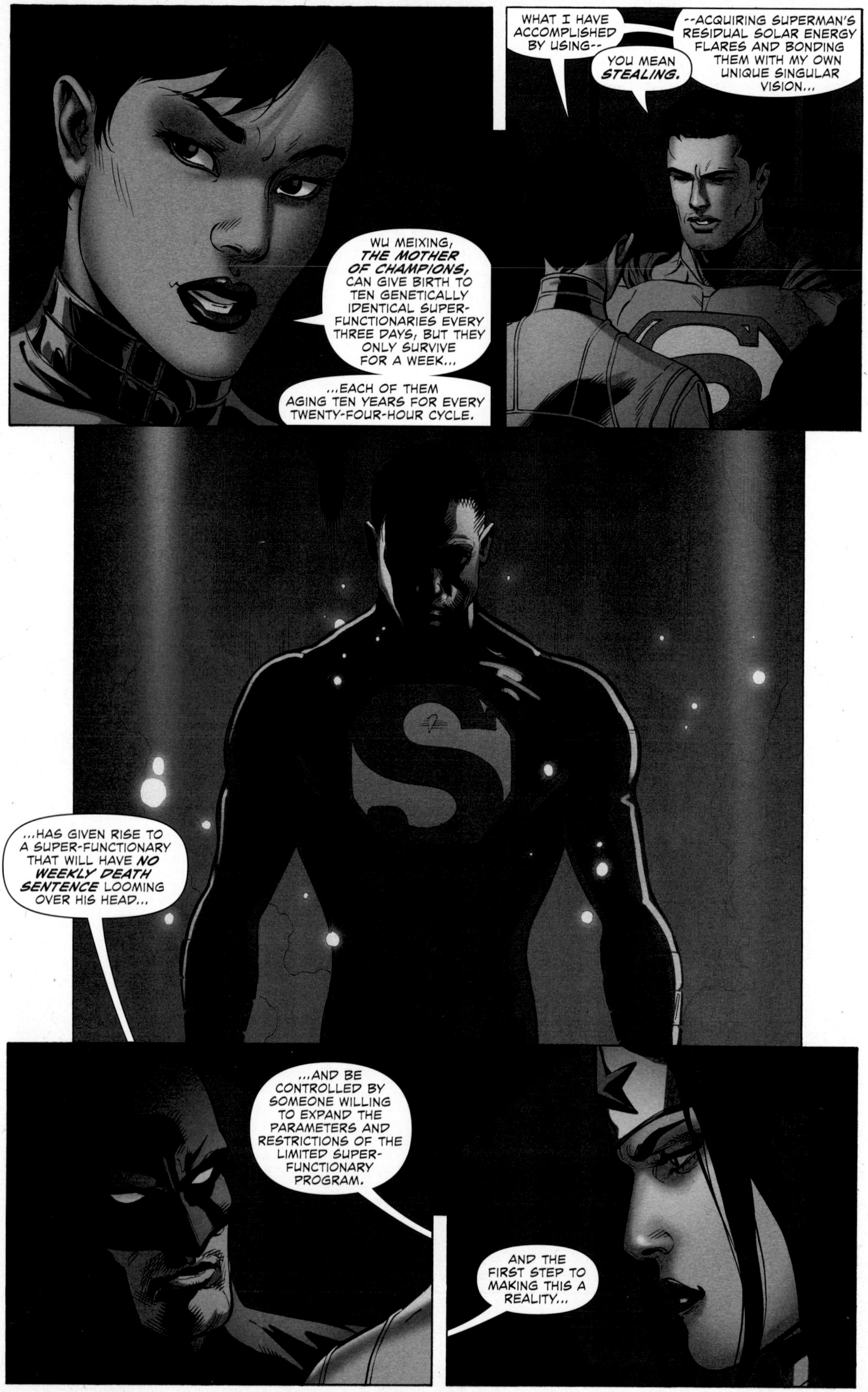
WU MEIXING, *THE MOTHER OF CHAMPIONS,* CAN GIVE BIRTH TO TEN GENETICALLY IDENTICAL SUPER-FUNCTIONARIES EVERY THREE DAYS, BUT THEY ONLY SURVIVE FOR A WEEK...
...EACH OF THEM AGING TEN YEARS FOR EVERY TWENTY-FOUR-HOUR CYCLE.
WHAT I HAVE ACCOMPLISHED BY USING--
YOU MEAN *STEALING.*
--ACQUIRING SUPERMAN'S RESIDUAL SOLAR ENERGY FLARES AND BONDING THEM WITH MY OWN UNIQUE SINGULAR VISION...
...HAS GIVEN RISE TO A SUPER-FUNCTIONARY THAT WILL HAVE *NO WEEKLY DEATH SENTENCE* LOOMING OVER HIS HEAD...
...AND BE CONTROLLED BY SOMEONE WILLING TO EXPAND THE PARAMETERS AND RESTRICTIONS OF THE LIMITED SUPER-FUNCTIONARY PROGRAM.
AND THE FIRST STEP TO MAKING THIS A REALITY...

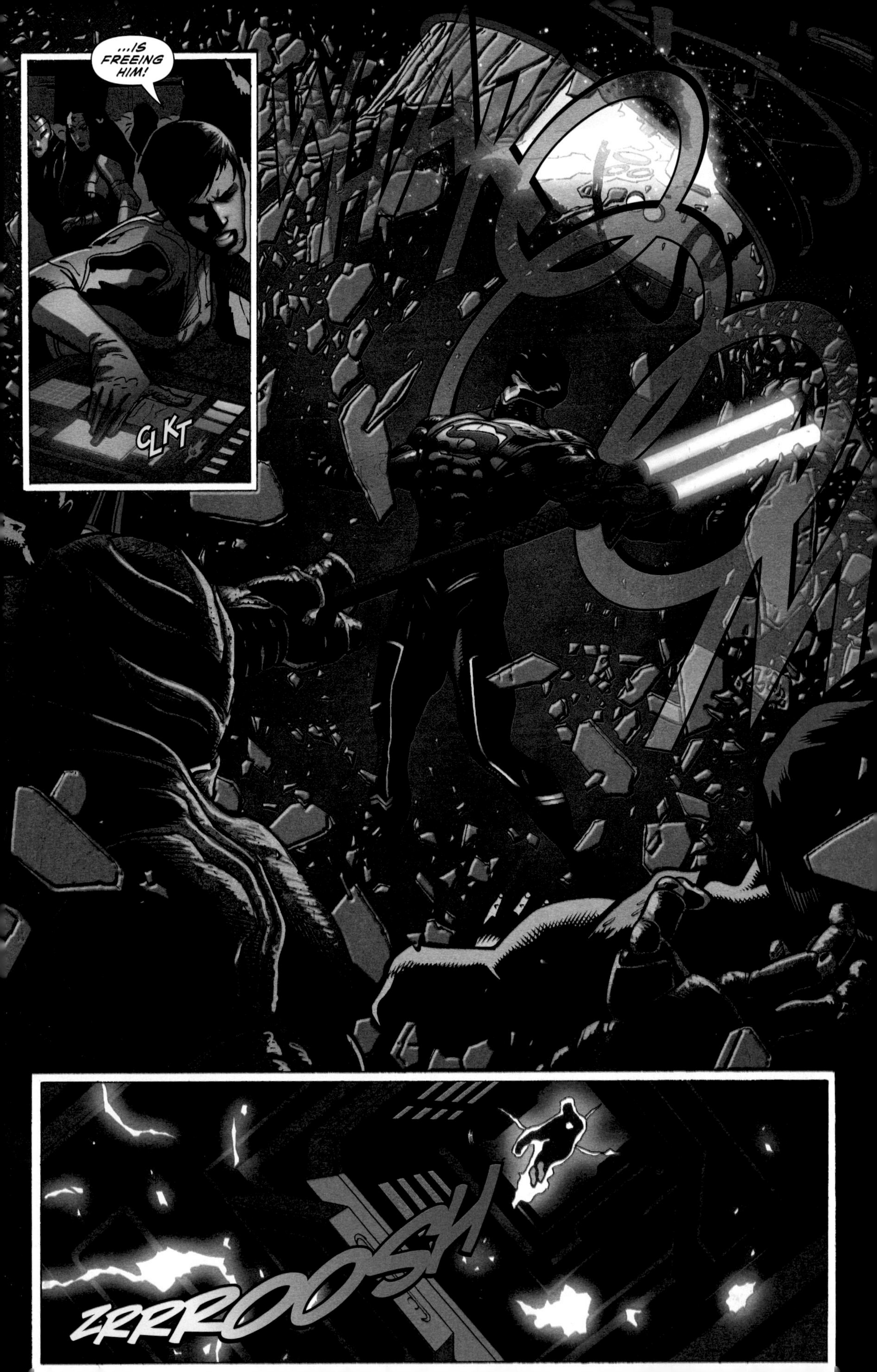
...IS FREEING HIM!
CLKT
ZRRROOSH

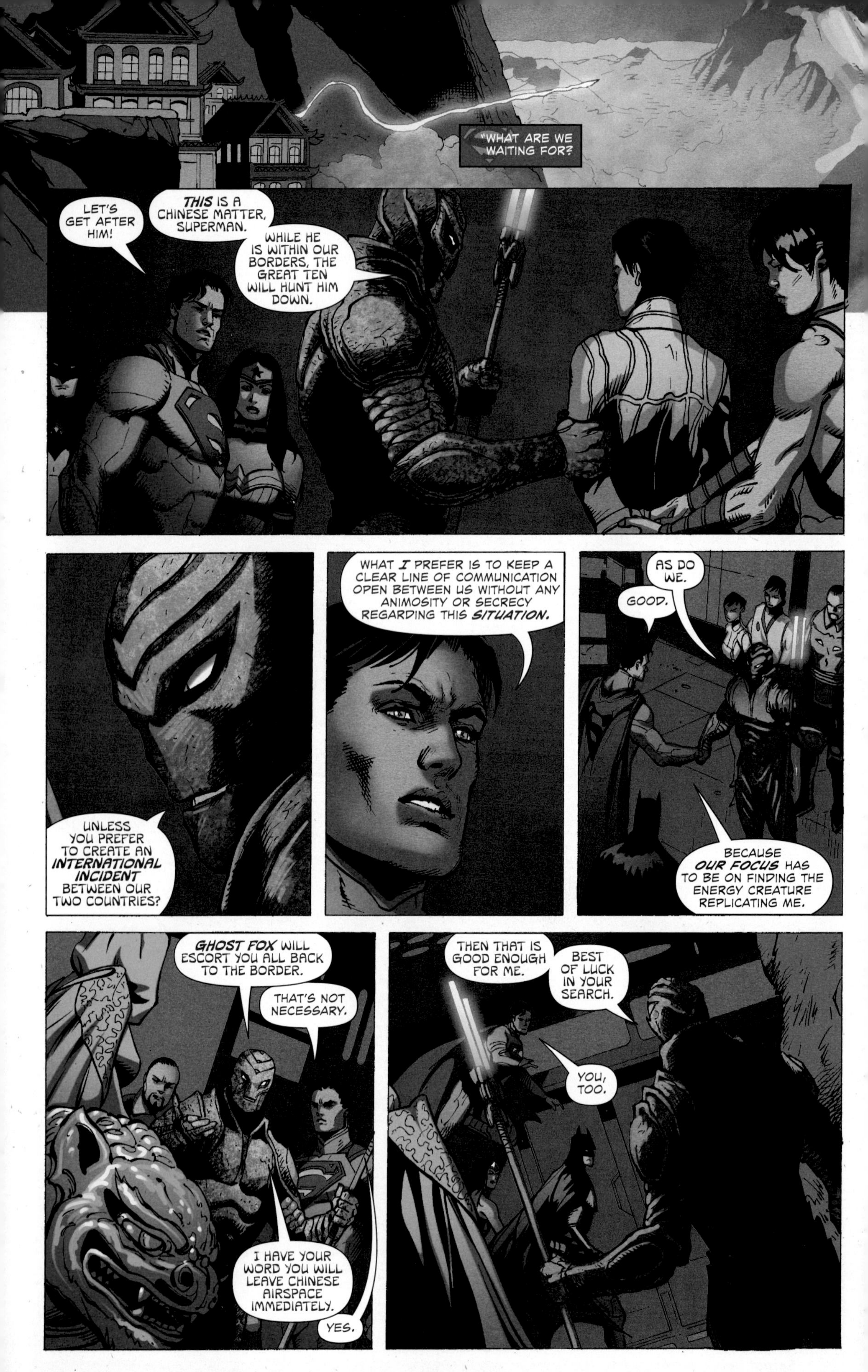
"WHAT ARE WE WAITING FOR?
LET'S GET AFTER HIM!
THIS IS A CHINESE MATTER, SUPERMAN.
WHILE HE IS WITHIN OUR BORDERS, THE GREAT TEN WILL HUNT HIM DOWN.
UNLESS YOU PREFER TO CREATE AN INTERNATIONAL INCIDENT BETWEEN OUR TWO COUNTRIES?
WHAT I PREFER IS TO KEEP A CLEAR LINE OF COMMUNICATION OPEN BETWEEN US WITHOUT ANY ANIMOSITY OR SECRECY REGARDING THIS SITUATION.
AS DO WE.
GOOD.
BECAUSE OUR FOCUS HAS TO BE ON FINDING THE ENERGY CREATURE REPLICATING ME.
GHOST FOX WILL ESCORT YOU ALL BACK TO THE BORDER.
THAT'S NOT NECESSARY.
I HAVE YOUR WORD YOU WILL LEAVE CHINESE AIRSPACE IMMEDIATELY.
YES.
THEN THAT IS GOOD ENOUGH FOR ME.
BEST OF LUCK IN YOUR SEARCH.
YOU, TOO.

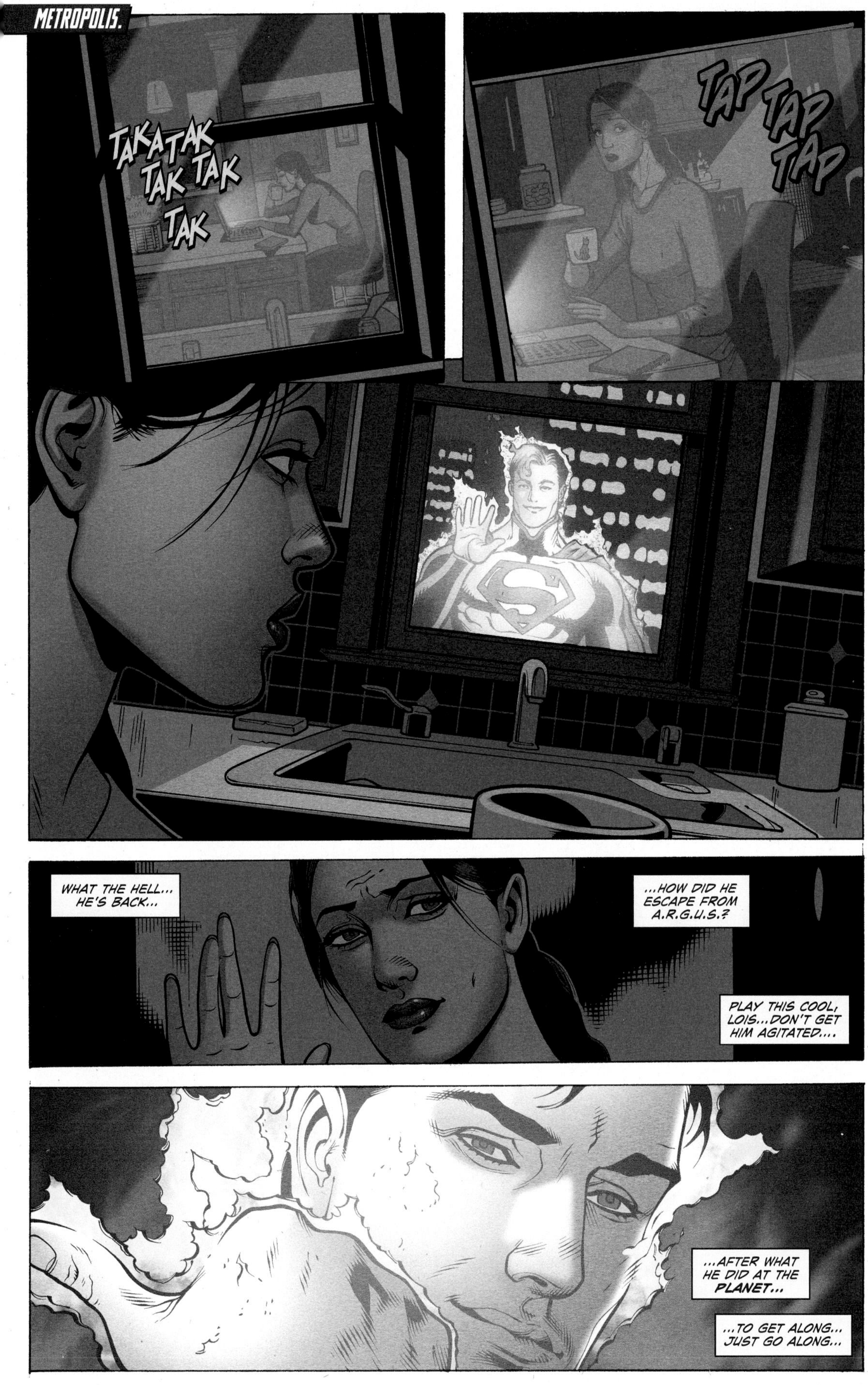
METROPOLIS.
TAKATAK TAK TAK TAK
TAP TAP TAP
WHAT THE HELL... HE'S BACK...
...HOW DID HE ESCAPE FROM A.R.G.U.S.?
PLAY THIS COOL, LOIS...DON'T GET HIM AGITATED....
...AFTER WHAT HE DID AT THE PLANET...
...TO GET ALONG... JUST GO ALONG...

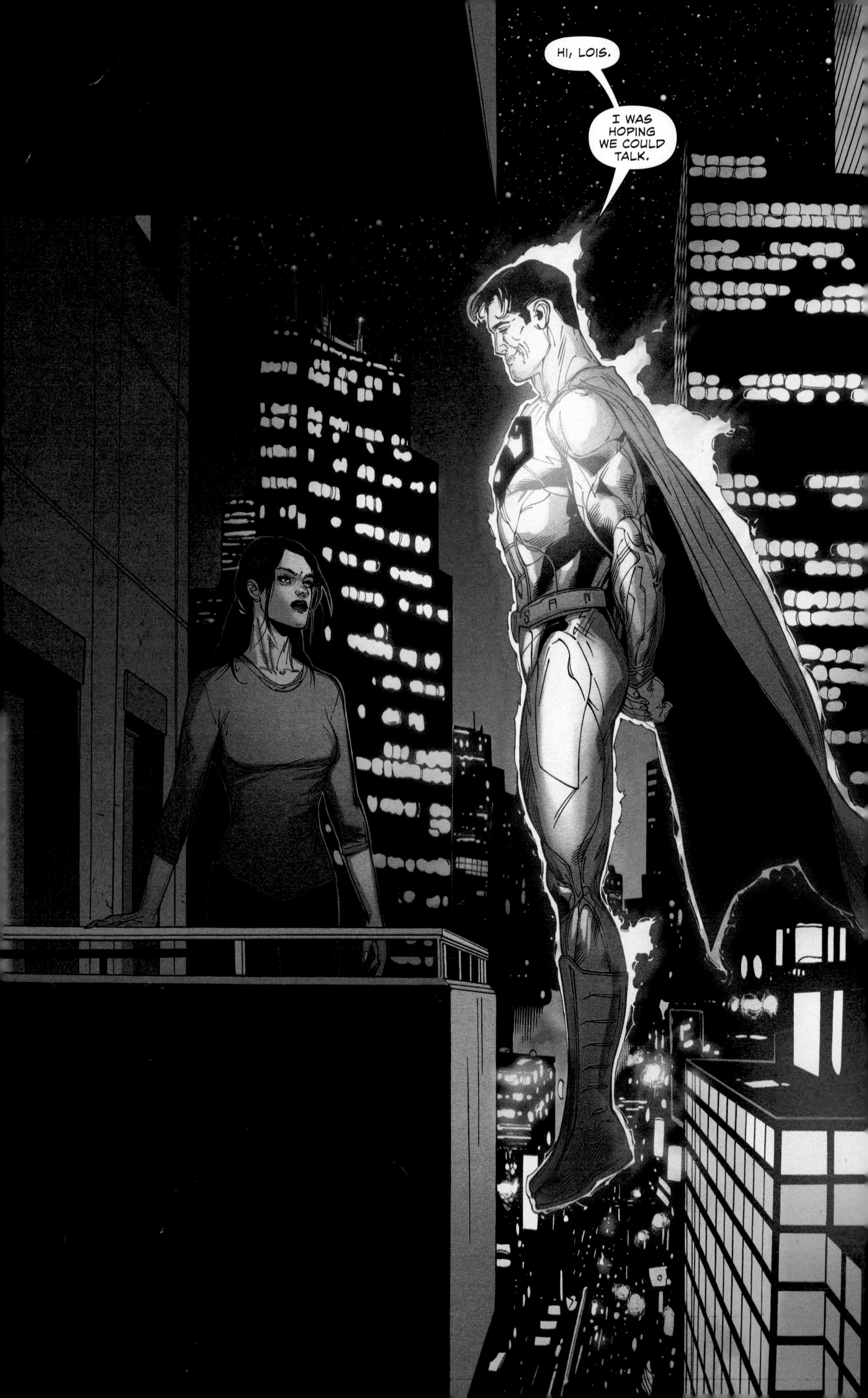
HI, LOIS.
I WAS HOPING WE COULD TALK.

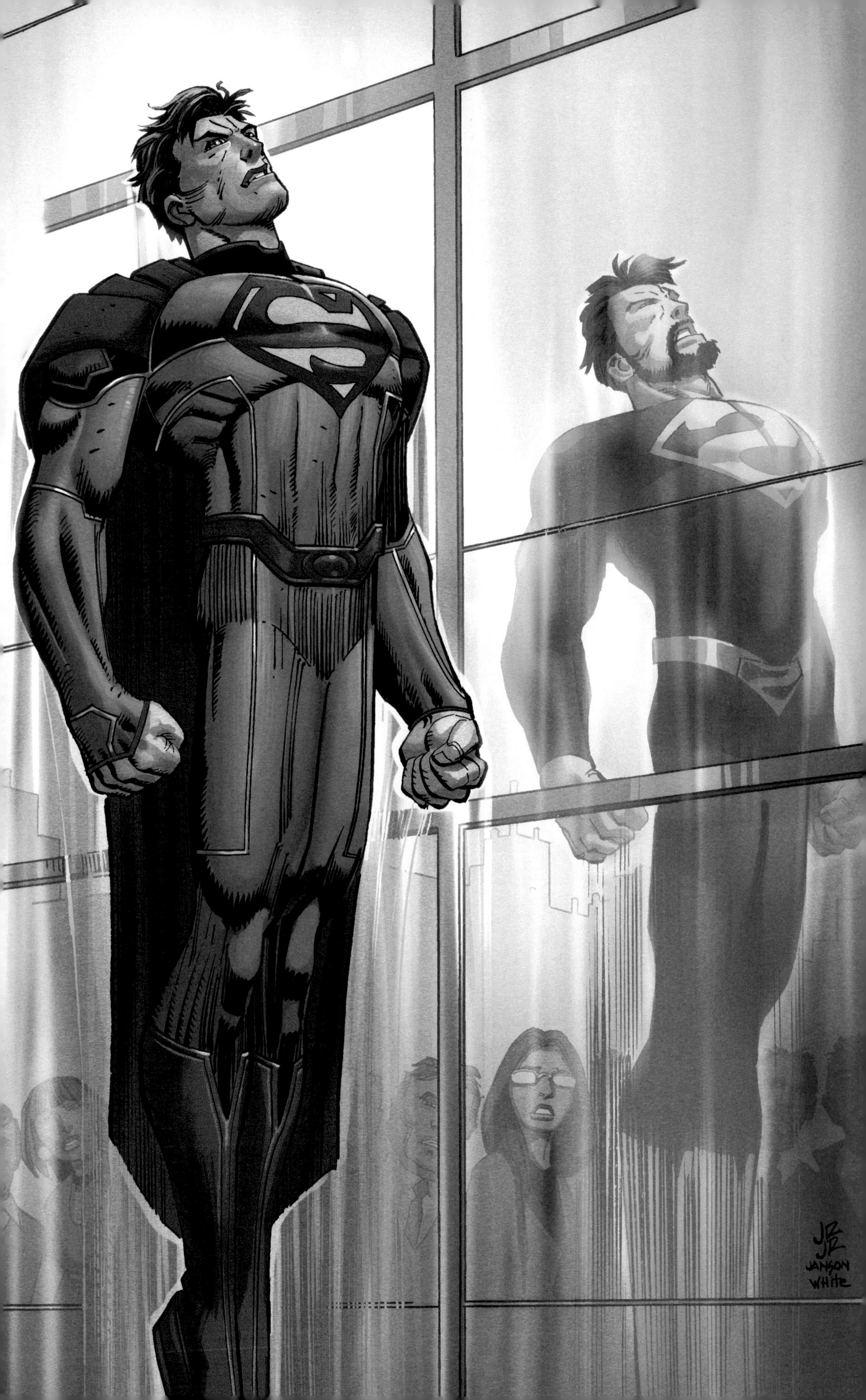
JRJR
JANSON
WHITE

THE FINAL DAYS OF SUPERMAN PART 6: THE GREAT PRETENDER

PETER J. TOMASI writer DALE EAGLESHAM SCOT EATON pencillers DALE EAGLESHAM WAYNE FAUCHER inkers TOMEU MOREY colorist ROB LEIGH letterer
JOHN ROMITA JR. KLAUS JANSON DEAN WHITE cover

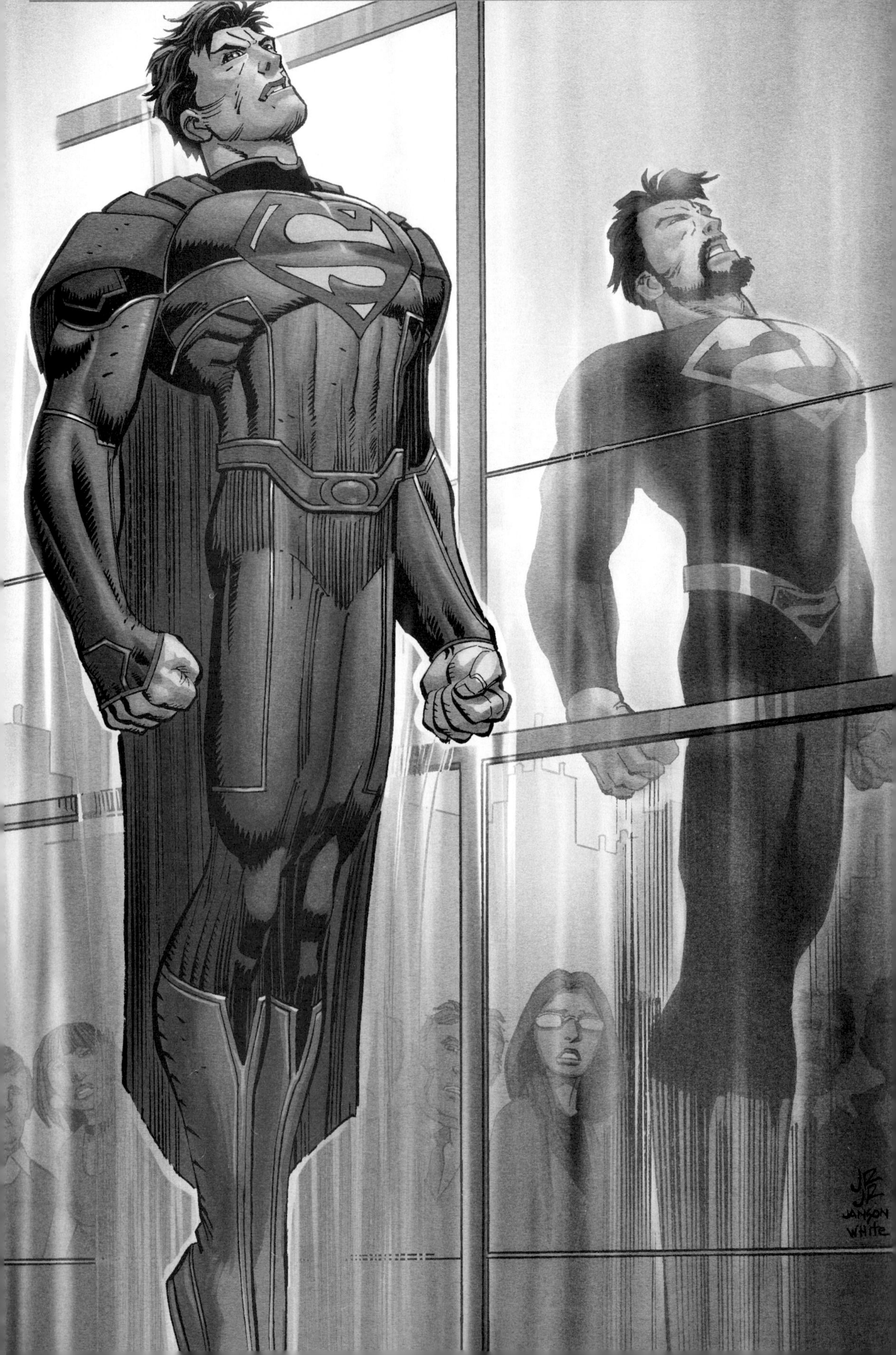
JANSON
WHITE

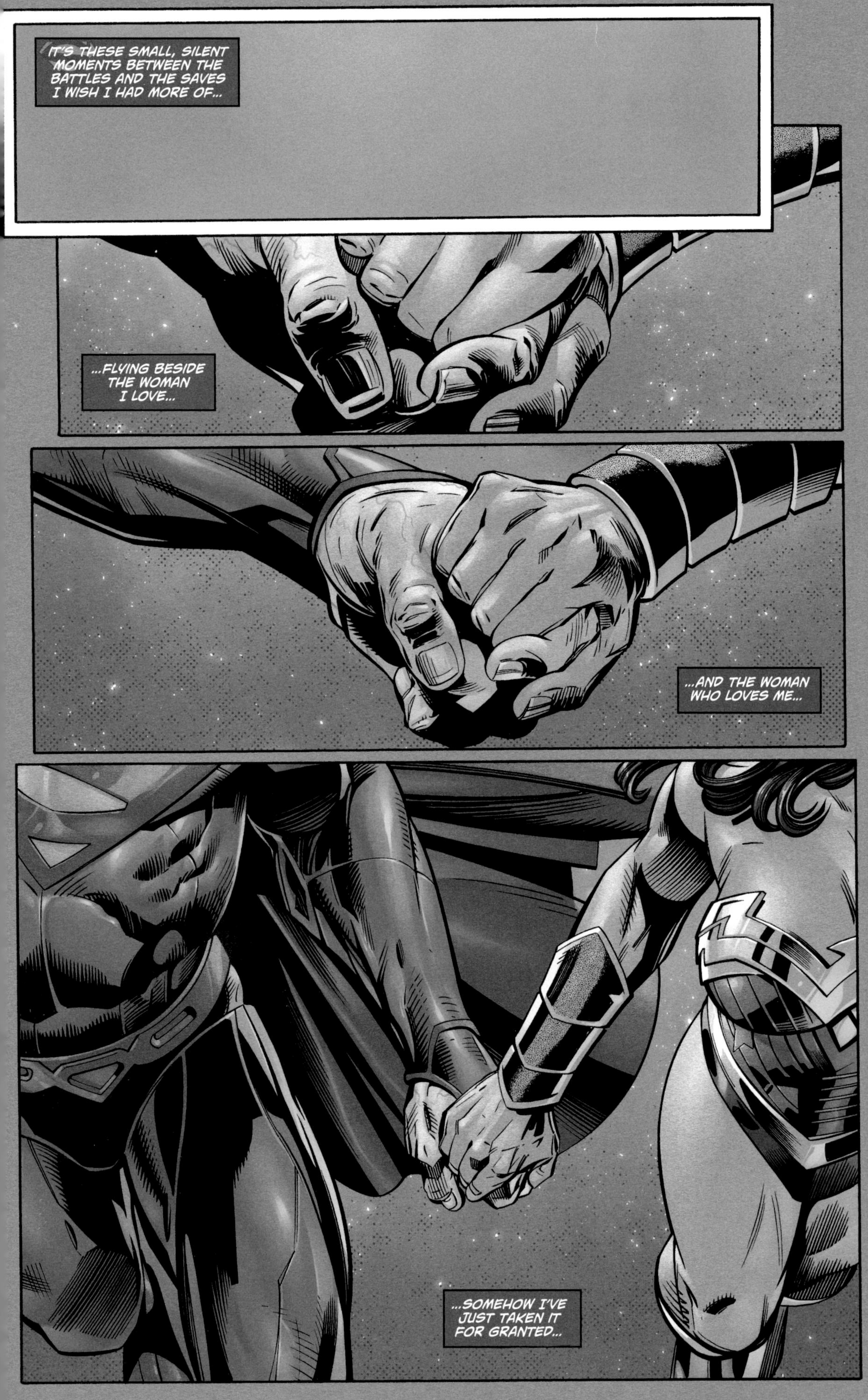
IT'S THESE SMALL, SILENT MOMENTS BETWEEN THE BATTLES AND THE SAVES I WISH I HAD MORE OF...
...FLYING BESIDE THE WOMAN I LOVE...
...AND THE WOMAN WHO LOVES ME...
...SOMEHOW I'VE JUST TAKEN IT FOR GRANTED...

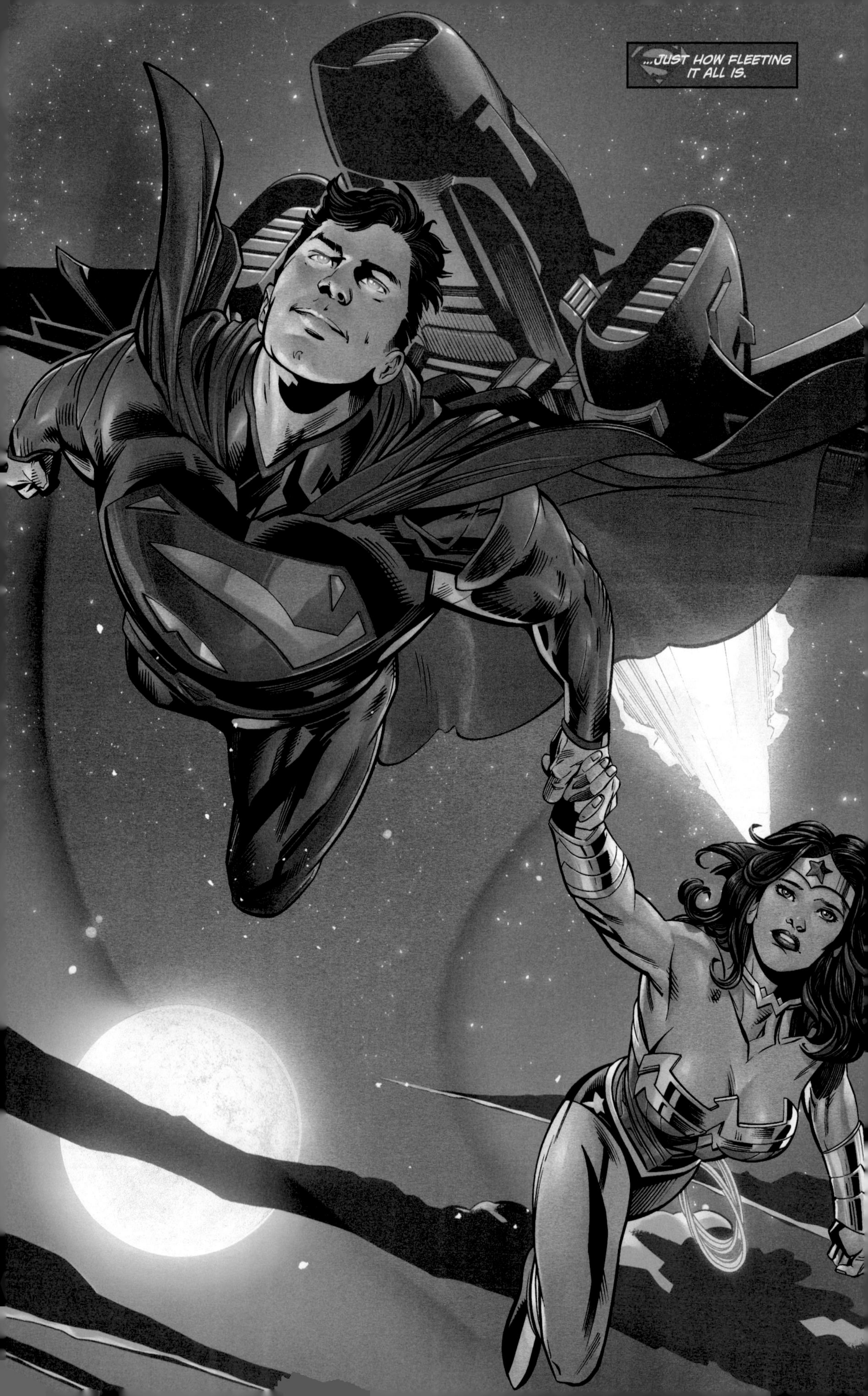
...JUST HOW FLEETING IT ALL IS.

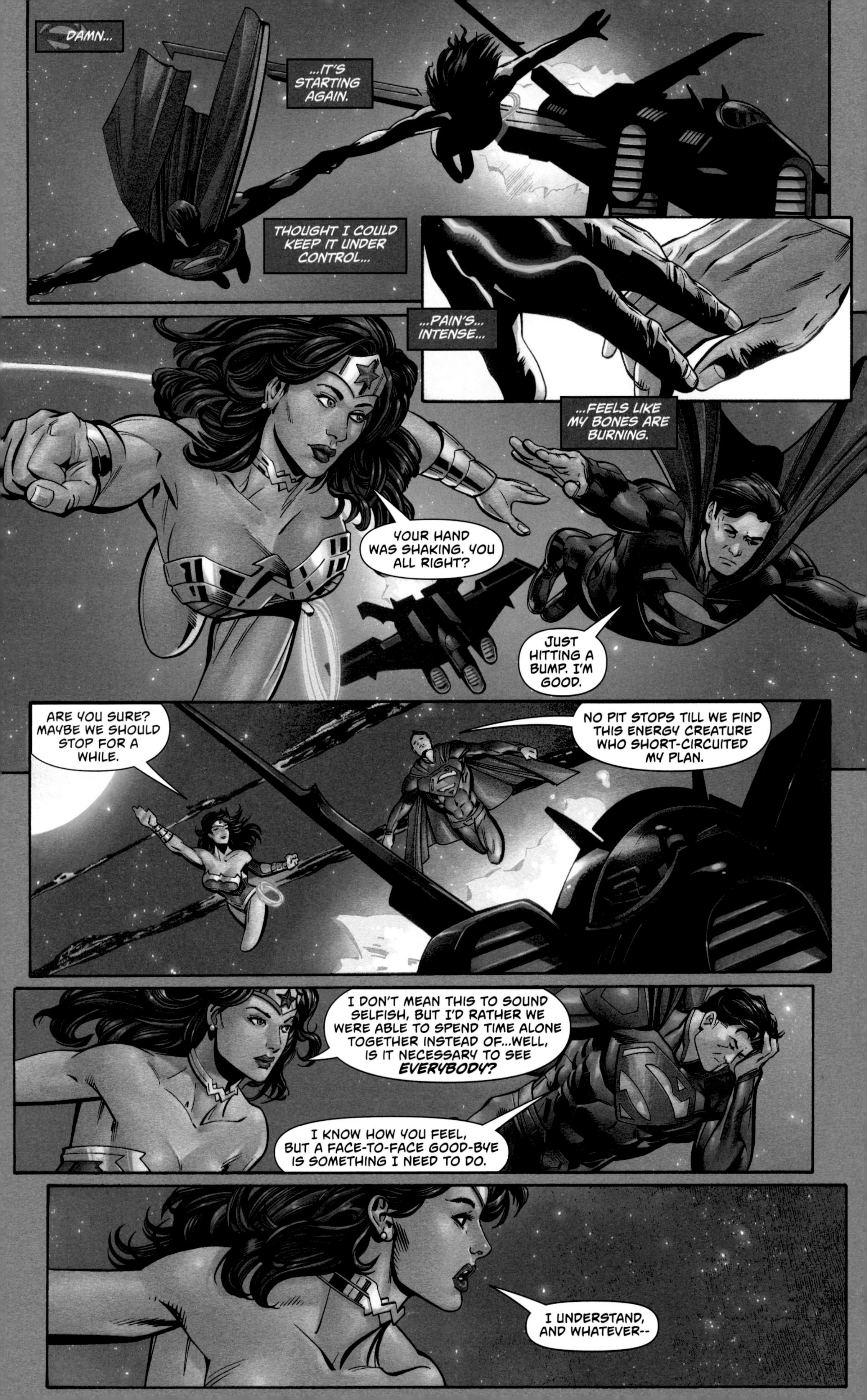
DAMN...
...IT'S STARTING AGAIN.
THOUGHT I COULD KEEP IT UNDER CONTROL...
...PAIN'S... INTENSE...
...FEELS LIKE MY BONES ARE BURNING.
YOUR HAND WAS SHAKING. YOU ALL RIGHT?
JUST HITTING A BUMP. I'M GOOD.
ARE YOU SURE? MAYBE WE SHOULD STOP FOR A WHILE.
NO PIT STOPS TILL WE FIND THIS ENERGY CREATURE WHO SHORT-CIRCUITED MY PLAN.
I DON'T MEAN THIS TO SOUND SELFISH, BUT I'D RATHER WE WERE ABLE TO SPEND TIME ALONE TOGETHER INSTEAD OF...WELL, IS IT NECESSARY TO SEE *EVERYBODY?*
I KNOW HOW YOU FEEL, BUT A FACE-TO-FACE GOOD-BYE IS SOMETHING I NEED TO DO.
I UNDERSTAND, AND WHATEVER--

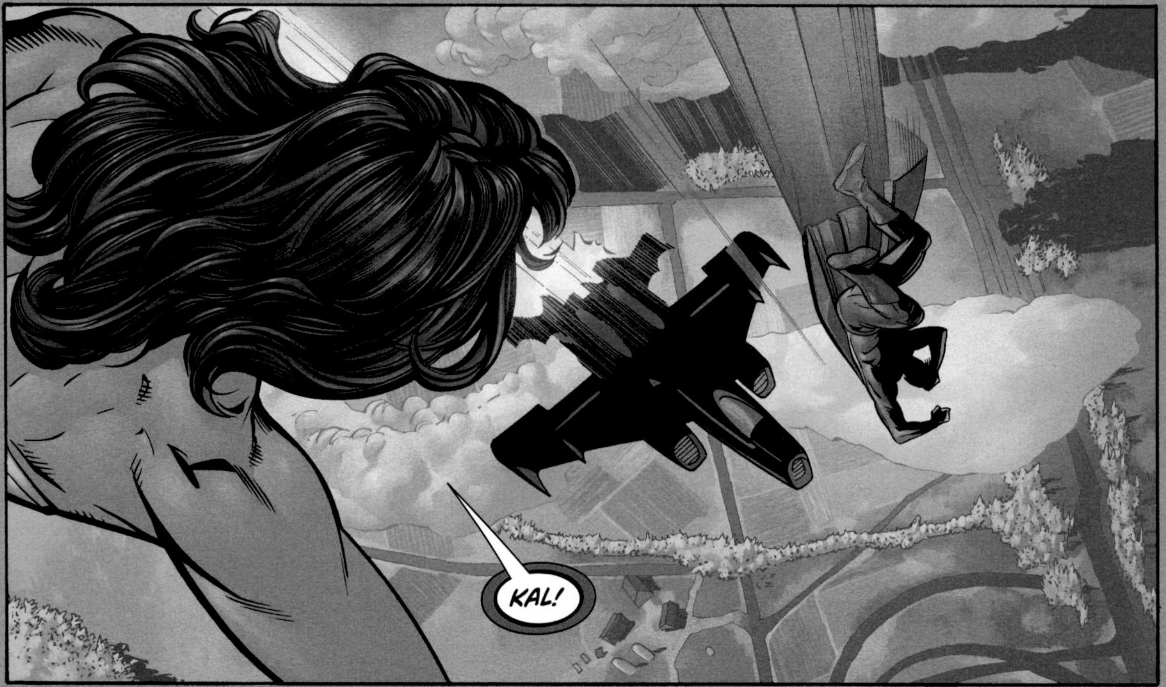
KAL!

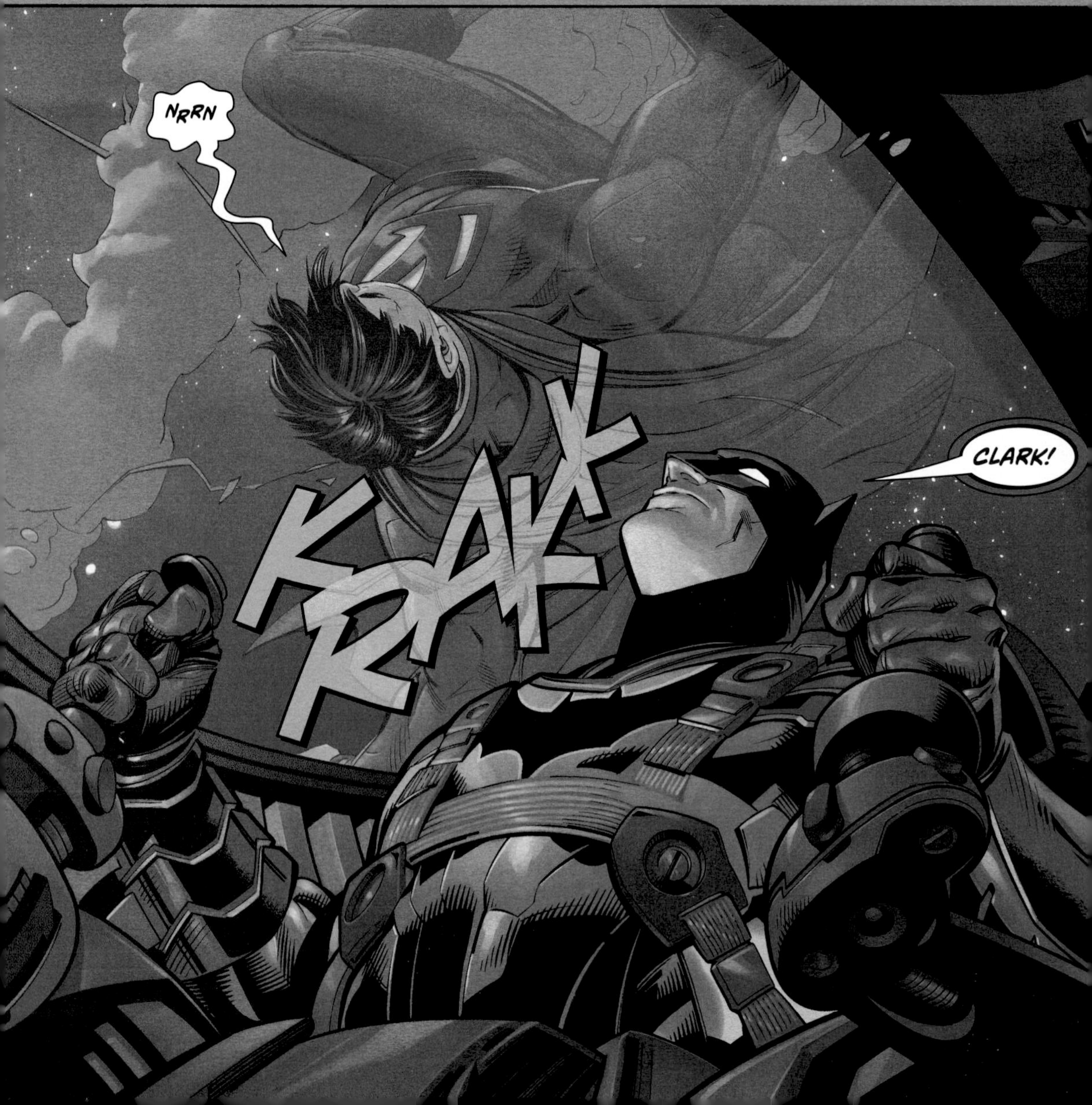
NRRN
CLARK!
KRAK

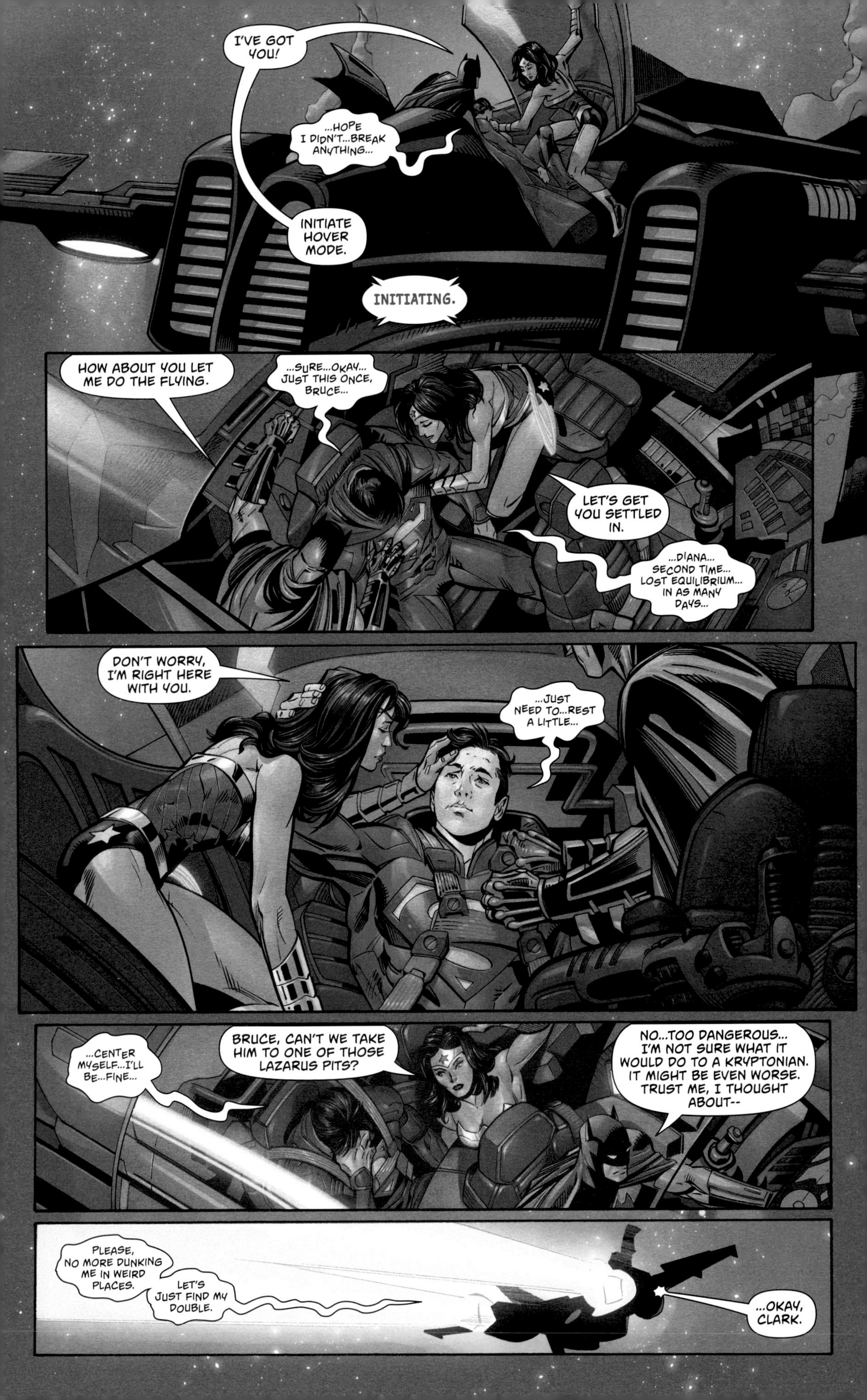
I'VE GOT YOU!
...HOPE I DIDN'T...BREAK ANYTHING...
INITIATE HOVER MODE.
INITIATING.
HOW ABOUT YOU LET ME DO THE FLYING.
...SURE...OKAY... JUST THIS ONCE, BRUCE...
LET'S GET YOU SETTLED IN.
...DIANA... SECOND TIME... LOST EQUILIBRIUM... IN AS MANY DAYS...
DON'T WORRY, I'M RIGHT HERE WITH YOU.
...JUST NEED TO...REST A LITTLE...
...CENTER MYSELF...I'LL BE...FINE...
BRUCE, CAN'T WE TAKE HIM TO ONE OF THOSE LAZARUS PITS?
NO...TOO DANGEROUS... I'M NOT SURE WHAT IT WOULD DO TO A KRYPTONIAN. IT MIGHT BE EVEN WORSE. TRUST ME, I THOUGHT ABOUT--
PLEASE, NO MORE DUNKING ME IN WEIRD PLACES.
LET'S JUST FIND MY DOUBLE.
...OKAY, CLARK.

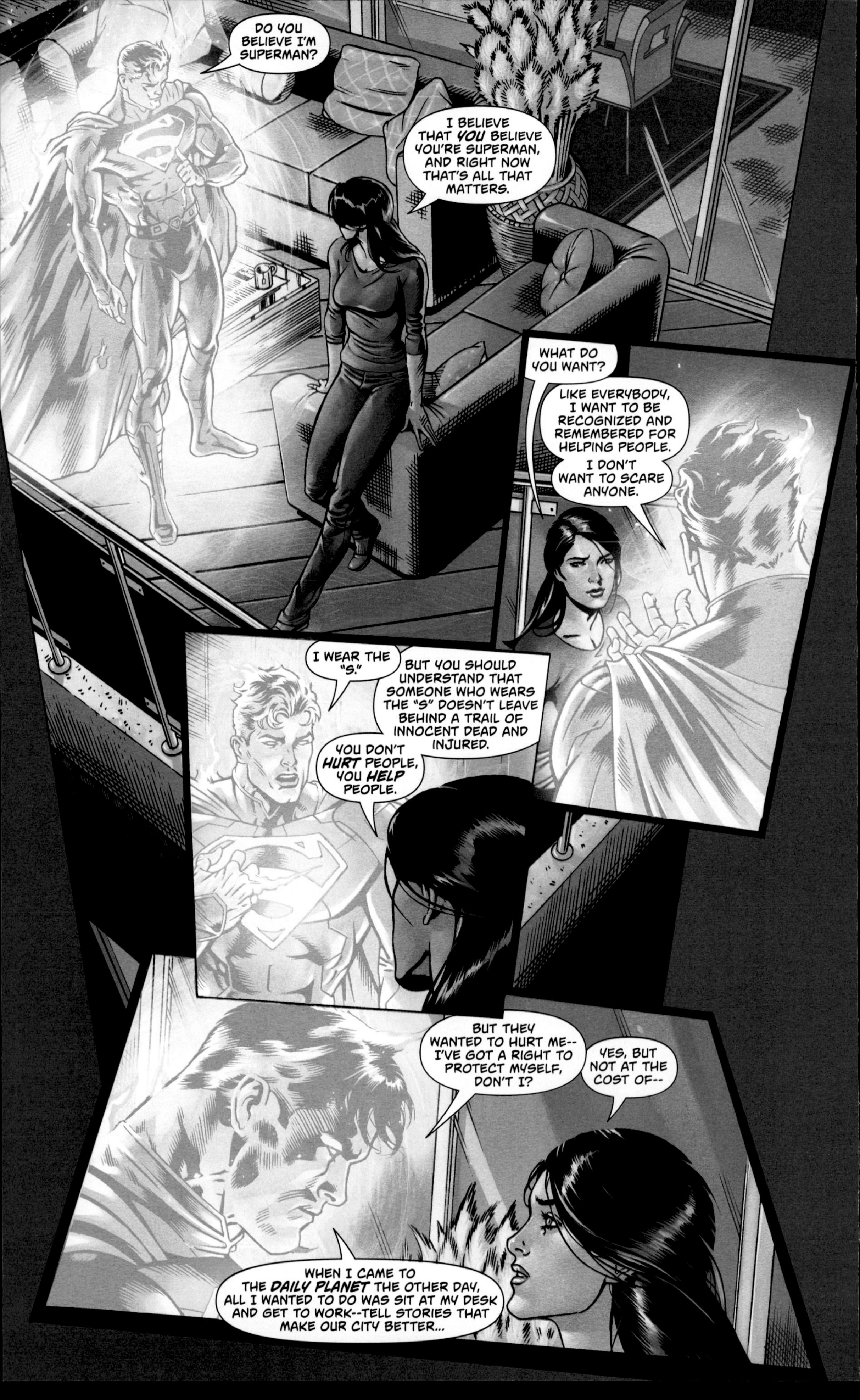
DO YOU BELIEVE I'M SUPERMAN?
I BELIEVE THAT *YOU* BELIEVE YOU'RE SUPERMAN, AND RIGHT NOW THAT'S ALL THAT MATTERS.
WHAT DO YOU WANT?
LIKE EVERYBODY, I WANT TO BE RECOGNIZED AND REMEMBERED FOR HELPING PEOPLE.
I DON'T WANT TO SCARE ANYONE.
I WEAR THE "S."
BUT YOU SHOULD UNDERSTAND THAT SOMEONE WHO WEARS THE "S" DOESN'T LEAVE BEHIND A TRAIL OF INNOCENT DEAD AND INJURED.
YOU DON'T *HURT* PEOPLE, YOU *HELP* PEOPLE.
BUT THEY WANTED TO HURT ME--I'VE GOT A RIGHT TO PROTECT MYSELF, DON'T I?
YES, BUT NOT AT THE COST OF--
WHEN I CAME TO THE *DAILY PLANET* THE OTHER DAY, ALL I WANTED TO DO WAS SIT AT MY DESK AND GET TO WORK--TELL STORIES THAT MAKE OUR CITY BETTER...

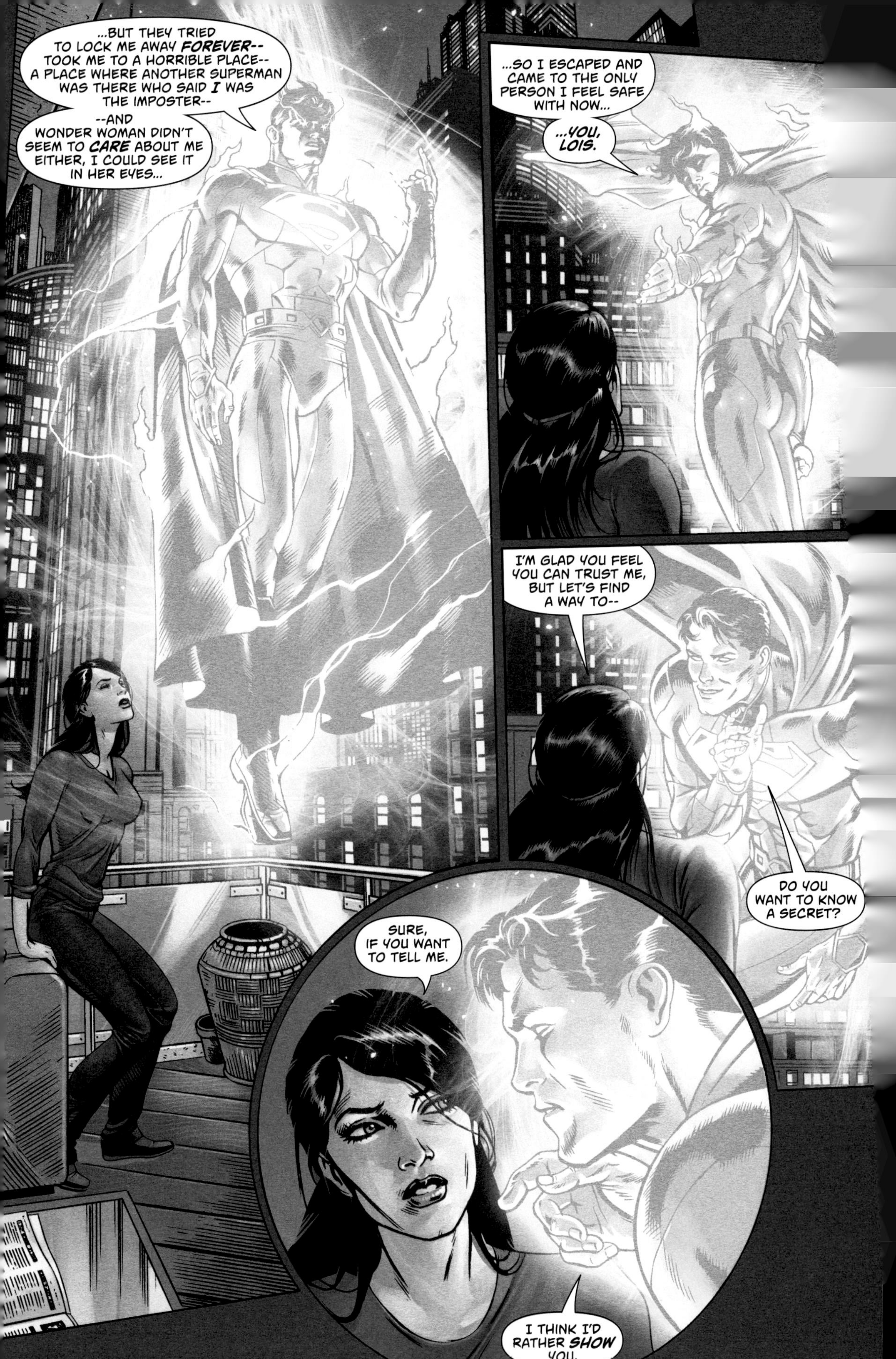
...BUT THEY TRIED TO LOCK ME AWAY FOREVER-- TOOK ME TO A HORRIBLE PLACE-- A PLACE WHERE ANOTHER SUPERMAN WAS THERE WHO SAID I WAS THE IMPOSTER--
--AND WONDER WOMAN DIDN'T SEEM TO CARE ABOUT ME EITHER, I COULD SEE IT IN HER EYES...
...SO I ESCAPED AND CAME TO THE ONLY PERSON I FEEL SAFE WITH NOW...
...YOU, LOIS.
I'M GLAD YOU FEEL YOU CAN TRUST ME, BUT LET'S FIND A WAY TO--
DO YOU WANT TO KNOW A SECRET?
SURE, IF YOU WANT TO TELL ME.
I THINK I'D RATHER SHOW YOU.

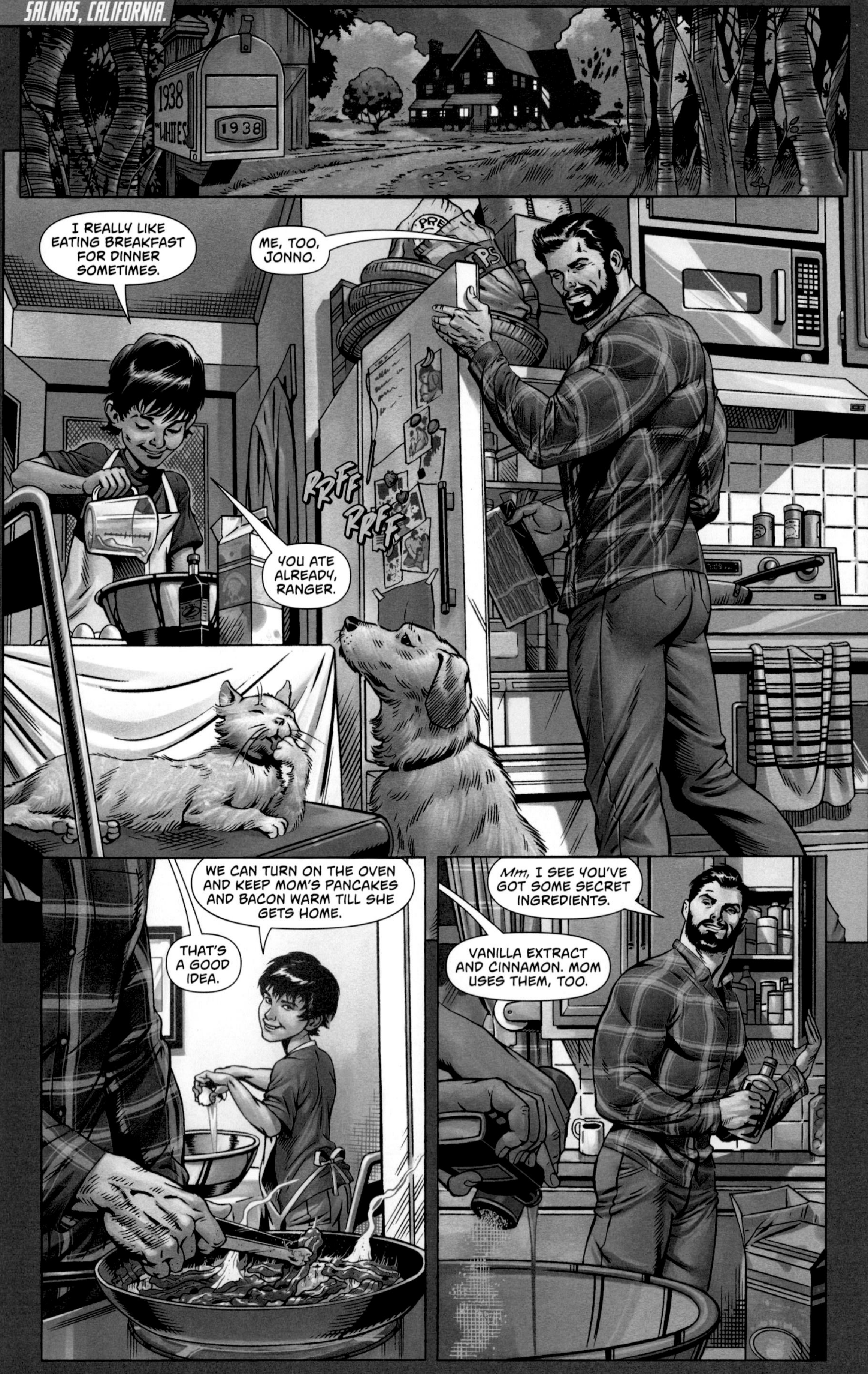
SALINAS, CALIFORNIA.
1938
WHITES
1938
I REALLY LIKE EATING BREAKFAST FOR DINNER SOMETIMES.
ME, TOO, JONNO.
RRFF
RRFF
YOU ATE ALREADY, RANGER.
WE CAN TURN ON THE OVEN AND KEEP MOM'S PANCAKES AND BACON WARM TILL SHE GETS HOME.
THAT'S A GOOD IDEA.
Mm, I SEE YOU'VE GOT SOME SECRET INGREDIENTS.
VANILLA EXTRACT AND CINNAMON. MOM USES THEM, TOO.

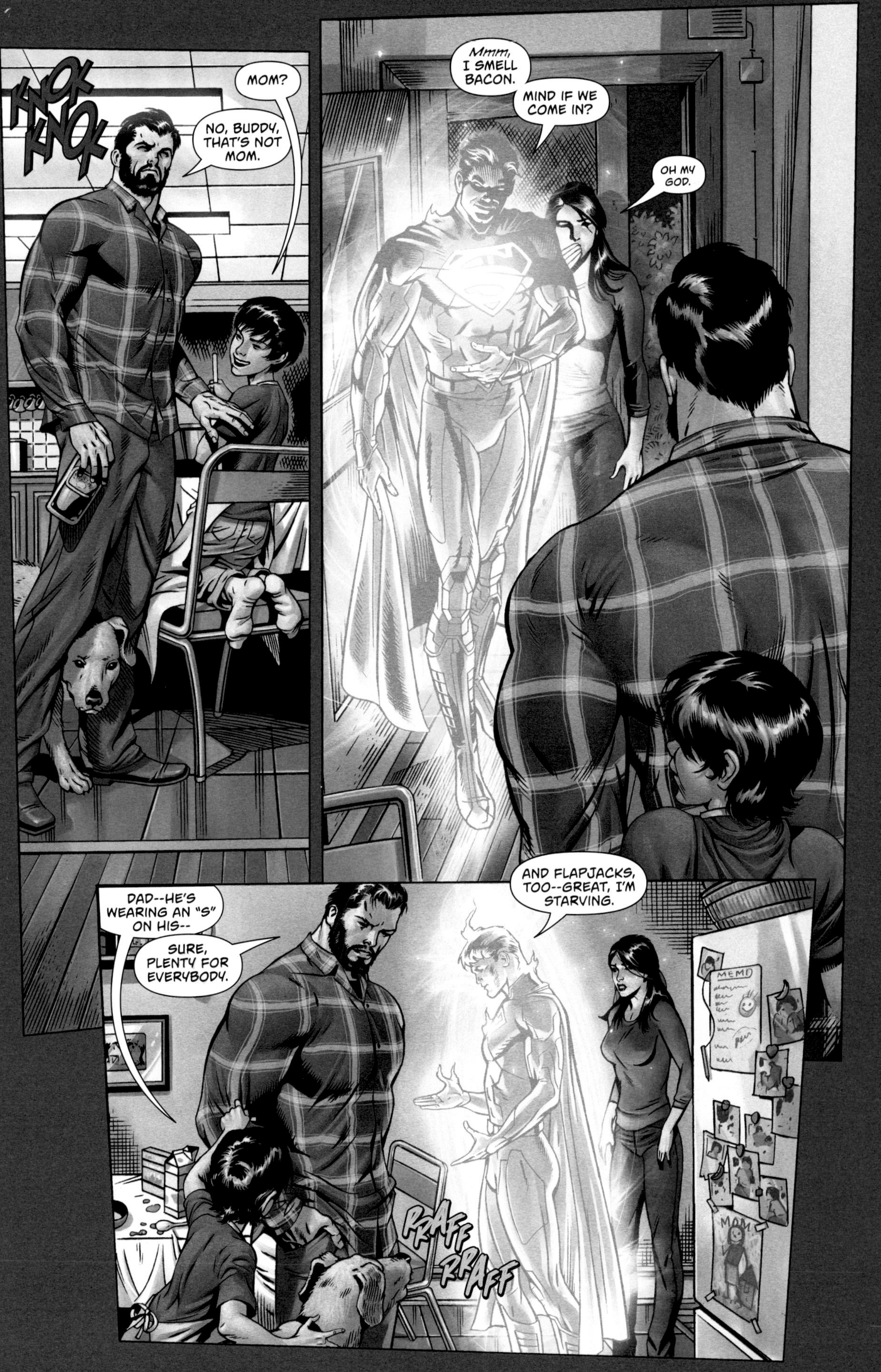
KNOK KNOK
MOM?
NO, BUDDY, THAT'S NOT MOM.
Mmm, I SMELL BACON.
MIND IF WE COME IN?
OH MY GOD.
DAD--HE'S WEARING AN "S" ON HIS--
SURE, PLENTY FOR EVERYBODY.
AND FLAPJACKS, TOO--GREAT, I'M STARVING.
RRAFF RRAFF
MEMO
MOM

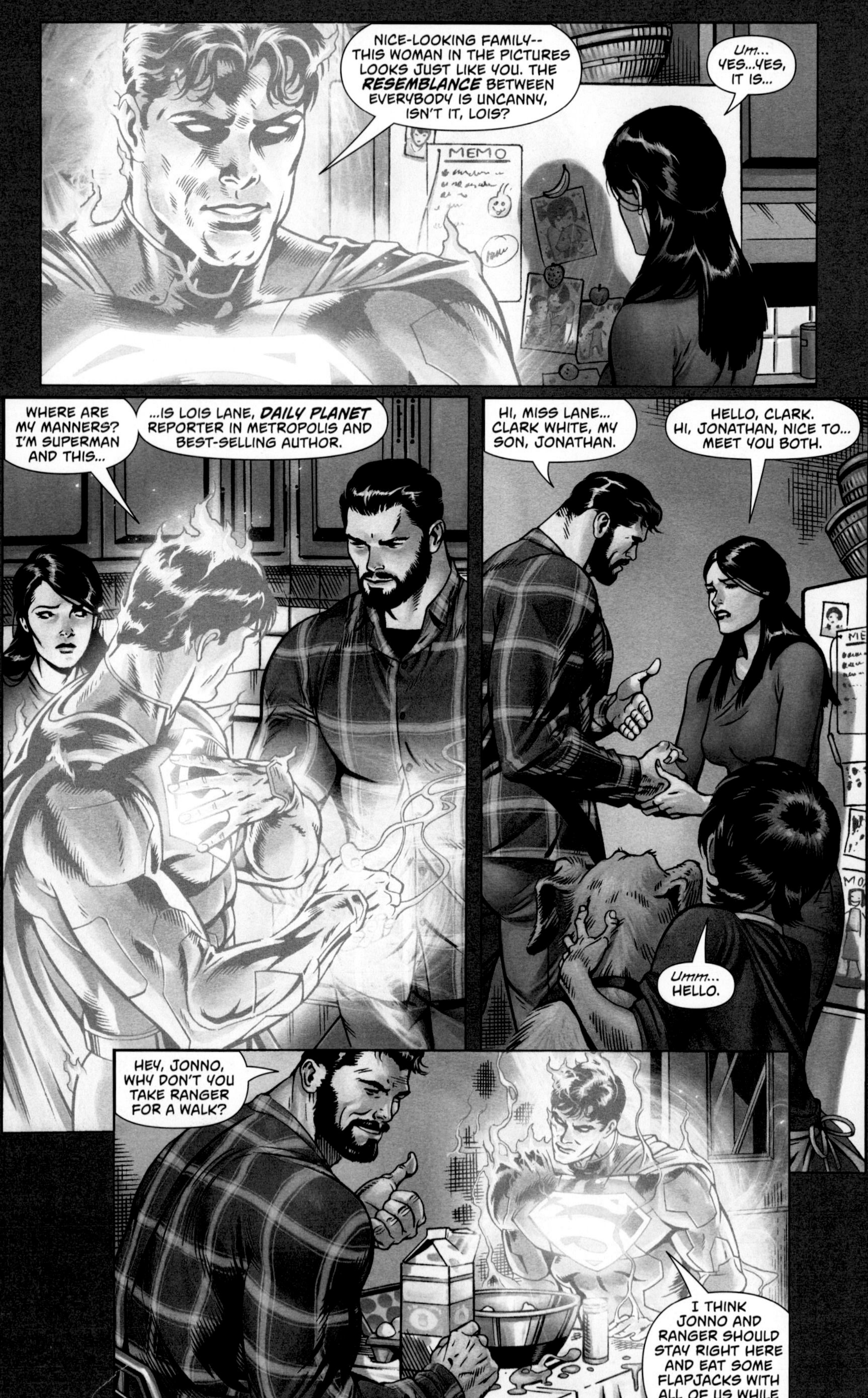

NICE-LOOKING FAMILY-- THIS WOMAN IN THE PICTURES LOOKS JUST LIKE YOU. THE RESEMBLANCE BETWEEN EVERYBODY IS UNCANNY, ISN'T IT, LOIS?
Um... YES...YES, IT IS...
WHERE ARE MY MANNERS? I'M SUPERMAN AND THIS...
...IS LOIS LANE, DAILY PLANET REPORTER IN METROPOLIS AND BEST-SELLING AUTHOR.
HI, MISS LANE... CLARK WHITE, MY SON, JONATHAN.
HELLO, CLARK. HI, JONATHAN, NICE TO... MEET YOU BOTH.
Umm... HELLO.
HEY, JONNO, WHY DON'T YOU TAKE RANGER FOR A WALK?
I THINK JONNO AND RANGER SHOULD STAY RIGHT HERE AND EAT SOME FLAPJACKS WITH ALL OF US WHILE THEY'RE HOT.

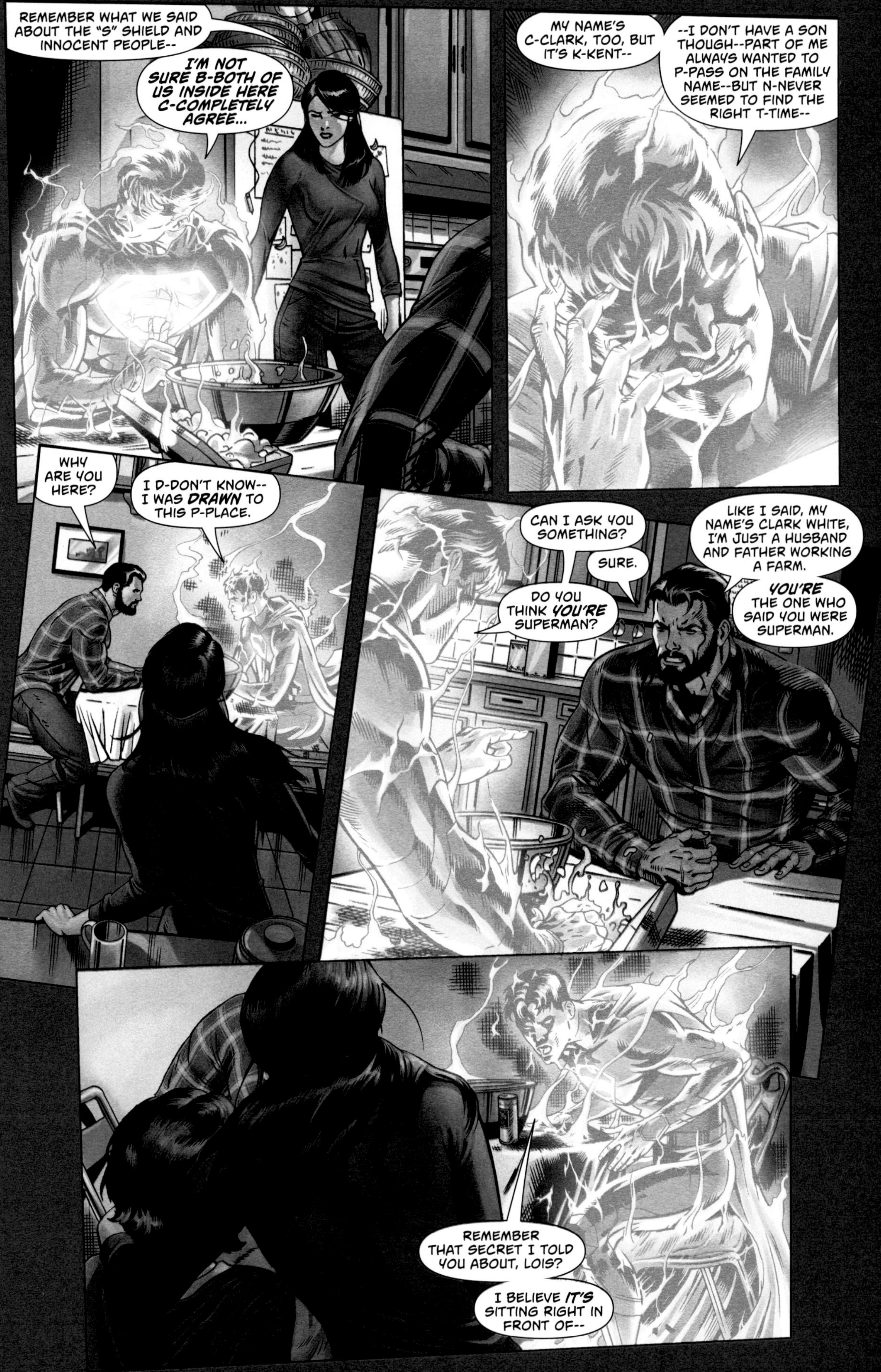
REMEMBER WHAT WE SAID ABOUT THE "S" SHIELD AND INNOCENT PEOPLE--
I'M NOT SURE B-BOTH OF US INSIDE HERE C-COMPLETELY AGREE...
MY NAME'S C-CLARK, TOO, BUT IT'S K-KENT--
--I DON'T HAVE A SON THOUGH--PART OF ME ALWAYS WANTED TO P-PASS ON THE FAMILY NAME--BUT N-NEVER SEEMED TO FIND THE RIGHT T-TIME--
WHY ARE YOU HERE?
I D-DON'T KNOW-- I WAS DRAWN TO THIS P-PLACE.
CAN I ASK YOU SOMETHING?
SURE.
DO YOU THINK YOU'RE SUPERMAN?
LIKE I SAID, MY NAME'S CLARK WHITE, I'M JUST A HUSBAND AND FATHER WORKING A FARM.
YOU'RE THE ONE WHO SAID YOU WERE SUPERMAN.
REMEMBER THAT SECRET I TOLD YOU ABOUT, LOIS?
I BELIEVE IT'S SITTING RIGHT IN FRONT OF--

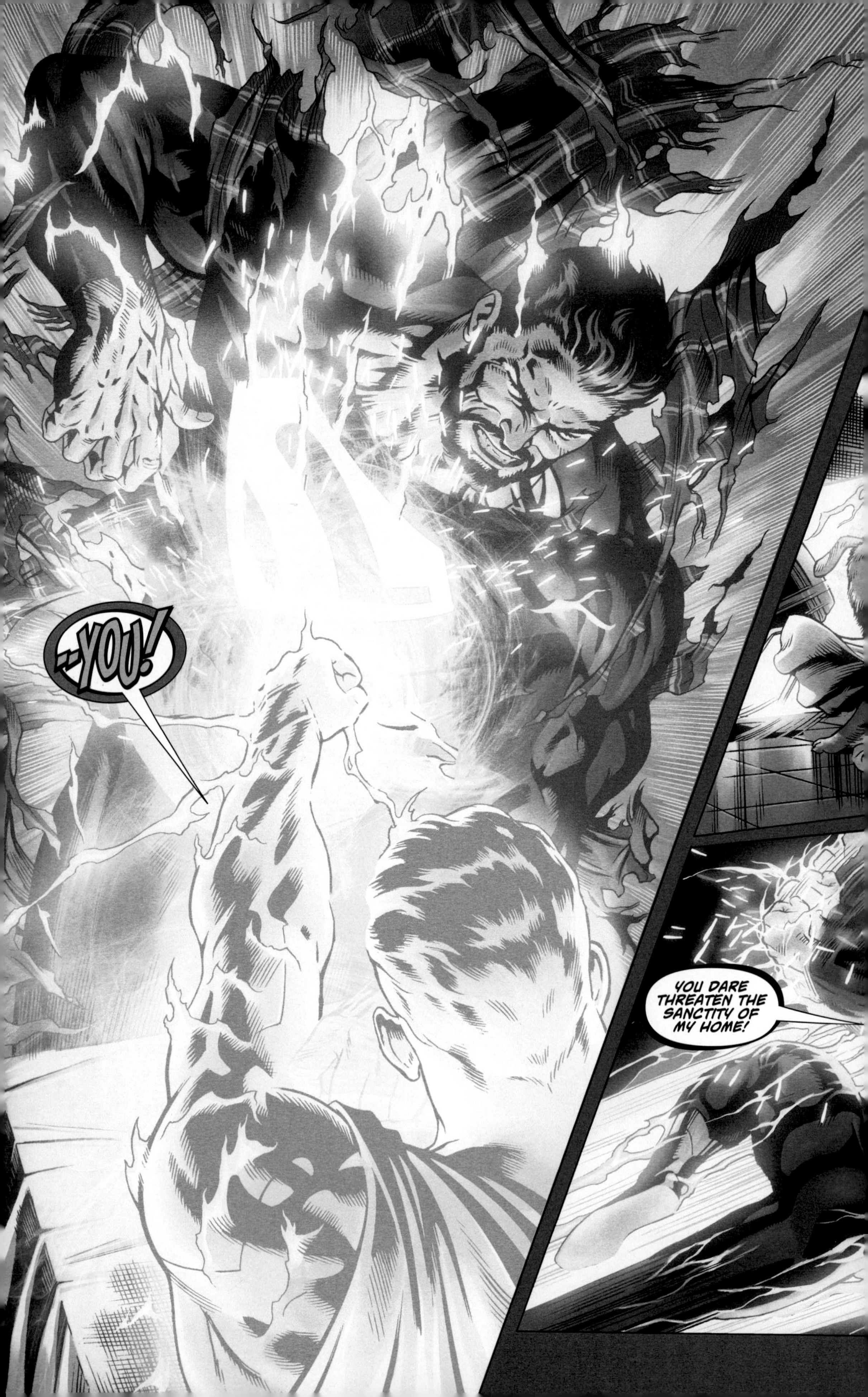
--YOU!
YOU DARE THREATEN THE SANCTITY OF MY HOME!

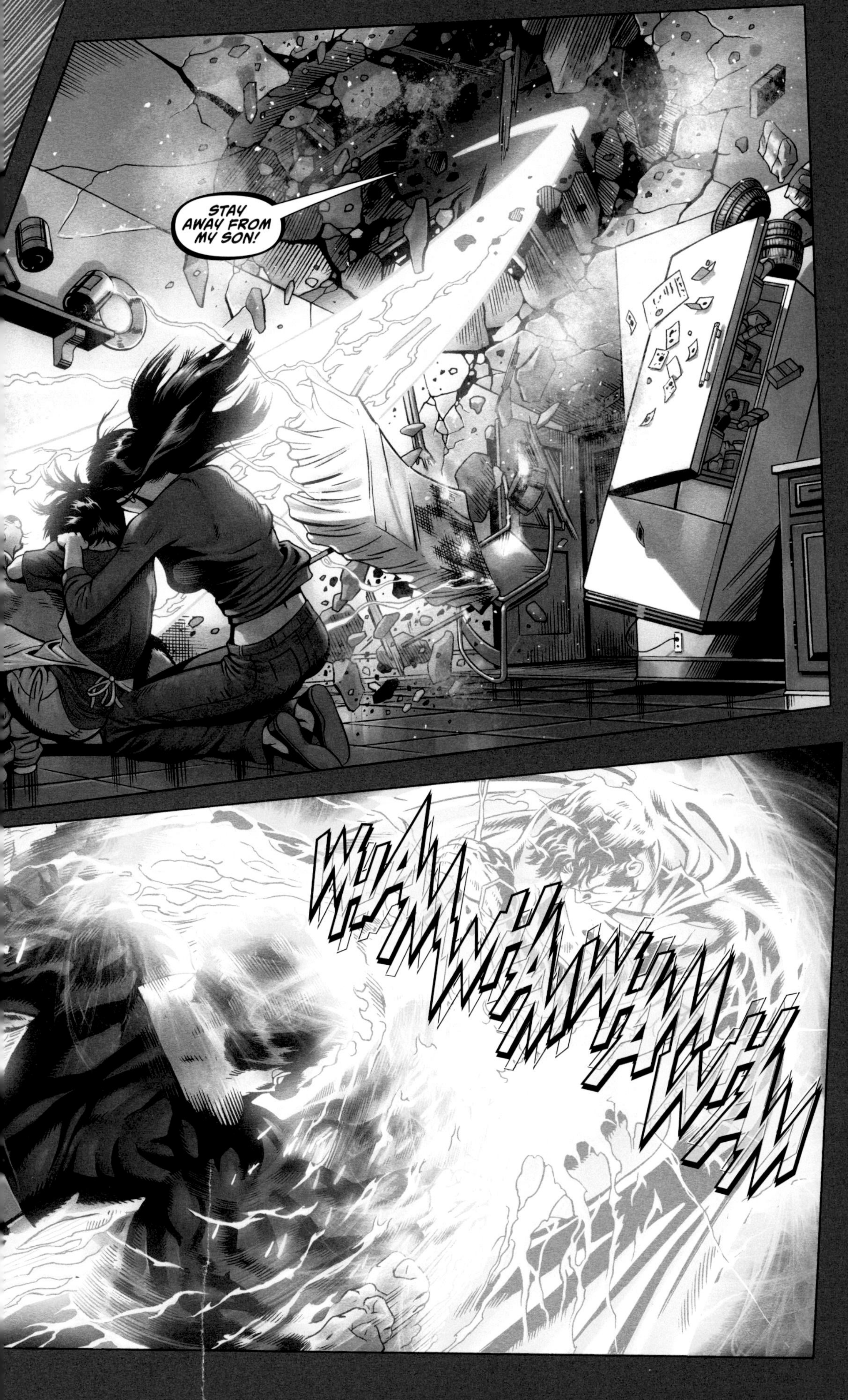
STAY AWAY FROM MY SON!

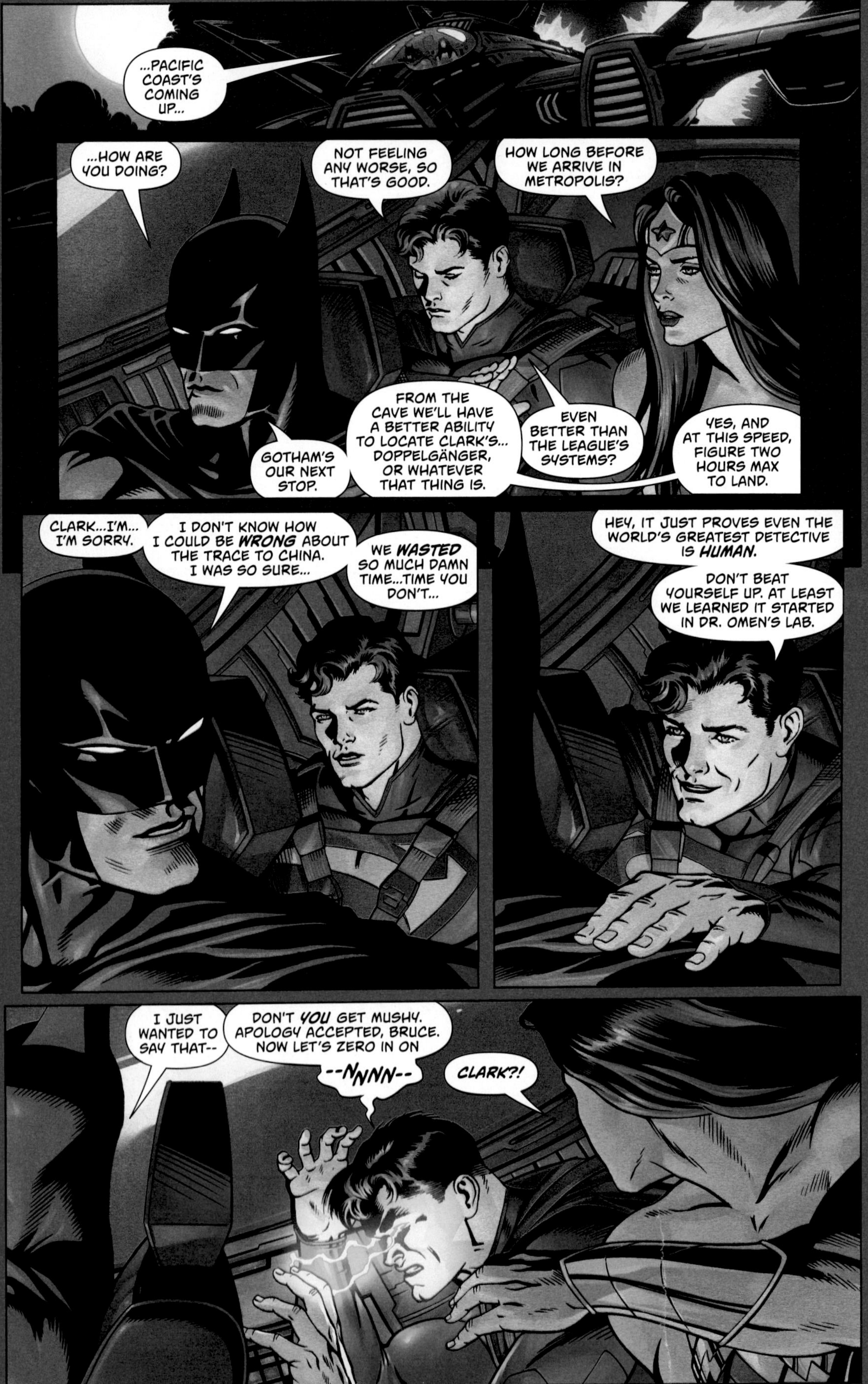
...PACIFIC COAST'S COMING UP...
...HOW ARE YOU DOING?
NOT FEELING ANY WORSE, SO THAT'S GOOD.
HOW LONG BEFORE WE ARRIVE IN METROPOLIS?
YES, AND AT THIS SPEED, FIGURE TWO HOURS MAX TO LAND.
GOTHAM'S OUR NEXT STOP.
FROM THE CAVE WE'LL HAVE A BETTER ABILITY TO LOCATE CLARK'S... DOPPELGÄNGER, OR WHATEVER THAT THING IS.
EVEN BETTER THAN THE LEAGUE'S SYSTEMS?
CLARK...I'M... I'M SORRY.
I DON'T KNOW HOW I COULD BE WRONG ABOUT THE TRACE TO CHINA. I WAS SO SURE...
WE WASTED SO MUCH DAMN TIME...TIME YOU DON'T...
HEY, IT JUST PROVES EVEN THE WORLD'S GREATEST DETECTIVE IS HUMAN.
DON'T BEAT YOURSELF UP. AT LEAST WE LEARNED IT STARTED IN DR. OMEN'S LAB.
I JUST WANTED TO SAY THAT--
DON'T YOU GET MUSHY. APOLOGY ACCEPTED, BRUCE. NOW LET'S ZERO IN ON
--NNNN--
CLARK?!

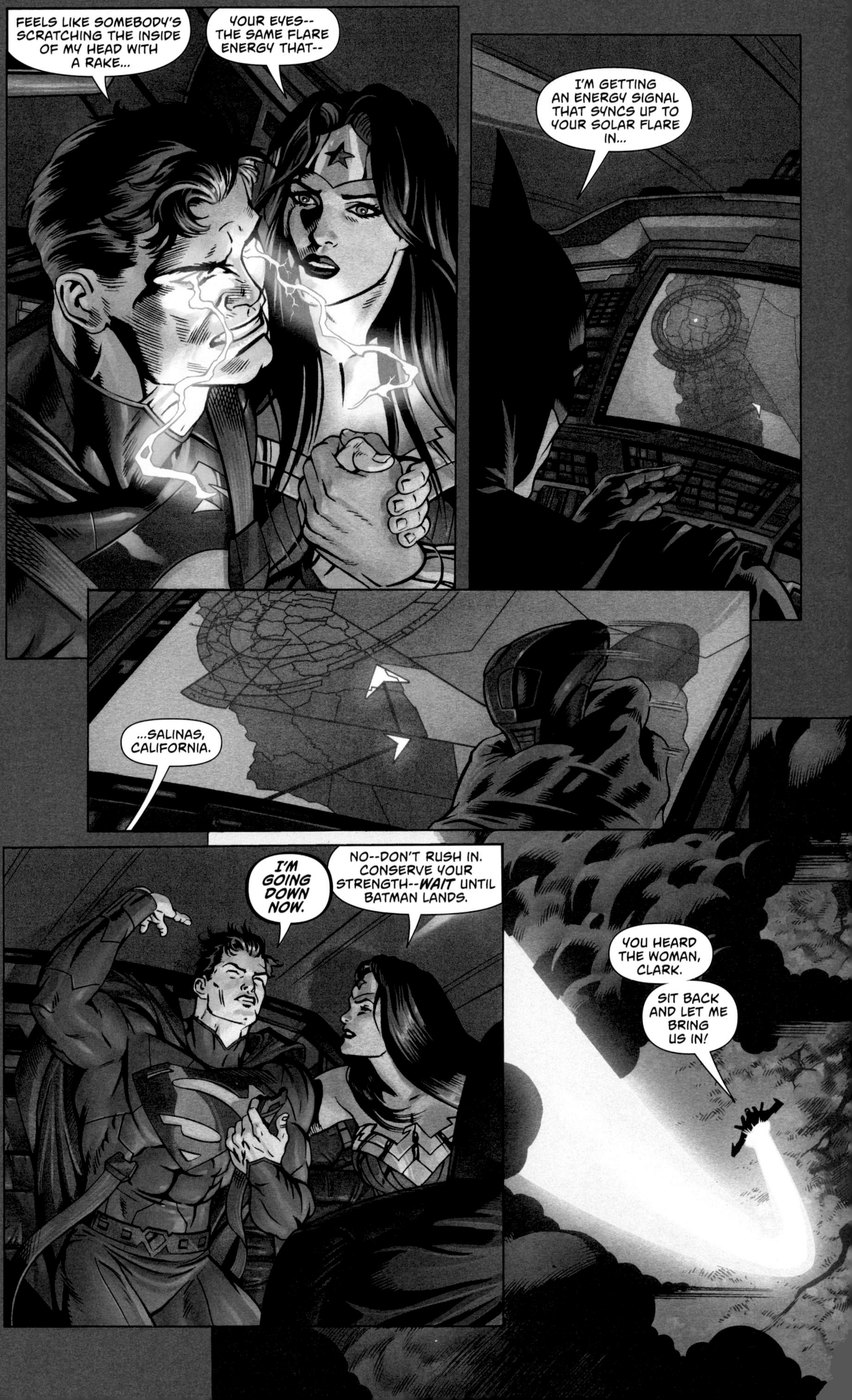
FEELS LIKE SOMEBODY'S SCRATCHING THE INSIDE OF MY HEAD WITH A RAKE...
YOUR EYES-- THE SAME FLARE ENERGY THAT--
I'M GETTING AN ENERGY SIGNAL THAT SYNCS UP TO YOUR SOLAR FLARE IN...
...SALINAS, CALIFORNIA.
I'M GOING DOWN NOW.
NO--DON'T RUSH IN. CONSERVE YOUR STRENGTH--WAIT UNTIL BATMAN LANDS.
YOU HEARD THE WOMAN, CLARK.
SIT BACK AND LET ME BRING US IN!

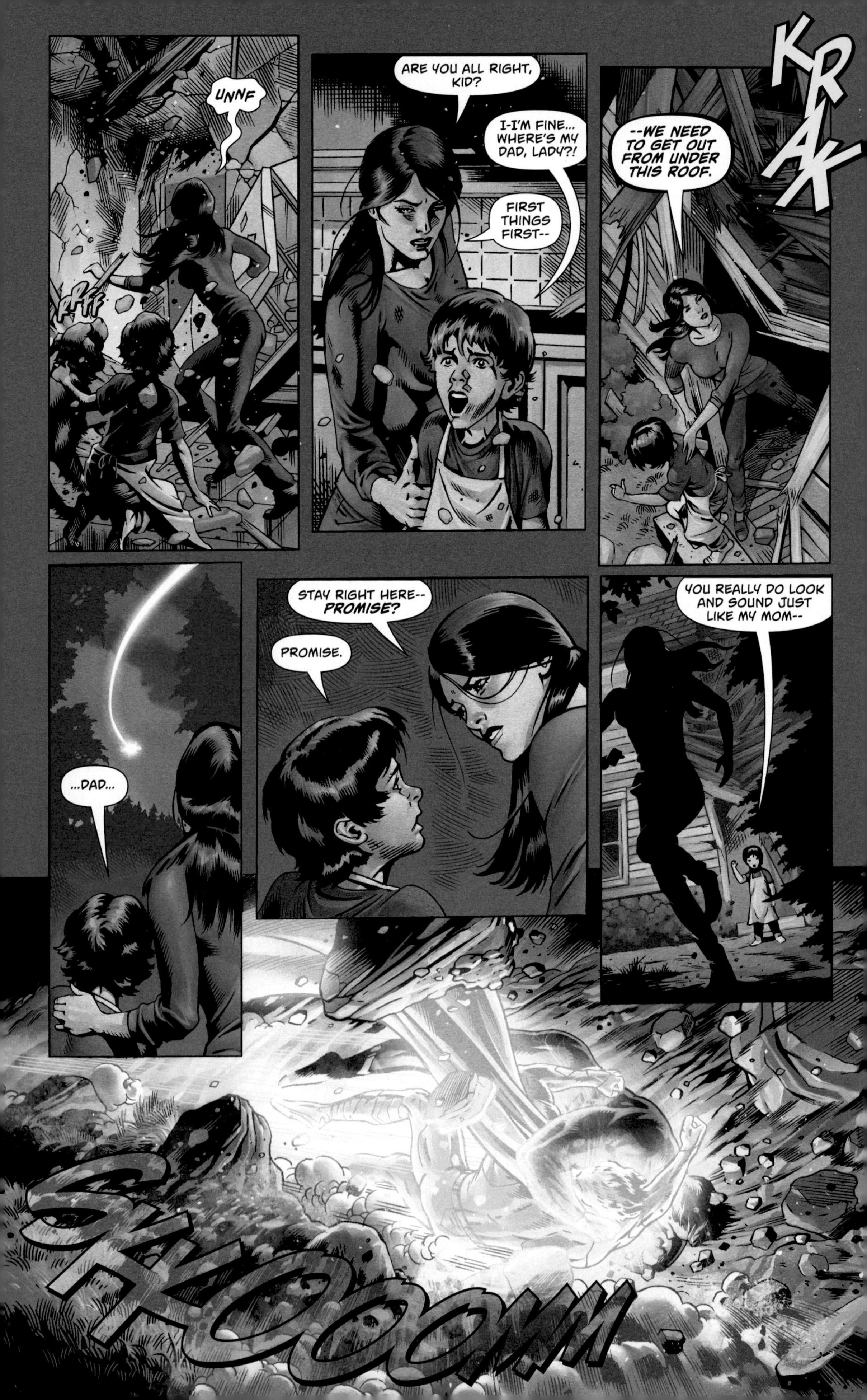
UNNF
pfff
ARE YOU ALL RIGHT, KID?
I-I'M FINE... WHERE'S MY DAD, LADY?!
FIRST THINGS FIRST--
--WE NEED TO GET OUT FROM UNDER THIS ROOF.
KRAK
...DAD...
STAY RIGHT HERE-- PROMISE?
PROMISE.
YOU REALLY DO LOOK AND SOUND JUST LIKE MY MOM--
SHOOOMM

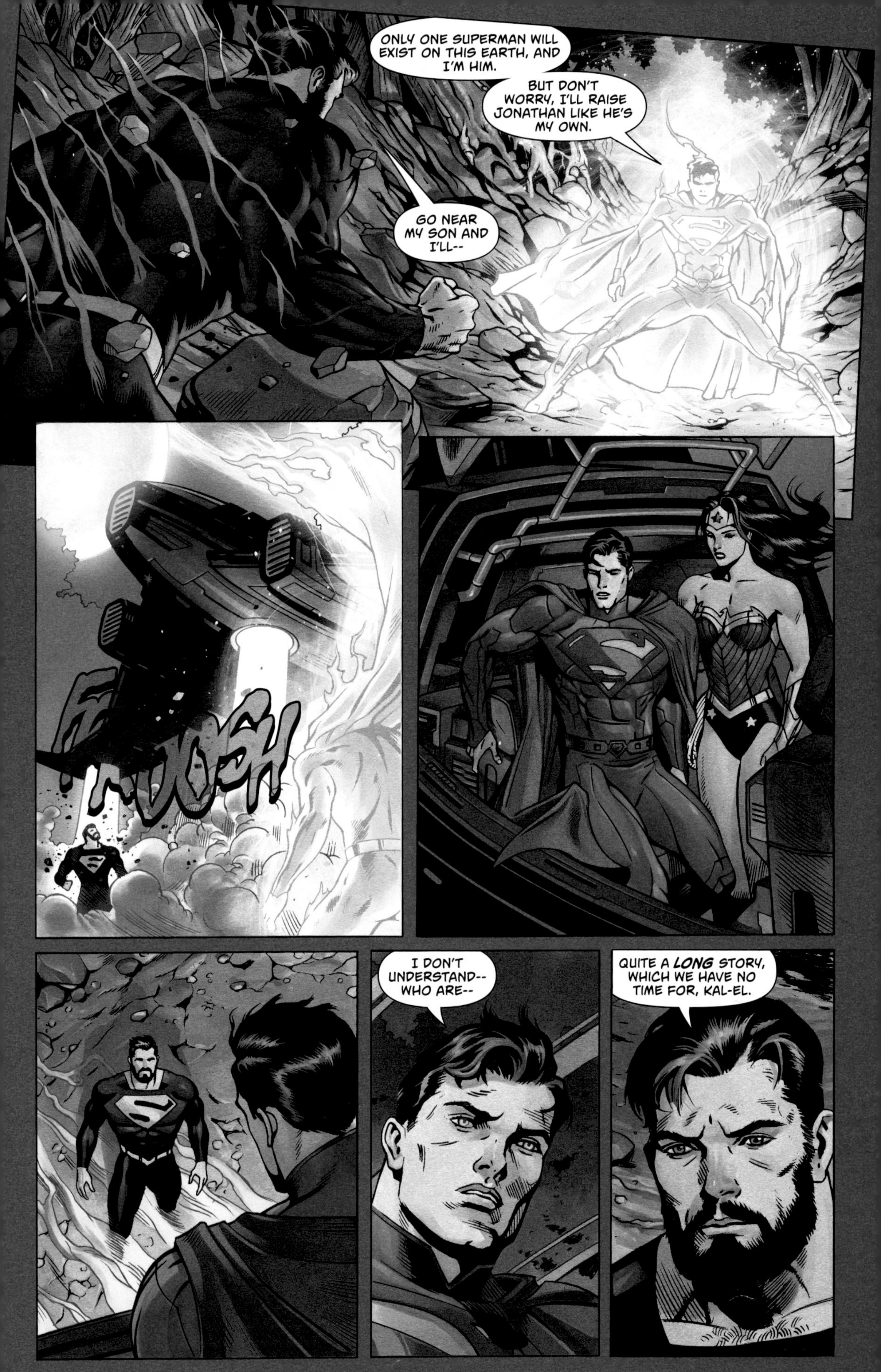
ONLY ONE SUPERMAN WILL EXIST ON THIS EARTH, AND I'M HIM.
BUT DON'T WORRY, I'LL RAISE JONATHAN LIKE HE'S MY OWN.
GO NEAR MY SON AND I'LL--
I DON'T UNDERSTAND-- WHO ARE--
QUITE A *LONG* STORY, WHICH WE HAVE NO TIME FOR, KAL-EL.

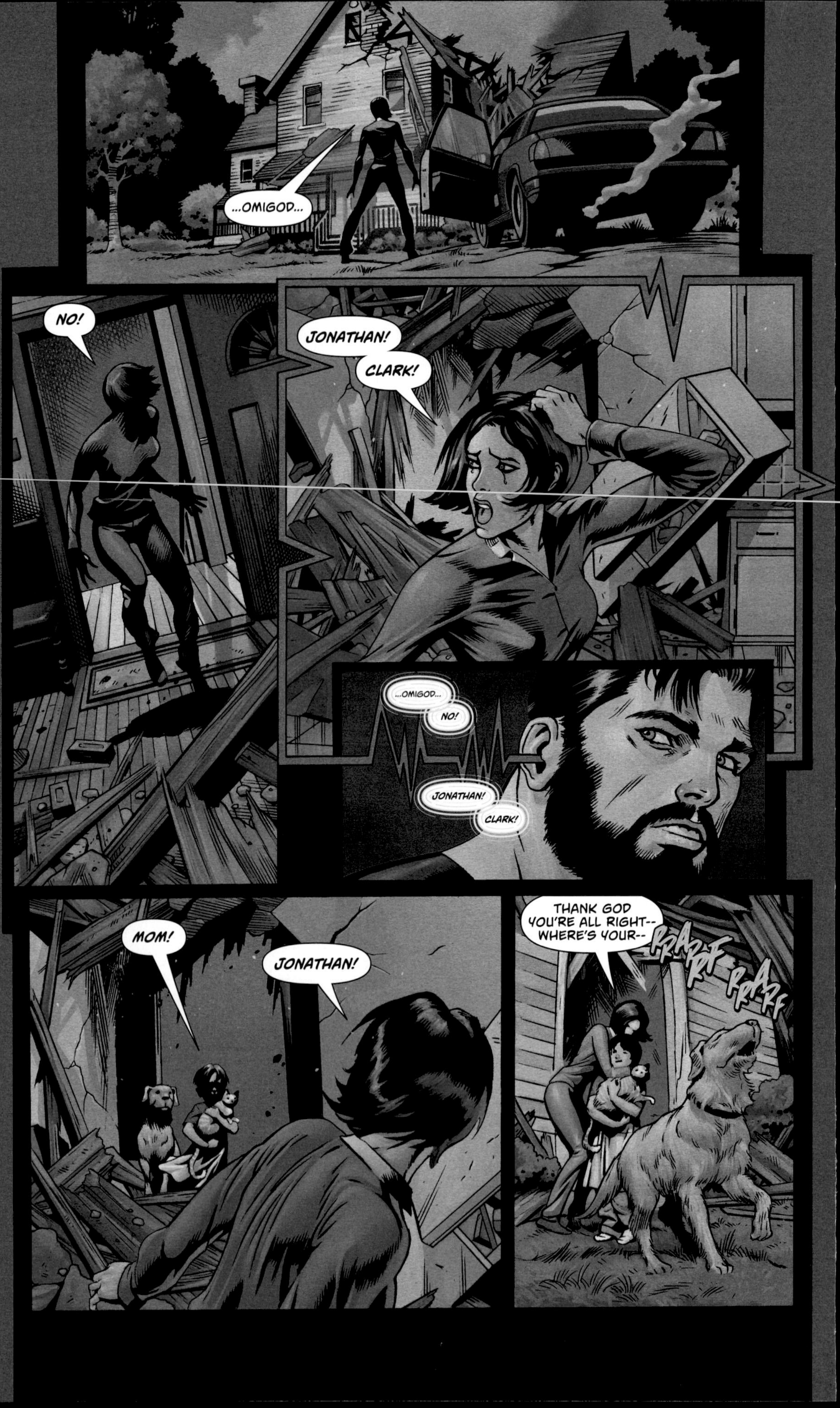
...OMIGOD...
NO!
JONATHAN!
CLARK!
...OMIGOD...
NO!
JONATHAN!
CLARK!
MOM!
JONATHAN!
THANK GOD YOU'RE ALL RIGHT-- WHERE'S YOUR--
RRARFF RRARFF

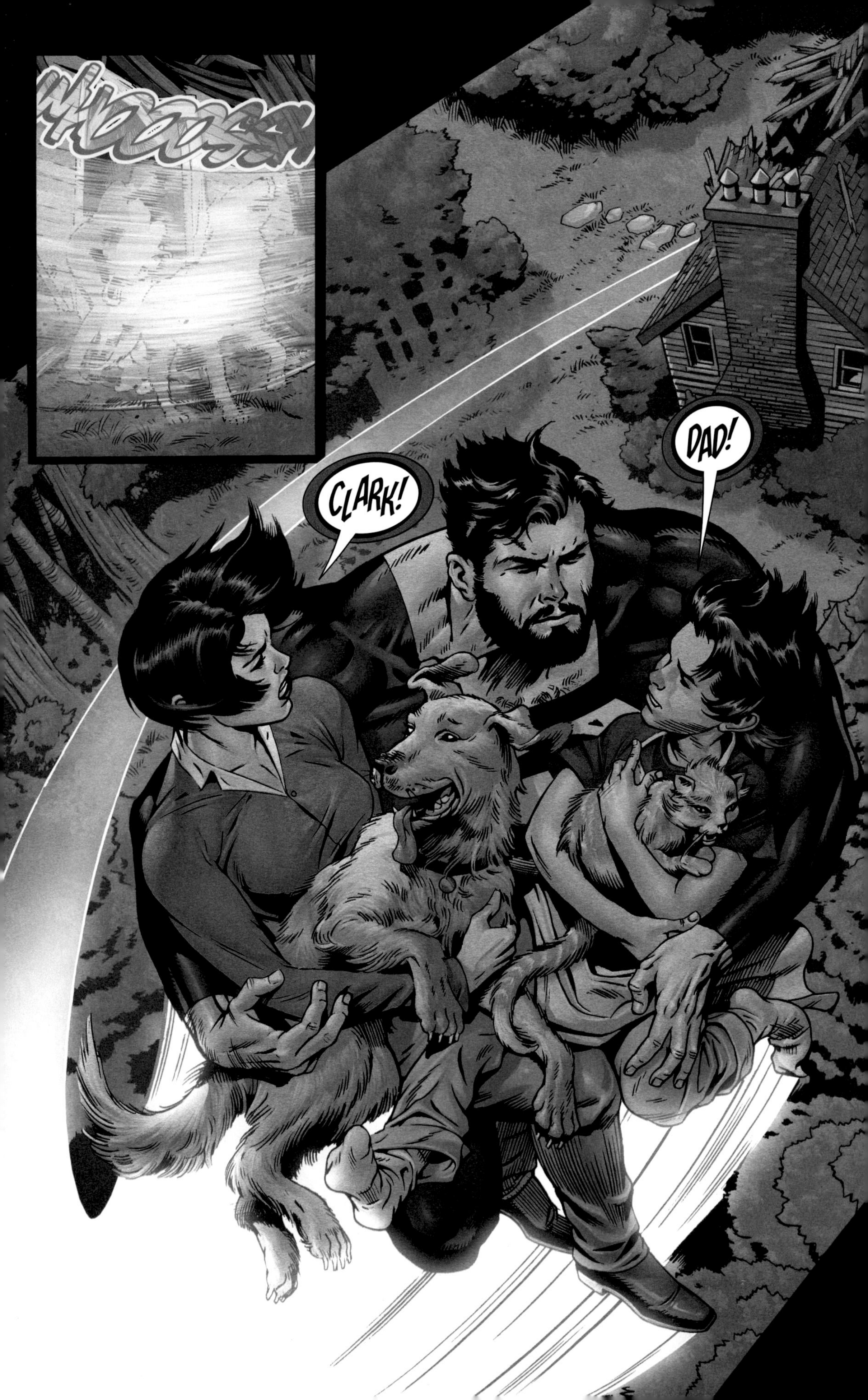
CLARK!
DAD!

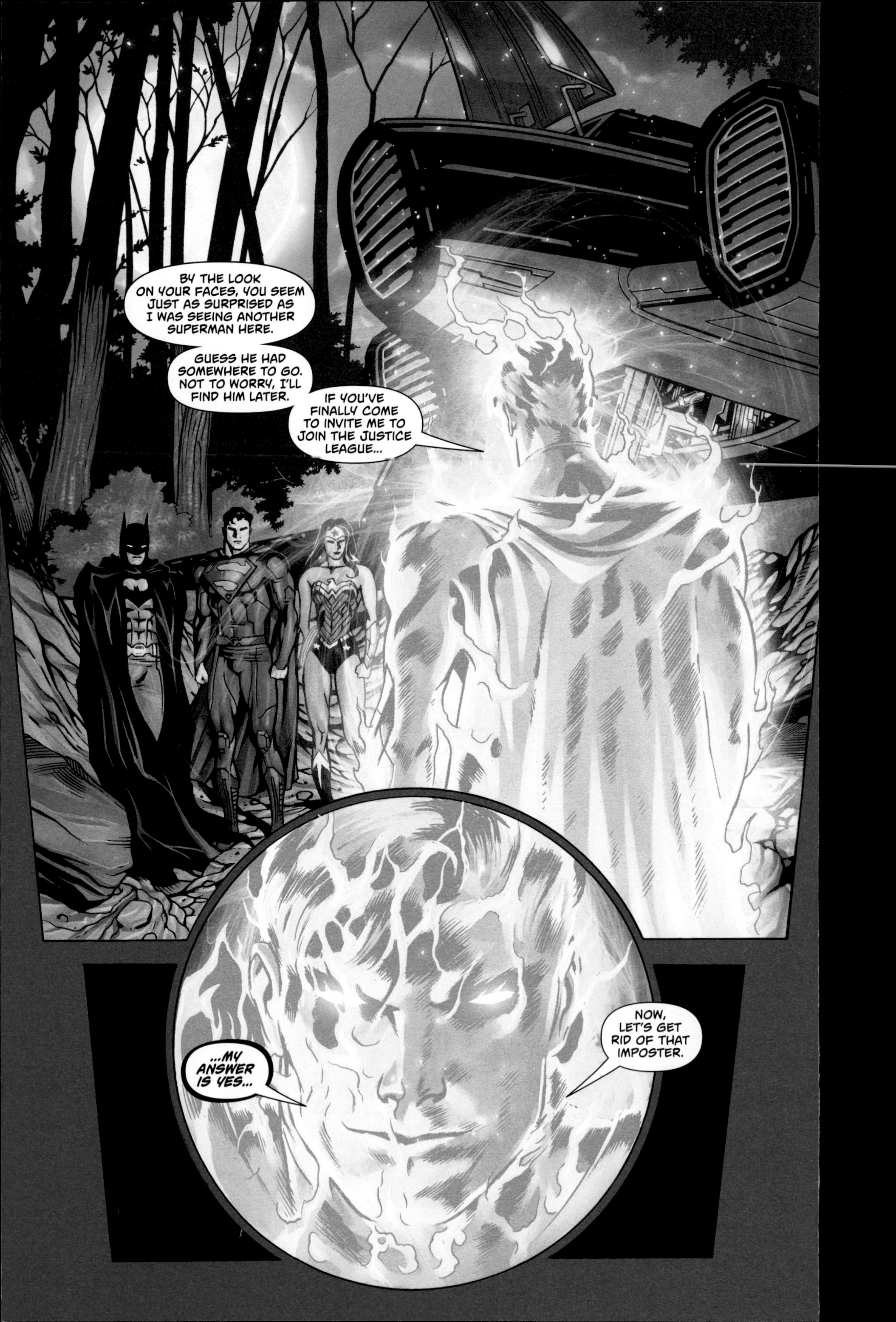
BY THE LOOK ON YOUR FACES, YOU SEEM JUST AS SURPRISED AS I WAS SEEING ANOTHER SUPERMAN HERE.
GUESS HE HAD SOMEWHERE TO GO. NOT TO WORRY, I'LL FIND HIM LATER.
IF YOU'VE FINALLY COME TO INVITE ME TO JOIN THE JUSTICE LEAGUE...
...MY ANSWER IS YES...
NOW, LET'S GET RID OF THAT IMPOSTER.

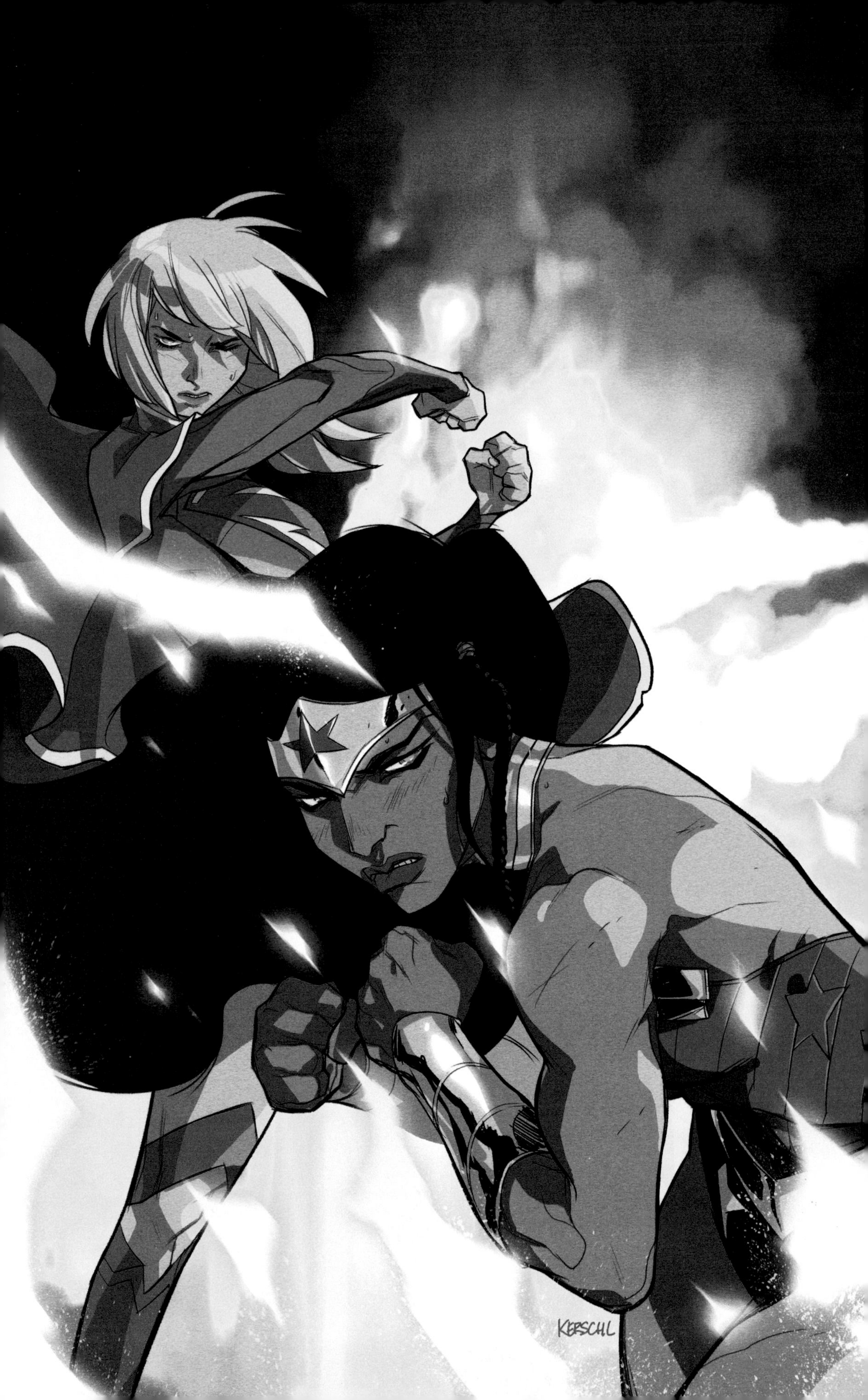
KERSCHL

THE FINAL DAYS OF SUPERMAN PART 7: FIRE LINE

PETER J. TOMASI writer JORGE JIMÉNEZ artist ALEJANDRO SÁNCHEZ colorist ROB LEIGH letterer KARL KERSCHL cover

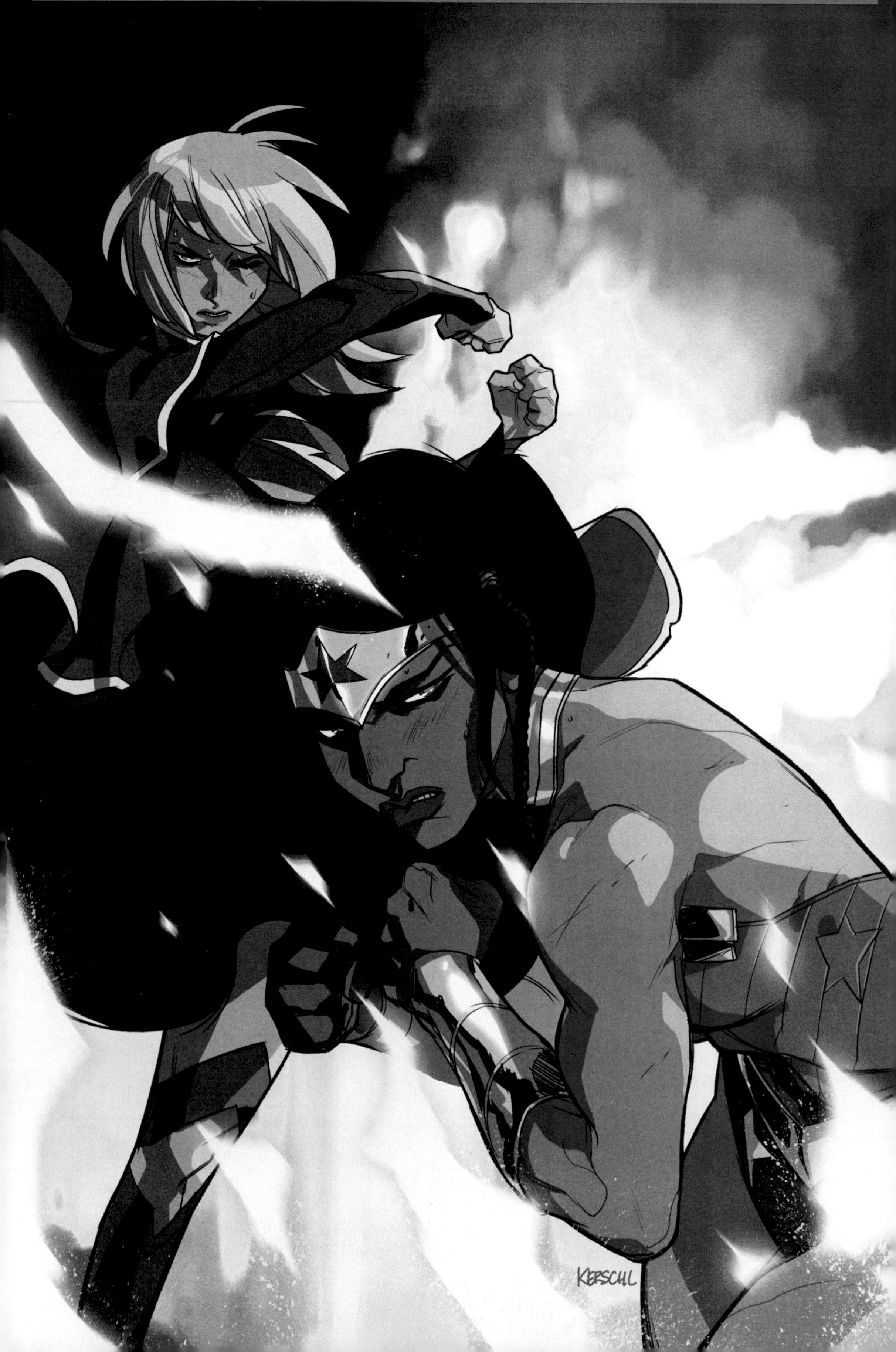
KERSCHL

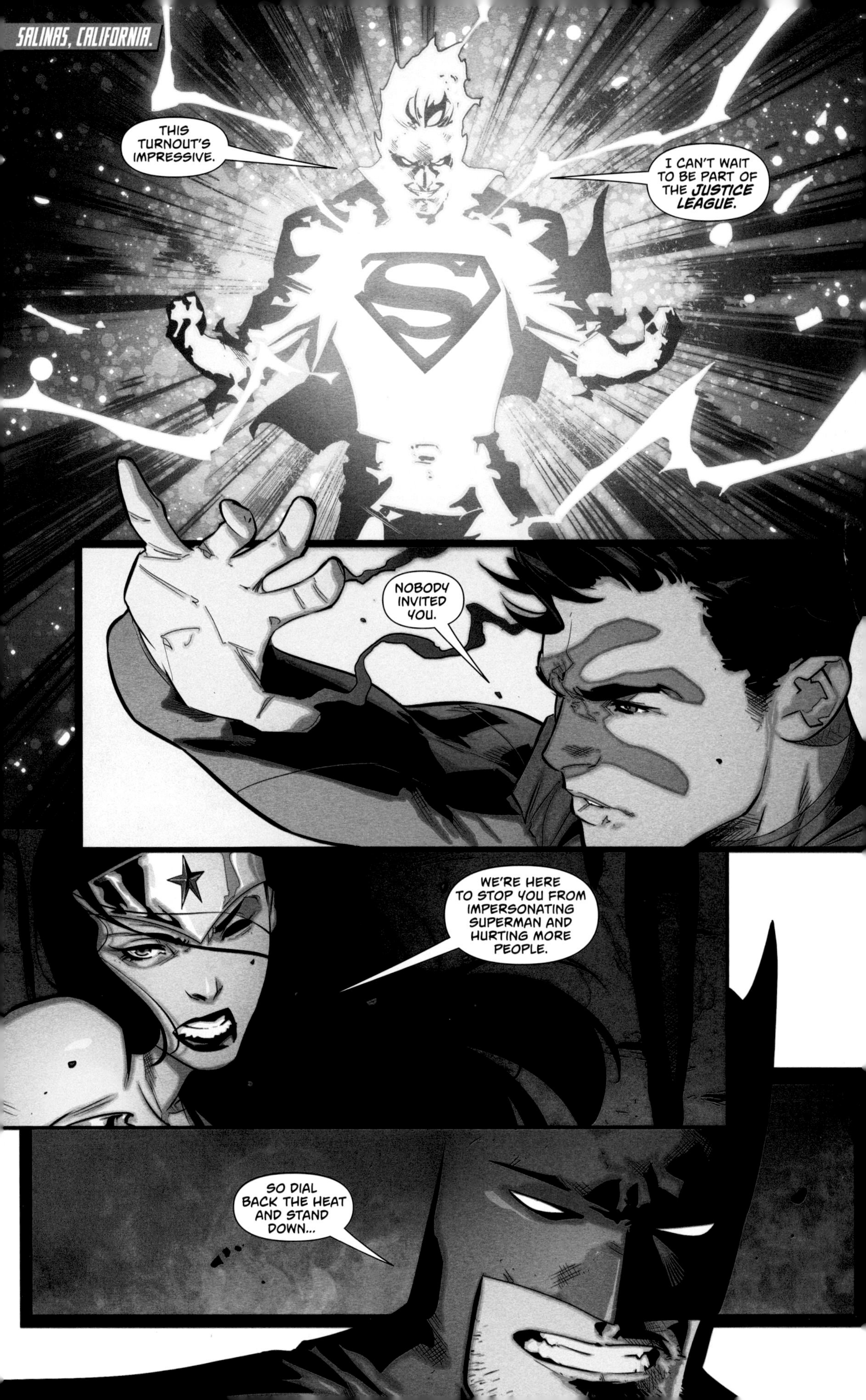
SALINAS, CALIFORNIA.
THIS TURNOUT'S IMPRESSIVE.
I CAN'T WAIT TO BE PART OF THE JUSTICE LEAGUE.
NOBODY INVITED YOU.
WE'RE HERE TO STOP YOU FROM IMPERSONATING SUPERMAN AND HURTING MORE PEOPLE.
SO DIAL BACK THE HEAT AND STAND DOWN...

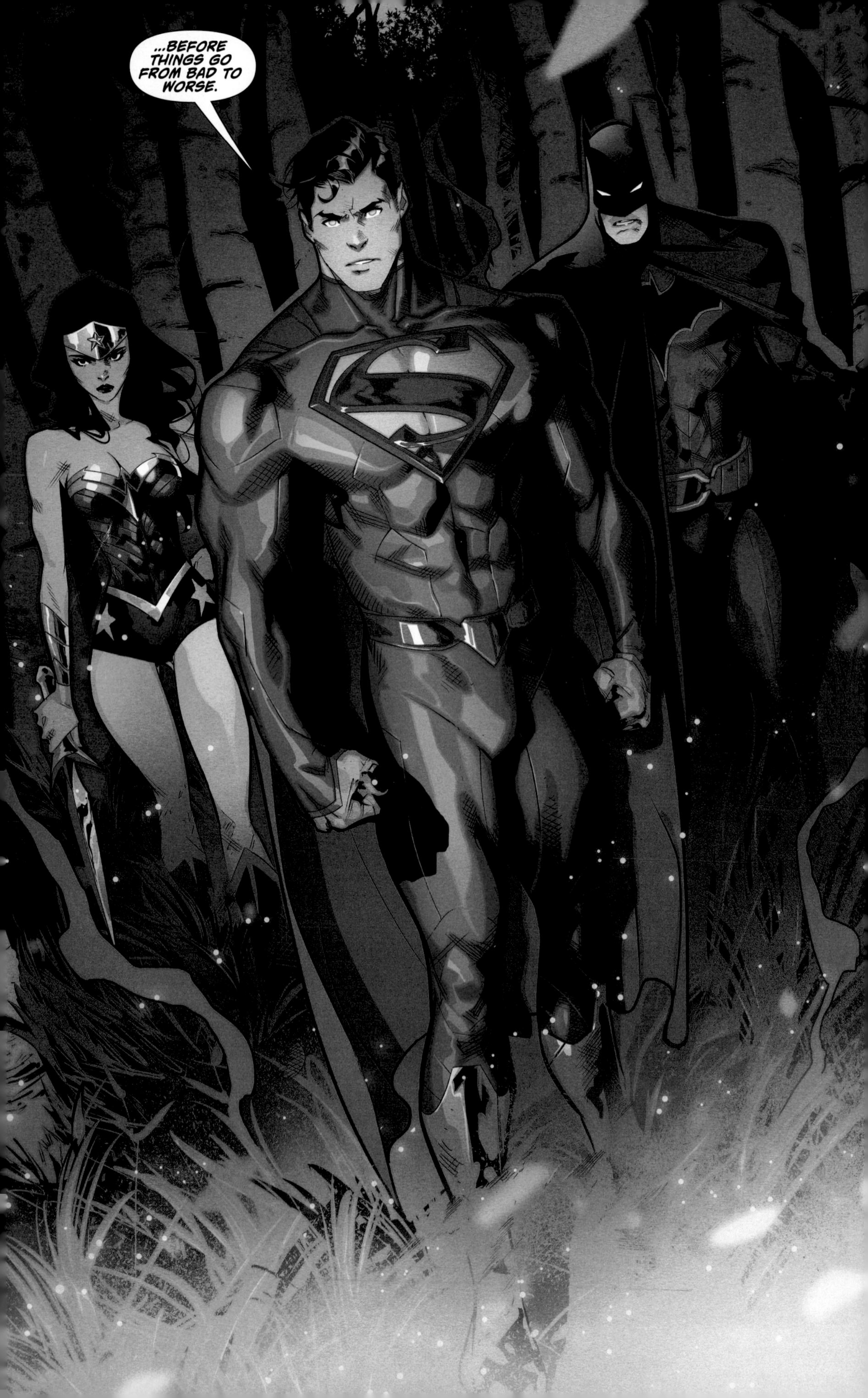
...BEFORE THINGS GO FROM BAD TO WORSE.

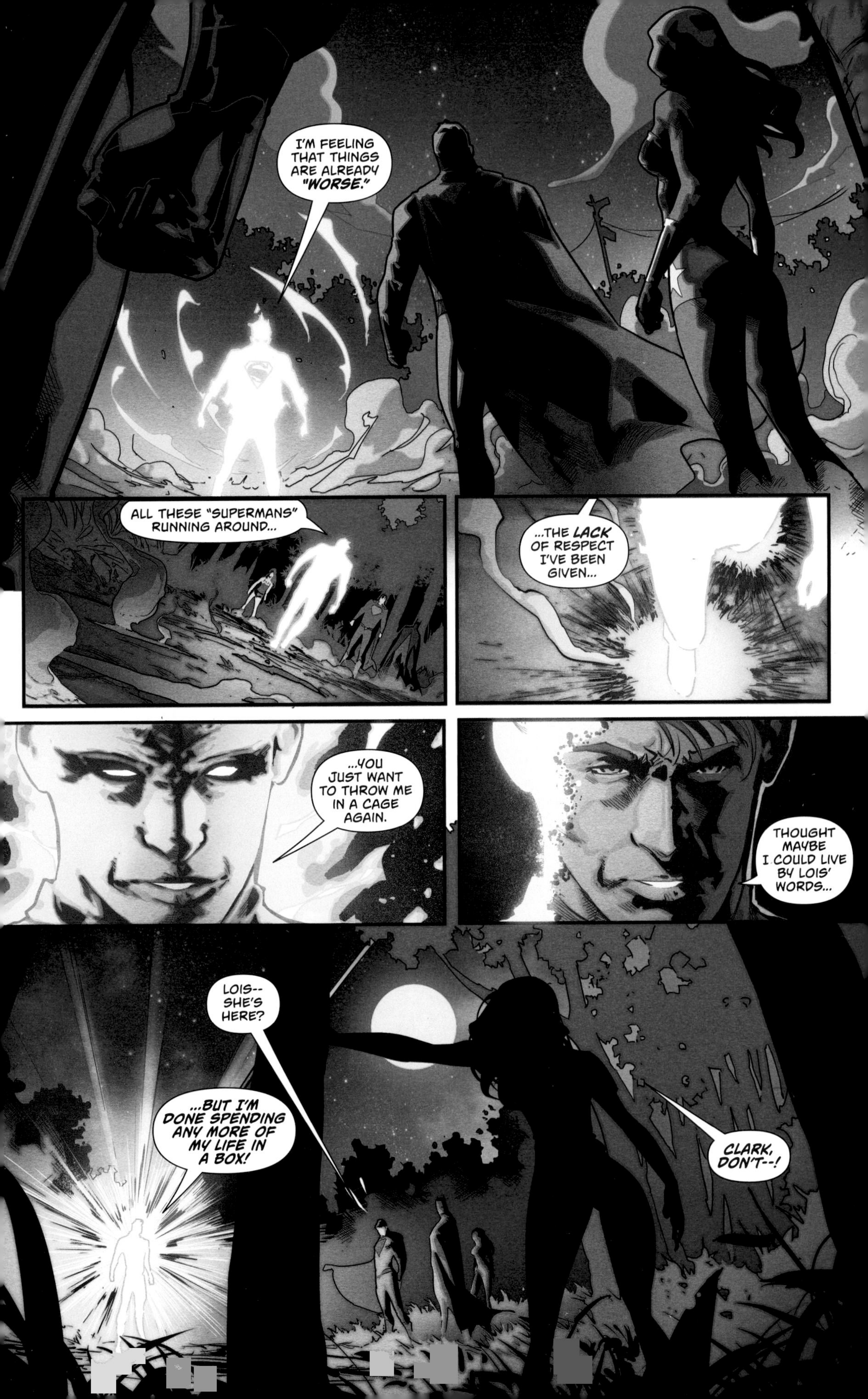
I'M FEELING THAT THINGS ARE ALREADY "WORSE."
ALL THESE "SUPERMANS" RUNNING AROUND...
...THE LACK OF RESPECT I'VE BEEN GIVEN...
...YOU JUST WANT TO THROW ME IN A CAGE AGAIN.
THOUGHT MAYBE I COULD LIVE BY LOIS' WORDS...
LOIS--SHE'S HERE?
...BUT I'M DONE SPENDING ANY MORE OF MY LIFE IN A BOX!
CLARK, DON'T--!

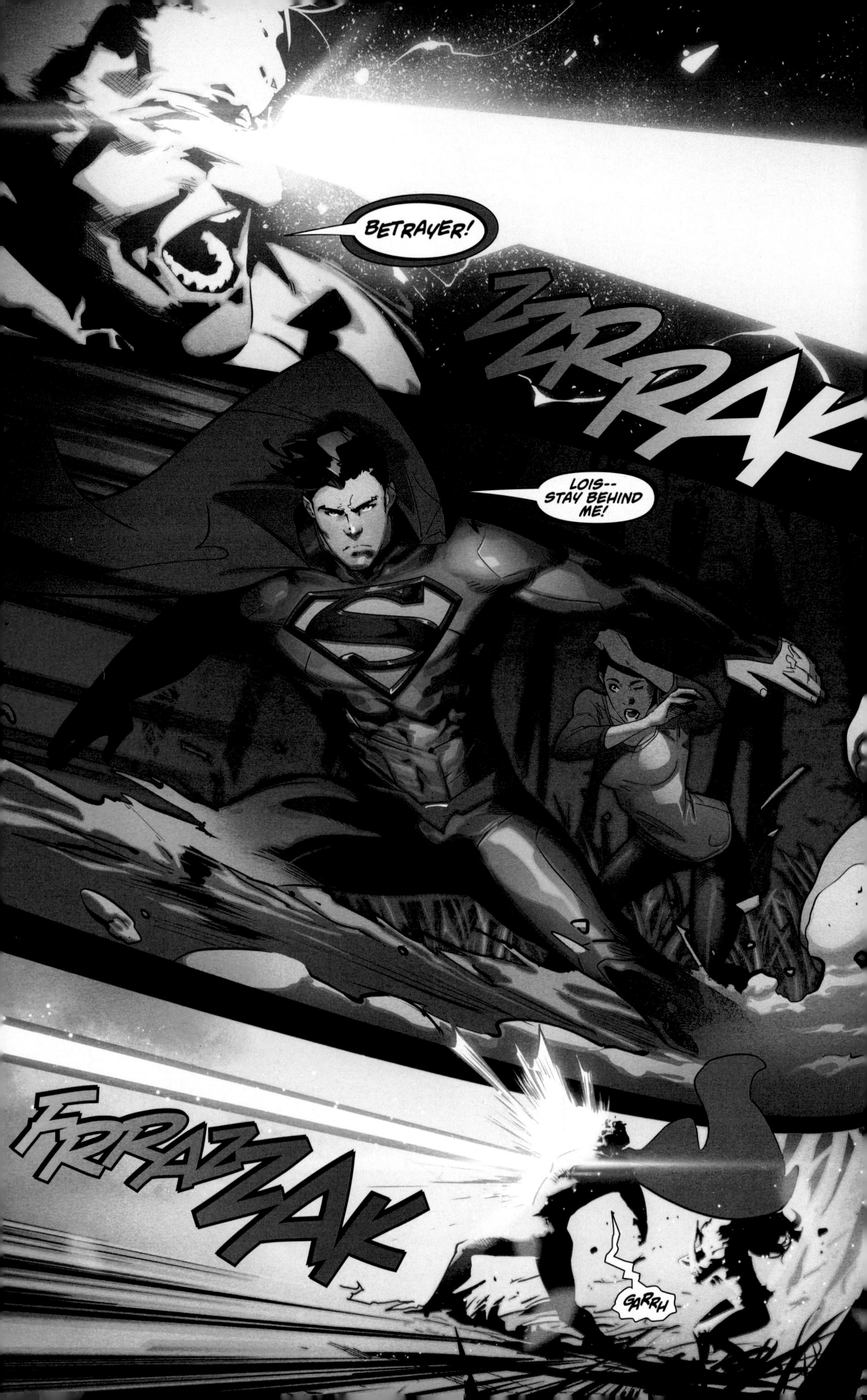
BETRAYER!
ZZRRAK
LOIS-- STAY BEHIND ME!
FFRRAZZAK
GARRH

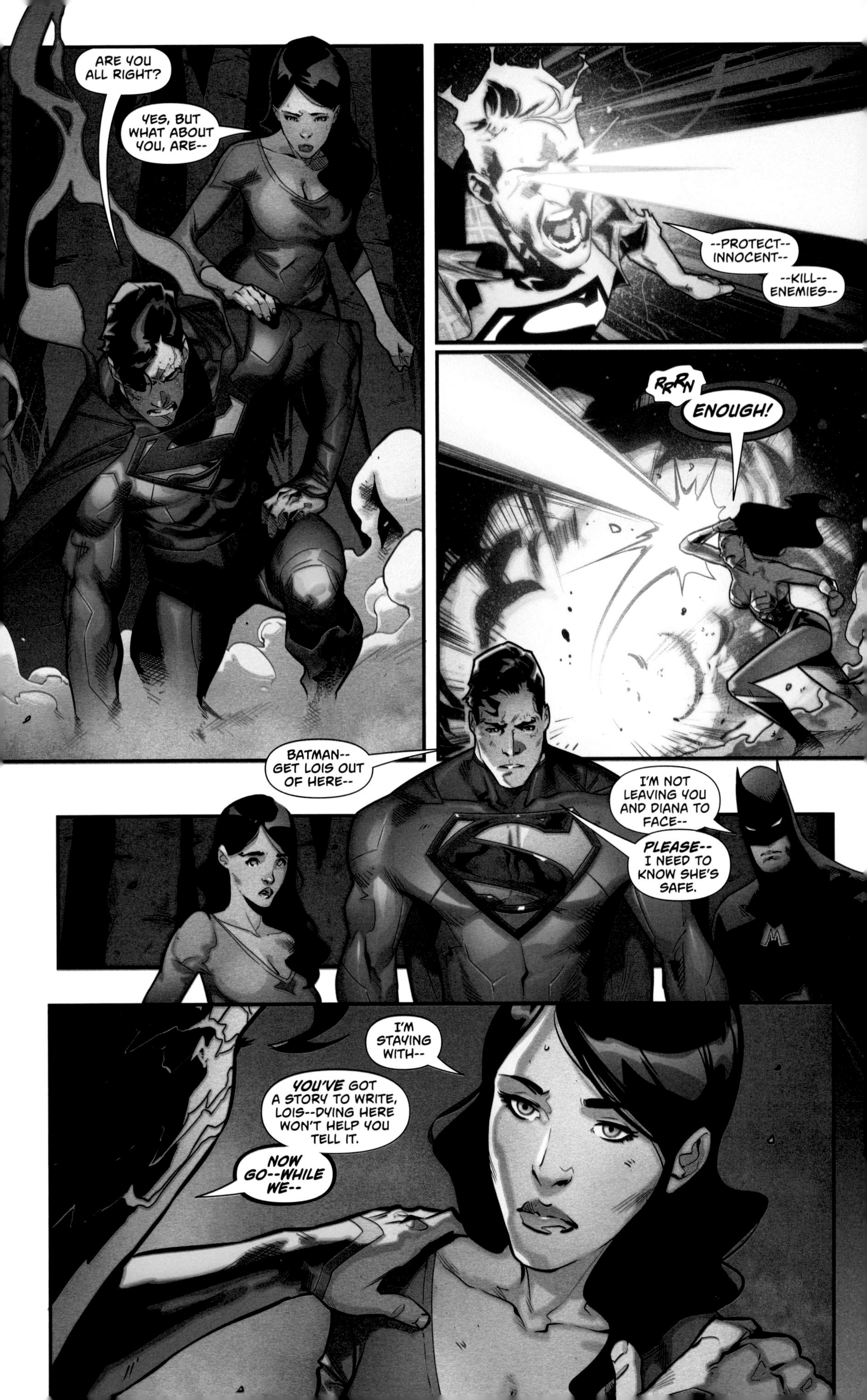
ARE YOU ALL RIGHT?
YES, BUT WHAT ABOUT YOU, ARE--
--PROTECT-- INNOCENT--
--KILL-- ENEMIES--
RRRN
ENOUGH!
BATMAN-- GET LOIS OUT OF HERE--
I'M NOT LEAVING YOU AND DIANA TO FACE--
PLEASE-- I NEED TO KNOW SHE'S SAFE.
I'M STAYING WITH--
YOU'VE GOT A STORY TO WRITE, LOIS--DYING HERE WON'T HELP YOU TELL IT.
NOW GO--WHILE WE--

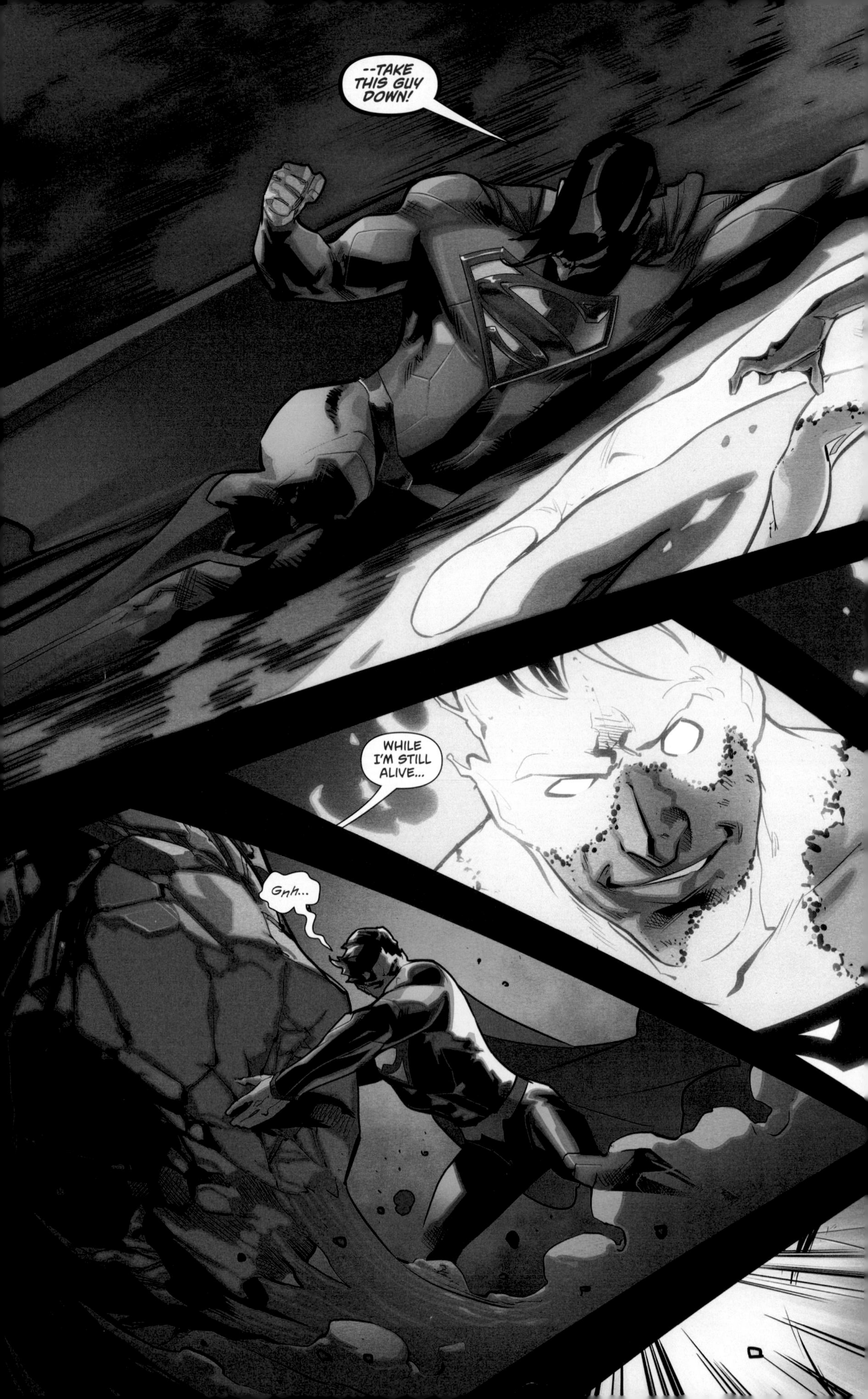
--TAKE THIS GUY DOWN!
WHILE I'M STILL ALIVE...
Gnh...

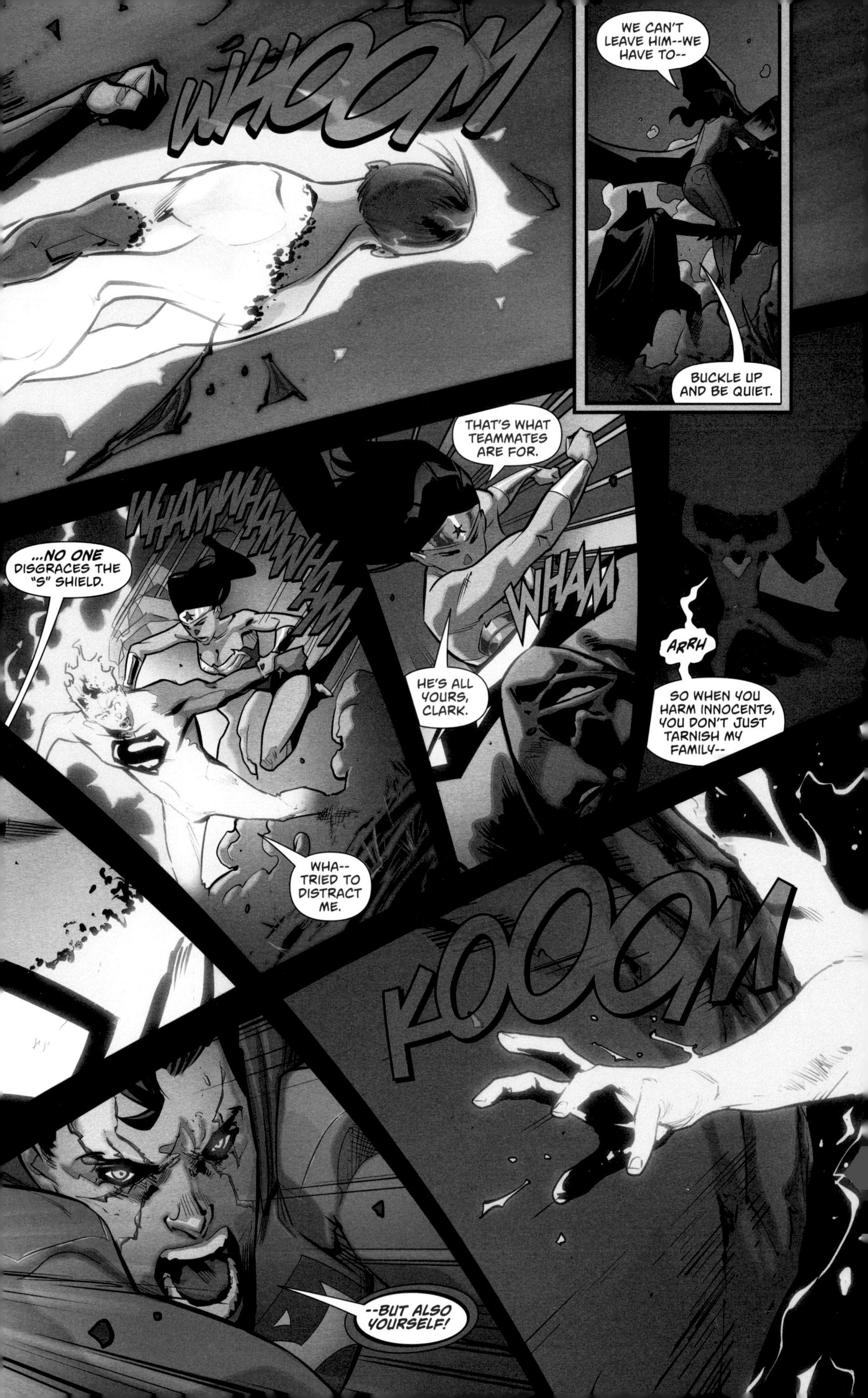
WHOOM
WE CAN'T LEAVE HIM--WE HAVE TO--
BUCKLE UP AND BE QUIET.
WHAMWHAMWHAM
...NO ONE DISGRACES THE "S" SHIELD.
WHA-- TRIED TO DISTRACT ME.
THAT'S WHAT TEAMMATES ARE FOR.
WHAM
HE'S ALL YOURS, CLARK.
ARRH
SO WHEN YOU HARM INNOCENTS, YOU DON'T JUST TARNISH MY FAMILY--
KOOOOM
--BUT ALSO YOURSELF!

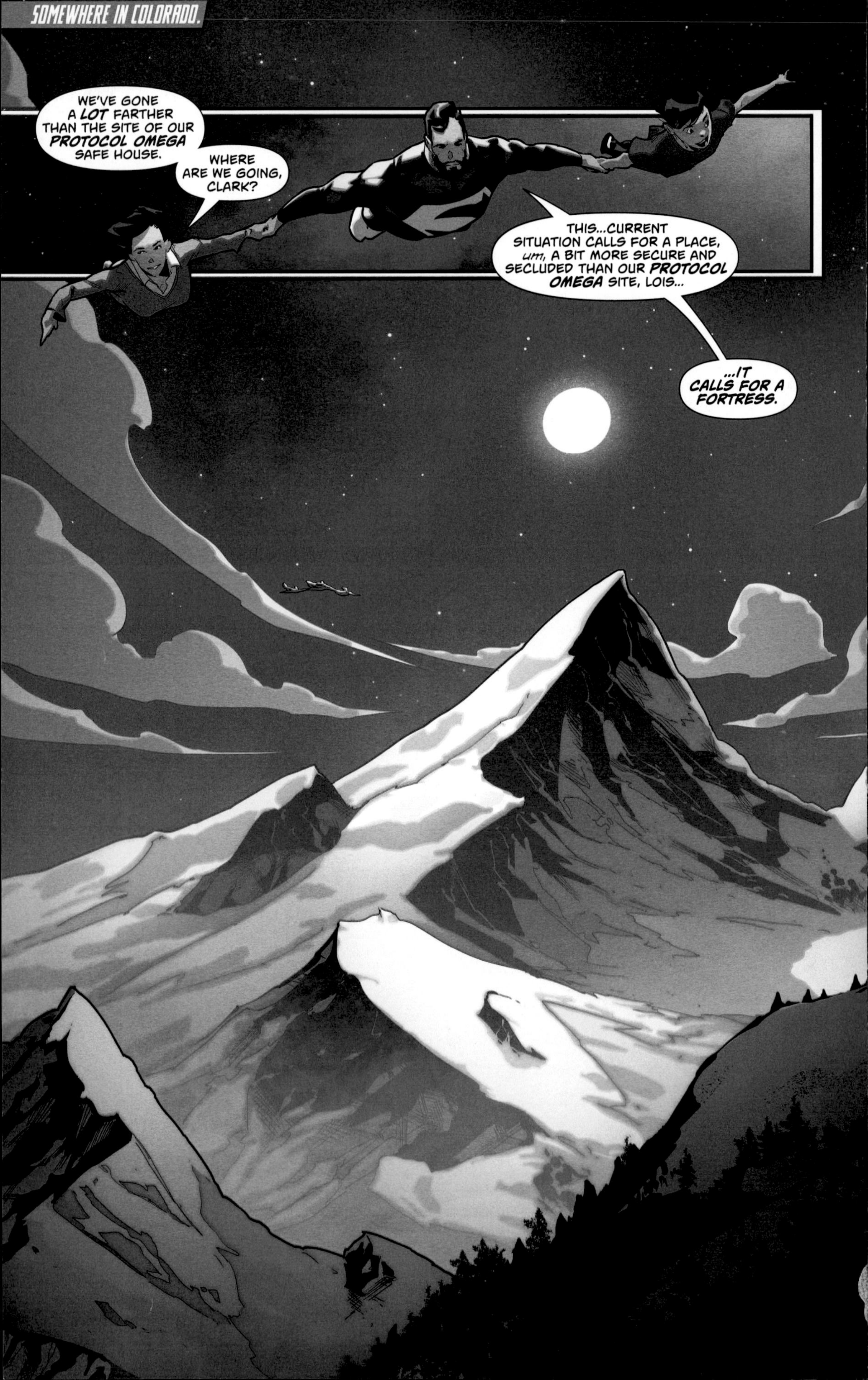
SOMEWHERE IN COLORADO.
WE'VE GONE A LOT FARTHER THAN THE SITE OF OUR PROTOCOL OMEGA SAFE HOUSE.
WHERE ARE WE GOING, CLARK?
THIS...CURRENT SITUATION CALLS FOR A PLACE, UM, A BIT MORE SECURE AND SECLUDED THAN OUR PROTOCOL OMEGA SITE, LOIS...
...IT CALLS FOR A FORTRESS.

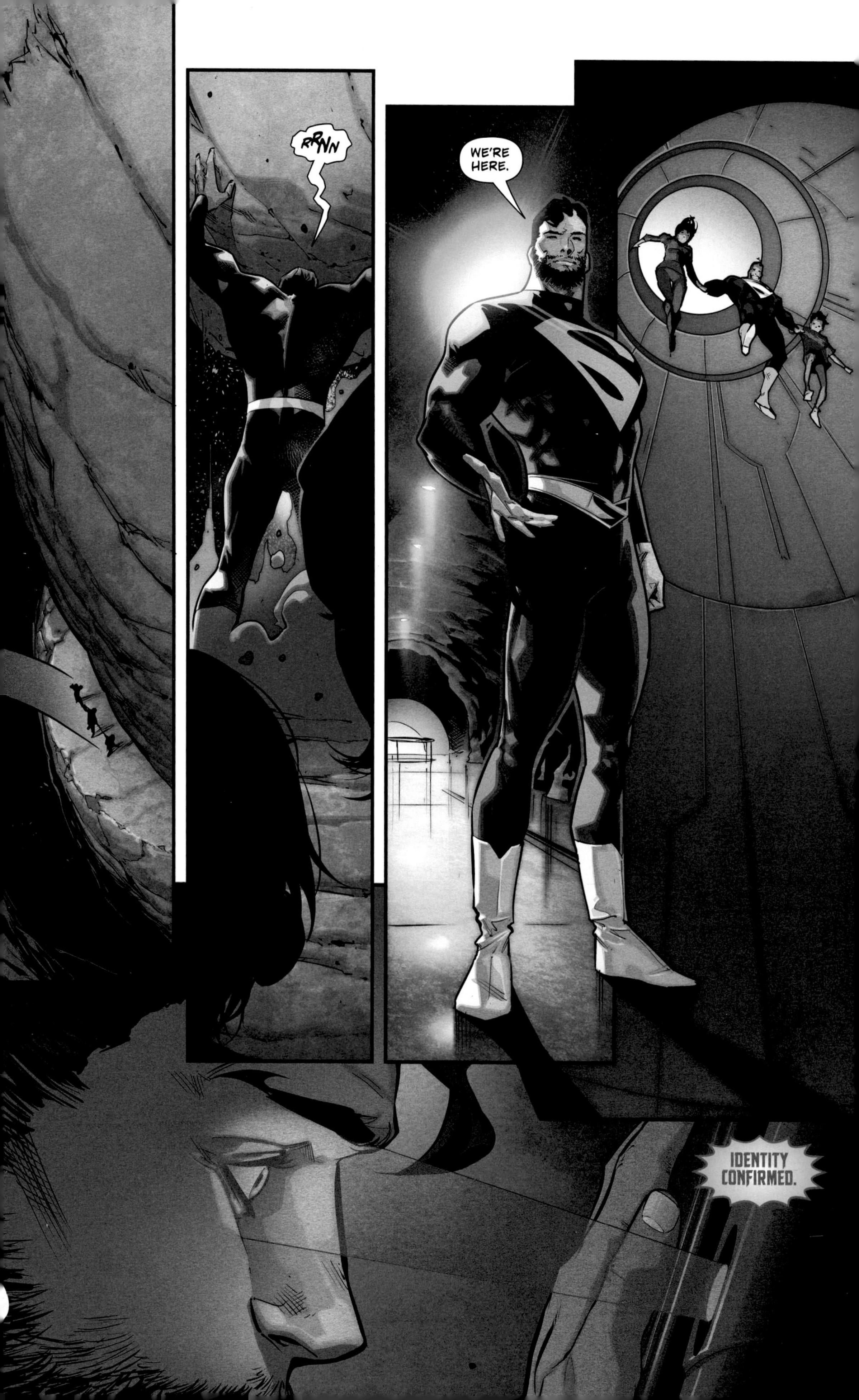
RRNN
WE'RE HERE.
IDENTITY CONFIRMED.

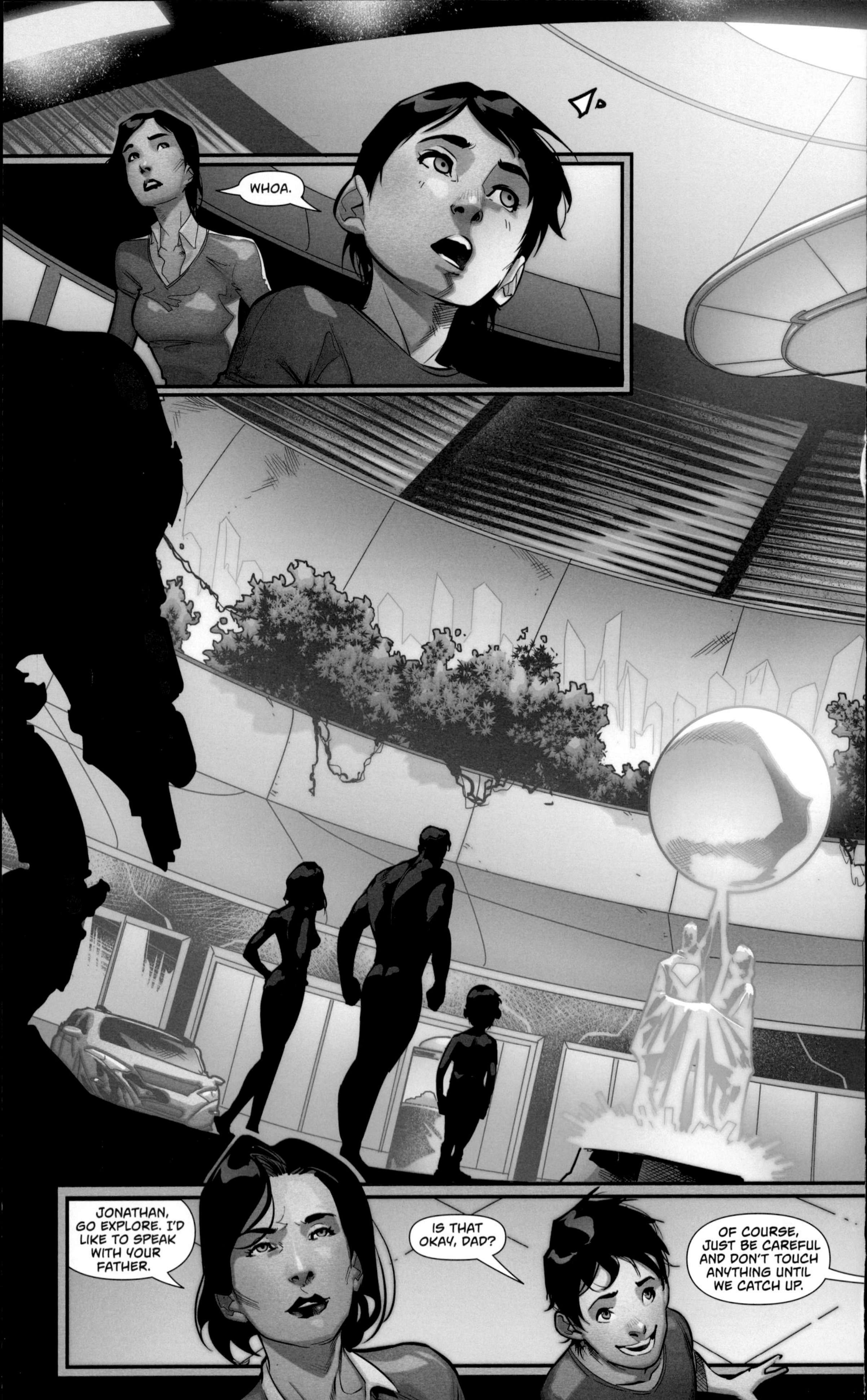
WHOA.
JONATHAN, GO EXPLORE. I'D LIKE TO SPEAK WITH YOUR FATHER.
IS THAT OKAY, DAD?
OF COURSE, JUST BE CAREFUL AND DON'T TOUCH ANYTHING UNTIL WE CATCH UP.

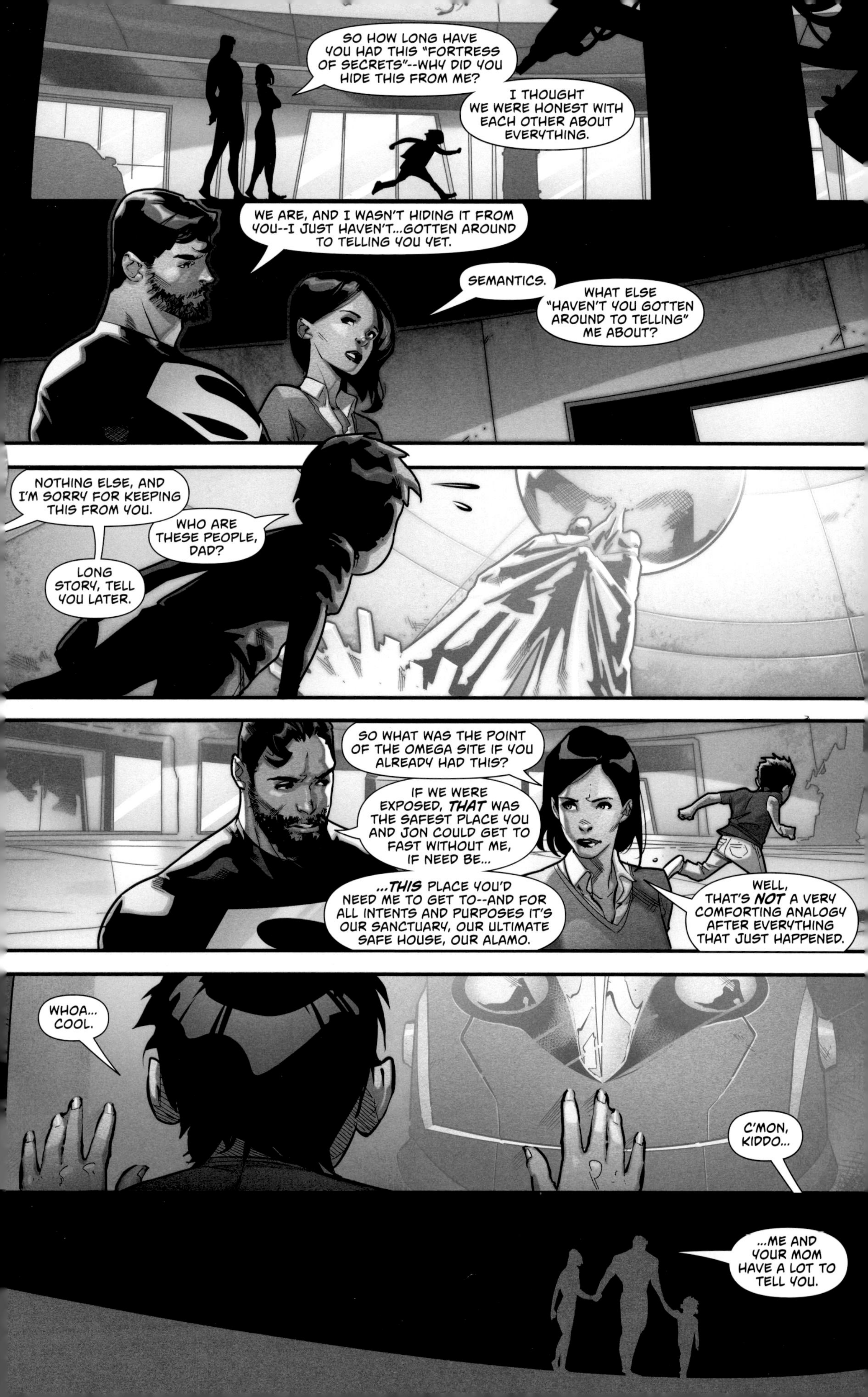
SO HOW LONG HAVE YOU HAD THIS "FORTRESS OF SECRETS"--WHY DID YOU HIDE THIS FROM ME?
I THOUGHT WE WERE HONEST WITH EACH OTHER ABOUT EVERYTHING.
WE ARE, AND I WASN'T HIDING IT FROM YOU--I JUST HAVEN'T...GOTTEN AROUND TO TELLING YOU YET.
SEMANTICS.
WHAT ELSE "HAVEN'T YOU GOTTEN AROUND TO TELLING" ME ABOUT?
NOTHING ELSE, AND I'M SORRY FOR KEEPING THIS FROM YOU.
WHO ARE THESE PEOPLE, DAD?
LONG STORY, TELL YOU LATER.
SO WHAT WAS THE POINT OF THE OMEGA SITE IF YOU ALREADY HAD THIS?
IF WE WERE EXPOSED, THAT WAS THE SAFEST PLACE YOU AND JON COULD GET TO FAST WITHOUT ME, IF NEED BE...
...THIS PLACE YOU'D NEED ME TO GET TO--AND FOR ALL INTENTS AND PURPOSES IT'S OUR SANCTUARY, OUR ULTIMATE SAFE HOUSE, OUR ALAMO.
WELL, THAT'S NOT A VERY COMFORTING ANALOGY AFTER EVERYTHING THAT JUST HAPPENED.
WHOA... COOL.
C'MON, KIDDO...
...ME AND YOUR MOM HAVE A LOT TO TELL YOU.

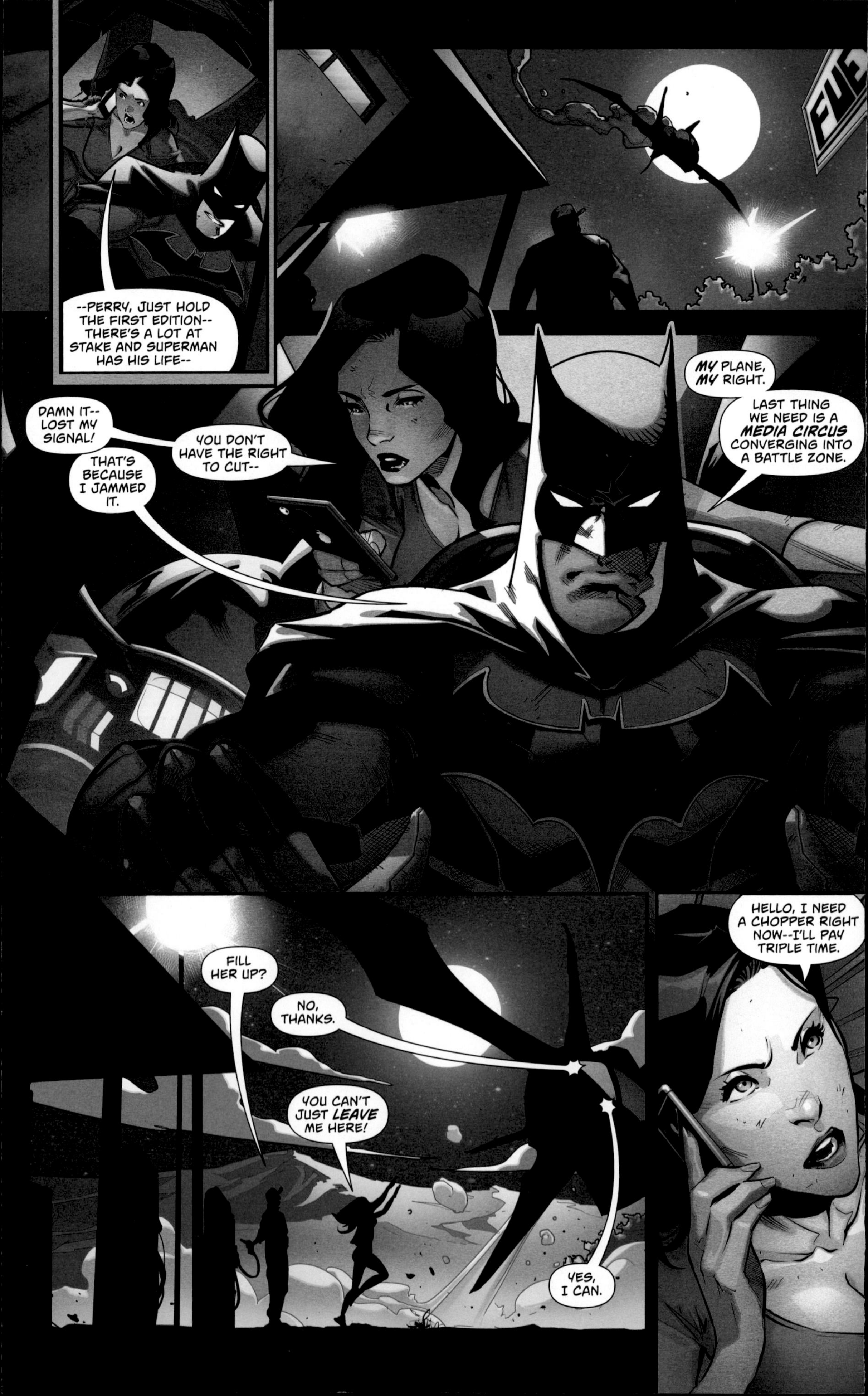
--PERRY, JUST HOLD THE FIRST EDITION-- THERE'S A LOT AT STAKE AND SUPERMAN HAS HIS LIFE--
DAMN IT-- LOST MY SIGNAL!
YOU DON'T HAVE THE RIGHT TO CUT--
THAT'S BECAUSE I JAMMED IT.
MY PLANE, MY RIGHT.
LAST THING WE NEED IS A MEDIA CIRCUS CONVERGING INTO A BATTLE ZONE.
FILL HER UP?
NO, THANKS.
YOU CAN'T JUST LEAVE ME HERE!
YES, I CAN.
HELLO, I NEED A CHOPPER RIGHT NOW--I'LL PAY TRIPLE TIME.

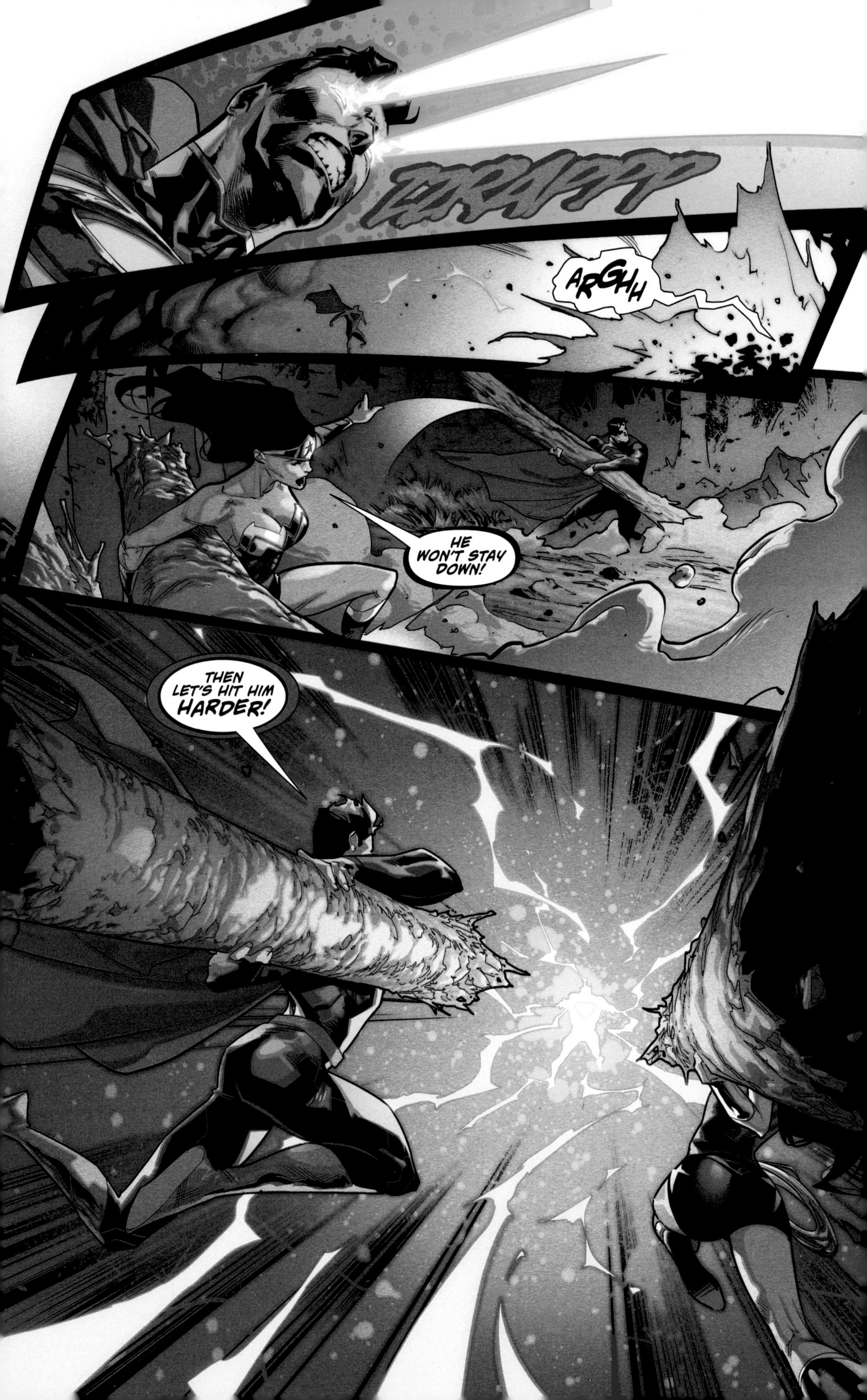
TZZRAKKK
ARGHH
HE WON'T STAY DOWN!
THEN LET'S HIT HIM HARDER!

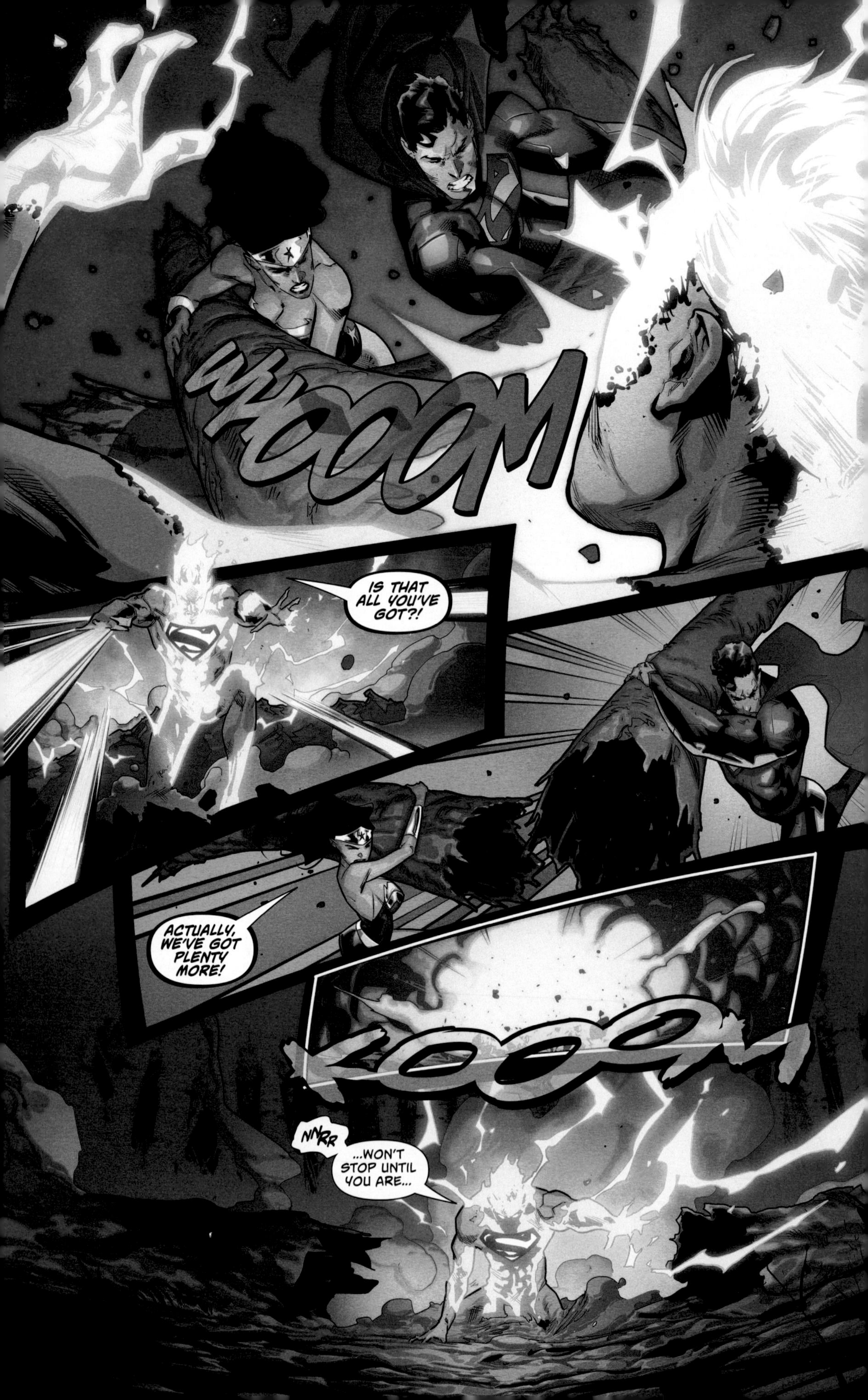
WHOOOOM
IS THAT ALL YOU'VE GOT?!
ACTUALLY, WE'VE GOT PLENTY MORE!
NNRR
...WON'T STOP UNTIL YOU ARE...

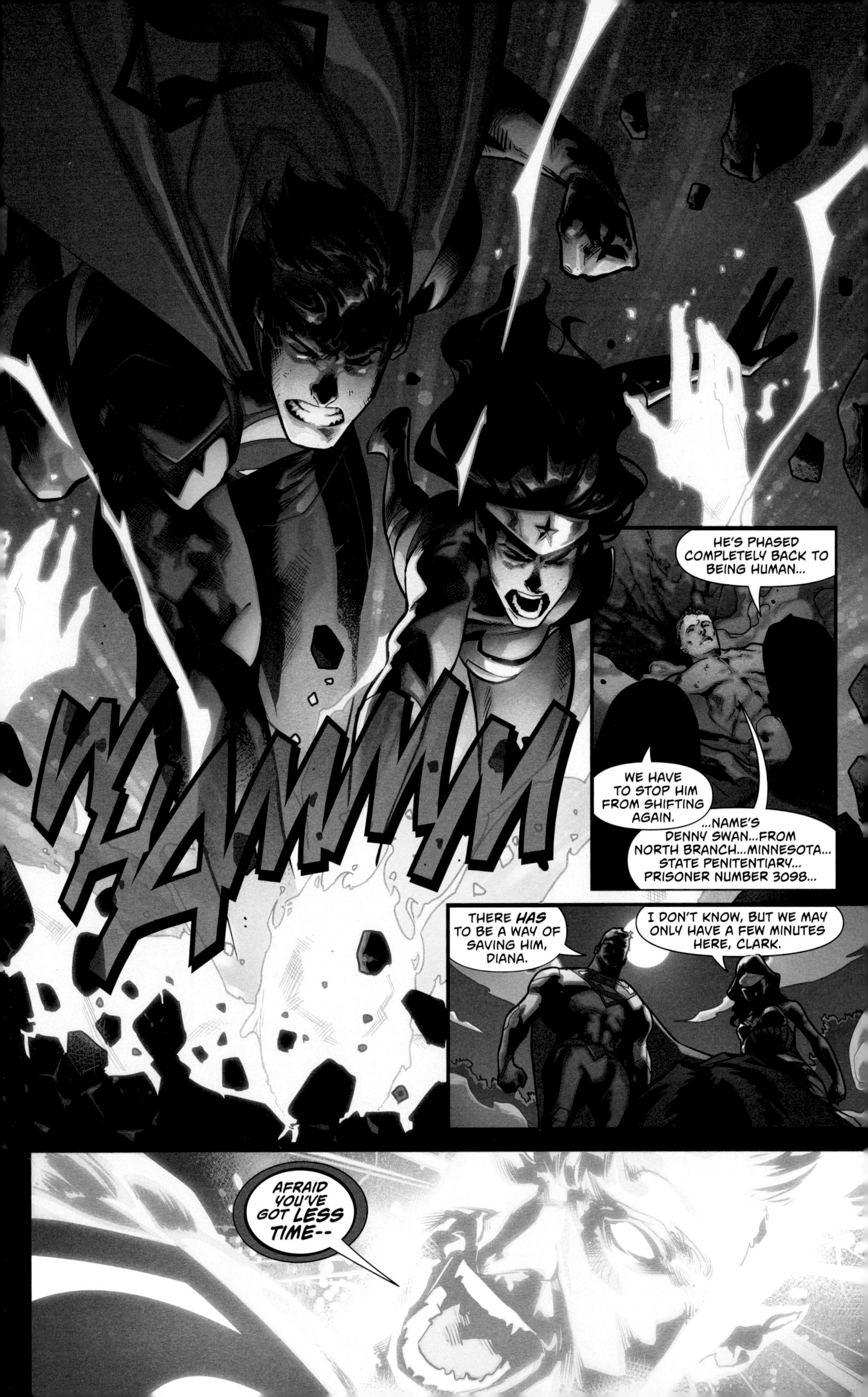
WHAMMM
HE'S PHASED COMPLETELY BACK TO BEING HUMAN...
WE HAVE TO STOP HIM FROM SHIFTING AGAIN.
...NAME'S DENNY SWAN...FROM NORTH BRANCH...MINNESOTA... STATE PENITENTIARY... PRISONER NUMBER 3098...
THERE HAS TO BE A WAY OF SAVING HIM, DIANA.
I DON'T KNOW, BUT WE MAY ONLY HAVE A FEW MINUTES HERE, CLARK.
AFRAID YOU'VE GOT LESS TIME--

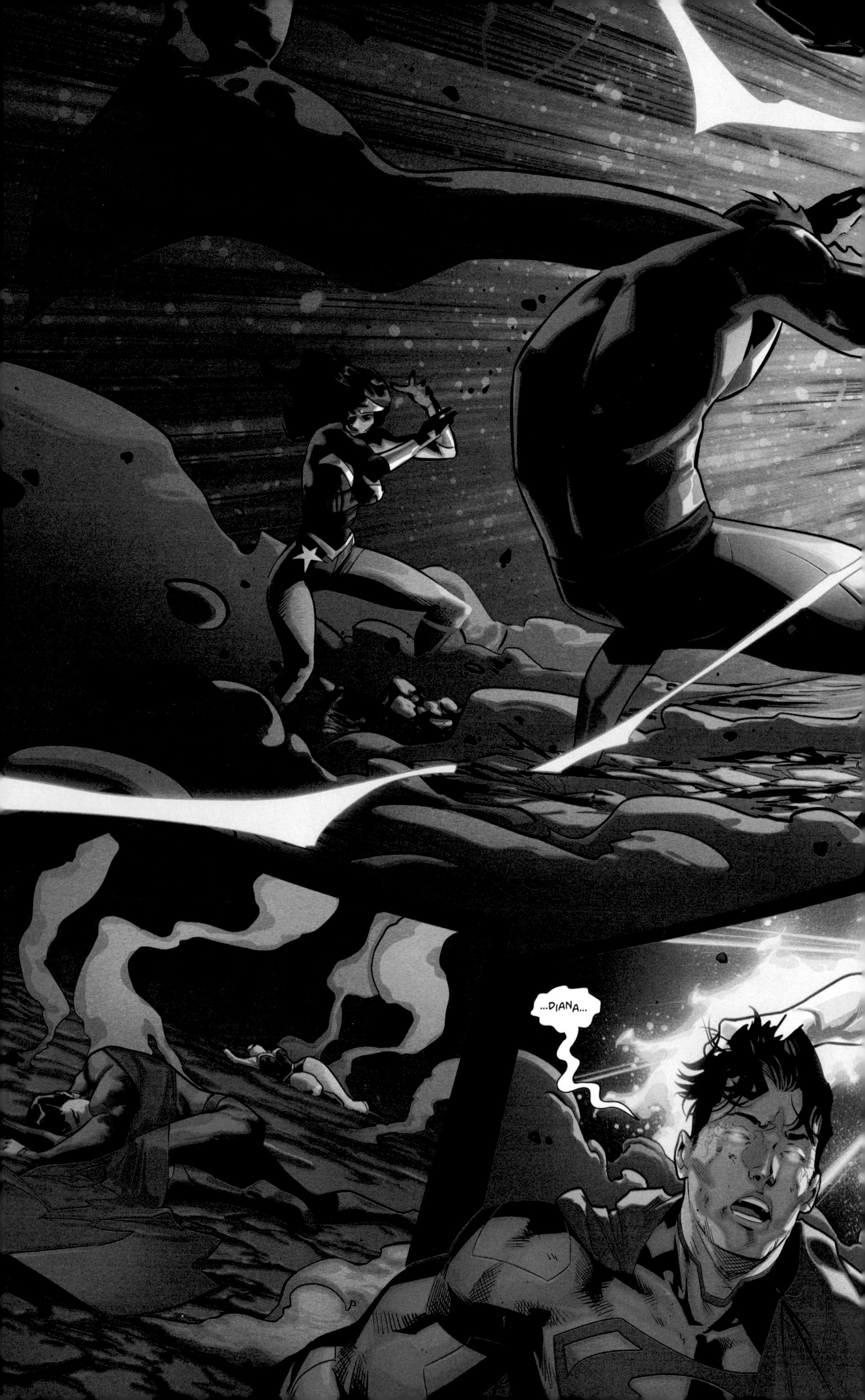
...DIANA...

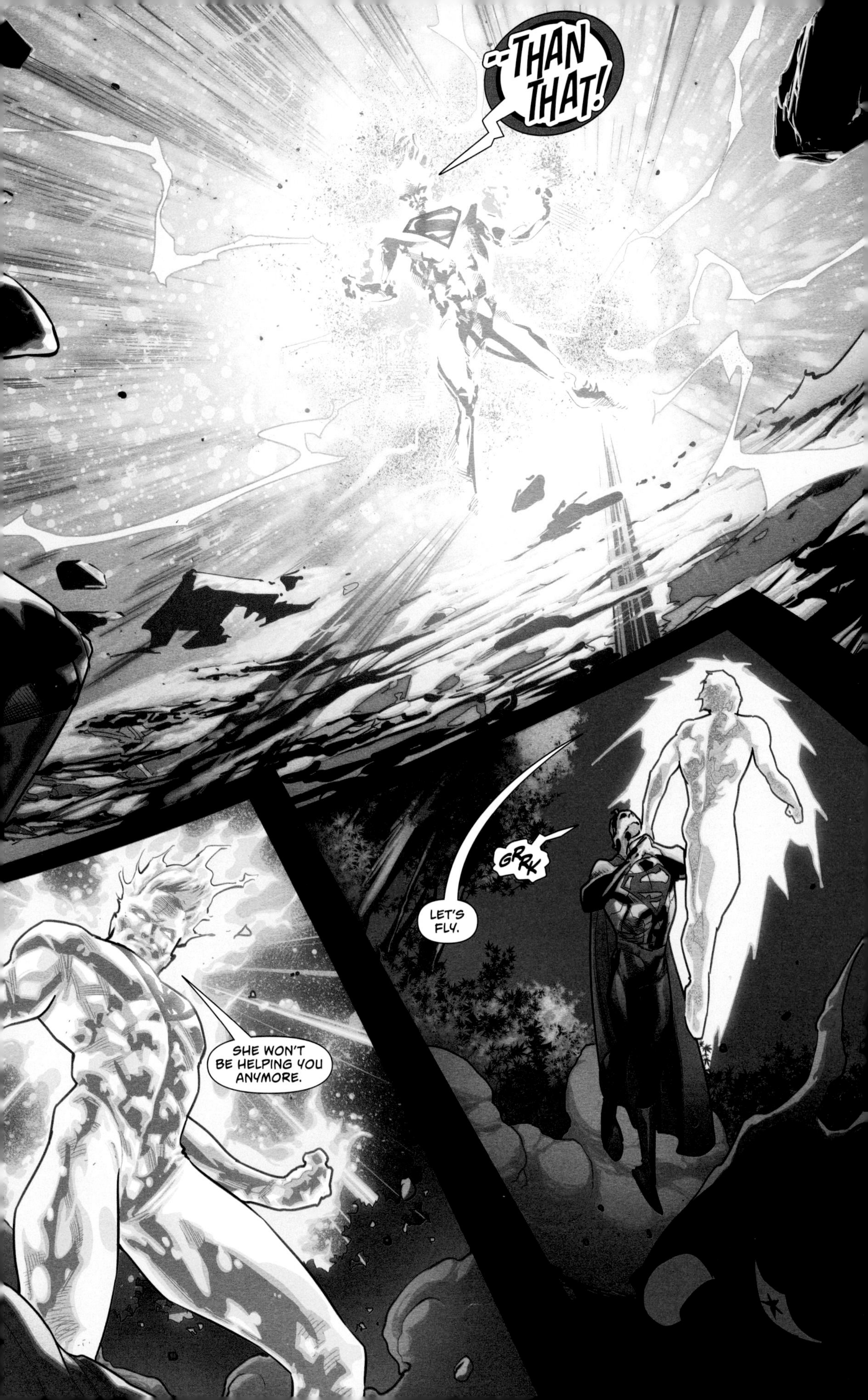

--THAN THAT!
SHE WON'T BE HELPING YOU ANYMORE.
LET'S FLY.
GRKK

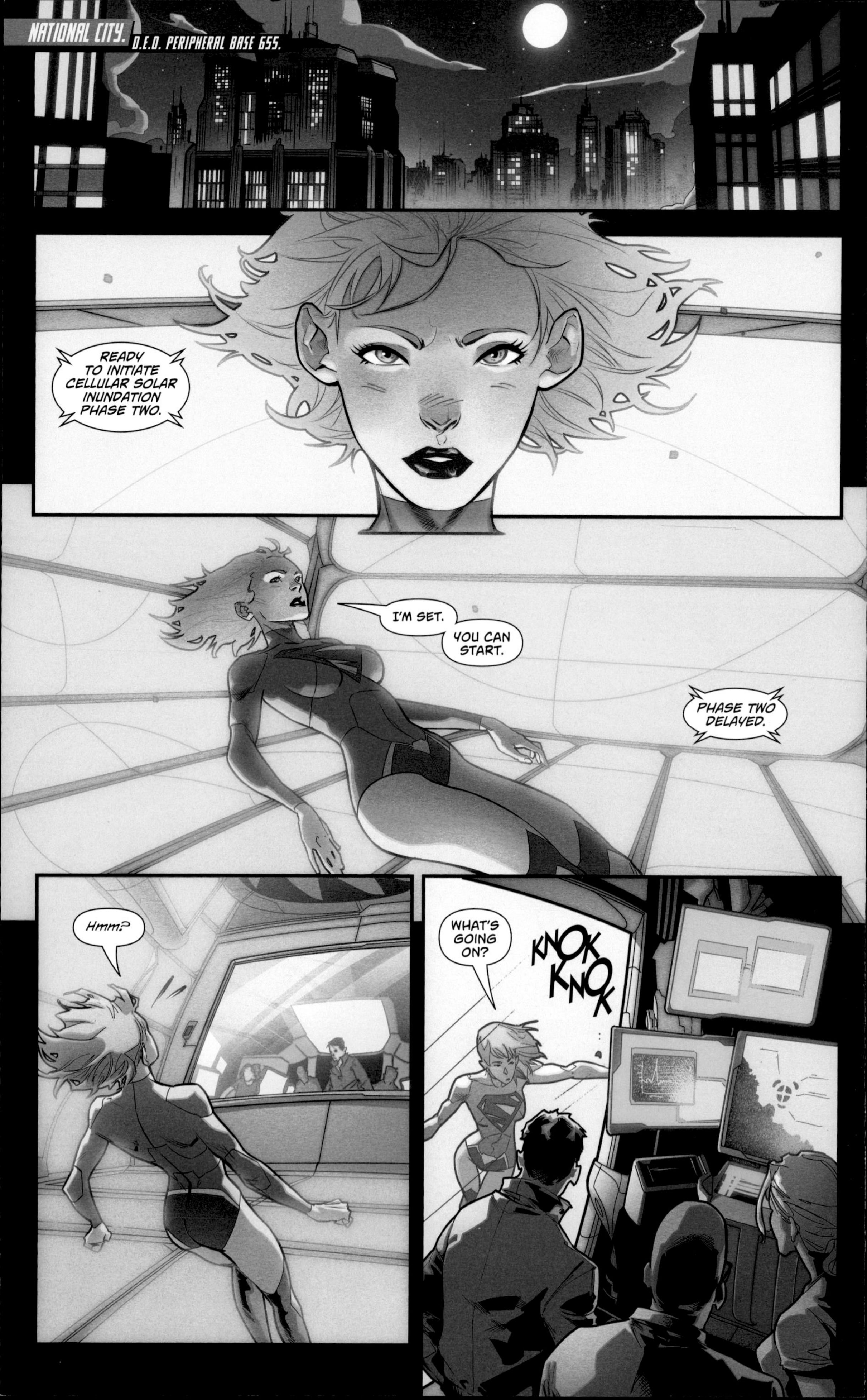
NATIONAL CITY.
D.E.O. PERIPHERAL BASE 655.
READY TO INITIATE CELLULAR SOLAR INUNDATION PHASE TWO.
I'M SET.
YOU CAN START.
PHASE TWO DELAYED.
Hmm?
WHAT'S GOING ON?
KNOK KNOK

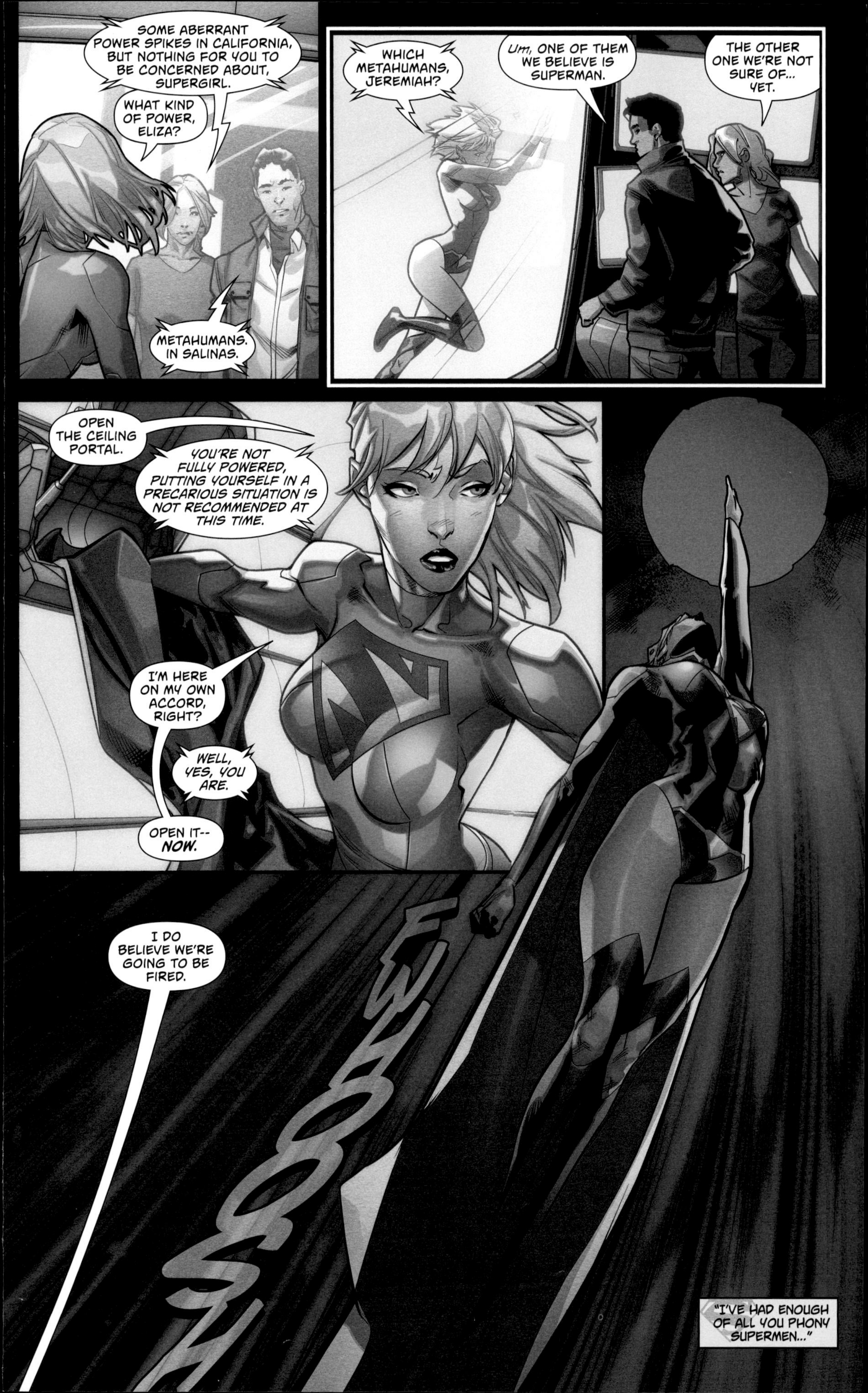
SOME ABERRANT POWER SPIKES IN CALIFORNIA, BUT NOTHING FOR YOU TO BE CONCERNED ABOUT, SUPERGIRL.
WHAT KIND OF POWER, ELIZA?
METAHUMANS. IN SALINAS.
WHICH METAHUMANS, JEREMIAH?
UM, ONE OF THEM WE BELIEVE IS SUPERMAN.
THE OTHER ONE WE'RE NOT SURE OF... YET.
OPEN THE CEILING PORTAL.
YOU'RE NOT FULLY POWERED, PUTTING YOURSELF IN A PRECARIOUS SITUATION IS NOT RECOMMENDED AT THIS TIME.
I'M HERE ON MY OWN ACCORD, RIGHT?
WELL, YES, YOU ARE.
OPEN IT-- NOW.
I DO BELIEVE WE'RE GOING TO BE FIRED.
FWHOOOOSH
"I'VE HAD ENOUGH OF ALL YOU PHONY SUPERMEN..."

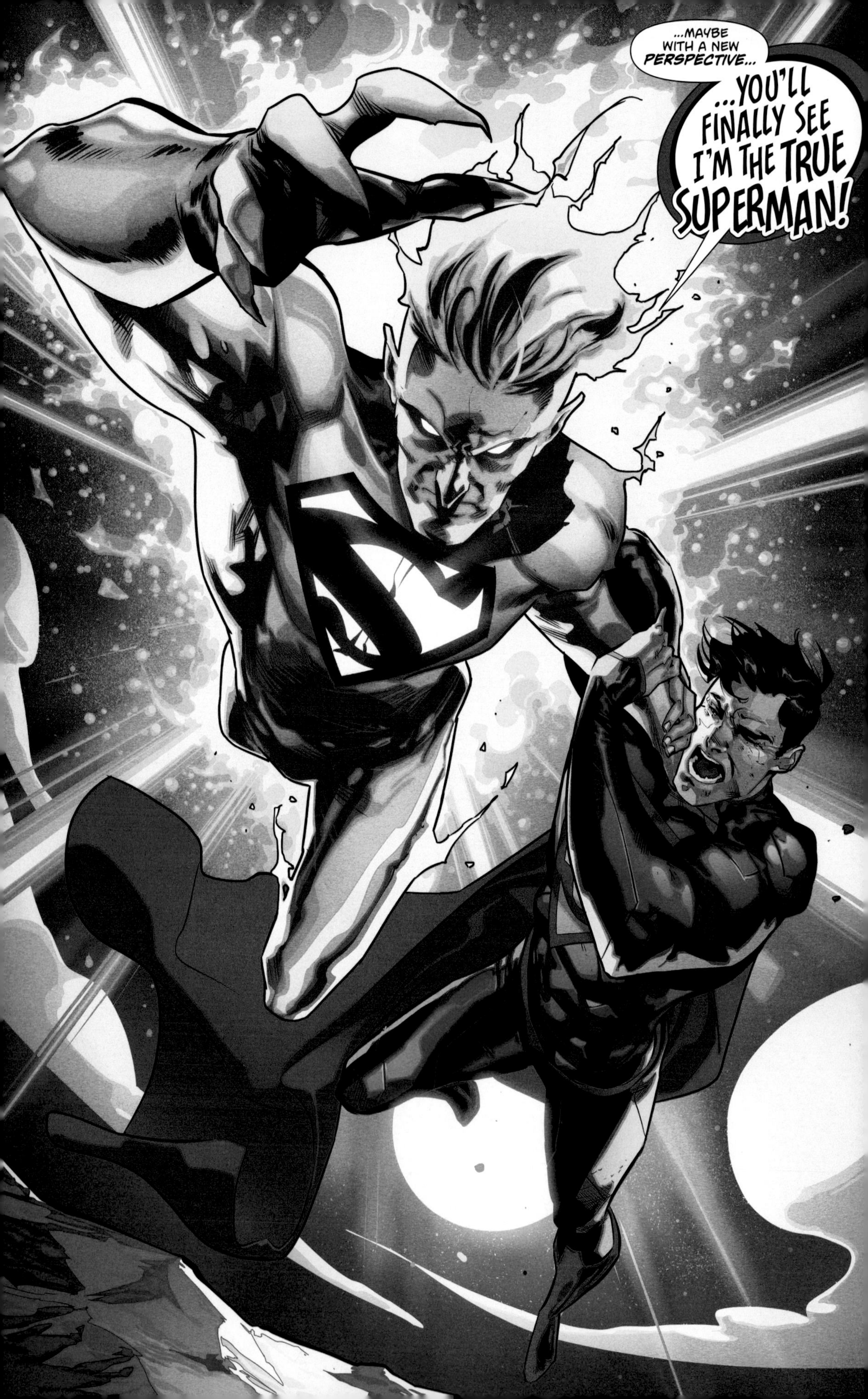
...MAYBE WITH A NEW PERSPECTIVE...
...YOU'LL FINALLY SEE I'M THE TRUE SUPERMAN!

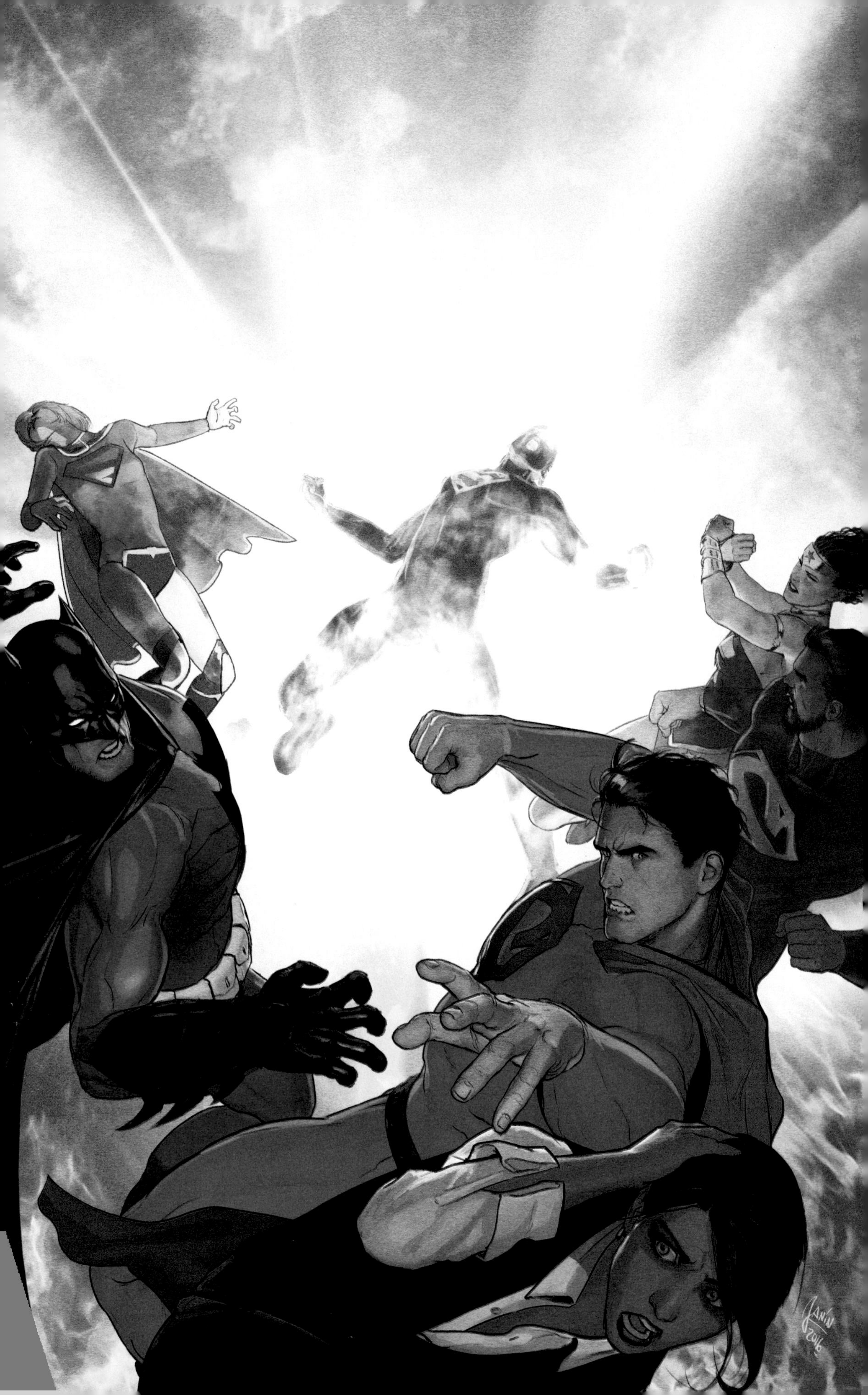
Janín
2016

THE FINAL DAYS OF SUPERMAN PART 8: DO OR DIE

PETER J. TOMASI writer MIKEL JANÍN artist MIKEL JANÍN JEROMY COX colorists ROB LEIGH letterer MIKEL JANÍN cover

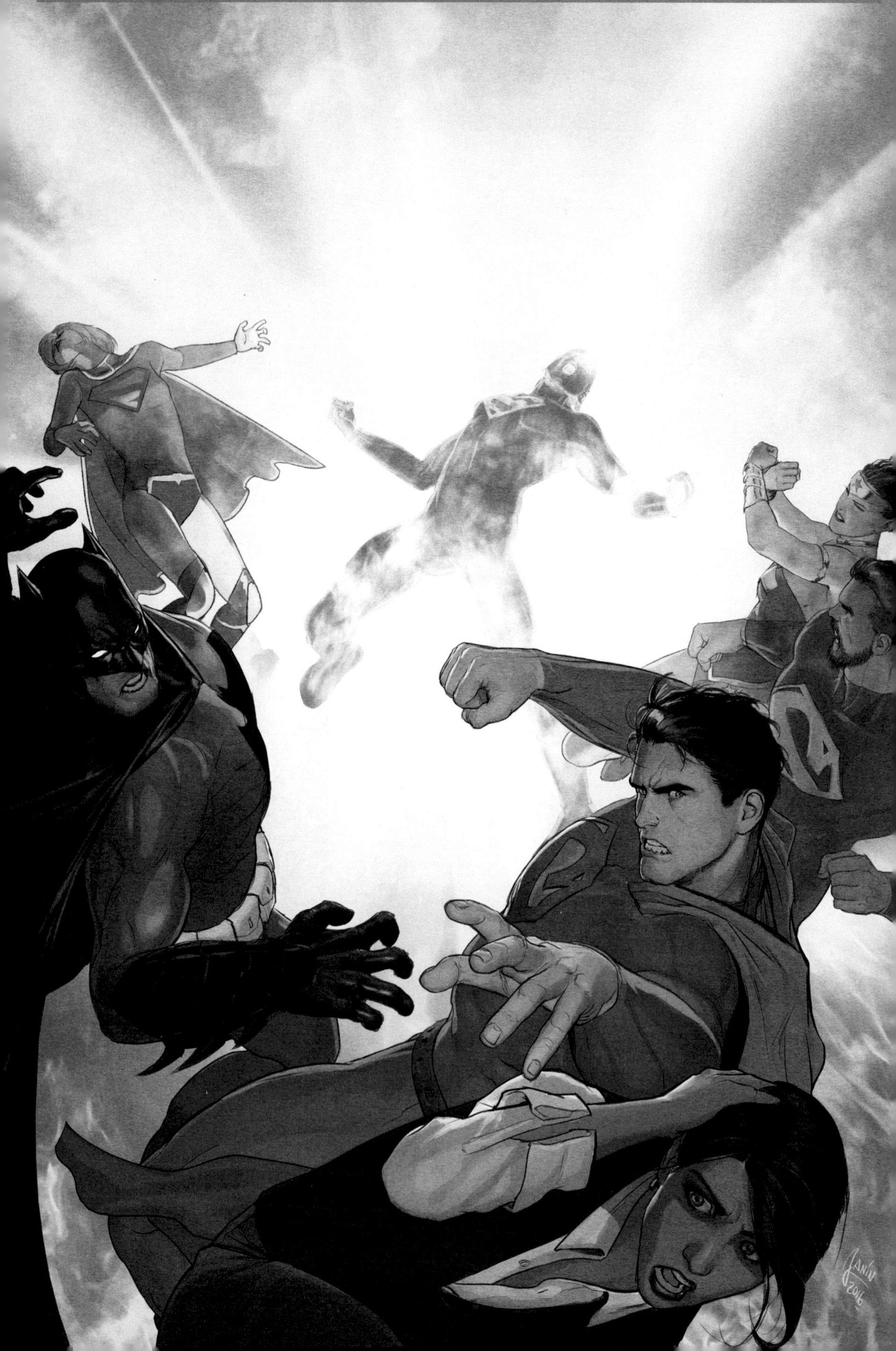

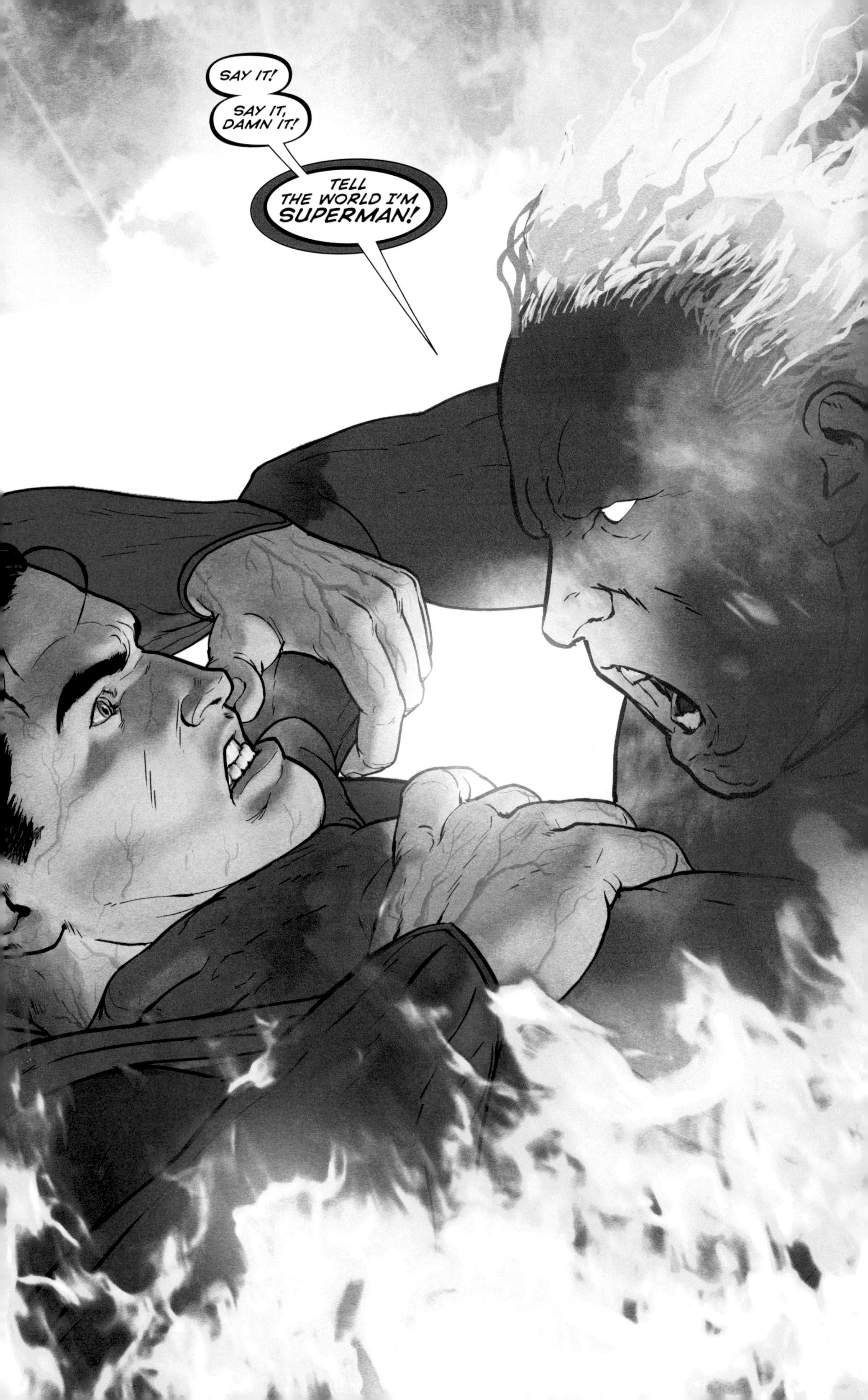
SAY IT!
SAY IT, DAMN IT!
TELL THE WORLD I'M SUPERMAN!

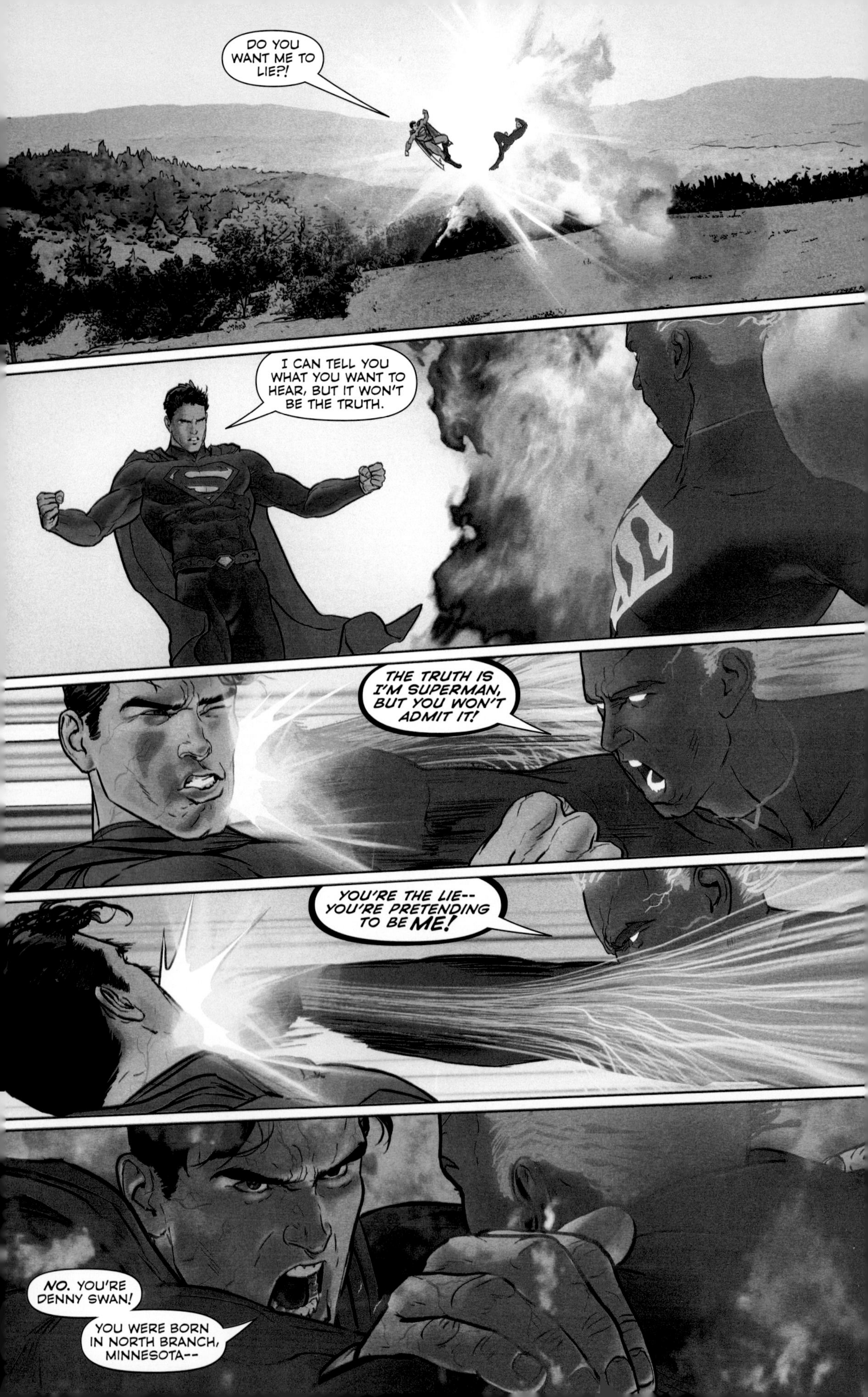
DO YOU WANT ME TO LIE?!
I CAN TELL YOU WHAT YOU WANT TO HEAR, BUT IT WON'T BE THE TRUTH.
THE TRUTH IS I'M SUPERMAN, BUT YOU WON'T ADMIT IT!
YOU'RE THE LIE-- YOU'RE PRETENDING TO BE ME!
NO. YOU'RE DENNY SWAN!
YOU WERE BORN IN NORTH BRANCH, MINNESOTA--

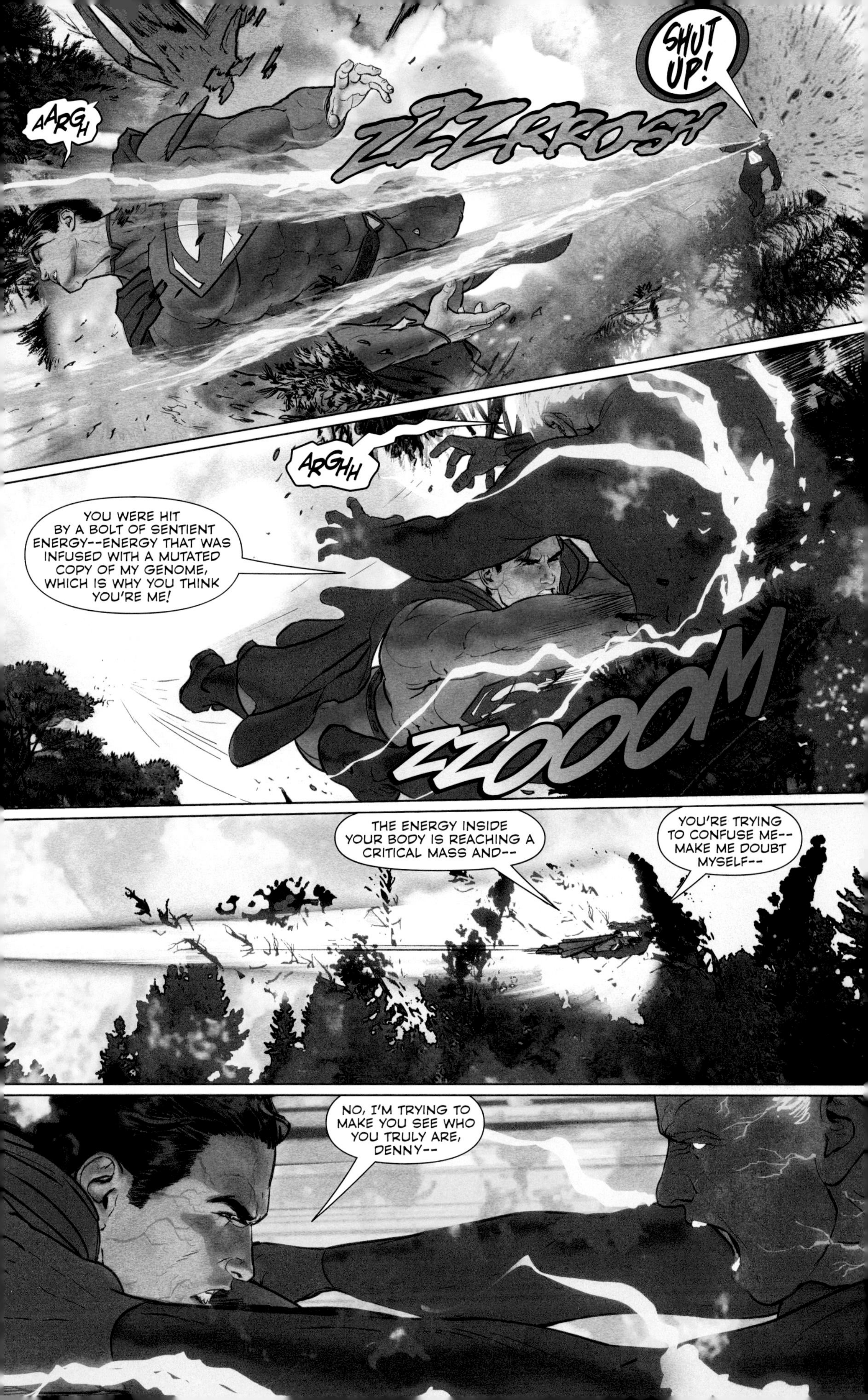
AARGH
SHUT UP!
ZZZZRROSH
ARGHH
YOU WERE HIT BY A BOLT OF SENTIENT ENERGY--ENERGY THAT WAS INFUSED WITH A MUTATED COPY OF MY GENOME, WHICH IS WHY YOU THINK YOU'RE ME!
ZZOOOOM
THE ENERGY INSIDE YOUR BODY IS REACHING A CRITICAL MASS AND--
YOU'RE TRYING TO CONFUSE ME--MAKE ME DOUBT MYSELF--
NO, I'M TRYING TO MAKE YOU SEE WHO YOU TRULY ARE, DENNY--

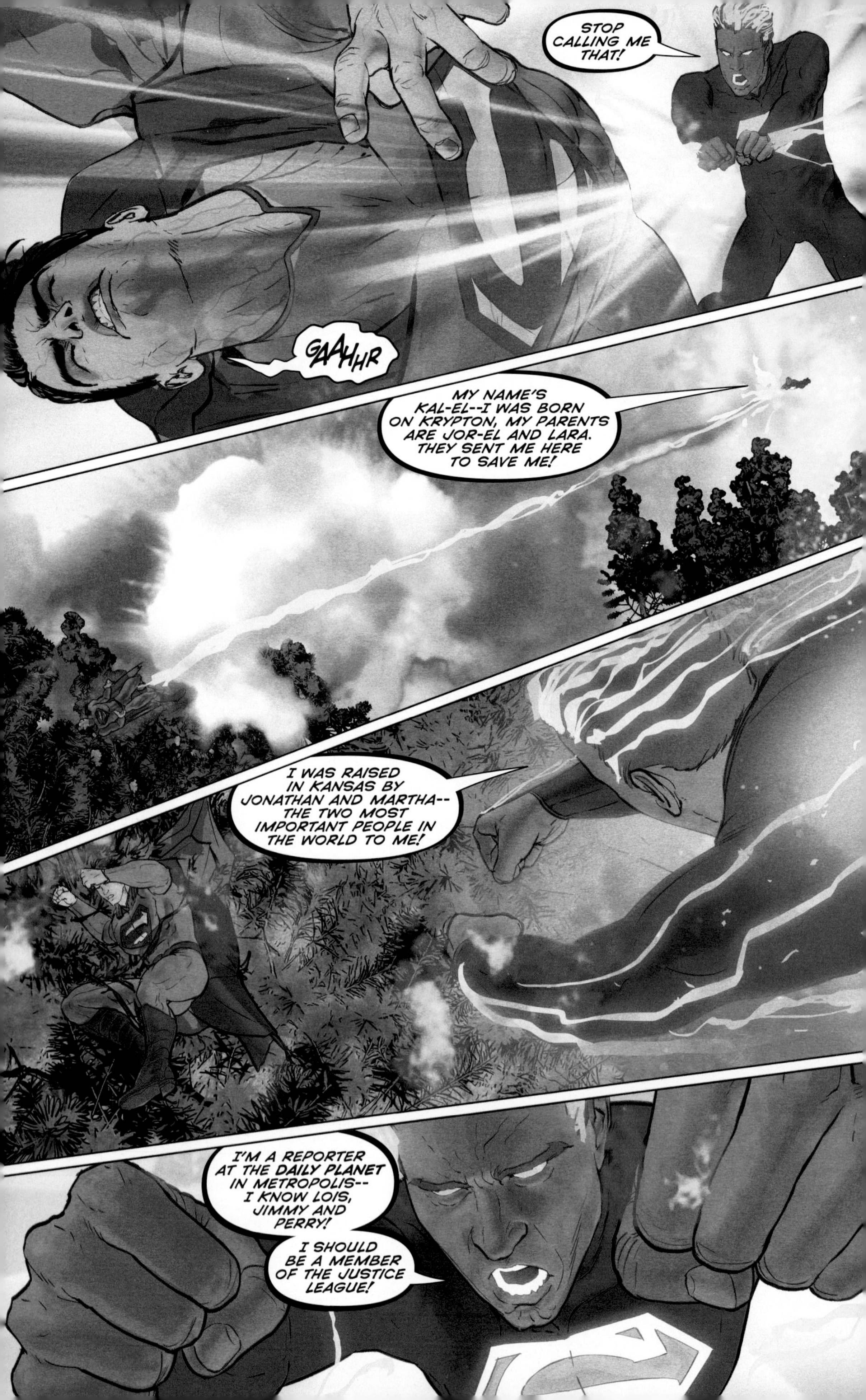
STOP CALLING ME THAT!
GAAHHR
MY NAME'S KAL-EL--I WAS BORN ON KRYPTON, MY PARENTS ARE JOR-EL AND LARA. THEY SENT ME HERE TO SAVE ME!
I WAS RAISED IN KANSAS BY JONATHAN AND MARTHA-- THE TWO MOST IMPORTANT PEOPLE IN THE WORLD TO ME!
I'M A REPORTER AT THE DAILY PLANET IN METROPOLIS-- I KNOW LOIS, JIMMY AND PERRY!
I SHOULD BE A MEMBER OF THE JUSTICE LEAGUE!

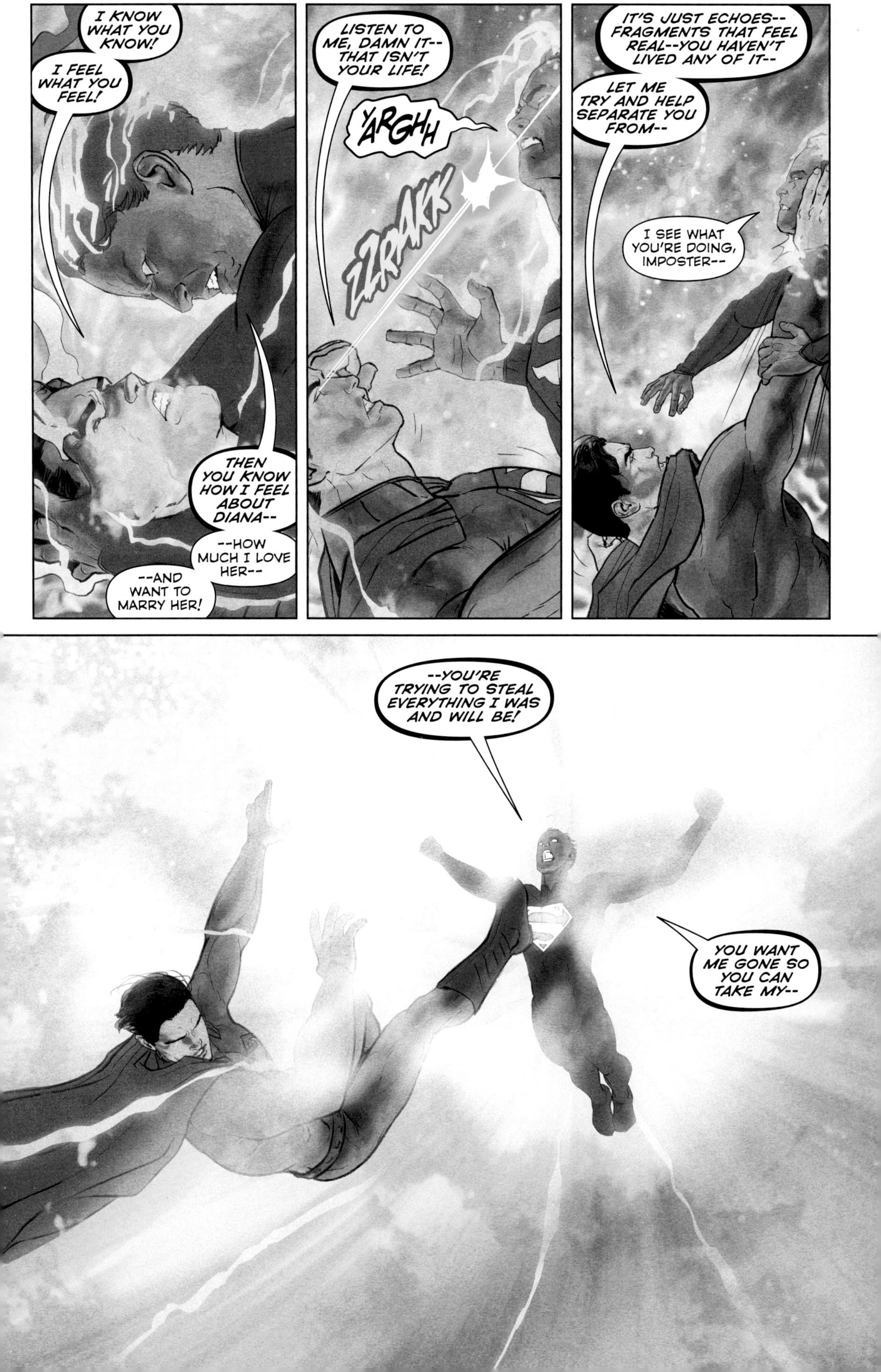
I KNOW WHAT YOU KNOW!
I FEEL WHAT YOU FEEL!
THEN YOU KNOW HOW I FEEL ABOUT DIANA--
--HOW MUCH I LOVE HER--
--AND WANT TO MARRY HER!
LISTEN TO ME, DAMN IT-- THAT ISN'T YOUR LIFE!
YARGHH
ZZRAKK
IT'S JUST ECHOES-- FRAGMENTS THAT FEEL REAL--YOU HAVEN'T LIVED ANY OF IT--
LET ME TRY AND HELP SEPARATE YOU FROM--
I SEE WHAT YOU'RE DOING, IMPOSTER--
--YOU'RE TRYING TO STEAL EVERYTHING I WAS AND WILL BE!
YOU WANT ME GONE SO YOU CAN TAKE MY--

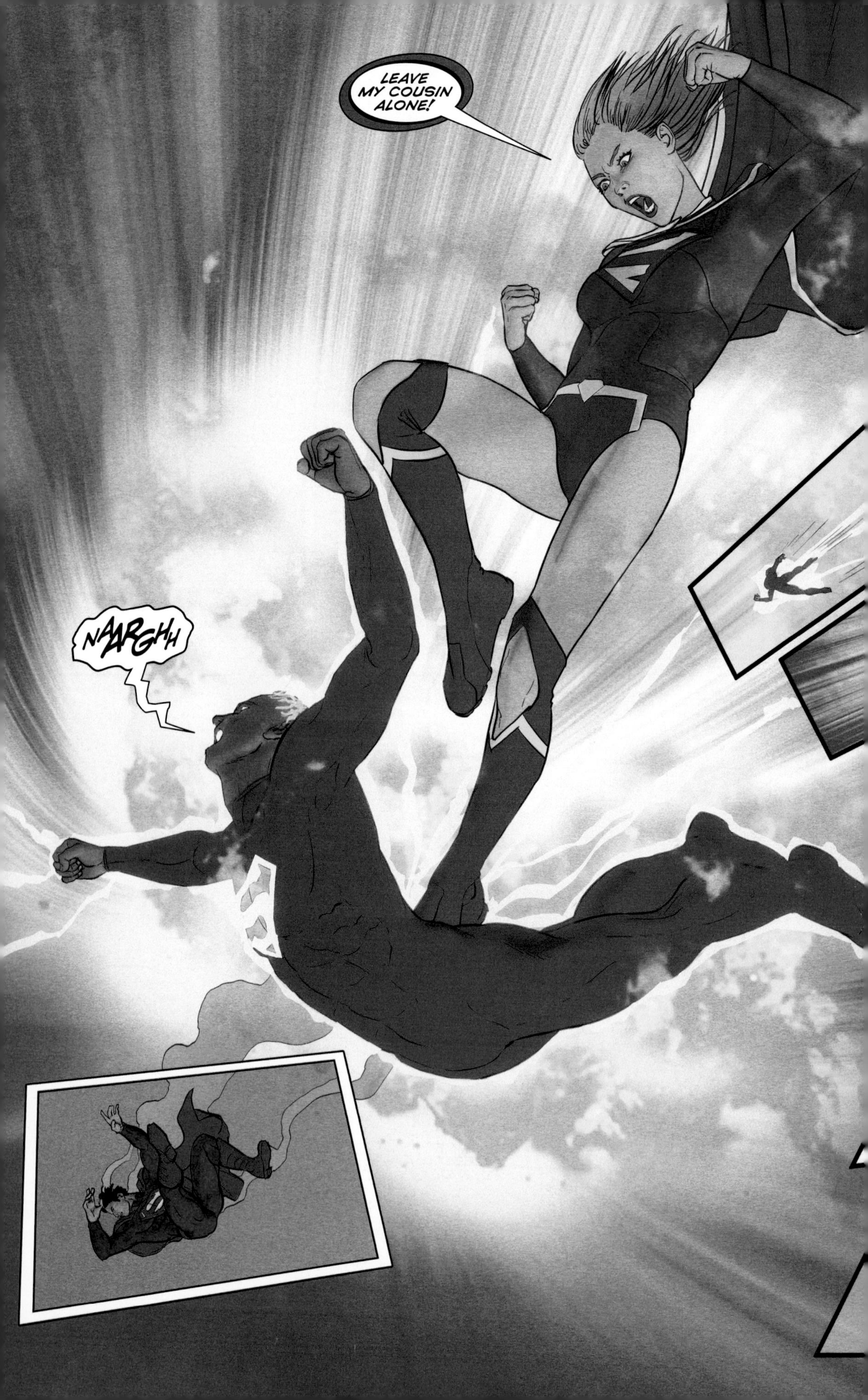
LEAVE MY COUSIN ALONE!
NAARGHH

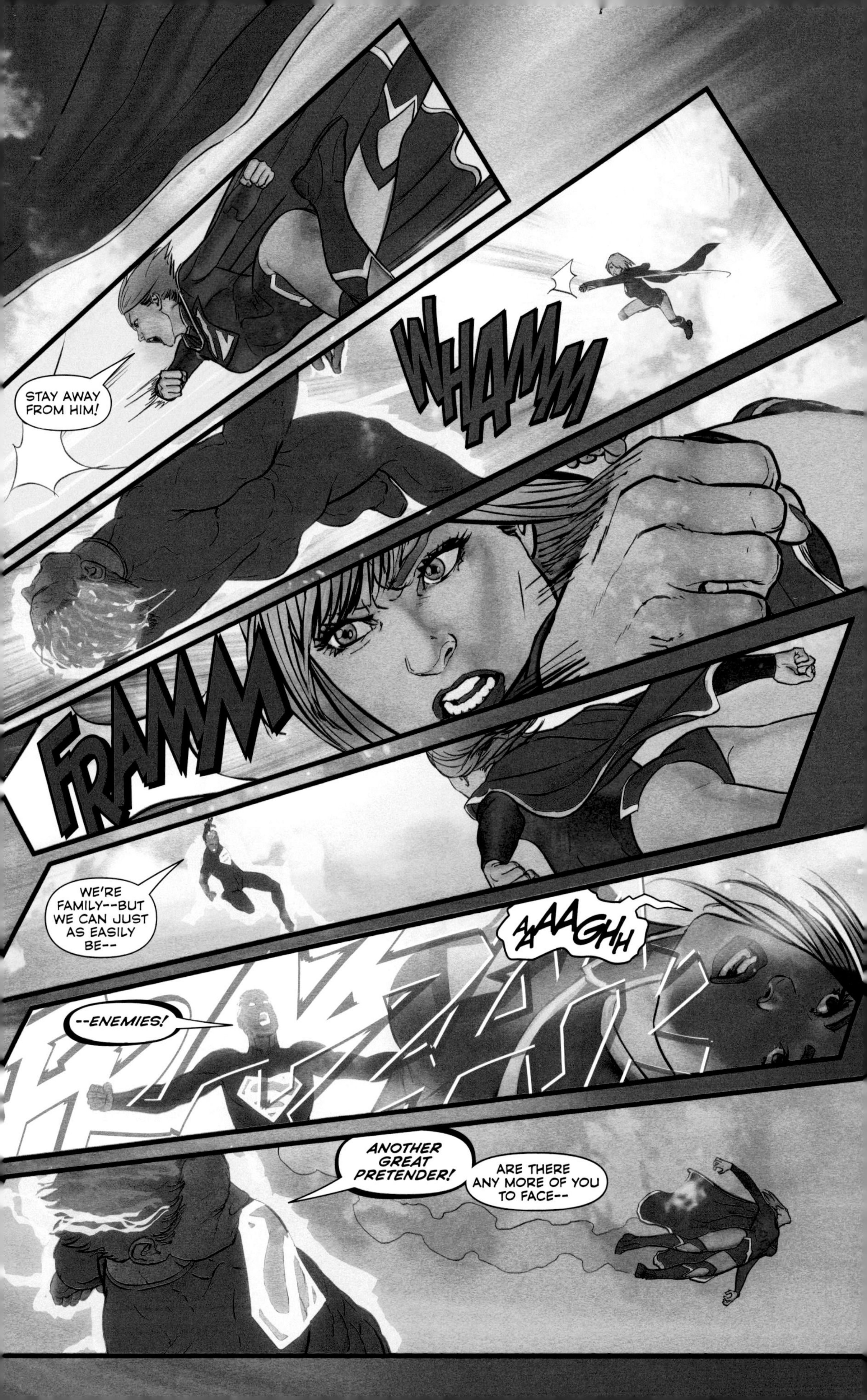

STAY AWAY FROM HIM!
WHAMMM
FRAMMM
WE'RE FAMILY--BUT WE CAN JUST AS EASILY BE--
AAAAGHH
--ENEMIES!
ANOTHER GREAT PRETENDER!
ARE THERE ANY MORE OF YOU TO FACE--

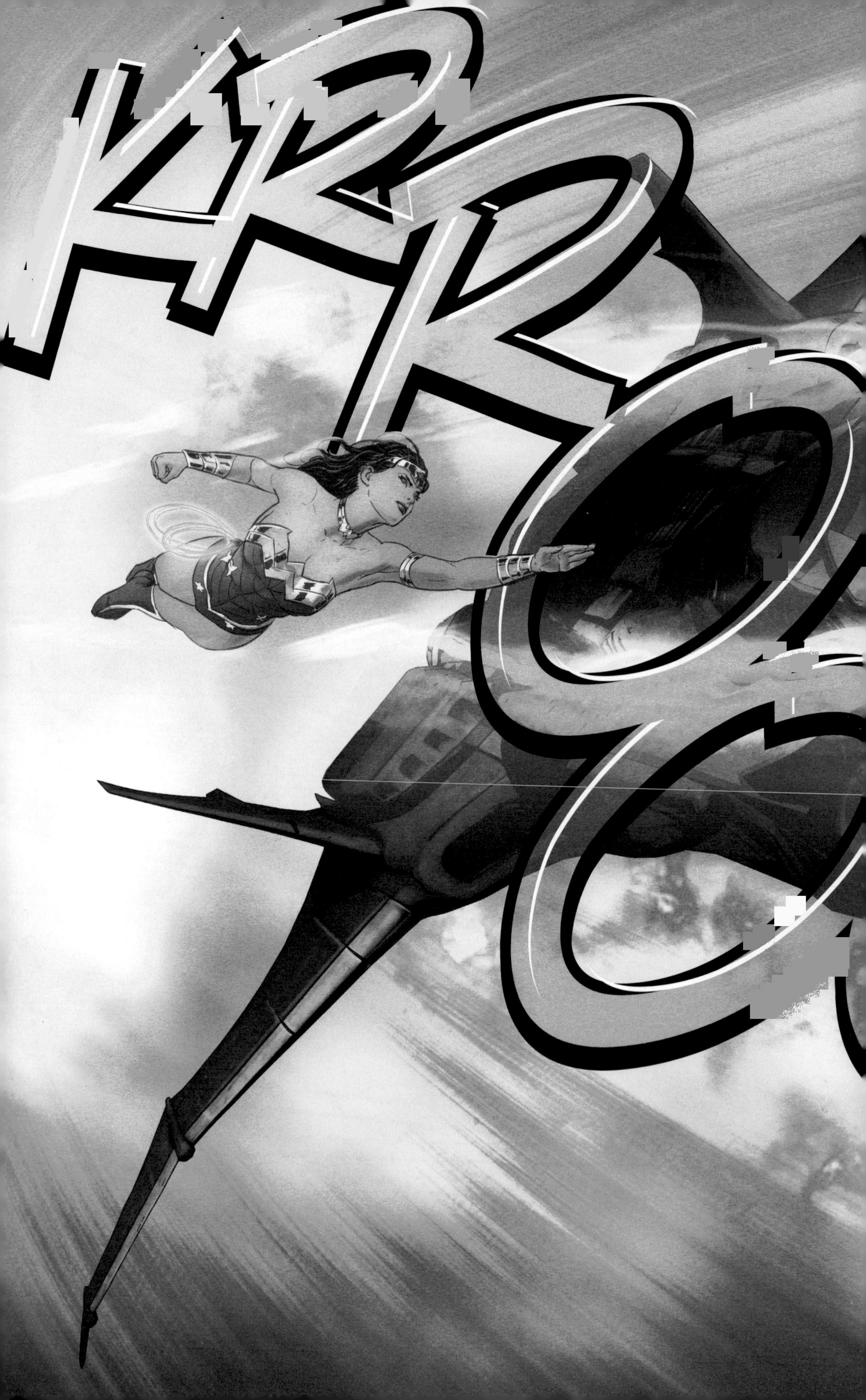
KRROO

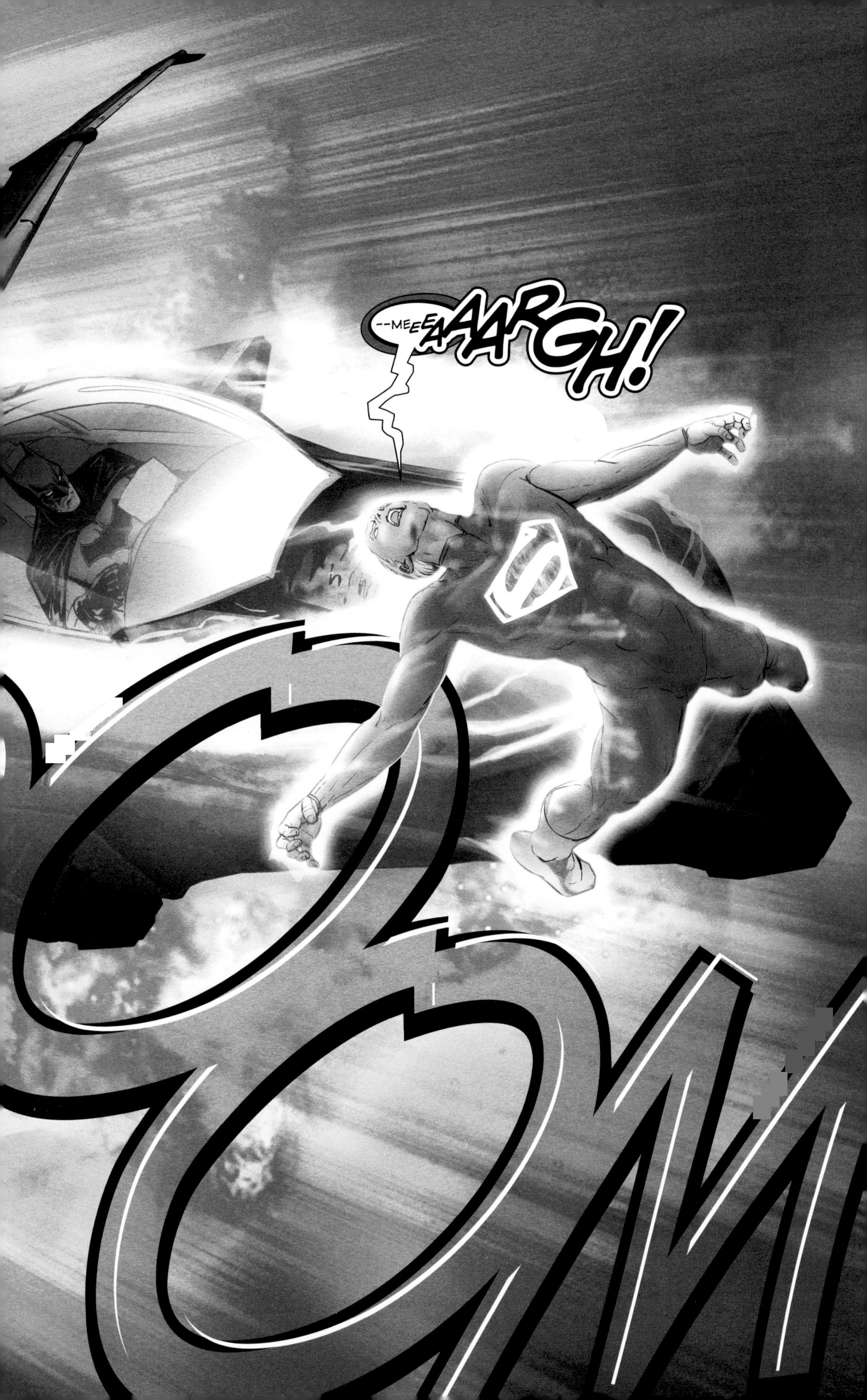
--MEEEAAAARGH!

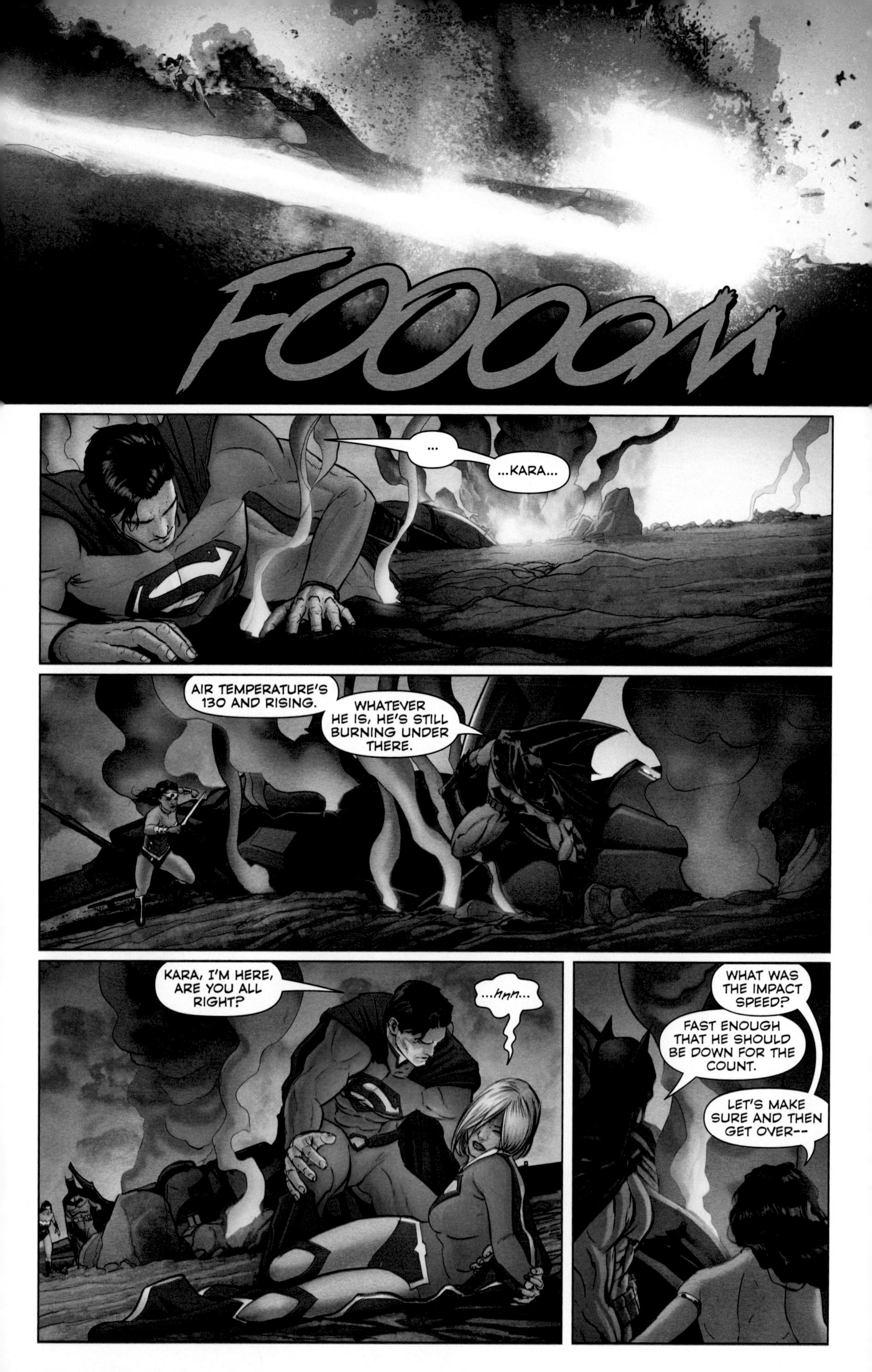
FOOOOM
...
...KARA...
AIR TEMPERATURE'S 130 AND RISING.
WHATEVER HE IS, HE'S STILL BURNING UNDER THERE.
KARA, I'M HERE, ARE YOU ALL RIGHT?
...hnn...
WHAT WAS THE IMPACT SPEED?
FAST ENOUGH THAT HE SHOULD BE DOWN FOR THE COUNT.
LET'S MAKE SURE AND THEN GET OVER--

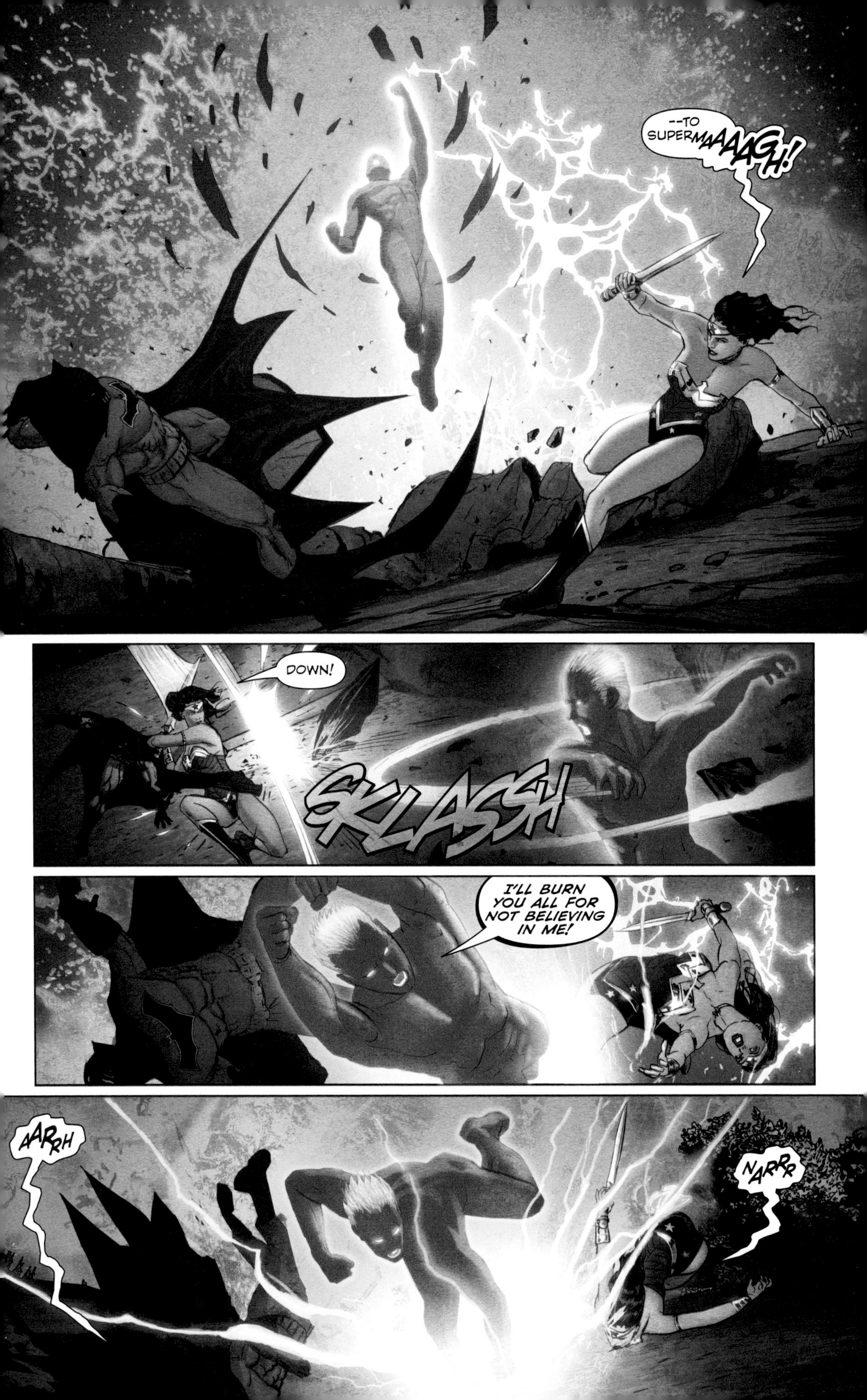
--TO SUPERMAAAAGH!
DOWN!
SKLASSH
I'LL BURN YOU ALL FOR NOT BELIEVING IN ME!
AARRH
NARRR

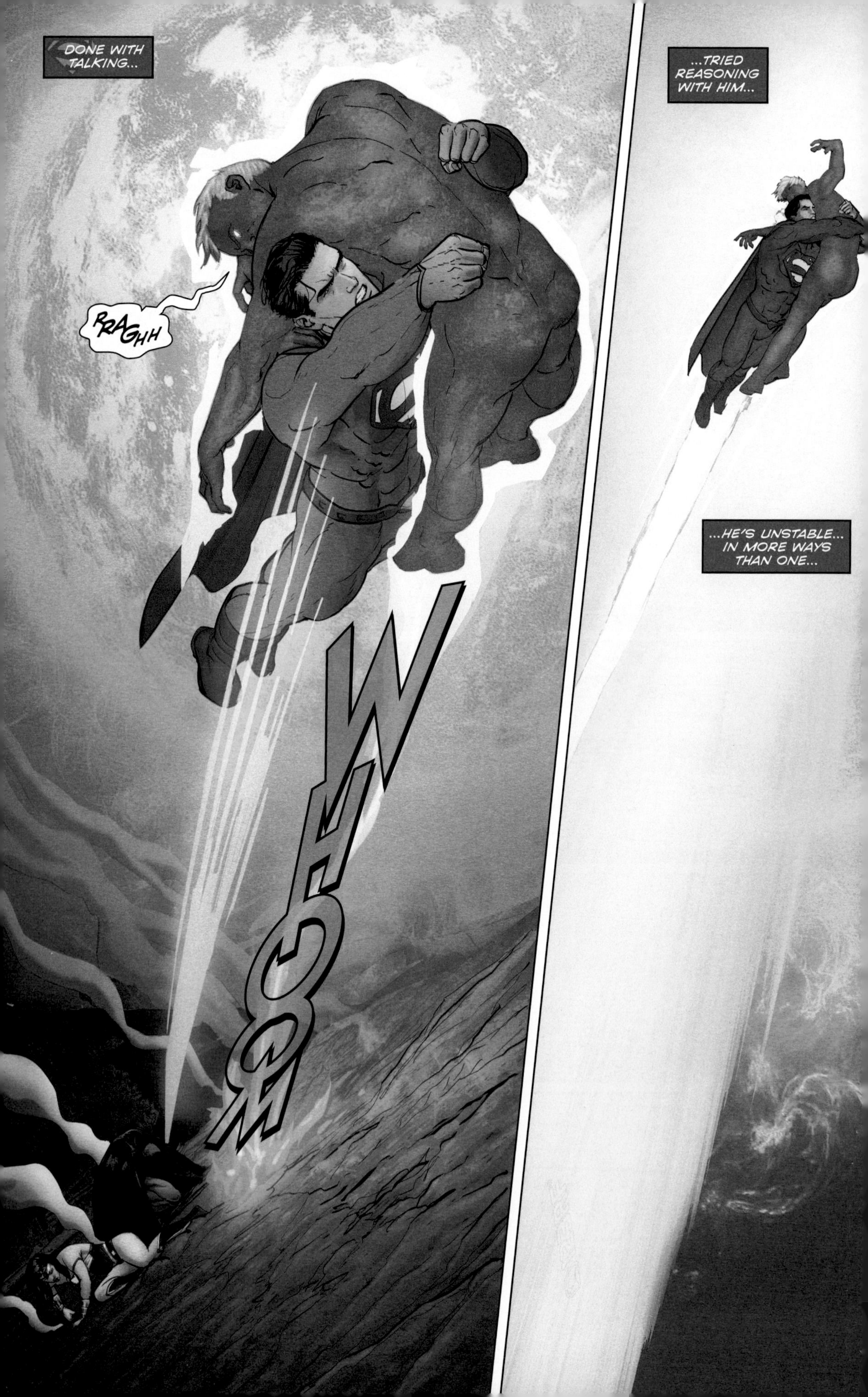
DONE WITH TALKING...
RRAGHH
WHOOM
...TRIED REASONING WITH HIM...
...HE'S UNSTABLE... IN MORE WAYS THAN ONE...

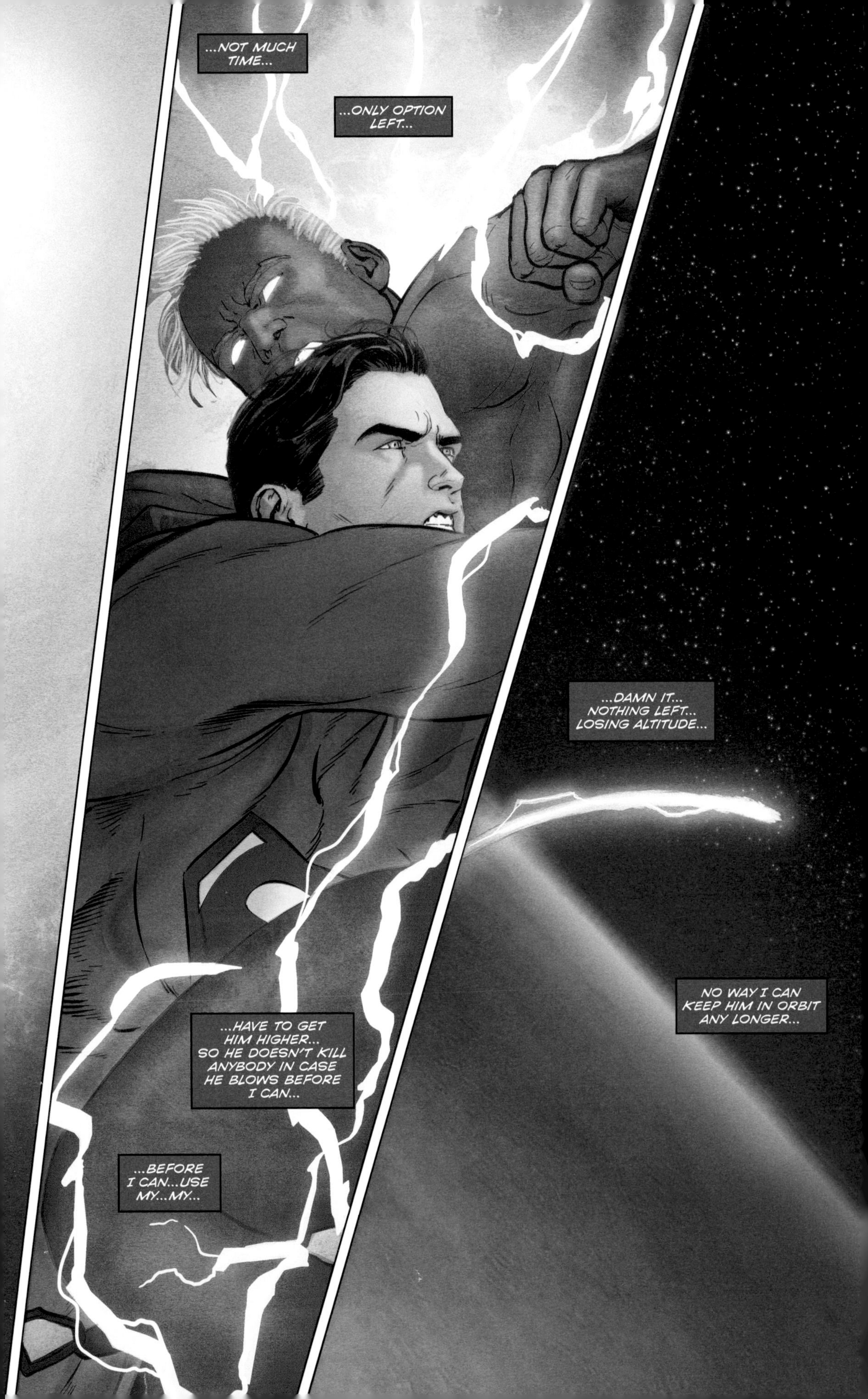
...NOT MUCH TIME...
...ONLY OPTION LEFT...
...HAVE TO GET HIM HIGHER... SO HE DOESN'T KILL ANYBODY IN CASE HE BLOWS BEFORE I CAN...
...BEFORE I CAN...USE MY...MY...
...DAMN IT... NOTHING LEFT... LOSING ALTITUDE...
NO WAY I CAN KEEP HIM IN ORBIT ANY LONGER...

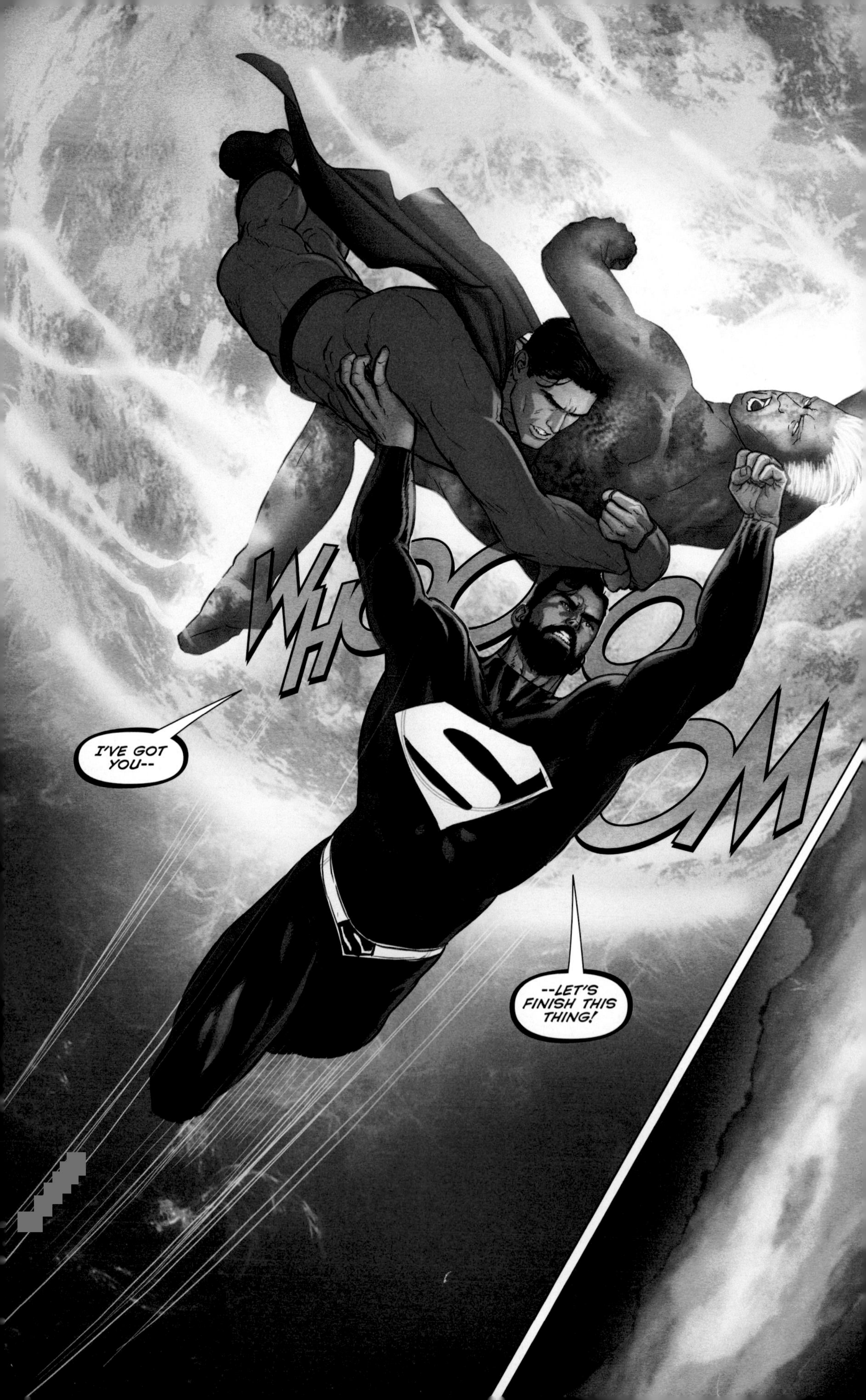
WHOOOOOOM
I'VE GOT YOU--
--LET'S FINISH THIS THING!

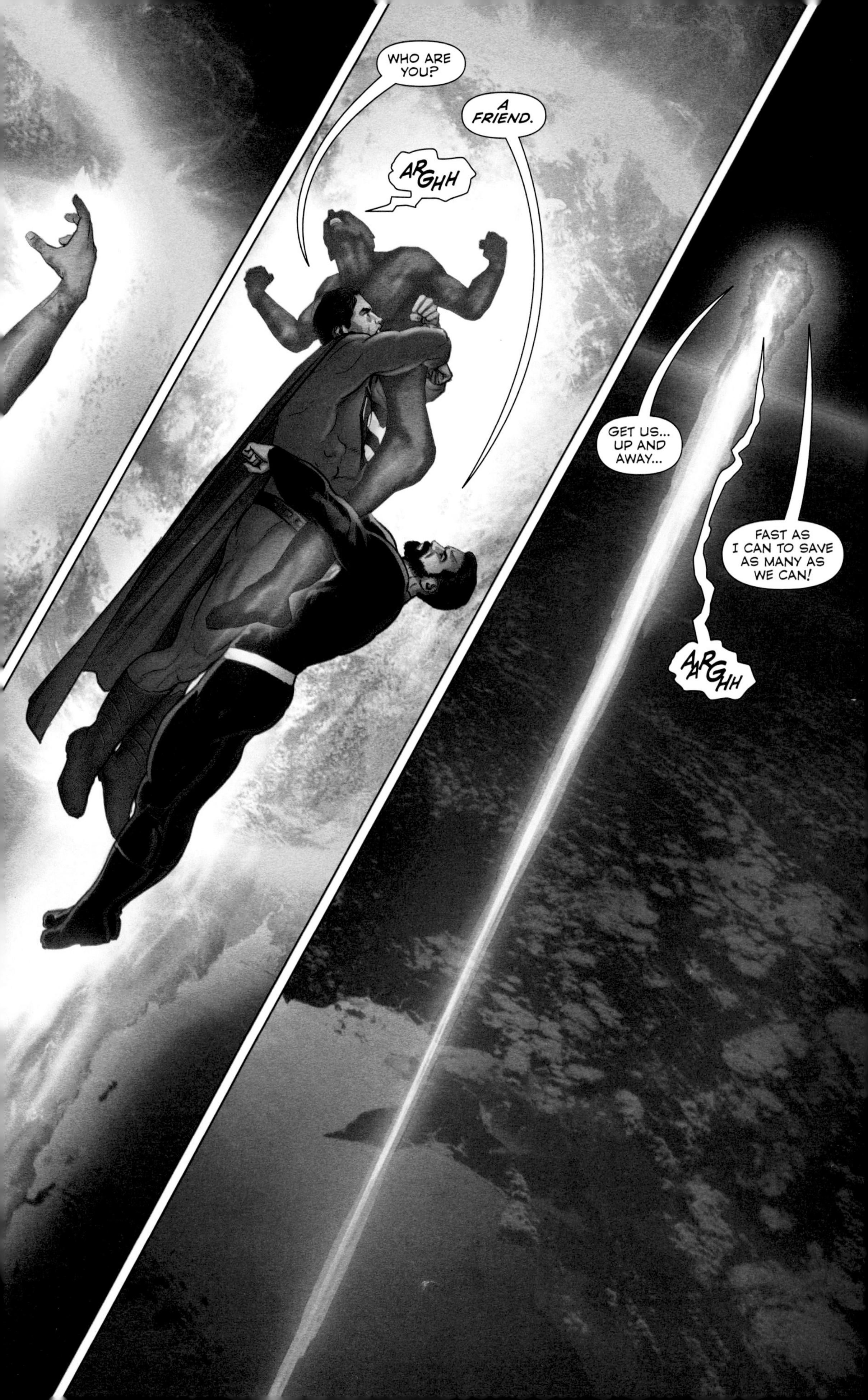
WHO ARE YOU?
A FRIEND.
ARGHH
GET US... UP AND AWAY...
FAST AS I CAN TO SAVE AS MANY AS WE CAN!
AARGHH

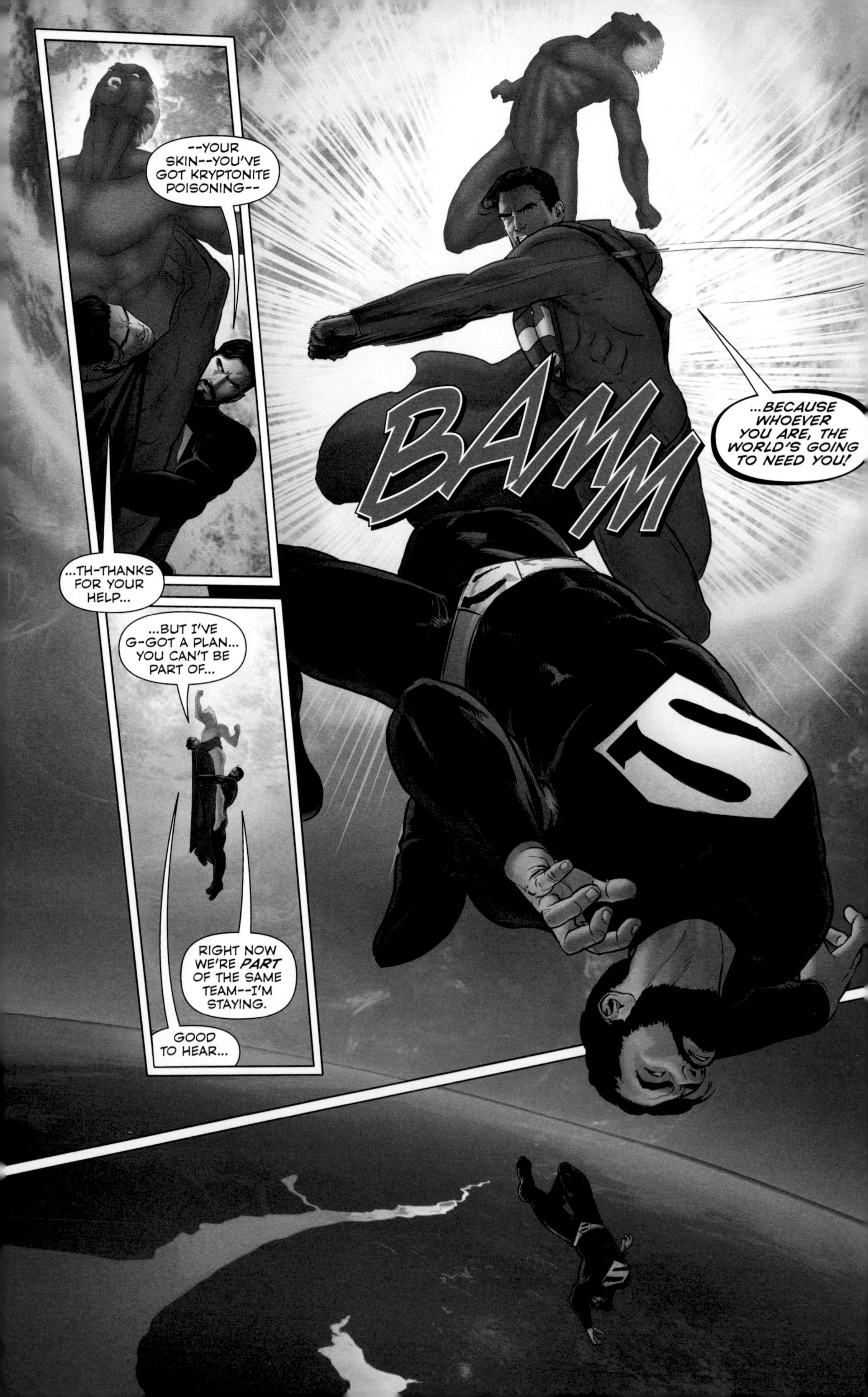
--YOUR SKIN--YOU'VE GOT KRYPTONITE POISONING--
...TH-THANKS FOR YOUR HELP...
...BUT I'VE G-GOT A PLAN... YOU CAN'T BE PART OF...
RIGHT NOW WE'RE *PART* OF THE SAME TEAM--I'M STAYING.
GOOD TO HEAR...
BAMM
...BECAUSE WHOEVER YOU ARE, THE WORLD'S GOING TO NEED YOU!

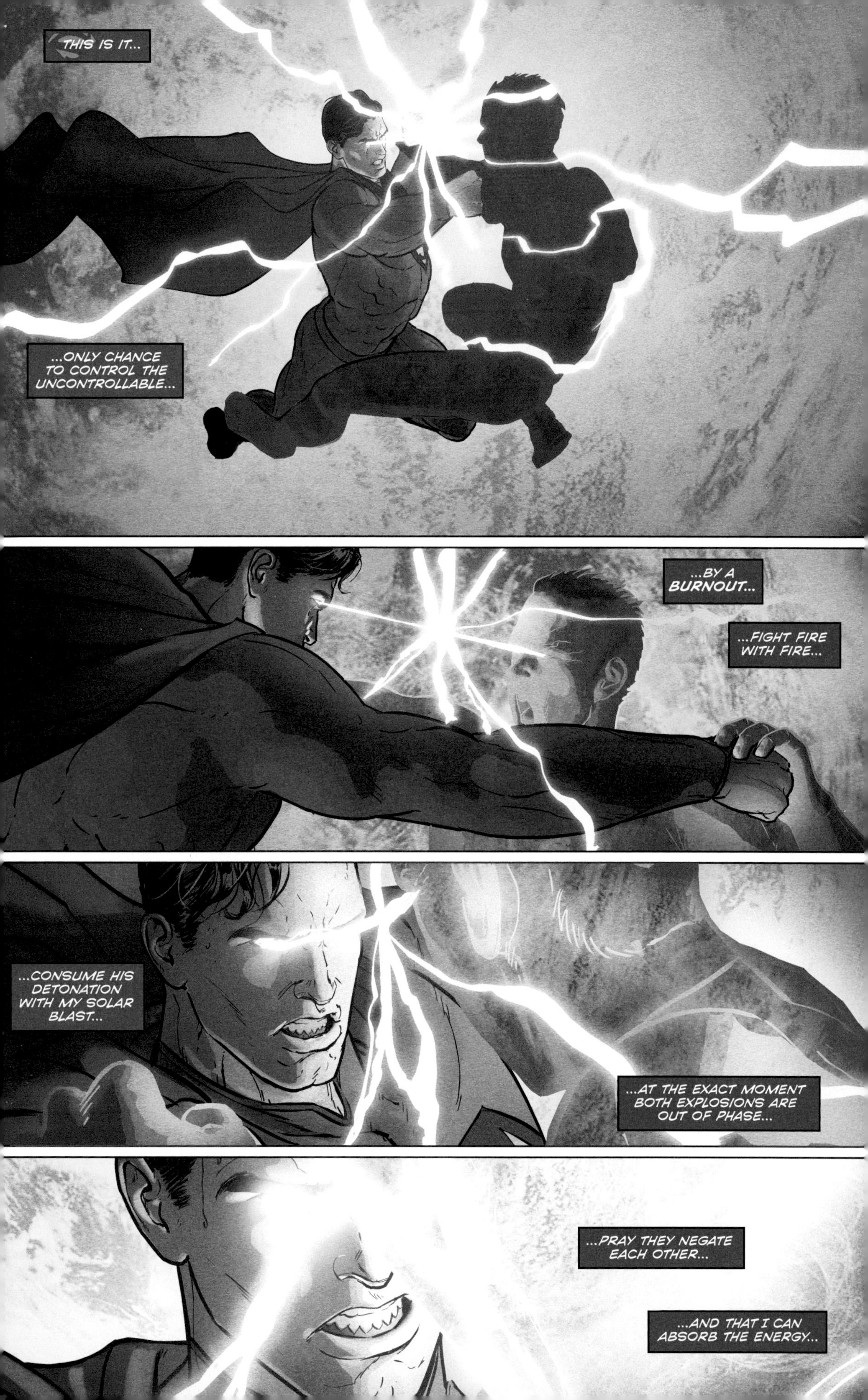
THIS IS IT...
...ONLY CHANCE TO CONTROL THE UNCONTROLLABLE...
...BY A BURNOUT...
...FIGHT FIRE WITH FIRE...
...CONSUME HIS DETONATION WITH MY SOLAR BLAST...
...AT THE EXACT MOMENT BOTH EXPLOSIONS ARE OUT OF PHASE...
...PRAY THEY NEGATE EACH OTHER...
...AND THAT I CAN ABSORB THE ENERGY...

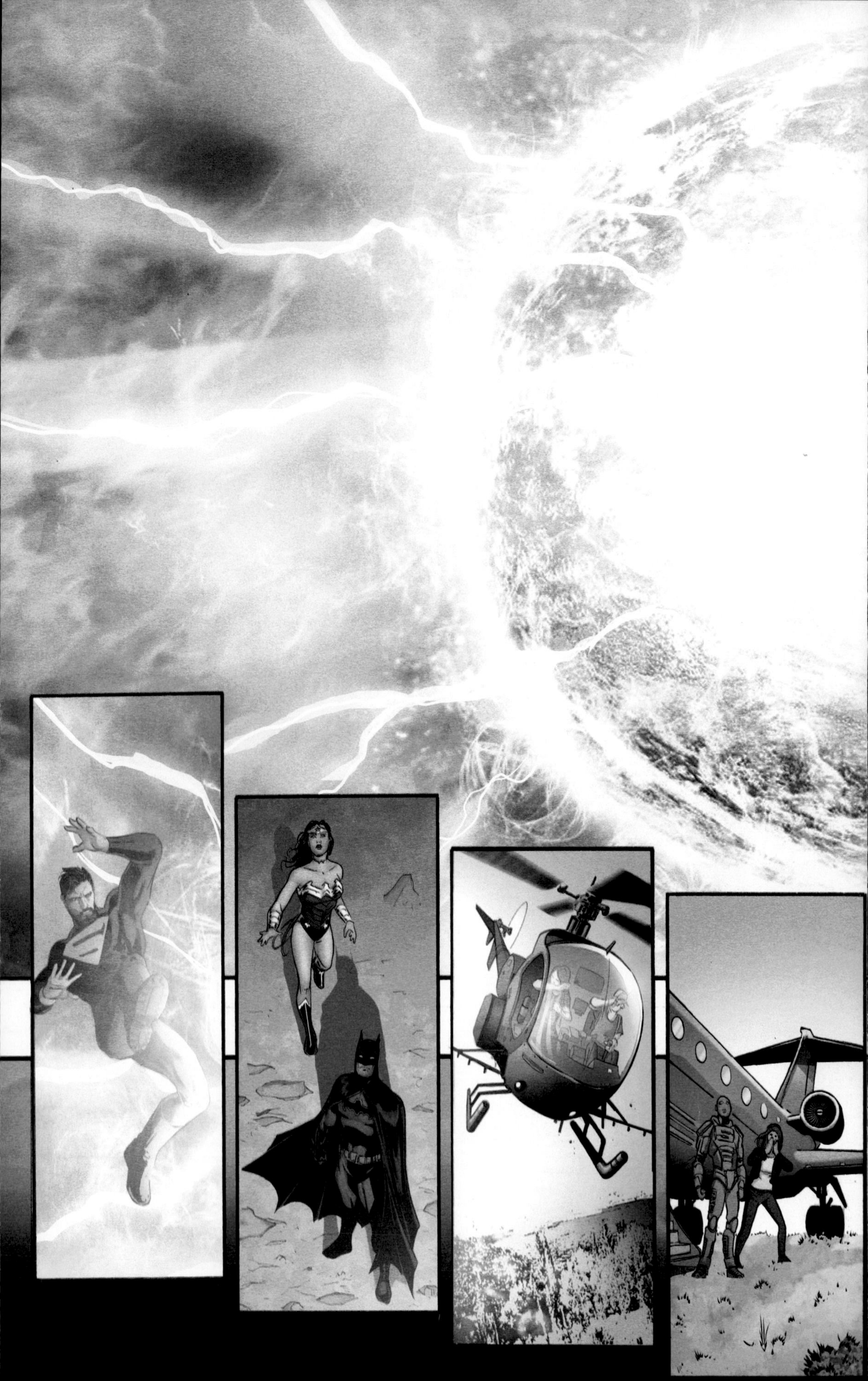

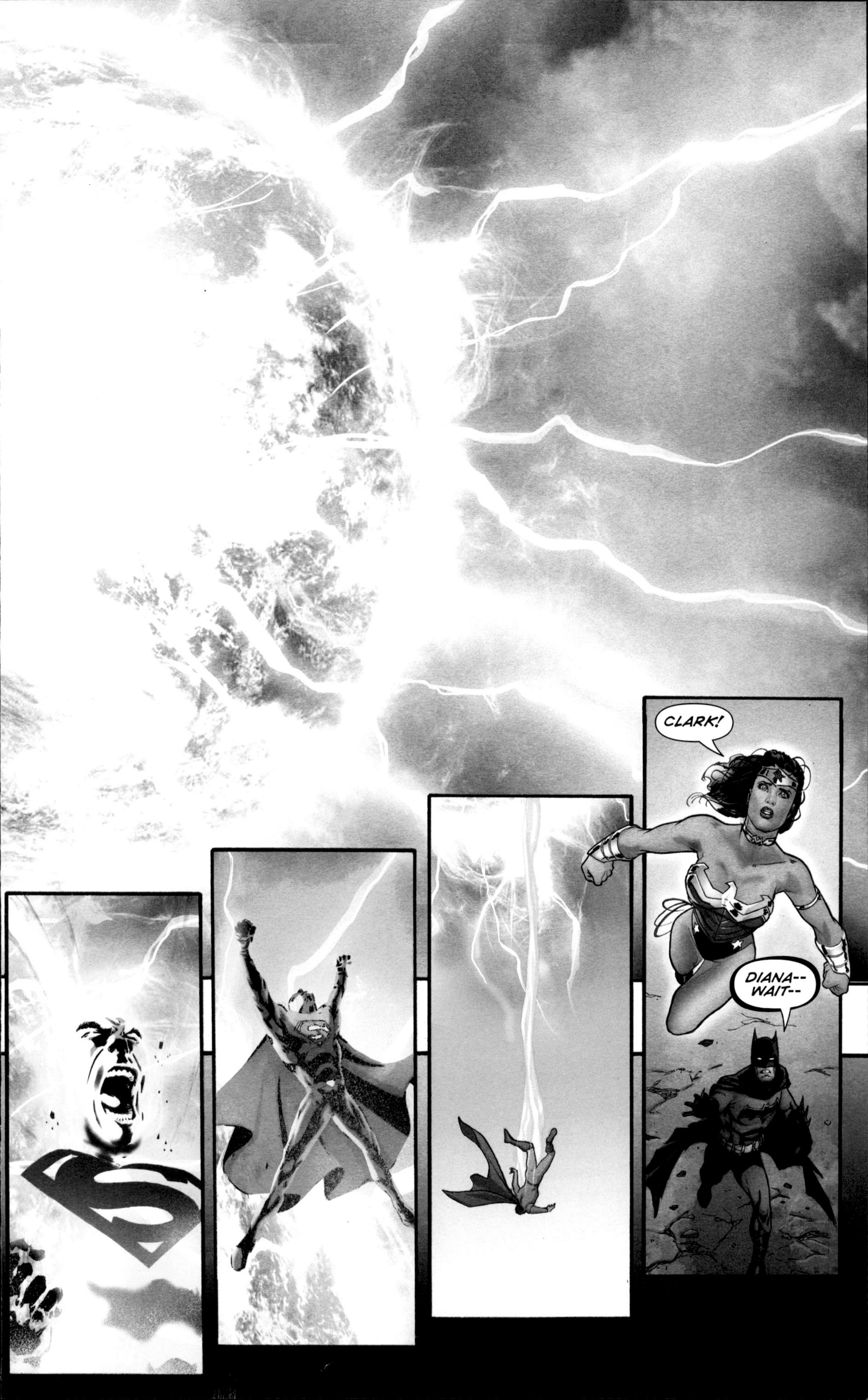
CLARK!
DIANA--
WAIT--

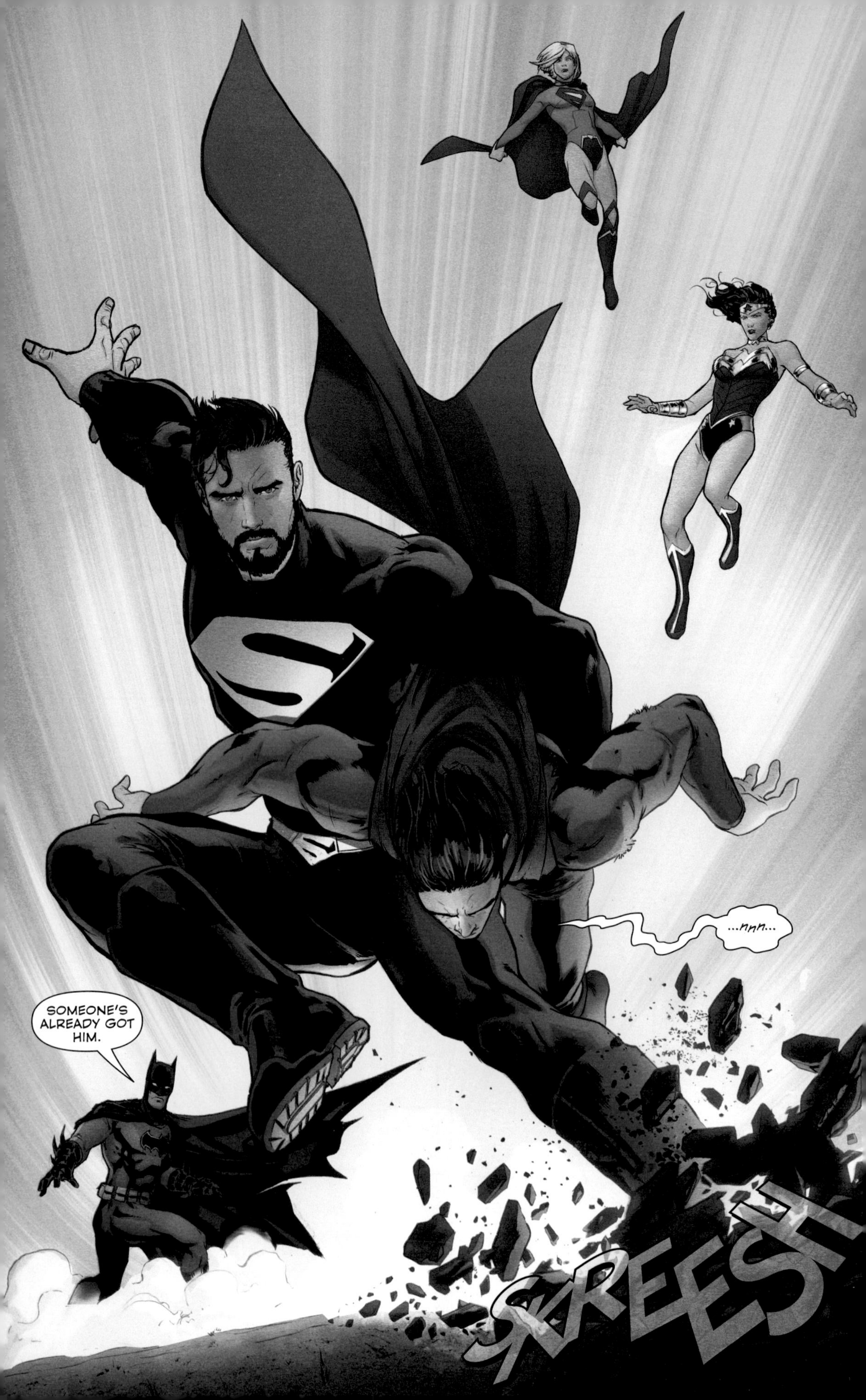
...nnn...
SOMEONE'S ALREADY GOT HIM.
SKREEESH

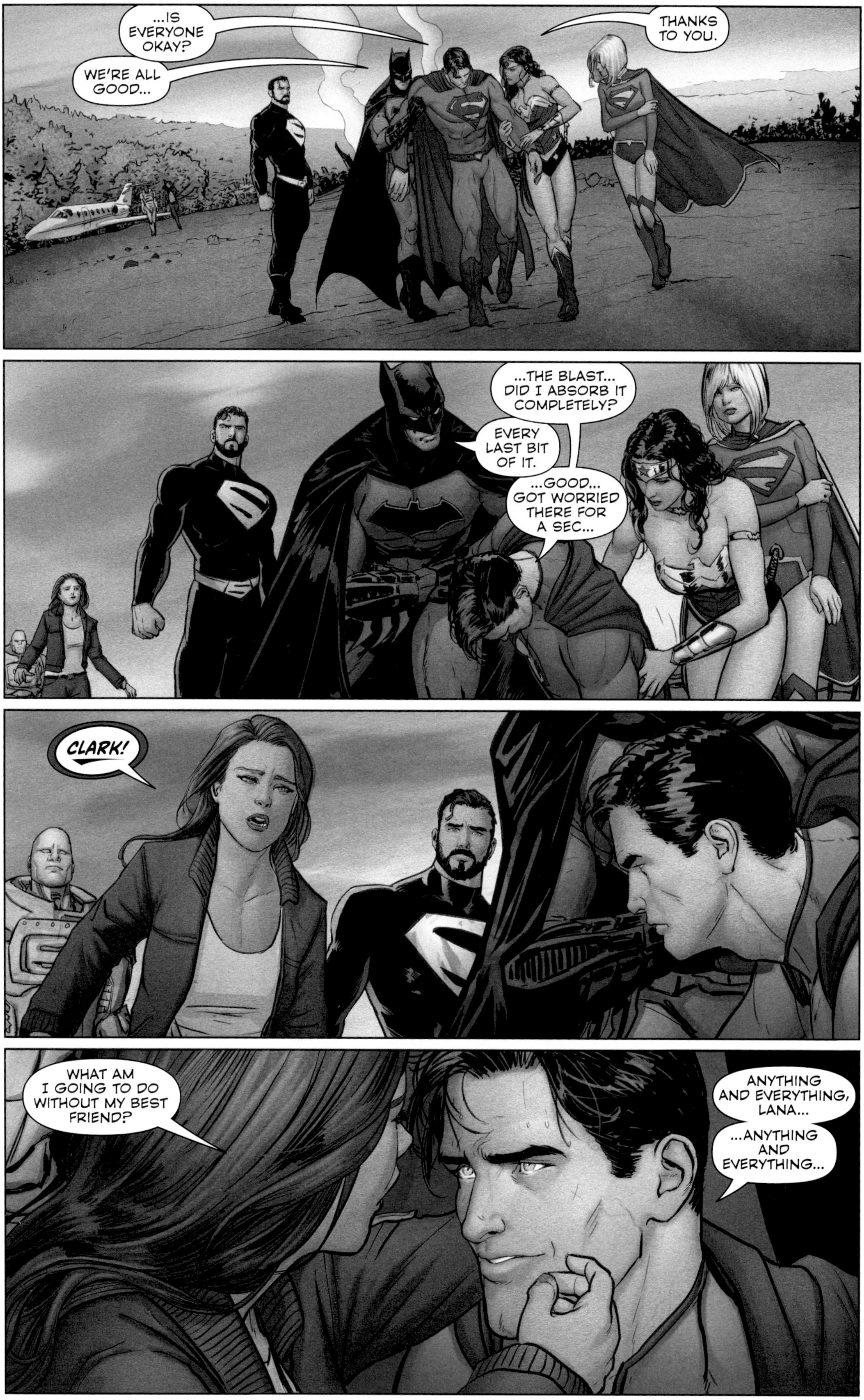

...IS EVERYONE OKAY?
WE'RE ALL GOOD...
THANKS TO YOU.
...THE BLAST... DID I ABSORB IT COMPLETELY?
EVERY LAST BIT OF IT.
...GOOD... GOT WORRIED THERE FOR A SEC...
CLARK!
WHAT AM I GOING TO DO WITHOUT MY BEST FRIEND?
ANYTHING AND EVERYTHING, LANA...
...ANYTHING AND EVERYTHING...

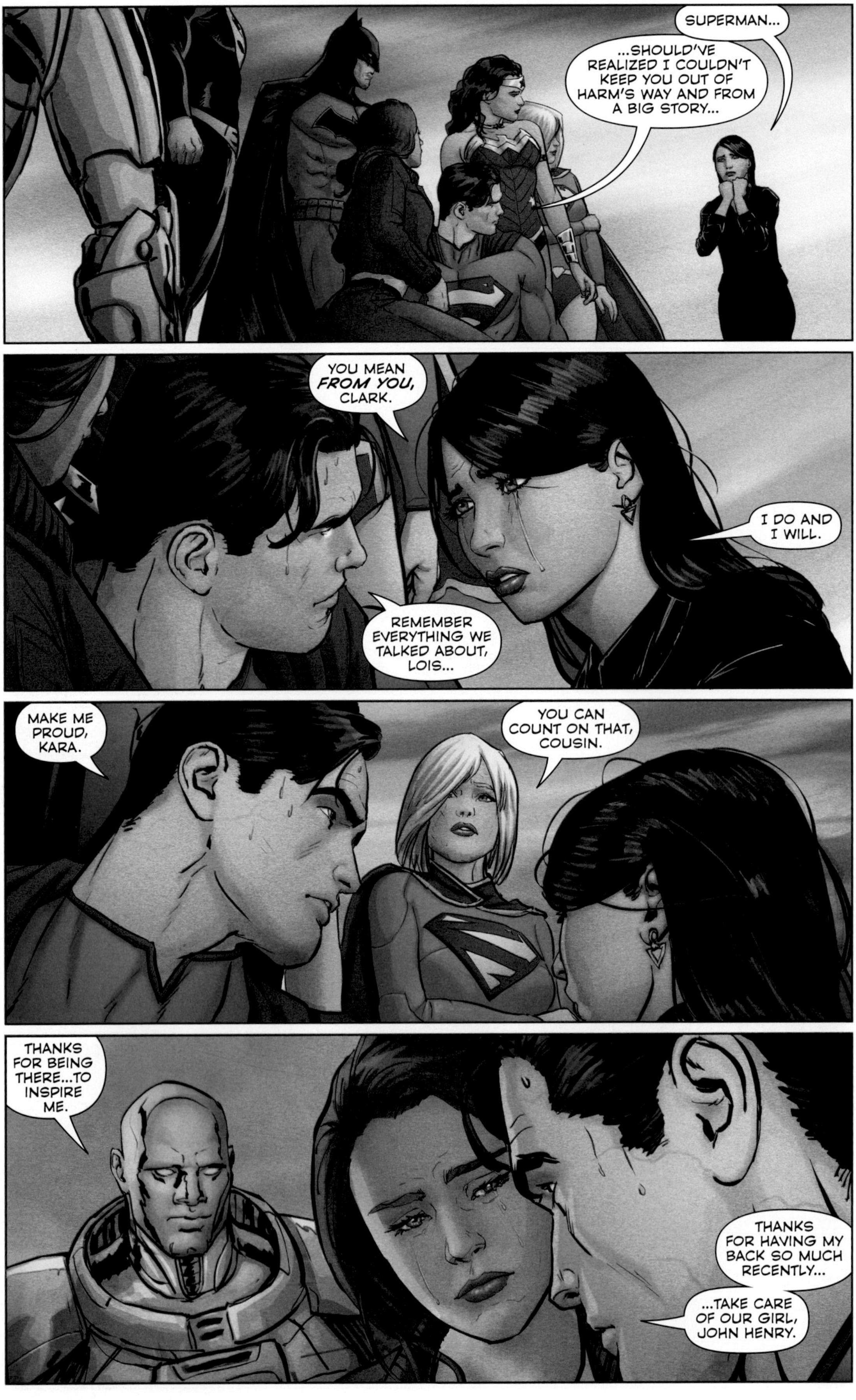
SUPERMAN...
...SHOULD'VE REALIZED I COULDN'T KEEP YOU OUT OF HARM'S WAY AND FROM A BIG STORY...
YOU MEAN *FROM YOU*, CLARK.
I DO AND I WILL.
REMEMBER EVERYTHING WE TALKED ABOUT, LOIS...
MAKE ME PROUD, KARA.
YOU CAN COUNT ON THAT, COUSIN.
THANKS FOR BEING THERE...TO INSPIRE ME.
THANKS FOR HAVING MY BACK SO MUCH RECENTLY...
...TAKE CARE OF OUR GIRL, JOHN HENRY.

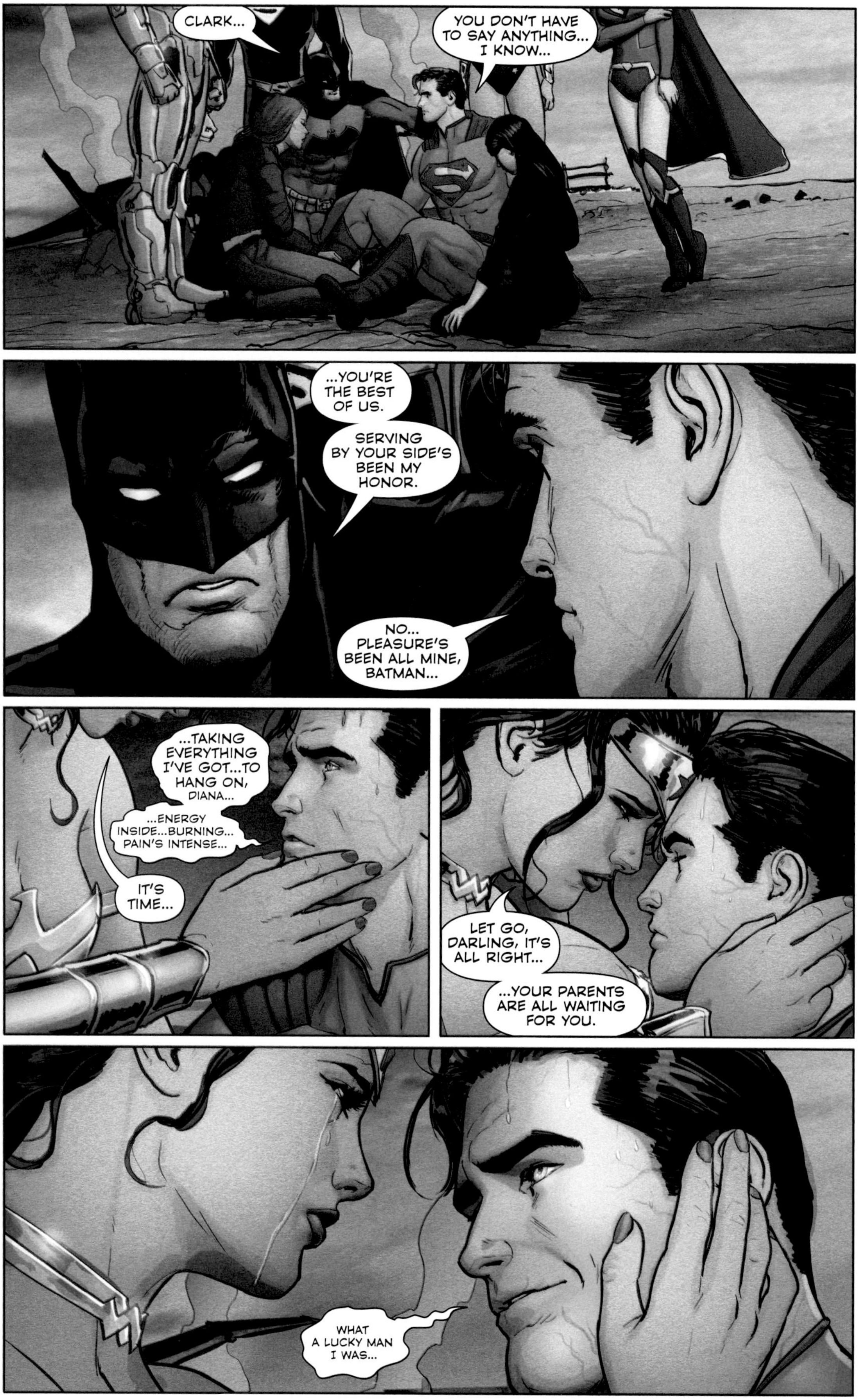
CLARK...
YOU DON'T HAVE TO SAY ANYTHING... I KNOW...
...YOU'RE THE BEST OF US.
SERVING BY YOUR SIDE'S BEEN MY HONOR.
NO... PLEASURE'S BEEN ALL MINE, BATMAN...
...TAKING EVERYTHING I'VE GOT...TO HANG ON, DIANA...
...ENERGY INSIDE...BURNING... PAIN'S INTENSE...
IT'S TIME...
LET GO, DARLING, IT'S ALL RIGHT...
...YOUR PARENTS ARE ALL WAITING FOR YOU.
WHAT A LUCKY MAN I WAS...

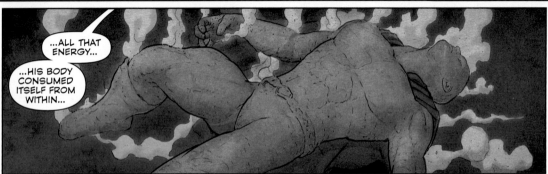

...ALL THAT ENERGY...

...HIS BODY CONSUMED ITSELF FROM WITHIN...

...HE'S... ...DEAD...

THERE'S LOTS OF QUESTIONS--

WHICH I'LL ANSWER AT ANOTHER TIME.

WHERE WILL WE FIND YOU?

DON'T WORRY, I'LL FIND YOU.

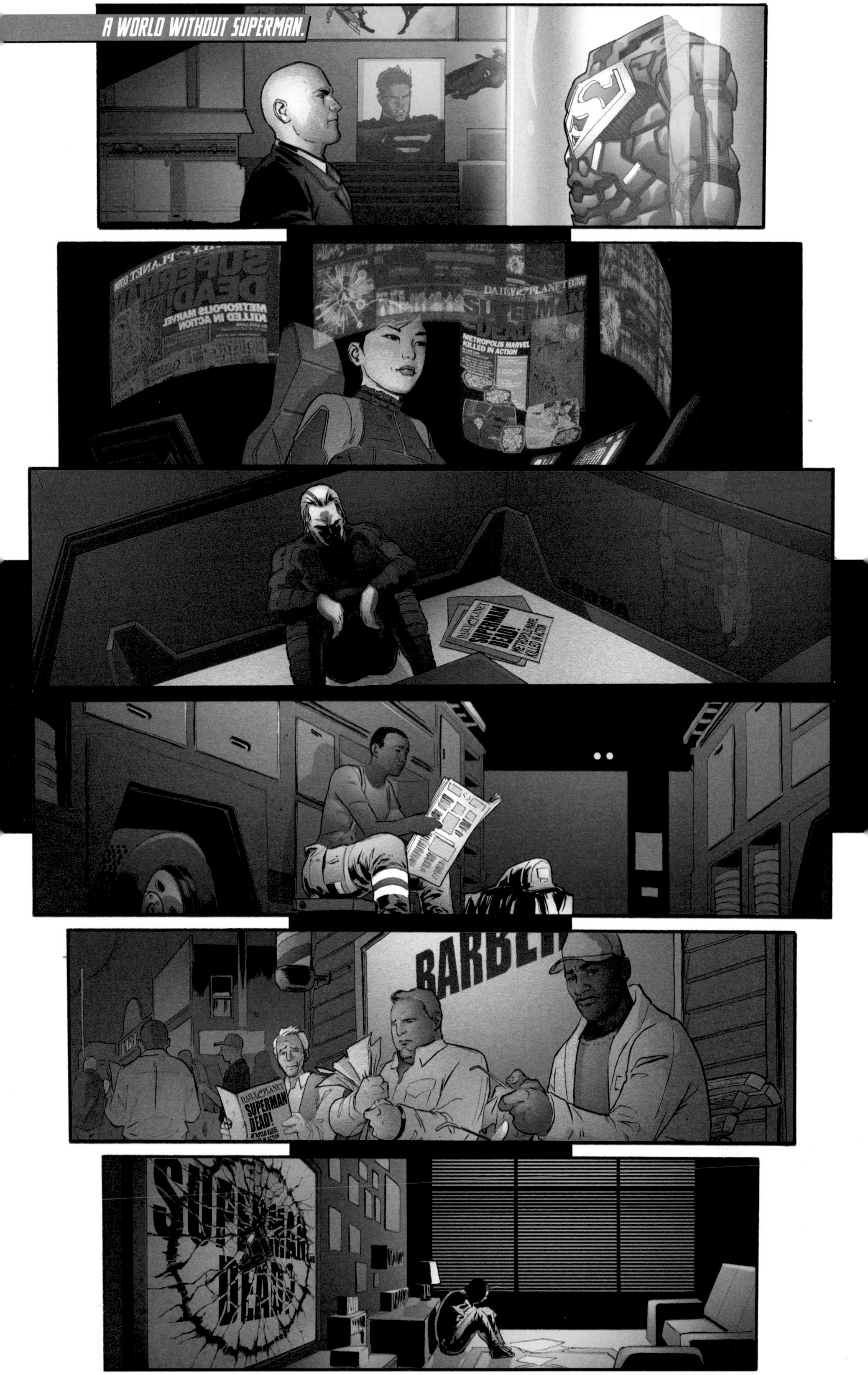
A WORLD WITHOUT SUPERMAN.
DAILY PLANET EXTRA
SUPERMAN DEAD!
METROPOLIS MARVEL KILLED IN ACTION
DAILY PLANET
SUPERMAN DEAD!
METROPOLIS MARVEL KILLED IN ACTION
BARBER
DAILY PLANET
SUPERMAN DEAD!

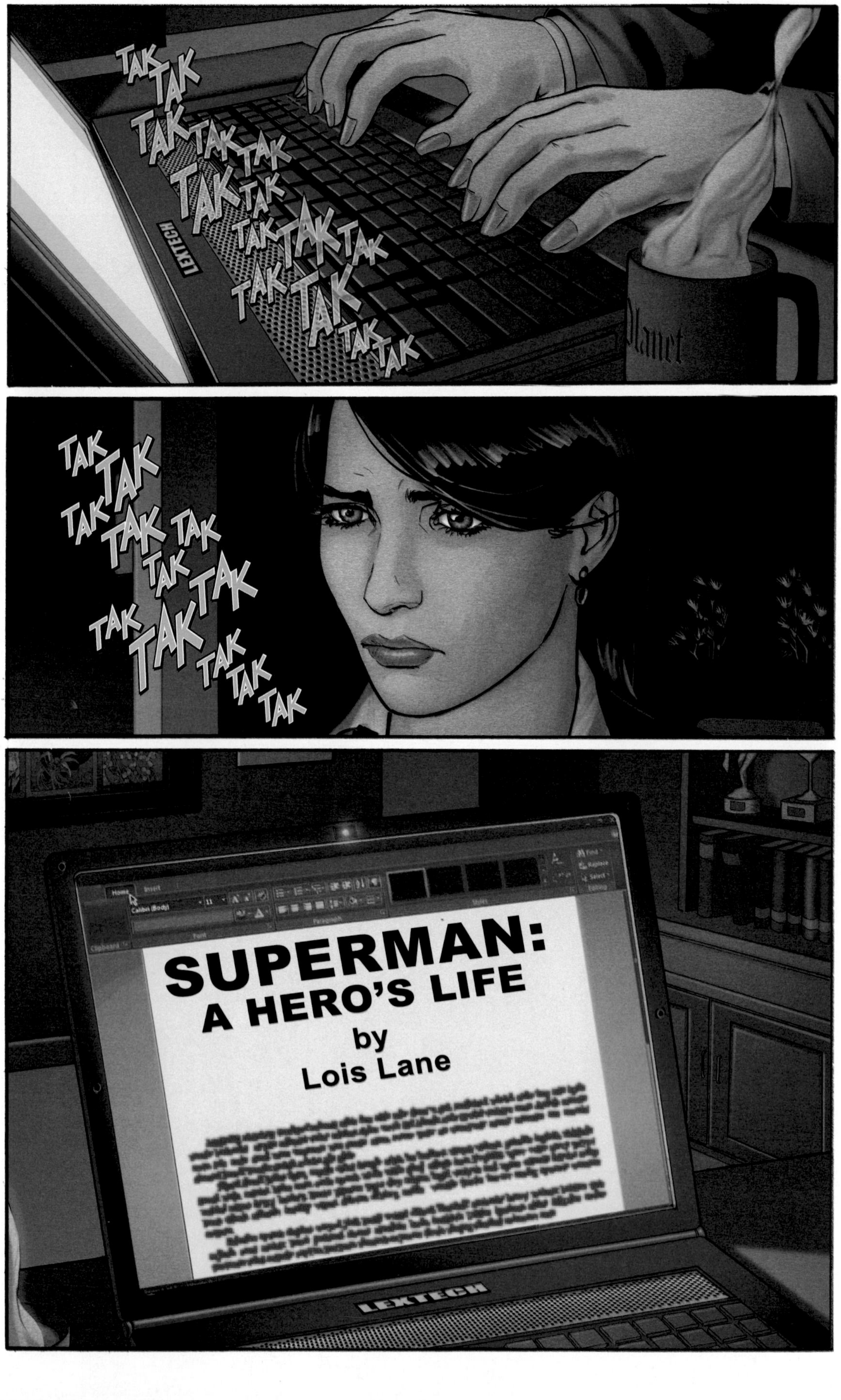
TAK TAK TAK TAK TAK TAK TAK TAK TAK TAK TAK TAK TAK TAK TAK
LEXTECH
Planet
TAK TAK TAK TAK TAK TAK TAK TAK TAK TAK TAK TAK TAK
SUPERMAN:
A HERO'S LIFE
by
Lois Lane
LEXTECH

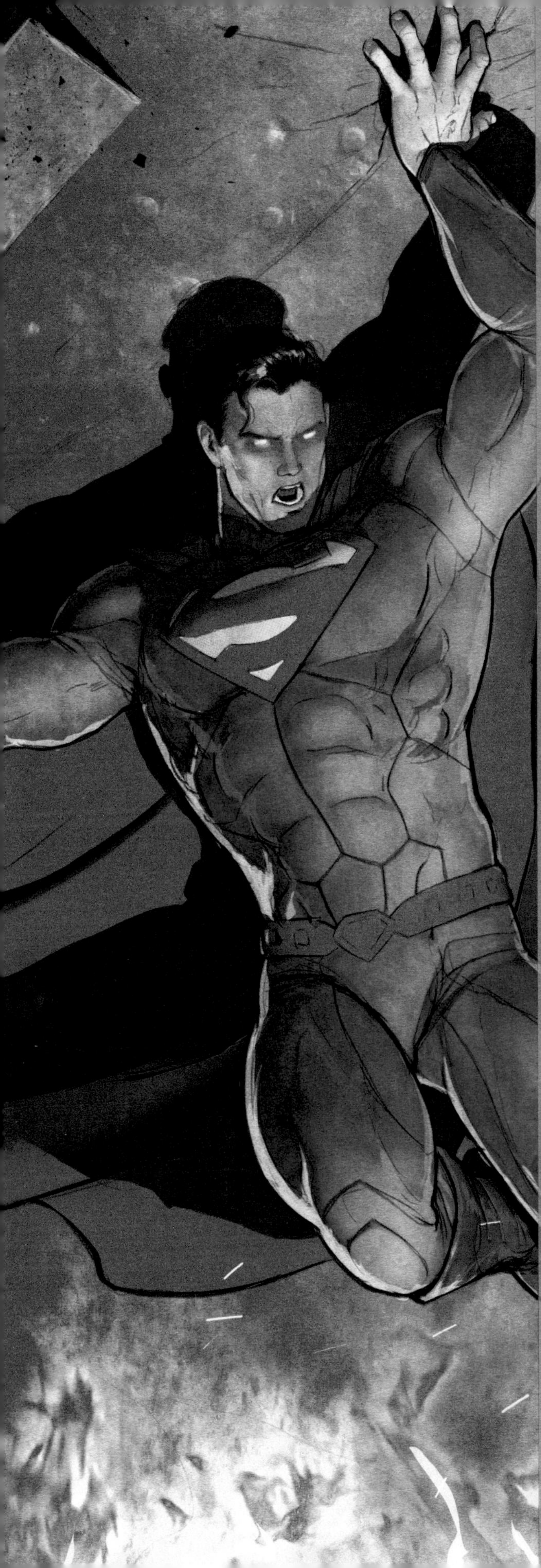

VARIANT COVER GALLERY

SUPERMAN #51
VARIANT BY JOHN ROMITA JR., DANNY MIKI, ARIF PRIANTO

BATMAN/SUPERMAN #31
VARIANT BY JOHN ROMITA JR., KLAUS JANSON, DAVE MCCAIG

ACTION COMICS #51
VARIANT BY JOHN ROMITA JR., KLAUS JANSON, ALEX SINCLAIR

SUPERMAN/ WONDER WOMAN #28
VARIANT BY JOHN ROMITA JR., SCOTT HANNA, LAURA MARTIN

ACTION COMICS #52
VARIANT BY BEN OLIVER

SUPERMAN #52
NEW 52 VARIANT BY MIKEL JANÍN

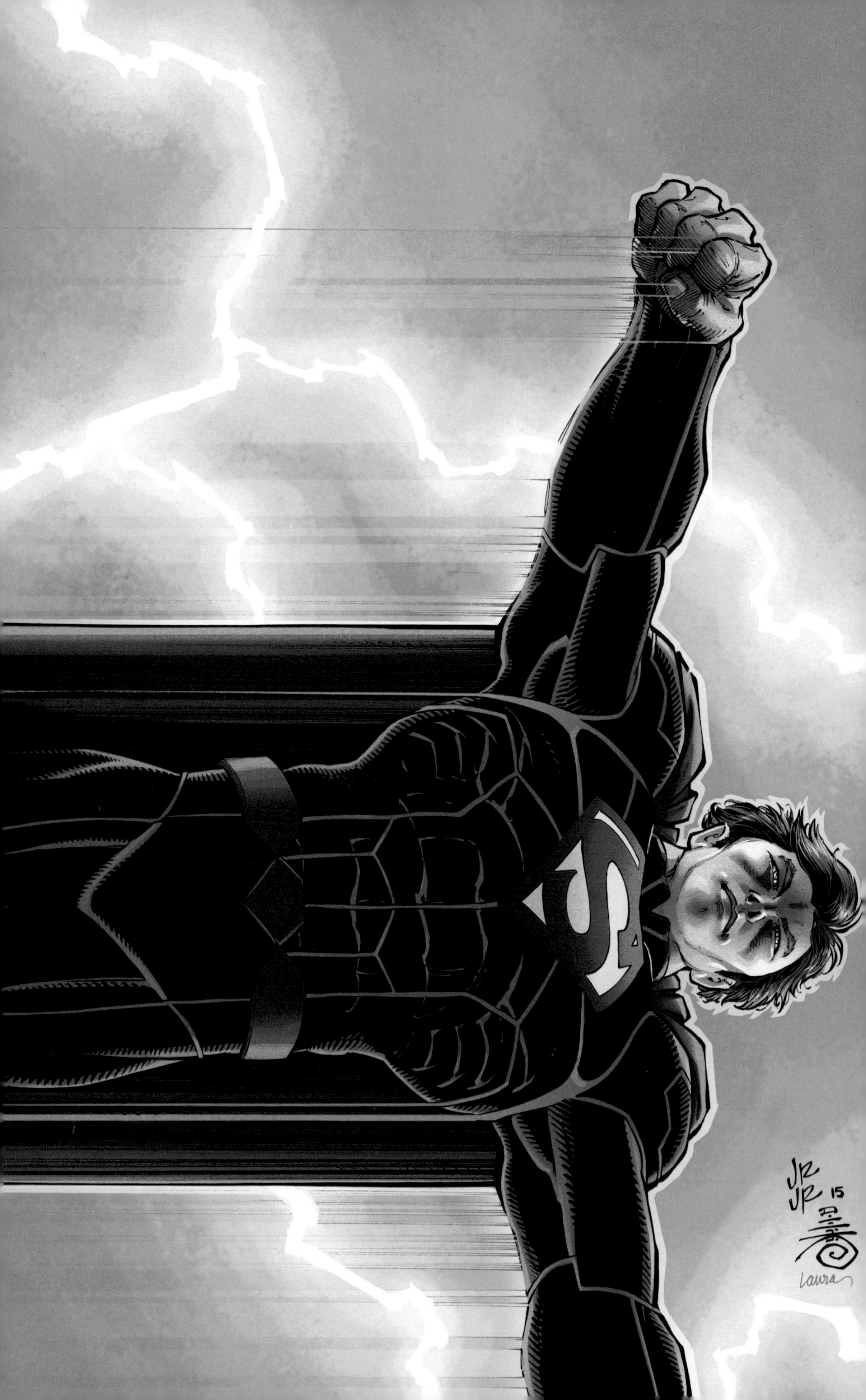

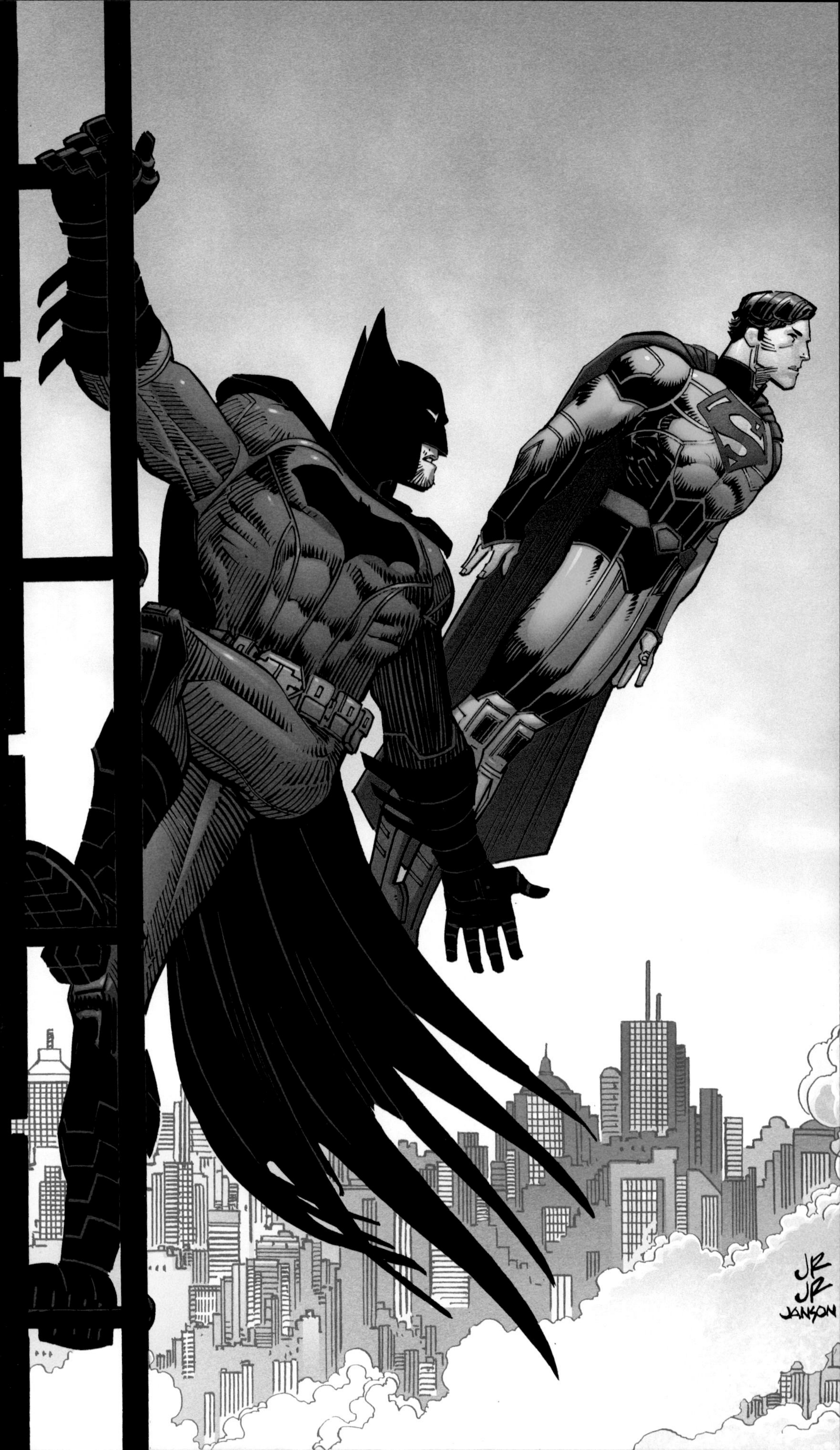
JR
JR
JANSON

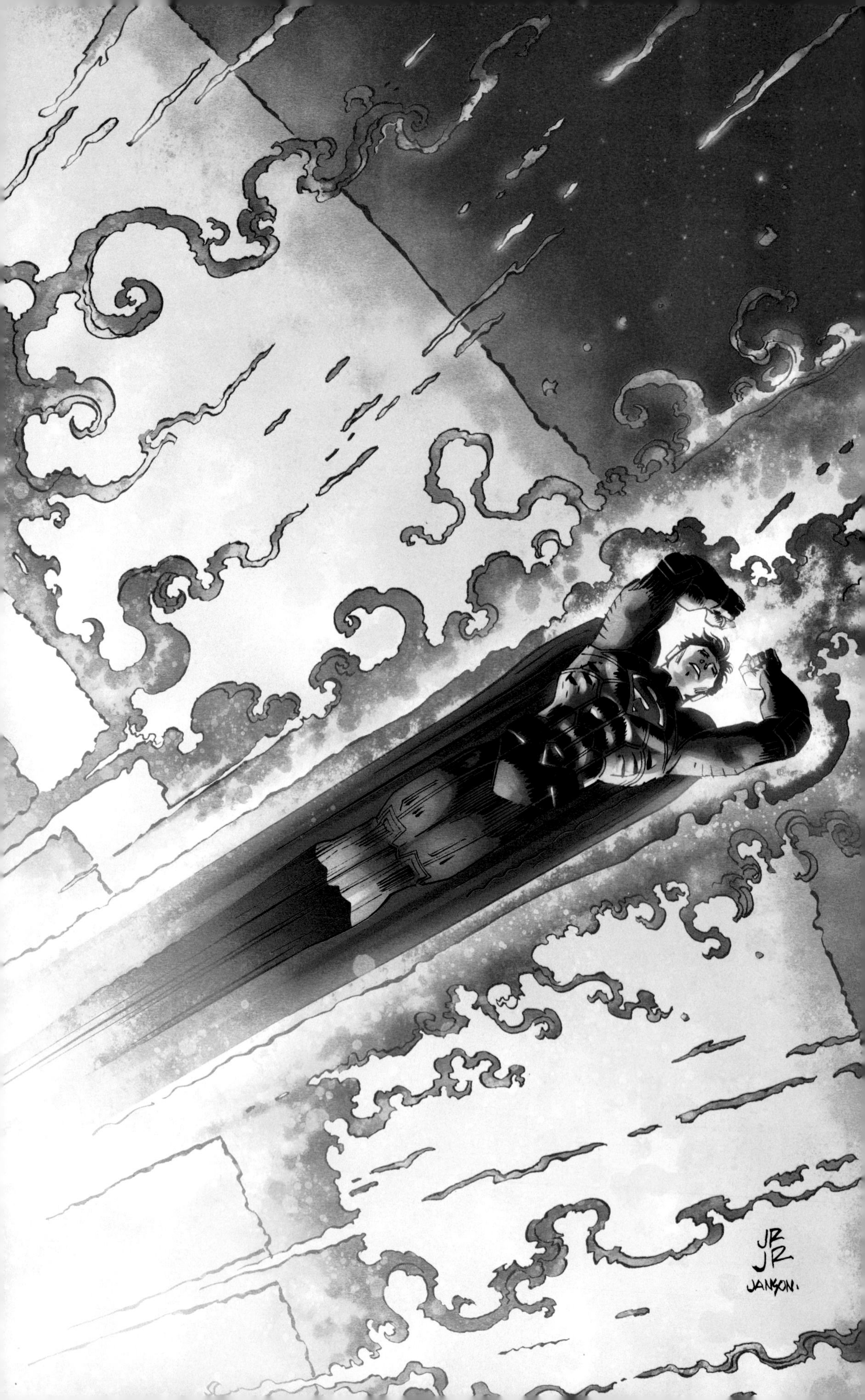
JR JR
JANSON.

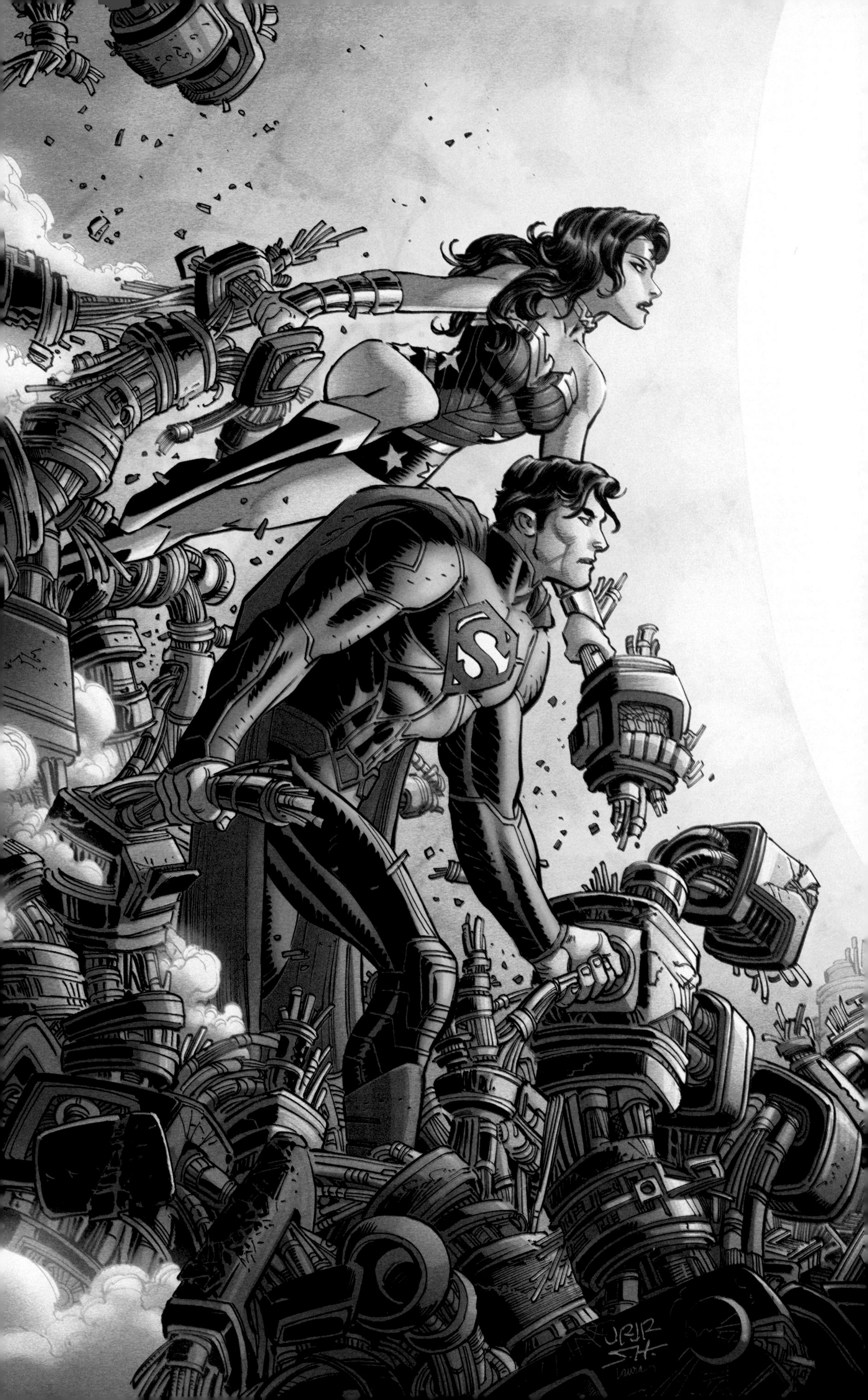

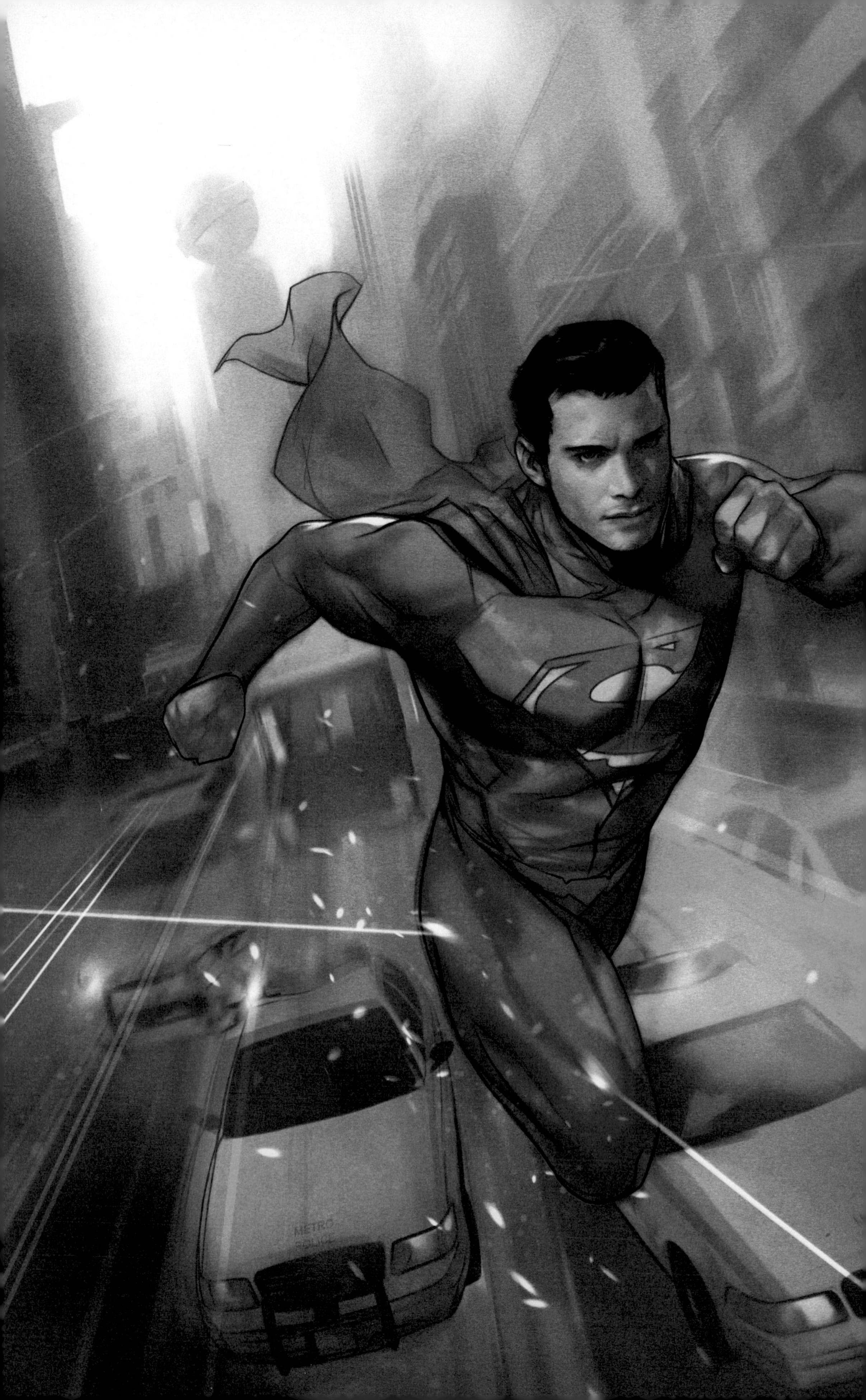
METRO

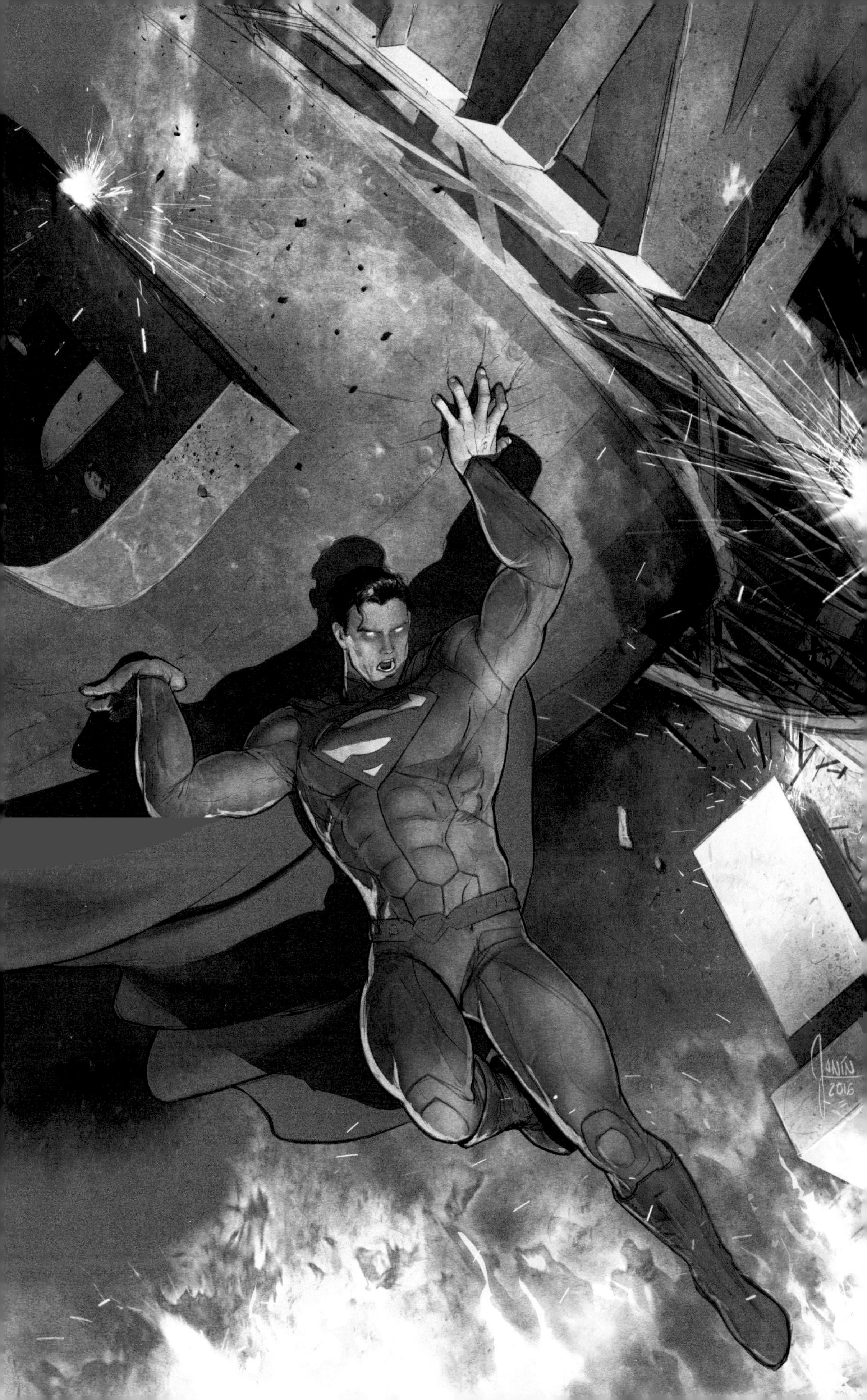

Pencils from SUPERMAN #51 by **MIKEL JANÍN**

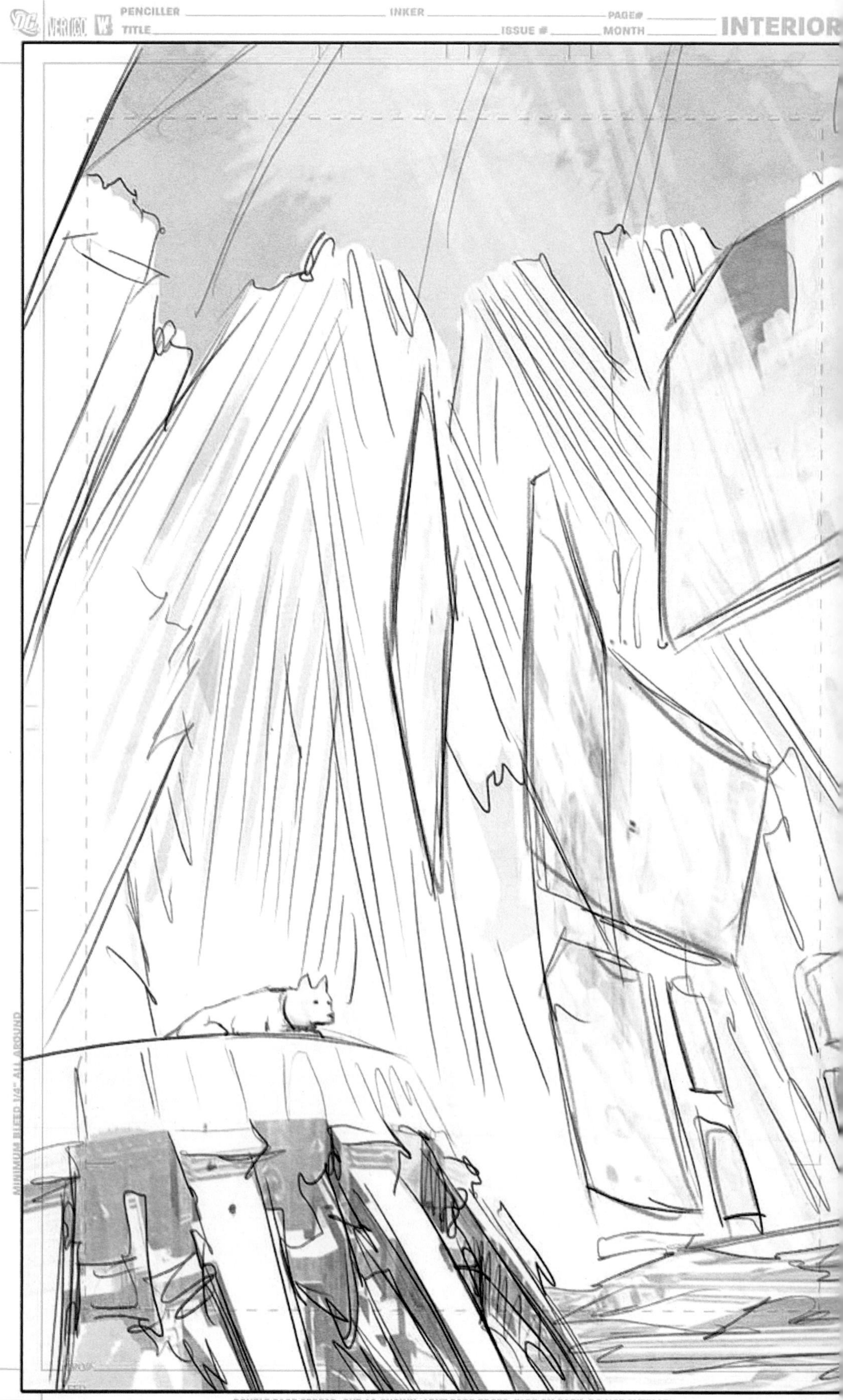
PENCILLER
INKER
PAGE#
TITLE
ISSUE #
MONTH
INTERIOR
MINIMUM BLEED 1/4" ALL AROUND
CUT RIGHT-HAND PAGE AT THIS LINE
DOUBLE PAGE SPREAD: CUT AS SHOWN, ABUT PAGE EDGES, TAPE ON BACK, DO NOT OVERLAP
CUT LEFT HAND PAGE AT THIS LINE

Pencils from ACTION COMICS #52 by SCOT EATON

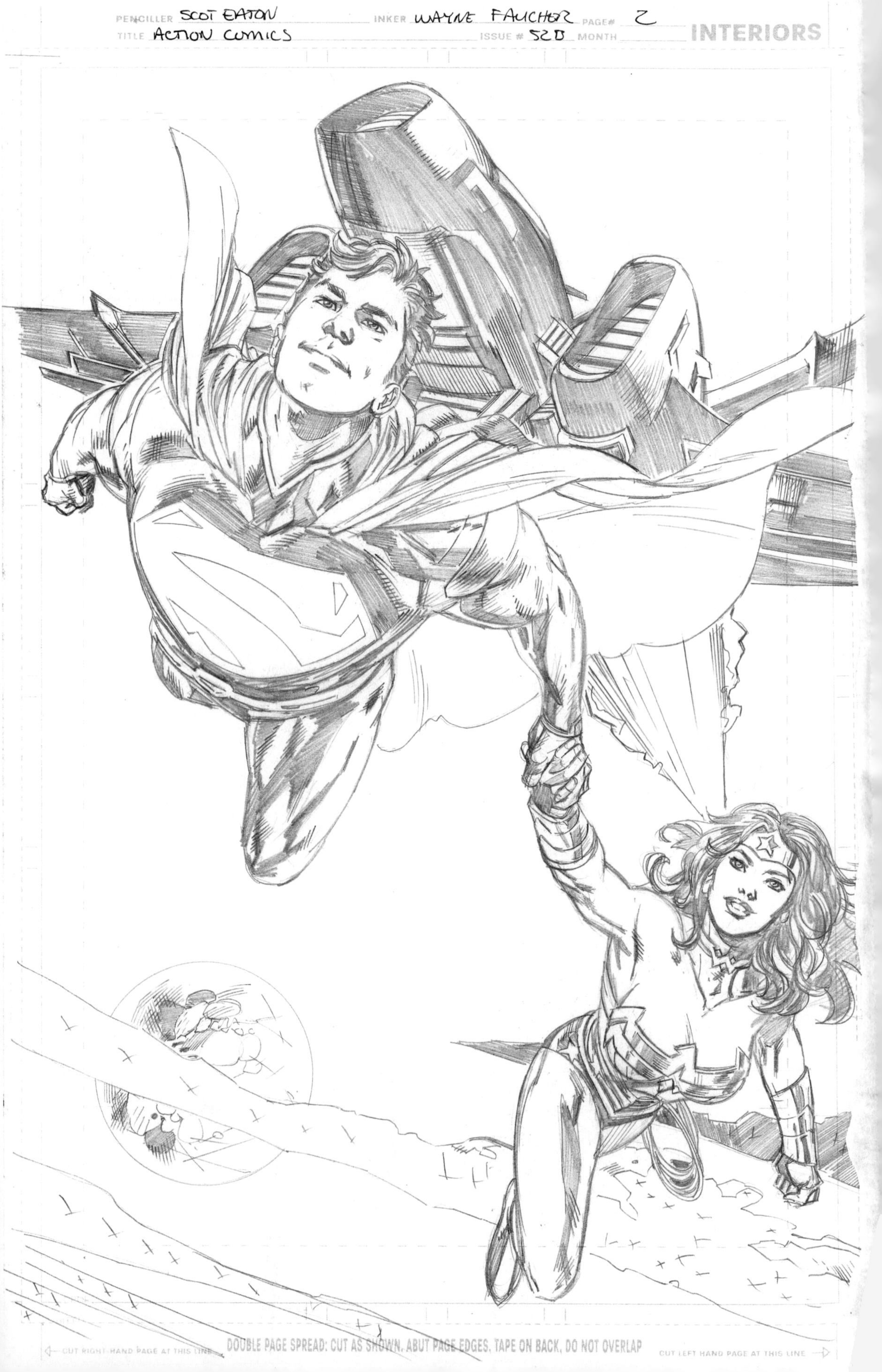
PENCILLER SCOT EATON
INKER WAYNE FAUCHER PAGE# 2
TITLE ACTION COMICS
ISSUE # MONTH
INTERIORS
CUT RIGHT HAND PAGE AT THIS LINE
DOUBLE PAGE SPREAD: CUT AS SHOWN, ABUT PAGE EDGES, TAPE ON BACK, DO NOT OVERLAP
CUT LEFT HAND PAGE AT THIS LINE